COURSE 1
B

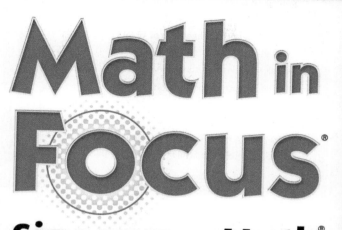

Math in Focus®

Singapore Math®
by Marshall Cavendish

Teacher's Edition

Consultant and Author
Dr. Fong Ho Kheong

Authors
Gan Kee Soon and Dr. Ng Wee Leng

U.S. Consultants
Dr. Richard Bisk
Andy Clark

Marshall Cavendish
Education

Distributor

Houghton
Mifflin
Harcourt

COMMON
CORE

© 2013 Marshall Cavendish International (Singapore) Private Limited
© 2014 Marshall Cavendish Education Pte Ltd

**Published by Marshall Cavendish Education**
Times Centre, 1 New Industrial Road, Singapore 536196
Customer Service Hotline: (65) 6213 9444
US Office Tel: (1-914) 332 8888 | Fax: (1-914) 332 8882
E-mail: tmesales@mceducation.com
Website: www.mceducation.com

Distributed by
**Houghton Mifflin Harcourt**
222 Berkeley Street
Boston, MA 02116
Tel: 617-351-5000
Website: www.hmheducation.com/mathinfocus

Cover: © Stéphane Maréchal/Photolibrary

First published 2013

*Math in Focus*® Course 1 Teacher's Edition B
ISBN 978-0-547-56096-0

Printed in United States of America

9  10  11          1401          19  18
4500703025                       B  C  D  E

COMMON CORE

CHAPTER

**8**

# Equations and Inequalities

COMMON CORE

In Student Book A and Student Book B, look for

| Practice and Problem Solving | Assessment Opportunities |
|---|---|
| • **Practice** in every lesson<br>• Real-world and mathematical problems in every chapter<br>• Brain @ Work in every chapter<br>• *Math Journal* exercises | • **Quick Check** at the beginning of every chapter to assess chapter readiness<br>• **Guided Practice** after every Learn to assess readiness to continue lesson<br>• **Chapter Review/Test** in every chapter to review or test chapter material<br>• **Cumulative Reviews** four times during the year |

# Math in Focus®: Singapore Math®

| **LESSON** | **Standards for Mathematical Practice** |
|---|---|
| **8.1** | 4. Model mathematics. 8. Express regularity in reasoning |
| **8.2** | 4. Model mathematics. 6. Attend to precision. 7. Look for and use structure. |
| **8.3** | 2. Reason. 3. Construct arguments. 4. Model mathematics. |
| **8.4** | 1. Solve problems/persevere. 4. Model mathematics. |

# Course 1B

CHAPTER

**9**

# The Coordinate Plane

COMMON CORE

Standards for Mathematical Content

MATHEMATICAL PRACTICES

| LESSON | Standards for Mathematical Practice |
|---|---|
| 9.1 | 6. Attend to precision. 4. Model mathematics. 7. Look for and use structure. |
| 9.2 | 2. Reason. 4. Model mathematics. 5. Use tools strategically. |
| 9.3 | 1. Solve problems/persevere. 2. Reason. 4. Model mathematics. |

# Math in Focus®: Singapore Math®

## CHAPTER 10 — Area of Polygons

MATHEMATICAL PRACTICES

**LESSON**    **Standards for Mathematical Practice**
**10.1-10-2**   4. Model mathematics. 7. Look for and use structure.
**10.3-10.4**   1. Solve problems/persevere. 6. Attend to precision. 8. Express regularity in reasoning.

Standards for Mathematical Content

# Course 1B

**CHAPTER**

## 11 Circumference and Area of a Circle

**Chapter Opener** Have you ever seen a rainbow? . . . . . . . . . . . . . . . . . . . . . . **118**

**Big Idea** A circle is a geometric figure that has many useful applications in the real world.

**Recall Prior Knowledge** • Adding decimals • Subtracting decimals • Multiplying decimals • Dividing decimals • Rounding numbers to the nearest whole number • Rounding numbers to the nearest tenth . . . . . . . . . . . . . . . . . . . . . . . . . . . . . **119**

**11.1 Radius, Diameter, and Circumference of a Circle** DAYS **2** . . . . . . . . . . . **122**

**Learn** • Identify the center and radius of a circle • Identify the diameter of a circle • Identify the circumference of a circle • Find the circumference of a circle • Recognize that half of a circle is a semicircle and a quarter of a circle is a quadrant • Find the lengths of a semicircular arc and the arc of a quadrant

**Hands-On Activities** • Drawing Circles Using a Compass • Investigating the Relationship Between the Circumference and Diameter of a Circle • Drawing Semicircles and Quadrants

**11.2 Area of a Circle** DAYS **2** . . . . . . . . . . . . . . . . . . . . . . . . . . . . . . . . . . . **136**

**Learn** • Derive the formula for the area of a circle • Find the area of a circle • Find the area of a semicircle

# Math in Focus®: Singapore Math®

**Standards for Mathematical Content**

| LESSON | Standards for Mathematical Practice |
|--------|-------------------------------------|
| **11.1** | 2. Reason. 3. Construct arguments. 5. Use tools strategically. |
| **11.2** | 4. Model mathematics. 3. Construct arguments. 8. Express regularity in reasoning. |
| **11.3** | 1. Solve problems/persevere. 2. Reason. 6. Attend to precision. |

# Course 1B

COMMON CORE

# Math in Focus® : Singapore Math®

|  | LESSON | Standards for Mathematical Practice |
|---|---|---|
| | **12.1** | 3. Construct arguments. 4. Model mathematics. 6. Attend to precision. |
| | **12.2** | 2. Reason. 8. Express regularity in reasoning. |
| | **12.3** | 4. Model mathematics. 6. Attend to precision. 8. Express regularity in reasoning. |
| | **12.4** | 1. Solve problems/persevere. 2. Reason. 5. Use tools strategically. |

# Course 1B

COMMON CORE

| MATHEMATICAL PRACTICES | LESSON | Standards for Mathematical Practice |
|---|---|---|
| | **13.1** | 4. Model mathematics. 5. Use tools strategically. |
| | **13.2** | 2. Reason. 3. Construct arguments. 4. Model mathematics. |
| | **13.3** | 4. Model mathematics. 5. Use tools strategically. |

# Math in Focus®: Singapore Math®

**MATHEMATICAL PRACTICES**

| **LESSON** | **Standards for Mathematical Practice** |
|---|---|
| **14.1** | 1. Solve problems/persevere. 2. Reason. 3. Construct arguments. 4. Model mathematics. |
| **14.2** | 2. Reason. 4. Model mathematics. 5. Use tools strategically. 8. Express regularity in reasoning. |
| **14.3** | 3. Construct arguments. 4. Model mathematics. 5. Use tools strategically. |
| **14.4** | 1. Solve problems/persevere. 5. Use tools strategically. 7. Look for and use structure. 8. Express regularity in reasoning. |

# Course 1B

**Standards for Mathematical Content**

# Chapter at a Glance

| | CHAPTER OPENER<br>**Equations and Inequalities**<br>**Recall Prior Knowledge** | LESSON 8.1<br>**Solving Algebraic Equations**<br>Pages 5–12 | LESSON 8.2<br>**Writing Linear Equations**<br>Pages 13–21 |
|---|---|---|---|
| **LESSON AT A GLANCE** Pacing | 2 days | 2 days | 2 days |
| Objectives | 💡 Equations and inequalities can be used to describe situations and solve real-world problems. | • Solve equations in one variable. | • Express the relationship between two quantities as a linear equation.<br>• Use a table or graph to represent a linear equation. |
| Vocabulary | | equation, solution | linear equation, independent variable, dependent variable |
| **RESOURCES** Materials | | algebra tiles, balance scale | TRT15–17* |
| Lesson Resources | Student Book A, pp. 1–4<br>*Assessments*, Chapter 8 Pre-Test<br>*Transition Guide*, Course 1, Skills 31–34 | Student Book B, pp. 5–12<br>*Extra Practice B*, Lesson 8.1<br>*Reteach B*, Lesson 8.1 | Student Book A, pp. 13–21<br>*Extra Practice B*, Lesson 8.2<br>*Reteach B*, Lesson 8.2<br>*Activity Book*, Lesson 8.2 |
| **Common Core** Standards for Mathematical Content | **6.EE.2a**<br>Foundational for **6.EE.5, 6.EE.8, 6.EE.9** | **6.EE.2c** Evaluate expressions at specific values of their variables.<br>**6.EE.5** Understand solving an equation ... as a process of answering a question... Use substitution to determine whether a given number ... makes an equation... true. | **6.EE.7** Solve ... problems by writing and solving equations of the form $x + p = q$ and $px = q$.<br>**6.EE.9** ...Write an equation to express one quantity ... in terms of the other.... Analyze the relationship using graphs and tables. |
| **Mathematical Practices** | **4.** Model mathematics.<br>**6.** Attend to precision. | **3.** Construct arguments. **4.** Model mathematics. **8.** Express regularity in reasoning. | **4.** Model mathematics. **6.** Attend to precision. **7.** Look for and use structure. |

*\*Teacher Resource Tools (TRT) are available on the Teacher One Stop.*

# Concepts and Skills Across the Courses

| GRADE 5 | COURSE 1 | COURSE 2 |
|---|---|---|
| • Evaluate, interpret, and write numerical expressions with symbols. (5.OA.1, 5.OA.2)<br>• Analyze patterns and relationships using rules. (5.OA.3)<br>• Solve real-world and mathematical problems using equations and other models. (5.NBT.6, 5.NF.6, 5.NF.7) | • Use variables to write expressions when solving real-world or mathematical problems. (6.EE.6)<br>• Solve real-world or mathematical problems by writing and solving equations and inequalities. (6.EE.5, 6.EE.7, 6.EE.8)<br>• Represent and analyze quantitative relationships between two quantities that change. (6.EE.9) | • Use equations and inequalities to solve multi-step problems with rational numbers. (7.EE.3)<br>• Use variables to represent quantities in real-world or mathematical problems and construct simple tequations and inequalities by reasoning about the quantities. (7.EE.4, 7.EE.4a, 7.EE.4b) |

| LESSON 8.3<br>**Solving Simple Inequalities**<br>Pages 22–28 | LESSON 8.4<br>**Real-World Problems:**<br>**Equations and Inequalities**<br>Pages 29–34 | CHAPTER<br>**WRAP UP/REVIEW/TEST**<br>**Brain@Work**<br>Pages 34–37 |
|---|---|---|
| 2 days | 2 days | 2 days |
| • Use substitution to determine whether a given number is a solution of an inequality.<br>• Represent the solutions of an inequality on a number line. | • Solve real-world problems by writing equations.<br>• Solve real-world problems by writing inequalities. | Reinforce, consolidate, and extend chapter skills and concepts. |
| inequality | | |
| algebra tiles, balance scale, TRT1* | TRT1* | |
| Student Book B, pp. 22–28<br>*Extra Practice B,* Lesson 8.3<br>*Reteach B,* Lesson 8.3 | Student Book B, pp. 29–34<br>*Extra Practice B,* Lesson 8.4<br>*Reteach B,* Lesson 8.4 | Student Book B pp. 34–37<br>*Activity Book,* Chapter 8 Project<br>*Enrichment,* Chapter 8<br>*Assessments,* Chapter 8 Test<br> ExamView® Assessment Suite Course 1 |
| **6.EE.5** Understand solving an inequality ... Use substitution to determine whether a given number ... makes an inequality... true.<br>**6.EE.7** ... Represent solutions of inequalities on number line diagrams. | **6.EE.7** Solve ... problems by writing and solving equations of the form $x + p = q$ and $px = q$.<br>**6.EE.8** Write an inequality of the form $x > c$ or $x < c$ to represent ... a real-world or mathematical problem. | |
| **2.** Reason. **3.** Construct arguments.<br>**4.** Model mathematics. | **1.** Solve problems/persevere.<br>**4.** Model mathematics. | **1.** Solve problems/persevere.<br>**5.** Use tools strategically. |

# Additional Chapter Resources

## TECHNOLOGY

- Online Student eBook

- Interactive Whiteboard Lessons

- Virtual Manipulatives

- Teacher One Stop

- ExamView® Assessment Suite Course 1

- Online Professional Development Videos

## Every Day Counts®
## ALGEBRA READINESS

**The February activities in the Pacing Chart provide:**

- **Review** of visual modes for decimals, fractions, and percents (**Ch. 6, 6.RP.3**)
- **Practice** writing equations for linear relationships (**Ch. 8, 6.EE.7, 6.EE.9**)
- **Preview** of data analysis and graphs (**Ch. 13, 6.SP.4, 6.SP.5**)

# Chapter 8 Equations and Inequalities

## Balancing Expressions

- In this chapter, students learn to write inequalities. They use substitution to evaluate simple equations and solve real-world problems by writing and solving both equations and inequalities.

### Deeper meaning for =

- Students are familiar with sentences such as 3 + 4 = ?, where = signals to them that they should compute. In Lesson 8.1, they learn to think of the = symbol as meaning that two expressions have the same value. This leap in abstraction should be accompanied by as much work with a balance scale as possible.

- Students use inverse operations to "get the variable alone" on one side of an equal sign to solve an equation. This reliance on the properties of equality establishes a strong base for future work in algebra.

### Exploring inequality

- Students learn to think of the symbols > and < as meaning that two expressions are unbalanced, or have different values. This should involve extensive work with an *unbalanced* balance scale.

- Students extend their use of substitution to determine whether a given number is a solution to an inequality.

- Students are introduced to the symbols ≥ and ≤, expanding their conception of how two quantities, or expressions, may compare.

### Visualizing solutions

- Students are introduced to the term *linear equation*. They learn that the graphed solutions of simple equations are lines.

- Students use number lines to represent solutions to inequalities.

- Students learn that linear equations and inequalities, as represented by lines and rays, have infinite solutions, including not just whole numbers, but also fractions, mixed numbers, and decimals.

- In real-world problems, students learn that solutions to linear equations and inequalities may not be infinite. Problem contexts may, for example, impose upper or lower limits, or limit solutions to integers or positive numbers. Graphing supports this concept.

## Multiple Models

- In this chapter, students use scales and bar models to solve simple equations and inequalities.

### Solving equations with balance scales

- Students learn to express the relationship between two quantities as a linear equation. They use balance models to solve equations with one variable.

The expression for the left side is $x + 3$. The expression for the right side is 8. So, $x + 3 = 8$.

$$x = 8 - 3$$
$$x = 5$$

### Solving equations with bar models

- Students solve real-world problems by writing equations and solving them with bar models.

  Jared is $x$ years old. Eric is 3 years younger. If Eric is $p$ years old, express $x$ in terms of $p$.

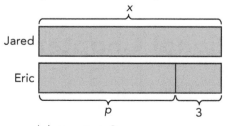

From the model: $x = p + 3$

### Representing inequalities

- Students use substitution to determine if given numbers are solutions to an inequality. Then they represent the solutions by using a number line.

  Draw a number line to represent $t < 12$.

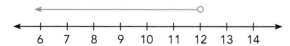

#  Differentiated Instruction

## Assessment and Intervention

| | ASSESSMENT | RtI STRUGGLING LEARNERS |
|---|---|---|
| **DIAGNOSTIC** | • Quick Check in Recall Prior Knowledge in Student Book B, pp. 1–4<br>• Chapter 8 Pre-Test in *Assessments* | • Skills 31–34 in *Transition Guide, Course 1* |
| **ON-GOING** | • Guided Practice<br>• Lesson Check<br>• Ticket Out the Door | • Reteach worksheets<br>• Extra Practice worksheets<br>• *Activity Book*, Chapter 8 |
| **END-OF-CHAPTER** | • Chapter Review/Test<br>• Chapter 8 Test in *Assessments*<br>• ExamView® Assessment Suite Course 1 | • Reteach worksheets |

### ELL ENGLISH LANGUAGE LEARNERS

Review the terms *equation* and *inequality*.

**Say** An *equation* is a mathematical statement that two quantities are *equal*, that they have the same value.

**Model** Write the equation $x + 2 = 5$. Then model the equation using a balance scale. Point out that the scale is balanced, so the amounts on the two sides of the scale must be the same. They are equal: $x + 2 = 5$.

**Say** An *inequality* is a mathematical statement that two quantities are *not equal*, that they do *not* have the same value.

**Model** Write the inequality $x + 3 > 8$. Then model the inequality using a balance scale. Point out that the scale is unbalanced, so the amounts on the two sides of the scale must be different. The amount on the left side is heavier than the amount on the right, so $x + 3 > 8$.

For definitions, see Glossary, page 301, and  Online Multilingual Glossary.

### ADVANCED LEARNERS

• Have students write their own real-world problems that involve inequalities. Challenge them to come up with problems where the real-world situation places limitations on the solution set, such as excluding non-integers and/or negative numbers. For example:

> Simone bought a 1-gallon container of milk. She put it in her refrigerator and used the milk. Write an inequality that best describes the amount of milk in the container, $c$, while it was in Simone's refrigerator. ($0 \leq c \leq 1$.) Draw a number line to represent the inequality.

• As needed, provide direction for students. Demonstrate compound inequalities. Also suggest a list of questions to consider: Is there a lower limit to the solution set? An upper limit? Can the solutions include fractions or decimals? Negative numbers?

**To provide additional challenges use:**
• *Enrichment*, Chapter 8
• Student Book A, Brain@Work problem

CHAPTER

# 8 Equations and Inequalities

## Going on a vacation?

If you travel to another country, you can use linear equations and inequalities to help you plan your finances. Before you leave, you might want to change your U.S. dollars into a different currency. The amount of money you get in the new currency depends on how many U.S. dollars you start with and also on the currency exchange rate. To find out how much money you get in the new currency, you use a linear equation.

While on your trip, you may want to set aside money to spend on souvenirs. You can use a linear inequality to find how many souvenirs you can buy. Planning finances, travel times, and distances can all be made easier by using linear equations and inequalities.

## Chapter Vocabulary

Vocabulary terms are used in context in the student text. For definitions, see the Glossary at the end of the Student Book and the Online Multilingual Glossary.

**equation** A statement that two mathematical expressions are equal

**inequality** A mathematical sentence that compares two unequal expressions

**solution** A value that makes an equation or an inequality true when substituted for the variable

**linear equation** An algebraic equation that has a dependent and an independent variable. The variables each have an exponent of 1 and are not multiplied together. The graph of a linear equation is a straight line.

**dependent variable** A variable whose value depends on the value of a related independent variable

**independent variable** A variable whose value determines the value of a related dependent variable

**BIG IDEA**

▶ Equations and inequalities can be used to describe situations and solve real-world problems.

## CHAPTER OPENER

Use the chapter opener to talk about the use of equations and inequalities in real life situations.

**Ask** Has anyone visited another country? How much money does a person need when he or she goes to another country? Possible answer: Yes. It depends on the currency exchange rate and how much the person needs to spend while he or she is abroad.

**Explain** Many countries use different currencies. How much you get of each currency for one US dollar depends on the exchange rate. For example, if you travel to Singapore, and the exchange rate for US$1.00 is S$1.30, it means that for every US dollar, you can get $1.30 in Singapore dollars. You can express this exchange rate as $s = 1.3u$, where $s$ represents the number of Singapore dollars and $u$ represents the number of US dollars.

In this chapter, you will learn how to write and solve algebraic equations and inequalities for many situations, as summarized in the **Big Idea**.

# Recall Prior Knowledge

## Comparing numbers with symbols

| Symbol | Meaning | Example |
|--------|---------|---------|
| = | is equal to | $12 \times 4 = 48$ ➔ $12 \times 4$ is equal to 48. |
| ≠ | is not equal to | $6 - 2 \neq 2 - 6$ ➔ $6 - 2$ is not equal to $2 - 6$. |
| > | is greater than | $0 > -9$ ➔ 0 is greater than $-9$. |
| < | is less than | $-5 < -1$ ➔ $-5$ is less than $-1$. |

### ✓ Quick Check

**Complete with =, >, or <.**

**1** 25 ? $-26$ $>$

**2** $12 + 12 + 12$ ? $3 \cdot 12$ $=$

**3** $40 \div 8$ ? $8 \div 40$ $>$

**4** $-16$ ? $-7$ $<$

## Using variables to write algebraic expressions

| Statement | Expression |
|-----------|------------|
| The sum of $x$ and 7 | $x + 7$ |
| The difference "14 less than $y$" | $y - 14$ |
| The product of 8 and $w$ | $8w$ |
| Divide $z$ by 6 | $\dfrac{z}{6}$ |

### ✓ Quick Check

**Write an algebraic expression for each of the following.**

**5** The sum of 15 and $p$  $15 + p$

**6** The difference "$q$ less than 10"  $10 - q$

**7** The product of $r$ and 23  $23r$

**8** Divide $s$ by 11.  $\dfrac{s}{11}$

## RECALL PRIOR KNOWLEDGE

Use the ✓ **Quick Check** exercises or Chapter Pre-Test in *Assessments, Course 1*, to assess students' chapter readiness. For intervention suggestions see the chart below and on the next page.

🖱 Additional online Reteach and Extra Practice worksheets from previous grades are also available. See the *Transition Guide*, Resource Planner for more information.

## RtI Assessing Prior Knowledge

| ✓ Quick Check | Assessments Course 1, Ch.8 Pre-Test Items | Skill Objective | Intervene with | |
|---------------|-------------------------------------------|-----------------|----------------|--|
| | | | Transition Guide | 🖱 Online Resources Grades 4 and 5 |
| **1** to **4** | 1–8 | Compare numbers with symbols. | Skill 31 | |
| **5** to **8** | 9–14 | Use variables to write algebraic expressions. | Skill 32 | Reteach 5A, pp. 143–146; Extra Practice 5A, Lesson 5.1 |

## Evaluating algebraic expressions

Evaluate $4y + 1$ when

a) $y = 7$,
b) $y = 10$.

a) When $y = 7$,

$$4y + 1 = (4 \cdot 7) + 1 \qquad \text{Substitute.}$$
$$= 28 + 1 \qquad \text{Multiply inside parentheses.}$$
$$= 29 \qquad \text{Add.}$$

b) When $y = 10$,

$$4y + 1 = (4 \cdot 10) + 1 \qquad \text{Substitute.}$$
$$= 40 + 1 \qquad \text{Multiply inside parentheses.}$$
$$= 41 \qquad \text{Add.}$$

### ✔ Quick Check

**Evaluate each expression for the given values of the variable.**

**9** $3x + 5$ when $x = 9$ and $x = 12$  $x = 9, 3x + 5 = 32; x = 12, 3x + 5 = 41$

**10** $28 - 4x$ when $x = 4$ and $x = 7$  $x = 4, 28 - 4x = 12; x = 7, 28 - 4x = 0$

## Plotting points on a coordinate plane

Plot points $A$ (2, 4) and $B$ (3, 2) on a coordinate plane.

To locate point $A$ (2, 4), move 2 units to the right of the $y$-axis and 4 units above the $x$-axis. Then mark the point with a dot.

To locate point $B$ (3, 2), move 3 units to the right of the $y$-axis and 2 units above the $x$-axis. Then mark the point with a dot.

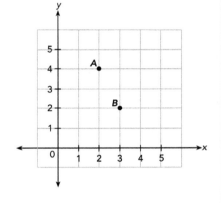

**11**

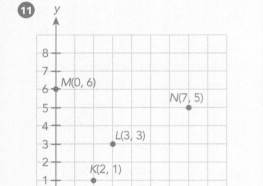

### ✔ Quick Check

**Plot the points on a coordinate plane.**

**11** $K$ (2, 1), $L$ (3, 3), $M$ (0, 6), and $N$ (7, 5)  See margin.

---

### ▲ RtI Assessing Prior Knowledge

| ✔ Quick Check | Assessments Course 1, Ch.8 Pre-Test Items | Skill Objective | Intervene with | |
| --- | --- | --- | --- | --- |
| | | | Transition Guide | ⊙ Online Resources Grades 4 and 5 |
| **9** to **10** | 15–18 | Evaluate algebraic expressions. | Skill 33 | Reteach 5A, pp. 147–152; Extra Practice 5A, Lesson 5.2 |
| **11** | 19–20 | Plot points on a coordinate plane. | Skill 34 | Reteach 4A, pp. 91–94; Extra Practice 4A, Lesson 4.3 |

**Lesson Objective**

• Solve equations in one variable.

**Vocabulary**

equation
solution

## KEY CONCEPT

• The solutions of an equation are the values of the variable that make the equation true.

## PACING

DAY **1** Pages 5–8

DAY **2** Pages 9–12

**Materials:** algebra tiles, balance scale

 **Use substitution to solve simple algebraic equations.**

a) The figure shows a balance scale. Find the value of x such that the left side balances the right side.

■ represents 1 counter.
x represents x counters.

There are $(x + 5)$ counters on the left side.

There are 8 counters on the right side.

Since the two sides balance each other,

$x + 5 = 8$.

$x + 5 = 8$ is called an equation.

To solve the equation, you need to find the value of x that makes $x + 5 = 8$ true.

If $x = 1$,    $x + 5 = 1 + 5$
             $= 6$    $(\neq 8)$

If $x = 2$,    $x + 5 = 2 + 5$
             $= 7$    $(\neq 8)$

If $x = 3$,    $x + 5 = 3 + 5$
             $= 8$

The equation $x + 5 = 8$ holds true when $x = 3$.

$x = 3$ gives the **solution** of the equation $x + 5 = 8$.

You can think of an equation as a balance scale, where the left side is always balanced by the right side.

Another way to solve an equation like $x + 5 = 8$ is to ask yourself, 'What number can be added to 5 to equal 8?' Only 3 can be added to 5 to equal 8, so the only solution of the equation is 3.

**Continue on next page**

### 5-minute Warm Up

1. Evaluate these algebraic expressions:
   a) $x + 6$ when $x = 2$ and $x = 5$
      8; 11
   b) $4x$ when $x = 4$ and $x = 7$
      16; 28

2. Complete these equations.
   a) ___ $+ 3 = 9$ 6
   b) ___ $+ 6 = 10$ 4
   c) $4 \cdot$ ___ $= 8$ 2
   d) $3 \cdot$ ___ $= 15$ 5
   e) ___ $+ 5 = 12$ 7
   f) $6 \cdot$ ___ $= 18$ 3

⏱ Also available on Teacher One Stop.

---

DAY **1**

 **Use substitution to solve simple algebraic equations.**

a) **Ask** How many counters are there on the right of the balance scale? 8 How many counters are there on the left of the balance scale? $(x + 5)$ Since the two sides balance each other, what does this tell you? $x + 5 = 8$

**Explain** Explain that $x + 5 = 8$ is called an equation. To solve this equation, you have to find the value of x that makes $x + 5 = 8$ true. You can do this by substituting some values of x in the equation.

**Ask** Is the equation true if $x = 2$? No; $x + 5 = 2 + 5$ $= 7$, not 8. Is the equation true when $x = 3$? Yes; $x + 5 = 3 + 5 = 8$. So, 3 is the solution of the equation.

**Explain** You can also solve this equation by finding the missing number in ___ $+ 5 = 8$. Since $3 + 5 = 8$, x must be equal to 3.

## Guided Practice

1 Explain that when you substitute a value of $x$ in the equation, you are evaluating the expression on the left of the equal sign.

---

b) Solve the equation $3x = 12$.

The equation $3x = 12$ can be represented on a balance scale:

■ represents 1 counter.
x represents $x$ counters.

To solve the equation, you need to find the value of $x$ that makes $3x = 12$ true.

If $x = 1$, $\qquad 3x = 3 \cdot 1$
$\qquad\qquad\qquad = 3 \qquad (\neq 12)$

If $x = 2$, $\qquad 3x = 3 \cdot 2$
$\qquad\qquad\qquad = 6 \qquad (\neq 12)$

If $x = 4$, $\qquad 3x = 3 \cdot 4$
$\qquad\qquad\qquad = 12$

The equation $3x = 12$ holds true when $x = 4$.

$x = 4$ gives the solution of the equation $3x = 12$.

> The equation $3x = 12$ has only one solution, $x = 4$. The equation does not hold true for other values of $x$.

## Guided Practice

**Complete each ? with = or ≠, and each _?_ with the correct value.**

1 For what value of $x$ will $x + 3 = 7$ be true?

If $x = 1$, $\qquad x + 3 = \underline{?} + 3$ 1
$\qquad\qquad\qquad = \underline{?}$ ( ? 7) 4; ≠

If $x = 2$, $\qquad x + 3 = \underline{?} + 3$ 2
$\qquad\qquad\qquad = \underline{?}$ ( ? 7) 5; ≠

If $x = 4$, $\qquad x + 3 = \underline{?} + 3$ 4
$\qquad\qquad\qquad = \underline{?}$ 7

$x + 3 = 7$ is true when $x = \underline{?}$. 4

---

**Learn continued**

b) **Ask** How many counters are on the right side of the balance scale? 12 How many counters are on the left of the balance scale? $x + x + x = 3x$ Since the two sides balance each other, what does this tell you? $3x = 12$

**Explain** Explain that $3x = 12$ is also an equation. To solve this equation, you have to find the value of $x$ that makes $3x = 12$ true. Substitute some values of $x$ in the equation.

**Ask** Is the equation true if $x = 3$? No; $3x = 3 \cdot 3 = 9$, not 12. Is the equation true when $x = 4$? Yes; $3x = 3 \cdot 4 = 12$. So, 4 is the solution of the equation.

**Explain** You can also solve this equation by finding the missing number in $3 \cdot \underline{\quad} = 12$. Since $3 \cdot 4 = 12$, $x$ must be equal to 4.

**Solve each equation using the substitution method.**

**2** $p + 6 = 13$  $p = 7$     **3** $r + 4 = 12$  $r = 8$     **4** $k - 10 = 7$  $k = 17$

**5** $2m = 6$  $m = 3$     **6** $4n = 20$  $n = 5$     **7** $\frac{1}{5}z = 3$  $z = 15$

## *Learn* Solve algebraic equations involving addition or subtraction.

a) Solve the equation $x + 6 = 9$.

The equation $x + 6 = 9$ can be represented on a balance scale:

> ■ represents 1 counter.
> ■ x represents x counters.

When you remove 6 counters from the left side, the scale becomes unbalanced.

$$x + 6 - 6 < 9$$

To balance the scale, you will need to remove 6 counters from the right side.

$$x + 6 - 6 = 9 - 6$$

The steps above can be summarized as follows:

$$x + 6 = 9$$
$$x + 6 - 6 = 9 - 6 \quad \text{Subtract 6 from both sides.}$$
$$x = 3$$

$x = 3$ gives the solution of the equation $x + 6 = 9$.

**Check:** Substitute 3 for the value of $x$ into the equation.

$$x + 6 = 3 + 6$$
$$= 9$$

When $x = 3$, the equation $x + 6 = 9$ is true.
$x = 3$ gives the correct solution.

> **Math Note**
>
> Compare this with $3 + 6 = 9$.
>
> $$3 + 6 - 6 = 9 - 6$$
> $$3 = 9 - 6$$
>
> You can subtract the same number from both sides of the equation and the two sides will remain equal.

**Continue on next page**

## Guided Practice

**2** to **7** You may want to work a couple of these problems as a class. For **2**, remind students that they can solve by asking, "What number plus 6 equals 13?" Look out for students who don't understand that the equation in **7** means "$\frac{1}{5}$ times z equals 3." Point out that the equation also means "$\frac{1}{5}$ of some unknown number z is 3."

### Best Practices

You may want to describe the process of solving an equation in everyday terms. To find the value of $x$ in $x + 6 = 9$, you need to "get $x$ alone" on one side of the equation. **Ask:** How can you "get $x$ alone" on the left side of the equation? *(Subtract 6.)* Why do you also need to subtract 6 from the right side of the equation? *(To keep the equation balanced)*

## *Learn* Solve algebraic equations involving addition or subtraction.

a) **Ask** How many counters are there on the right side of the balance scale? 9 How many counters are there on the left side of the balance scale? $x + 6$ Since the two sides balance, what does this tell you? $x + 6 = 9$

**Explain** Point out that $x + 6 = 9$ is an equation. To find $x$, remove 6 counters from the left side. To balance the two sides, you must also remove 6 counters from the right side. You record what you have done as

$$x + 6 = 9$$
$$x + 6 - 6 = 9 - 6 \quad \text{Subtract 6 from both sides.}$$
$$x = 3$$

**Explain** To show $x + 6$ in the model, 6 counters were added to $x$ on the left of the balance scale. To solve for $x$, you removed 6 counters from both sides. When solving equations, you show this by subtracting 6 from both sides of the equation. You subtract 6, because the inverse operation of adding 6 is subtracting 6.

**Ask** How can you check that $x = 3$ gives the correct solution? By substituting 3 for $x$ in the original equation

**Explain** When you substitute 3 for $x$, you get $x + 6 = 3 + 6 = 9$. So, the equation is a true statement, and $x = 3$ gives the correct solution.

## DIFFERENTIATED INSTRUCTION

**Through Concrete Manipulatives**

You may want to to use algebra tiles or an actual balance scale to model the operations in **a)** and **b)**. Make sure students understand that the scale will stay balanced when any number of counters are added to or subtracted from each side. The important idea is that the same operation must be performed on both sides of the equal sign or equation.

## Guided Practice

**8** Remind students that they must add or subtract the same number from both sides of the equation.

**Caution** ////////

**8** Some students may add the number subtracted from the left side of the equation to the right side: $x + 8 = 19$; $x + 8 - 8 = 19 + 8$; $x = 27$. Emphasize that to keep the equation "balanced," the same number must be taken away from each side. Students must perform the same operation with the same number on each side.

**b)** Solve the equation $6 = x - 3$.

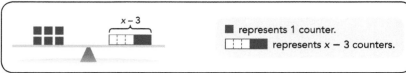

- ■ represents 1 counter.
- ⬚■ represents $x - 3$ counters.

$$6 = x - 3$$
$$6 + 3 = x - 3 + 3 \quad \text{Add 3 to both sides.}$$
$$9 = x$$

**Check:** Substitute 9 for the value of $x$ into the equation.

$$6 = x - 3$$
$$= 9 - 3$$
$$= 6$$

When $x = 9$, the equation $6 = x - 3$ holds true.

$x = 9$ gives the correct solution.

> **Math Note**
>
> Compare this with $6 = 9 - 3$.
>
> $$6 + 3 = 9 - 3 + 3$$
> $$6 + 3 = 9$$
>
> You can add the same number to both sides of the equation and the two sides will remain equal.

### Guided Practice

Complete each **?** with + or −, and each **?** with the correct value.

**8** Solve $x + 8 = 19$.

$$x + 8 = 19$$
$$x + 8 \; \boxed{?} \; \underline{?} = 19 \; \boxed{?} \; \underline{?} \qquad -; 8; -; 8$$
$$x = \underline{?} \quad 11$$

Solve each equation.

**9** $f + 5 = 14$ $f = 9$

**10** $26 = g + 11$ $g = 15$

**11** $w - 6 = 10$ $w = 16$

**12** $z - 9 = 21$ $z = 30$

---

**Learn continued**

**b) Ask** How many counters are there on the right side of the balance scale? $x - 3$ How many counters are there on the left side of the balance scale? 6 Since the two sides balance, what does this tell you?
$6 = x - 3$

**Explain** $6 = x - 3$ is another equation. To find $x$, you can add 3 to both sides of the equation like this:

$$6 = x - 3$$
$$6 + 3 = x - 3 + 3 \quad \text{Add 3 to both sides.}$$
$$9 = x$$

**Ask** Why did you add 3 to both sides? Because 3 has been subtracted from $x$, and adding 3 is the inverse of subtracting 3. **How** can you check that $x = 9$ gives the correct solution? By substituting 9 for $x$ in the original equation

**Explain** When you substitute 9 for $x$, you get $x - 3 = 9 - 3 = 6$. So, the equation is a true statement, and $x = 9$ gives the correct solution.

## Learn Solve algebraic equations involving multiplication or division.

a) Solve the equation $2x = 12$.

The equation $2x = 12$ can be represented on a balance scale:

■ represents 1 counter.
| x | represents x counters.

When you divide the number of counters on the left side by 2, the scale becomes unbalanced.

$2x \div 2 < 12$

To balance the scale, you will need to divide the number of counters on the right side by 2.

$2x \div 2 = 12 \div 2$

The steps above can be summarized as follows:

$$2x = 12$$
$$2x \div 2 = 12 \div 2 \qquad \text{Divide both sides by 2.}$$
$$x = 6$$

$x = 6$ gives the solution of the equation $2x = 12$.

**Check:** Substitute 6 for the value of x into the equation.

$$2x = 2 \cdot 6$$
$$= 12$$

When $x = 6$, the equation $2x = 12$ holds true.

$x = 6$ gives the correct solution.

### Math Note

Compare this with $6 \cdot 2 = 12$.

$$6 \cdot 2 \div 2 = 12 \div 2$$
$$6 = 12 \div 2$$

You can divide both sides of the equation by the same number (except 0) and the two sides will remain equal.

**Continue on next page**

Continue on next page

---

---

### DAY 2

## Learn Solve algebraic equations involving multiplication or division.

a) **Ask** What operation is being used in the equation $2x = 12$? multiplication What numbers are being multiplied? 2 and an unknown number x

**Ask** How many counters are on the right side of the balance scale? 12 How many counters are there on the left side of the balance scale? 2x Since the two sides balance, what does this tell you? $2x = 12$ In the equation $2x = 12$, what inverse operation do you need to use to find x? Dividing by 2

**Explain** $2x = 12$ is an equation. To find x, you can divide both sides of the equation by 2 like this:

$$2x = 12$$
$$\frac{2x}{2} = \frac{12}{2} \quad \text{Divide both sides by 2.}$$
$$x = 6$$

**Ask** How can you check that $x = 6$ gives the correct solution? By substituting 6 for x into the original equation

**Explain** When you substitute 6 for x, you get $2x = 2 \cdot 6 = 12$. So, the equation is a true statement, and $x = 6$ gives the correct solution.

b) Solve the equation $\frac{y}{3} = 4$.

■ represents 1 counter.

$\boxed{\frac{y}{3}\ \vdots}$ represents $\frac{y}{3}$ counters.

$\frac{y}{3} = 4$

$\frac{y}{3} \cdot 3 = 4 \cdot 3$   Multiply both sides by 3.

$y = 12$

**Check:** Substitute 12 for the value of $y$ into the equation.

$\frac{y}{3} = \frac{12}{3}$

$= 4$

When $y = 12$, the equation $\frac{y}{3} = 4$ holds true.

$y = 12$ gives the correct solution.

**Math Note**

Compare this with $\frac{12}{3} = 4$.

$\frac{12}{3} \cdot 3 = 4 \cdot 3$

$12 = 4 \cdot 3$

You can multiply both sides of the equation by the same number and the two sides will remain equal.

### Guided Practice

Complete each ? with × or ÷, and __?__ with the correct value.

13 Solve $3x = 27$.

$3x = 27$

$3x$ ⬤ __?__ $= 27$ ⬤ __?__   ÷; 3; ÷; 3

$x = $ __?__   9

**Solve each equation.**

14 $6a = 42$   $a = 7$

15 $65 = 13b$   $b = 5$

16 $\frac{m}{8} = 9$   $m = 72$

17 $12 = \frac{n}{7}$   $n = 84$

## Guided Practice

15 Remind students that they must multiply or divide both sides of the equation by the same non-zero number.

**Learn continued**

b) **Ask** What operation is being used in the equation $\frac{y}{3} = 4$? Division; an unknown number $y$ is divided by 3.

**Ask** How many counters are there on the right side of the balance scale? 4 How many counters are there on the left side of the balance scale? $\frac{y}{3}$ Since the two sides balance, what does this tell you? $\frac{y}{3} = 4$

**Explain** $\frac{y}{3} = 4$ is another equation. To find $y$, you can multiply both sides of the equation by 3 like this:

$\frac{y}{3} = 4$

$\frac{y}{3} \cdot 3 = 4 \cdot 3$

$y = 12$

**Ask** How can you check that $y = 12$ gives the correct solution? By substituting 12 for $y$ into the original equation

**Explain** When you substitute 12 for $y$, you get $\frac{y}{3} = \frac{12}{3} = 4$. So, the equation is a true statement, and $y = 12$ gives the correct solution.

**Learn** **Solve algebraic equations involving fractions.**

a) Solve the equation $x + \frac{1}{10} = \frac{3}{10}$. Write your answer in simplest form.

Decide which operation to use. Since $\frac{1}{10}$ was added to the variable, you need to subtract $\frac{1}{10}$ from each side of the equation.

$$x + \frac{1}{10} = \frac{3}{10}$$
$$x + \frac{1}{10} - \frac{1}{10} = \frac{3}{10} - \frac{1}{10} \qquad \text{Subtract } \frac{1}{10} \text{ from both sides.}$$
$$x = \frac{2}{10} \qquad \text{Simplify.}$$
$$= \frac{1}{5}$$

b) Solve the equation $3y = \frac{2}{3}$.

Decide which operation to use. Since $y$ was multiplied by 3, divide each side of the equation by 3.

$$3y = \frac{2}{3}$$
$$3y \div 3 = \frac{2}{3} \div 3 \qquad \text{Divide both sides by 3.}$$
$$y = \frac{2}{3} \cdot \frac{1}{3} \qquad \text{Multiply by the reciprocal of the divisor.}$$
$$= \frac{2}{9}$$

**Guided Practice**

Complete each ? with +, −, × or ÷, and __?__ with the correct value.

18 Solve $x + \frac{3}{7} = \frac{5}{7}$.

$$x + \frac{3}{7} = \frac{5}{7}$$
$$x + \frac{3}{7} \;?\; \underline{\;?\;} = \frac{5}{7} \;?\; \underline{\;?\;} \qquad -; \frac{3}{7}; -; \frac{3}{7}$$
$$x = \underline{\;?\;} \frac{2}{7}$$

Solve each equation. First tell which operation you will perform on each side of the equation. Write your answer in simplest form.

19 $k + \frac{1}{8} = \frac{7}{8}$  Subtract $\frac{1}{8}$; $k = \frac{3}{4}$

20 $4p = \frac{3}{4}$  Divide by 4; $p = \frac{3}{16}$

---

**DIFFERENTIATED INSTRUCTION**

**Through Enrichment**

Point out that when students subtract the same number from both sides of an equation or divide both sides of an equation by the same *non-zero* number, they are applying properties of equality. Subtraction Property of Equality If $a = b$, then $a - c = b - c$. Division Property of Equality If $a = b$, then $a \div c = b \div c$, $c \neq 0$.

**Guided Practice**

18 Remind students to first decide which inverse operation is needed to solve the equation.

---

**Learn** **Solve algebraic equations involving fractions.**

a) **Ask** How can you solve the equation

$x + \frac{1}{10} = \frac{3}{10}$? Subtract $\frac{1}{10}$ from both sides.

**Explain** Show students that

$$x + \frac{1}{10} = \frac{3}{10}$$
$$x + \frac{1}{10} - \frac{1}{10} = \frac{3}{10} - \frac{1}{10}$$
$$x = \frac{2}{10} = \frac{1}{5}$$

**Ask** How can you check your solution? Substitute $\frac{1}{5}$ or $\frac{2}{10}$ for $x$ into the equation.

**Explain** Show students that

$$x + \frac{1}{10} = \frac{2}{10} + \frac{1}{10} = \frac{3}{10}.$$

When $x = \frac{1}{5}$, $x + \frac{1}{10} = \frac{3}{10}$ is true.

$x = \frac{1}{5}$ is the correct solution.

b) **Ask** How can you solve the equation $3y = \frac{2}{3}$? Divide both sides by 3.

**Explain** Show students that

$$3y = \frac{2}{3}$$
$$\frac{3y}{3} = \frac{2}{3} \div 3$$
$$y = \frac{2}{3} \cdot \frac{1}{3} = \frac{2}{9}$$

**Ask** How can you check your solution? Substitute $\frac{2}{9}$ for $y$ into the equation.

## Practice 8.1

Basic ①–⑲
Intermediate ⑳–㉝
Advanced ㉞–㉟

### Assignment Guide

**DAY 1** All students should complete ① – ⑲.

**DAY 2** All students should complete ⑳ – ㉝.

㉞ – ㉟ provide additional challenge.

Optional: *Extra Practice 8.1*

**EXIT**

### Ticket Out the Door

Explain how inverse operations are used to solve equations in one variable. Include at least one example. Possible answer: You use inverse operations in order to get the variable alone on one side of the equation. For example, to solve the addition equation $x + 3 = 9$, you use subtraction, the inverse of addition. You subtract 3 from each side of the equation and find $x = 6$.

 Also available on Teacher One Stop.

---

## Practice 8.1

Solve each equation using the substitution method.

① $b + 7 = 10$  $b = 3$
② $17 = e + 9$  $e = 8$
③ $k - 4 = 11$  $k = 15$
④ $42 = 3p$  $p = 14$
⑤ $8t = 56$  $t = 7$
⑥ $\frac{1}{4}v = 5$  $v = 20$

Solve each equation using the concept of balancing.

⑦ $k + 12 = 23$  $k = 11$
⑧ $x - 8 = 17$  $x = 25$
⑨ $24 = f - 16$  $f = 40$
⑩ $5j = 75$  $j = 15$
⑪ $81 = 9m$  $m = 9$
⑫ $\frac{r}{6} = 11$  $r = 66$

Solve each equation using the concept of balancing. Write all fraction answers in simplest form.

⑬ $\frac{5}{6} = c + \frac{1}{6}$  $c = \frac{2}{3}$
⑭ $h + \frac{5}{14} = \frac{11}{14}$  $h = \frac{3}{7}$
⑮ $q - \frac{3}{10} = \frac{7}{10}$  $q = 1$
⑯ $7k = \frac{4}{7}$  $k = \frac{4}{49}$
⑰ $\frac{5}{12} = 5d$  $d = \frac{1}{12}$
⑱ $\frac{1}{2}x = \frac{1}{4}$  $x = \frac{1}{2}$
⑲ $\frac{8}{9} = \frac{1}{3}f$  $f = 2\frac{2}{3}$
⑳ $r + 2.1 = 4.7$  $r = 2.6$
㉑ $9.9 = x + 5.4$  $x = 4.5$
㉒ $11.2 = f - 1.8$  $f = 13$
㉓ $j - 3.7 = 20.4$  $j = 24.1$
㉔ $4w = 6.8$  $w = 1.7$
㉕ $13.9 = 2.5z$  $z = 5.56$
㉖ $3.2d = 40.8$  $d = 12.75$
㉗ $x + \frac{1}{2} = 1\frac{3}{4}$  $x = 1\frac{1}{4}$
㉘ $g + \frac{5}{3} = 3\frac{2}{3}$  $g = 2$
㉙ $2\frac{5}{7} = p - \frac{2}{7}$  $p = 3$
㉚ $e - \frac{18}{11} = 1\frac{6}{11}$  $e = 3\frac{2}{11}$
㉛ $\frac{4}{3}y = 36$  $y = 27$
㉜ $\frac{9}{10} = \frac{5}{6}v$  $v = 1\frac{2}{25}$
㉝ $\frac{2}{3}k = 28 \cdot \frac{4}{9}$  $k = 18\frac{2}{3}$

Solve.

㉞ Find five pairs of whole numbers, such that when they are inserted into the equation below, the solution of the equation is 3. Answers vary.
$$x + \underline{\ ?\ } = \underline{\ ?\ }$$
Sample: 1, 4; 2, 5; 3, 6; 4, 7; 5, 8

㉟ Find five pairs of numbers, such that when they are inserted into the equation below, the solution of the equation is $\frac{2}{5}$. Answers vary.
$$\underline{\ ?\ }x = \underline{\ ?\ }$$
Sample: 1, $\frac{2}{5}$; 2, $\frac{4}{5}$; 3, $1\frac{1}{5}$; 4, $1\frac{3}{5}$; 5, 2

---

### ▲RtI Lesson Check

| Before assigning homework, use the following ... | to make sure students ... | Intervene with ... |
|---|---|---|
| Exercises ① and ⑨ | • can find the value of the variable that makes an equation true | |
|  **EXIT** Ticket Out the Door | • can use inverse operations to solve equations in one variable | Reteach 8.1 |

# 8.2 Writing Linear Equations

## Lesson Objectives

- Express the relationship between two quantities as a linear equation.
- Use a table or graph to represent a linear equation.

**Vocabulary**

linear equation
independent variable
dependent variable

**Write a linear equation to represent a given situation.**

a) Caleb is $x$ years old. His sister is 10 years older than he is. If his sister is $y$ years old, write an equation that relates their two ages.

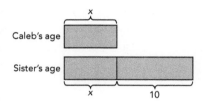

From the model, an expression for the sister's age is $x + 10$.

To make an equation using this expression, notice that the problem says that the sister's age is another variable $y$.

So you can write:

$y = x + 10$

The equation $y = x + 10$ is called a linear equation.

> In the equation, $x$ is called the **independent variable** and $y$ is called the **dependent variable** because the value of $y$ depends on the value of $x$.
>
> Writing $y$ as an expression using $x$ is called expressing $y$ in terms of $x$.

**Continue on next page** →

## KEY CONCEPTS

- In a linear equation, the two variables each has an exponent of 1 and the variables are not multiplied.

- A linear equation can be represented by a table or graph.

## PACING

DAY **1** Pages 13–15

DAY **2** Pages 15–21

**Materials:** TRT15–17

 **5-minute Warm Up**

Mary is $y$ years old.
Write an algebraic expression in terms of $y$ for the age of

a) her brother, who is 4 years older. $y + 4$

b) her mother, who is 3 times as old. $3y$

c) her sister, who is 2 years younger. $y - 2$

 Also available on Teacher One Stop.

---

DAY **1**

**Write a linear equation to represent a given situation.**

a) **Ask** How old is Caleb? x years old How many years older is his sister? 10 years older What is his sister's age in terms of x? (x + 10) years If you let his sister's age be y years, what is y equal to? y = x + 10

**Explain** Explain that $y = x + 10$ is called a linear equation. For every given value of x, a corresponding value of y can be found. For example, when x = 6, y = 6 + 10 = 16, when x = 12, y = 12 + 10 = 22. Note that the value of y (his sister's age) depends

on the value of x (Caleb's age). Since the value of y depends on the value of x, you call y the dependent variable and x the independent variable.

**Model** Remind students that a bar model can be used to represent the scenario.

b) A rhombus has sides of length $r$ centimeters. If the perimeter of the rhombus is $P$ centimeters, express $P$ in terms of $r$.

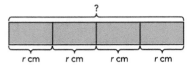

Expressing $P$ in terms of $r$ means that $r$ is the independent variable, and $P$ is the dependent variable.

$r$ cm

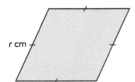

?

$r$ cm    $r$ cm    $r$ cm    $r$ cm

From the model, the perimeter of the rhombus = $r + r + r + r$
$$= 4r \text{ cm}$$

Because the perimeter of the rhombus is $P$ centimeters, you can write

$$P = 4r.$$

## Guided Practice

1 Remind students that the bar model can help them visualize the terms in the expression.

## Guided Practice

**Complete.**

1 Isaiah has $h$ baseball cards. Miguel has 7 more baseball cards than Isaiah.

a) Write an expression for the number of baseball cards that Miguel has in terms of $h$.

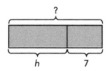

?

$h$        7

Miguel has __?__ baseball cards. $(h + 7)$

b) If Miguel has $k$ baseball cards, express $k$ in terms of $h$.

$k = $ __?__ $+$ __?__   $h; 7$

c) State the independent and dependent variables.

Independent variable: __?__ , dependent variable: __?__   $h; k$

---

**Learn continued**

b) **Model** Use a bar model to represent the perimeter of the rhombus.

**Ask** What is the length of one side of the rhombus? $r$ cm What is the perimeter of the rhombus in terms of $r$? $r + r + r + r$ or $4r$ cm If you let the perimeter of the rhombus be $P$ cm, what is $P$ equal to? $P = 4r$

**Explain** $P = 4r$ is another linear equation. For every value of $r$ (the length of one side), the corresponding value of $P$ can be found. For example, when $r = 5$, $P = 4 \cdot 5 = 20$, when $r = 7$, $P = 4 \cdot 7 = 28$. The value of $P$ depends on the value of $r$.

**Ask** Which is the dependent variable in the equation $P = 4r$? $P$ Which is the independent variable? $r$

**Write an equation for each of the following. Then state the independent and dependent variables for each equation.**

**2** Hannah took $p$ minutes to jog around a park. Sofia took 12 minutes longer to jog around the park. If Sofia took $t$ minutes to jog around the park, express $t$ in terms of $p$. $t = p + 12$; Independent variable: $p$, Dependent variable: $t$

**3** A bouquet of roses costs $30. A bouquet of tulips costs $m$ dollars less. If the cost of one bouquet of tulips is $n$ dollars, express $n$ in terms of $m$. $n = 30 - m$; Independent variable: $m$, Dependent variable: $n$

**4** Nathan has 7 boxes of marbles. Each box contains $b$ marbles. If he has $c$ marbles altogether, express $c$ in terms of $b$. $c = 7b$; Independent variable: $b$, Dependent variable: $c$

**5** A motel charges Mr. Kim $x$ dollars for his stay. Mr. Kim stayed at the motel for 12 nights. If the rate per night for a room is $y$ dollars, express $y$ in terms of $x$. $y = \dfrac{x}{12}$; Independent variable: $x$, Dependent variable: $y$

## Use tables and graphs to represent linear equations.

a) The length of a rectangular picture frame is 5 inches longer than its width. Write an equation to show how its width and length are related.

Let $w$ represent the width of the picture frame, in inches.
Let $\ell$ represent the length of the picture frame, in inches.

Since the length is 5 inches longer than the width,

$\ell = w + 5$.

Many pairs of $\ell$ and $w$ values will make this equation true.

| Width ($w$ in.) | | Length ($\ell$ in.) |
|---|---|---|
| 1 | $\xrightarrow{+5}$ | 6 |
| 2 | $\xrightarrow{+5}$ | 7 |
| 3 | $\xrightarrow{+5}$ | 8 |
| 4 | $\xrightarrow{+5}$ | 9 |
| 5 | $\xrightarrow{+5}$ | 10 |

> The length is dependent on the width.
>
> The width ($w$) is the independent variable, and the length ($\ell$) is the dependent variable.

**Continue on next page**

## Guided Practice

**2** to **5** For students who have difficulty identifying the independent and dependent variables, explain that when they are asked to express one variable "in terms of" a second variable, the words "in terms of" imply that the second variable is the independent variable.

 **DIFFERENTIATED INSTRUCTION**

**Through Home Connection**

Have students use both words and algebraic expressions to describe real-world math situations they experience at home. For example: My brother practices piano for the same length of time every day. How much time does he spend practicing in a week? (*7m, where m represents the number of minutes he practices each of the 7 days in a week*)

---

**DAY 2**

## Use tables and graphs to represent linear equations.

a) **Ask** How much longer than the width is the length of the frame? 5 in. If the width of the frame is $w$ inches, what is the length of the frame? ($w + 5$) in. If you let the length of the frame be $\ell$ inches, what is $\ell$ equal to? $\ell = w + 5$

**Explain** $\ell = w + 5$ is a linear equation. For every value of $w$, there is a corresponding value of $\ell$. For example, when $w = 1$, $\ell = 1 + 5 = 6$, when $w = 2$, $\ell = 2 + 5 = 7$.

**Ask** In this situation, $\ell$ is expressed in terms of $w$. How does this fact help you identify the dependent and independent variables? The value of $\ell$ depends on the value chosen for $w$, so $\ell$ is the dependent variable, and $w$ is the independent variable.

The data on the previous page can be represented in a table, as shown below. The first row of the table shows values of the independent variable. The second row shows values of the dependent variable.

| Width (w inches) | 1 | 2 | 3 | 4 | 5 |
|---|---|---|---|---|---|
| Length (ℓ inches) | 6 | 7 | 8 | 9 | 10 |

Use the data in the table to plot the ordered pairs (1, 6), (2, 7), (3, 8), (4, 9), and (5, 10) on a coordinate plane. Connect the points to draw a line.

The horizontal axis shows the width of the picture frame.
The vertical axis shows the length of the picture frame.

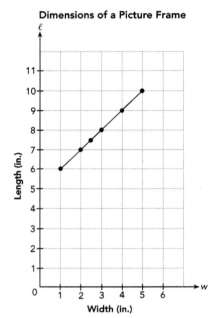

**Dimensions of a Picture Frame**

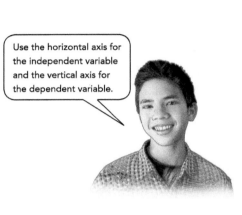

Use the horizontal axis for the independent variable and the vertical axis for the dependent variable.

All linear equations have graphs that are lines. The graph of a linear equation contains all the ordered pairs that make the equation true.

For example, the point (2.5, 7.5) is on the graph of the equation $\ell = w + 5$. You can see that these values make the equation true:

$$\ell = w + 5$$
$$7.5 = 2.5 + 5$$

The ordered pair (2.5, 7.5) also makes sense in this situation because you could have a picture frame that is 2.5 inches wide and 7.5 inches long.

**Learn continued**

**Explain** You can show the values of w and ℓ in a table. The table in the text shows the values of ℓ for values of w from 1 to 5.

You can use the table to draw a graph of the equation $\ell = w + 5$ on a coordinate plane.

**Model** Draw the graph. Then label the horizontal axis w and the vertical axis ℓ. Tell students that the horizontal axis always represents the independent variable and the vertical axis the dependent variable. Plot the points (1, 6), (2, 7) (3, 8), (4, 9), and (5, 10). Then connect them to draw a line.

**Ask** What is the shape of the graph? A straight line

**Explain** When you draw the graph of the equation $\ell = w + 5$, you can see that it is a straight line. For this reason, $\ell = w + 5$ is called a linear equation. At every point on the graph of $\ell = w + 5$, the coordinates of the point will make the equation true.

**Model** Mark a point on the graph and label it P. (P is the point (2.5, 7.5).)

**Ask** What are the coordinates of point P? (2.5, 7.5) When you substitute these values of w and ℓ into the equation $\ell = w + 5$, what do you find? 7.5 = 2.5 + 5 What does this tell you? These values make the equation true.

**b)** Each can of paint contains 5 gallons of paint. Write an equation to show the relationship between the number of cans and the volume of paint.

Let $v$ represent the volume of paint in gallons, and $c$ represent the number of cans of paint.

Since each can contains 5 gallons of paint,

$v = 5c$.

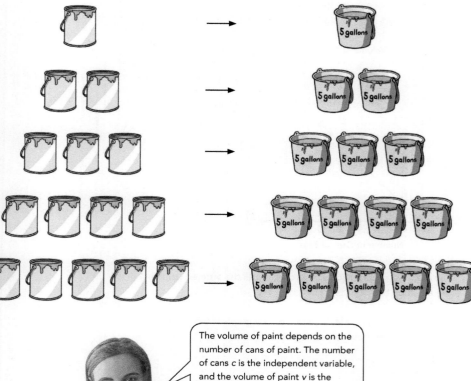

| Number of Cans (c) | Volume of Paint in Gallons (v) |
|---|---|

> The volume of paint depends on the number of cans of paint. The number of cans $c$ is the independent variable, and the volume of paint $v$ is the dependent variable.

**Continue on next page** ➡

**Learn continued**

**b)** **Ask** How many gallons of paint are there in 1 can? 5 gallons How can you find how many gallons there are in 2 cans? Since there are 5 gallons in 1 can, multiply 5 gallons by 2 for 2 cans: $5 \times 2 = 10$ gallons. Multiply 5 gallons by 3 for 3 cans: $5 \times 3 = 15$ gallons.

**Explain** Let $v$ represent the volume of paint and $c$ the number of cans of paint.

**Ask** How many gallons of paint are there in $c$ cans? $5c$ gallons If you let the amount of paint in $c$ cans be $v$ gallons, what is the value of $v$? $v = 5c$

**Explain** $v = 5c$ is another linear equation. For every value of $c$, there is a corresponding value of $v$

**Ask** When $c = 2$, what is the value of $v$? 10 When $c = 5$, what is the value of $v$? 25

**Through Multiple Representations**

Point out that the scale on the vertical axis of the graph is 0, 5, 10, 15... Explain that, for the equation $v = 5c$, this is a useful scale for the graph. Then display the graph of the equation using axes that are numbered in single units. Draw and label a coordinate grid that is 25 units tall and 5 units wide. Have volunteers plot each ordered pair from the table and then connect the points to draw a line. **Ask:** How did using increments of 5 along the vertical axis change the shape of the coordinate grid? *(It made the grid shorter, more compact.)* **Ask:** How did using increments of 3 along the vertical axis change the appearance of the graph of $v = 5c$? *(It made the lines less steep.)* Point out that while the two graphs appear to be different, they include the same values, the same ordered pairs.

The data on the previous page can be represented in a table, as shown below. The first row of the table shows values of the independent variable, and the second row shows values of the dependent variable.

| Number of Cans (c) | 1 | 2 | 3 | 4 | 5 |
|---|---|---|---|---|---|
| Volume of Paint (v gallons) | 5 | 10 | 15 | 20 | 25 |

You can write the data in the table as the ordered pairs (1, 5), (2, 10), (3, 15), (4, 20), and (5, 25). These ordered pairs can be plotted on a coordinate plane, and you can look for a pattern. You can connect the points to draw a line.

The horizontal axis shows the number of cans of paint.
The vertical axis shows the volume of paint in gallons.

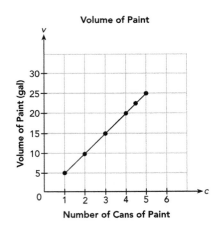

Volume of Paint

Use the horizontal axis for the independent variable and the vertical axis for the dependent variable.

The graph of the equation $v = 5c$ contains all the ordered pairs that make the equation true.

For example, the point (4.5, 22.5) is on the graph of the equation $v = 5c$. You can see that these values make the equation true:

$$v = 5c$$
$$22.5 = 5 \times 4.5$$

The ordered pair (4.5, 22.5) and other values of ordered pairs make sense in this situation.

It is possible to have 4.5 cans of paint that contain 22.5 gallons of paint.

It is also possible to have $2\frac{1}{3}$ cans of paint that contain $11\frac{2}{3}$ gallons of paint.

**Learn continued**

**Explain** You can show the values of c and v in a table. The table in the text shows the values of v for values of c from 1 to 5.

You can use the table to draw a graph of the equation $v = 5c$ on a coordinate plane.

**Ask** Which is the independent variable? c Which is the dependent variable? v

**Model** Draw the axes on a coordinate plane.

**Ask** How should you label the horizontal axis? c How should you label the vertical axis? v

**Model** Plot the points in the table on a coordinate plane. Then join the points.

**Ask** What is the shape of the graph? A straight line Why is $v = 5c$ a linear equation? Because its graph is a straight line.

**Explain** At every point on the graph of $v = 5c$, the coordinates of the point will make the equation true.

**Model** Mark the point (4.5, 22.5) on the graph.

**Ask** What are the coordinates of the point? (4.5, 22.5) When you substitute these values of c and v into the equation $v = 5c$, what do you find? $22.5 = 5 \times 4.5$ What does this tell you? These values make the equation true.

## Guided Practice

**Copy and complete the table. Then use the table to answer the questions.**

6 The width of a rectangular tank is 2 meters less than its length.

a) If the length is $p$ meters and the width is $q$ meters, write an equation relating $p$ and $q$. $q = p - 2$

| Length (p meters) | 3 | 4 | 5 | 6 | 7 | 8 |
|---|---|---|---|---|---|---|
| Width (q meters) | 1 | ? | ? | 4 | ? | ? |

2; 3; 5; 6

b) Use the data from **a)** to plot the points on a coordinate plane. Connect the points with a line. See margin.

c) The point (5.5, 3.5) is on the line you drew in **b)**. Does this point make sense in the situation? Yes, the rectangular tank can have a length of 5.5 meters and a width of 3.5 meters.

**Copy and complete each table. Then express the relationship between the two variables as an equation.**

7 Paul and Lee went to the library to borrow some books. Paul borrowed 6 more books than Lee.

| Number of Books Lee Borrowed (x) | 1 | 2 | 3 | 4 | 5 |
|---|---|---|---|---|---|
| Number of Books Paul Borrowed (y) | 7 | ? | 9 | ? | ? |

8; 10; 11; $y = x + 6$

8 At a crafts store, Zoey bought some boxes of red beads and some boxes of blue beads. The number of boxes of red beads was 4 times the number of boxes of blue beads.

| Number of Boxes of Blue Beads (b) | 2 | 3 | 4 | 5 | 6 |
|---|---|---|---|---|---|
| Number of Boxes of Red Beads (r) | 8 | ? | ? | ? | 24 |

12; 16; 20; $r = 4b$

**Use the data in the table to plot points on a coordinate plane. Connect the points to form a line. Then write an equation to show the relationship between the variables.**

9

| Time Taken (t hours) | 1 | 2 | 3 | 4 | 5 | 6 |
|---|---|---|---|---|---|---|
| Distance Traveled (d miles) | 50 | 100 | 150 | 200 | 250 | 300 |

See margin.
$d = 50t$

## Guided Practice

6 to 9 Remind students that each table shows the two variables of the problem situation, and letters are used to represent these variables. In 6, watch for students who incorrectly write the equation as $q = 2 - p$. Make sure they understand the problem statement, that the tank's width is "2 meters less than its length." Remind them that order is important in subtraction.

### Best Practices

9 Point out that writing an expression is similar to identifying a rule for a pattern. Each column individually may be described by a number of possible equations; students must find an equation that correctly describes *every* column in the table.

6 b)

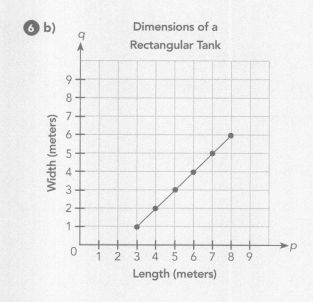

Dimensions of a Rectangular Tank

9

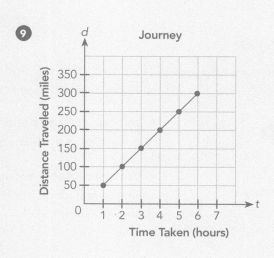

Journey

# Practice 8.2

Basic ① – ④
Intermediate ⑤ – ⑧
Advanced ⑨

**Solve.**

① Joshua is *w* years old. His brother is 3 years older than he is.

   a) If his brother is *x* years old, express *x* in terms of *w*. $x = w + 3$

   b) State the independent and dependent variables in the equation. Independent variable: *w*; Dependent variable: *x*

② Rita has *b* markers. Sandy has 11 fewer markers than she has.

   a) If Sandy has *h* markers, express *h* in terms of *b*. $h = b - 11$

   b) State the independent and dependent variables in the equation. Independent variable: *b*; Dependent variable: *h*

③ A small box of cereal weighs *k* grams. A jumbo box of cereal weighs 5 times as much.

   a) If the weight of the jumbo box of cereal is *m* grams, express *m* in terms of *k*. $m = 5k$

   b) State the independent and dependent variables in the equation. Independent variable: *k*; Dependent variable: *m*

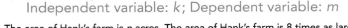
*m* grams     *k* grams

④ The area of Hank's farm is *n* acres. The area of Hank's farm is 8 times as large as the area of Stan's farm.

   a) If *s* represents the area of Stan's farm, express *s* in terms of *n*. $s = \dfrac{n}{8}$

   b) State the independent and dependent variables in the equation. Independent variable: *n*; Dependent variable: *s*

⑤ Ethan scored *x* points in a game. His younger sister scored 8 points when she played the same game. Their combined score was *y* points.

   a) Write an equation relating *x* and *y*. $y = x + 8$

   b) Copy and complete the table to show the relationship between *x* and *y*.

| Ethan's Scores (*x* points) | 10 | 11 | 12 | 13 | 14 | 15 |
|---|---|---|---|---|---|---|
| Combined Scores (*y* points) | ? | ? | ? | ? | ? | ? |

See below.

18; 19; 20; 21; 22; 23

## ⚠ RtI Lesson Check

| Before assigning homework, use the following ... | to make sure students ... | Intervene with ... |
|---|---|---|
| Exercises ① and ⑤ | • can express the relationship between two quantities as a linear equation | Reteach 8.2 |
| **EXIT** Ticket Out the Door | • can write a linear equation to describe a simple real-world math situation | |

**6** There are *x* sparrows in a tree. There are 50 sparrows on the ground beneath the tree. Let *y* represent the total number of sparrows in the tree and on the ground.

a) Express *y* in terms of *x*. $y = x + 50$

b) Make a table to show the relationship between *y* and *x*. Use values of *x* = 10, 20, 30, 40, and 50 in your table. See margin.

c) Graph the relationship between *y* and *x* in a coordinate plane. See margin.

**7** A rectangle has a perimeter of *P* centimeters. Its width is *b* centimeters. Its length is double its width.

a) Express *P* in terms of *b*. $P = 6b$

b) Copy and complete the table to show the relationship between *P* and *b*.

| Width (*b* centimeters) | 1 | 2 | 3 | 4 | 5 | 6 |
|---|---|---|---|---|---|---|
| Perimeter (*P* centimeters) | ? | ? | ? | ? | ? | ? |

See below.

6; 12; 18; 24; 30; 36

**8** Every month, Amaan spends 60% of what he earns and saves the rest. Amaan earns *n* dollars and saves *r* dollars each month.

a) Express *r* in terms of *n*. $r = \dfrac{2}{5}n$

spend

save

b) Make a table to show the relationship between *r* and *n*. Use values of *n* = 100, 200, 400, and 500 in your table. See margin.

c) Graph the relationship between *n* and *r* in a coordinate plane. See margin.

d) The point (287.5, 115) is on the line you drew in c). Does this point make sense in the situation? Explain. Yes. The point means Amaan earns $287.50 and saves $115 of it.

**9** The side length of a square is *t* inches. The perimeter of the square is *z* inches.

a) Express *z* in terms of *t*. $z = 4t$

b) Make a table to show the relationship between *z* and *t*. Use whole number values of *t* from 1 to 10. See margin.

c) Graph the relationship between *z* and *t* in a coordinate plane. See margin.

d) Use your graph to find the perimeter of the square when the length is 3.5 inches and 7.5 inches. Length: 3.5 in., Perimeter: 14 in.; Length: 7.5 in., Perimeter: 30 in.

**DIFFERENTIATED INSTRUCTION**

**Through Communication**

**7** You may want to use a series of prompts to guide students in writing an equation for this situation. **Ask:** What dimensions do you need to find the perimeter of a rectangle? *(Its length and width)* Does the problem give you either of those? *(Yes, the width is b cm.)* Knowing the width, *b*, what is the rectangle's length? *(2b)* Have students substitute these dimensions into the formula for the perimeter of a rectangle to write their equation.

**EXIT**

**Ticket Out the Door**

In your own words, describe a real-world math situation that involves two variables. Write a linear equation to describe the situation. Possible answer: Charlene is paid $8 an hour for working at a bookstore. Her pay *p* for any week is described by the equation *p* = 8*h*, where *h* is the number of hours she worked.

Also available on Teacher One Stop.

---

**6** b)

| No. of Sparrows in the Tree (*x*) | 10 | 20 | 30 | 40 | 50 |
|---|---|---|---|---|---|
| Total No. of Sparrows (*y*) | 60 | 70 | 80 | 90 | 100 |

c) **Number of Sparrows**

*(graph: Total No. of Sparrows vs. No. of Sparrows in the Tree, points plotted at (10,60), (20,70), (30,80), (40,90), (50,100))*

**8** b)

| Amount Amaan Earns (*n* dollars) | 100 | 200 | 400 | 500 |
|---|---|---|---|---|
| Amount Amaan Saves (*r* dollars) | 40 | 80 | 160 | 200 |

c) See Additional Answers.

**9** b)

| Length of Square (*t* inches) | 1 | 2 | 3 | 4 | 5 | 6 | 7 | 8 | 9 | 10 |
|---|---|---|---|---|---|---|---|---|---|---|
| Perimeter of Square (*z* inches) | 4 | 8 | 12 | 16 | 20 | 24 | 28 | 32 | 36 | 40 |

c) See Additional Answers.

# 8.3 Solving Simple Inequalities

## KEY CONCEPTS

- The solutions of an inequality are the values of the variable that make the inequality true.

- The solutions of an inequality can be represented by a number line.

## PACING

DAY **1** Pages 22–24

DAY **2** Pages 25–28

**Materials:** algebra tiles, balance scale, TRT1

### 5-minute Warm Up

Complete the following with **<** or **>**.

1. 6 ___ 8 <
2. 4.5 ___ 5 <
3. 8.6 ___ 7 >
4. 9 ___ 9.1 <
5. −4 ___ − 5 >
6. −3.5 ___ − 3 <
7. −7.6 ___ − 6 <
8. −8.1 ___ − 8 <

🖱 Also available on Teacher One Stop.

### Lesson Objectives

- Use substitution to determine whether a given number is a solution of an inequality.
- Represent the solutions of an inequality on a number line.

**Vocabulary**

inequality

**Learn** Determine solutions of inequalities of the form $x > c$ and $x < c$.

a) A bag of tomatoes weighs more than 5 pounds. Find the possible weights of the bag of tomatoes. Then represent the possible weights on a number line.

Let $x$ represent the possible weights, in pounds, of the tomatoes.

Since you know the bag of tomatoes weighs more than 5 pounds, you can write the inequality

$x > 5.$

To find the possible weights of the bag, you need to find the values of $x$ that make $x > 5$ true.

When $x = 5.1$,  $x > 5$ is true.
When $x = 5.2$,  $x > 5$ is true.
When $x = 5.3$,  $x > 5$ is true.
When $x = 6$,  $x > 5$ is true.
⋮        ⋮
When $x = 100$,  $x > 5$ is true.

When $x = 5$, the inequality is not true, since the bag of tomatoes must weigh **more than** 5 pounds.

The inequality $x > 5$ is true for any value of $x$ that is greater than 5.

Since the inequality has infinitely many solutions, you can represent the solutions on a number line as follows:

4  5  6  7  8  9  10  11  12  13

The number line above indicates that the inequality $x > 5$ is true for any value of $x$ that is greater than 5. This value can be a fraction or mixed number, decimal, or whole number.

For example, $5\frac{3}{8} > 5$, $5.6 > 5$, and $9 > 5$.

**Math Note**

The empty circle indicates that the value below the circle is not a solution of the inequality.

---

DAY **1**

**Learn** Determine solutions of inequalities of the form $x > c$ and $x < c$.

a) **Ask** What is the weight of the bag of tomatoes? More than 5 pounds If you let the weight of the bag of tomatoes be $x$ pounds, what can you say about $x$? $x$ is greater than 5. How do you write "$x$ is greater than 5" in symbols? $x > 5$

**Explain** $x > 5$ is an inequality. To solve it, you have to find the values of $x$ that make $x > 5$ true. To do this, substitute some values of $x$ into the inequality.

**Ask** Is $x = 4$ a solution of the inequality? No, because 4 > 5 is not a true statement. Is $x = 5$ a solution? No, because 5 > 5 is not a true statement.

Is $x = 5.1$ a solution? Yes, because 5.1 > 5 is a true statement. Can you name another number that is a solution? Yes; possible answer: 6

**Explain** You can see that any value of $x$ that is greater than 5 will make the inequality $x > 5$ true. You can use a graph to show all the solutions.

**Ask** How does the graph in your text show that 5 is not a solution of the inequality? An empty circle is shown at $x = 5$. How does the graph show that all numbers greater than 5 are solutions? The arrow points to the right of 5.

**b)** The figure shows a medicine bottle.

Store below
20°C

Find the possible temperatures at which the medicine should be stored.
Then represent the possible temperatures on a number line.

Let $w$ represent the possible temperatures, in °C, at which the medicine should be stored.

You can write an inequality to show that the medicine is to be stored below 20°C:

$w < 20$

To find the possible temperatures, you need to find the values of $w$ that make $w < 20$ true.

When $w = 19.9$,      $w < 20$ is true.
When $w = 19.8$,      $w < 20$ is true.
When $w = 19.7$,      $w < 20$ is true.
When $w = 19.5$,      $w < 20$ is true.
When $w = 19.4$,      $w < 20$ is true.
When $w = 10$,        $w < 20$ is true.
$\vdots$                    $\vdots$
When $w = -4$,        $w < 20$ is true.
When $w = -5$,        $w < 20$ is true.

The inequality $w < 20$ is true for any value of $w$ that is less than 20.

The solutions can be represented on a number line as shown:

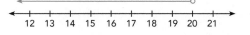

12   13   14   15   16   17   18   19   20   21

Learn continued

**b) Ask** About which temperature should the bottle of medicine be stored? It must be less than 20°C. If you store the medicine at $w$°C, what can you say about $w$? $w$ is less than 20. How do you write $w$ is less than 20 in symbols? $w < 20$

**Explain** $w < 20$ is another inequality. To solve this inequality, you have to find the values of $w$ that make $w < 20$ true. To do this, you have to substitute some values of $w$ into the inequality.

**Ask** Is $w = 21$ a solution of the inequality? No, because 21 < 20 is not a true statement.
Is $w = 20$ a solution? No, because 20 < 20 is not

a true statement. Is 19 a solution? Yes, because 19 < 20 is a true statement. Can you name another number that is a solution? Yes; possible answer: 18

**Explain** You can see that any value of $w$ that is less than 20 will make the inequality $w < 20$ true. You can use a graph to show all the solutions.

**Ask** How does the graph in your text show that 20 is not a solution of the inequality? An empty circle is shown at $x = 20$. How does the graph show that all numbers less than 20 are solutions? The arrow points to the left of 20.

**ELL** Vocabulary Highlight

Make sure that students understand the meaning of **inequality**. Point out that the prefix *in-* means "not." While an equation is a statement that two quantities are equal, an inequality is a statement that two quantities are *not* equal.

**Best Practices**

Students may wonder why these graphs are on a number line instead of a coordinate plane as in the previous lesson. Have students note that these equations have just one variable, not two. One-variable number sentences are graphed on a one-dimensional line, and two-variable number sentences are graphed in the two-dimensional coordinate plane.

## Guided Practice

**1** to **6** Students should be led to see that the solutions of each inequality are in fact given by the inequality.

### ✋ Hands-On Activity

Students should note that the value of $x$ is already determined to be 5. In **3**, the balance is not restored to its initial position. The 3 counters are removed from the 7 counters that are on the right side of the balance.

## Guided Practice

**Use substitution to determine the solutions of each inequality. Then represent the solution set of each inequality on a number line.**

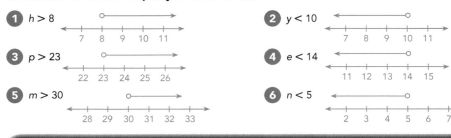

**1** $h > 8$

7  8  9  10  11

**2** $y < 10$

7  8  9  10  11

**3** $p > 23$

22  23  24  25  26

**4** $e < 14$

11  12  13  14  15

**5** $m > 30$

28  29  30  31  32  33

**6** $n < 5$

2  3  4  5  6  7

---

### ✋ Hands-On Activity

**WRITING INEQUALITIES**          **2** – **4** See margin.

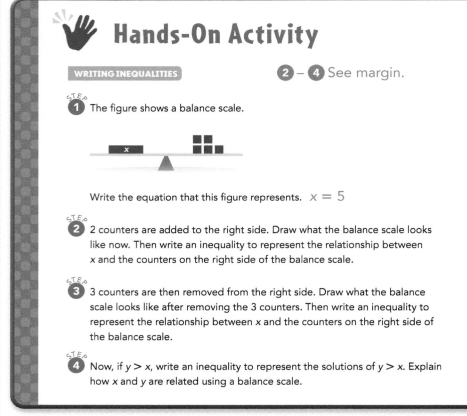

**STEP 1** The figure shows a balance scale.

Write the equation that this figure represents. $x = 5$

**STEP 2** 2 counters are added to the right side. Draw what the balance scale looks like now. Then write an inequality to represent the relationship between $x$ and the counters on the right side of the balance scale.

**STEP 3** 3 counters are then removed from the right side. Draw what the balance scale looks like after removing the 3 counters. Then write an inequality to represent the relationship between $x$ and the counters on the right side of the balance scale.

**STEP 4** Now, if $y > x$, write an inequality to represent the solutions of $y > x$. Explain how $x$ and $y$ are related using a balance scale.

---

**2**

$x < 7$

**3**
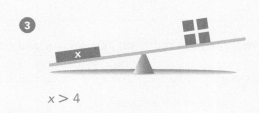
$x > 4$

**4** $y > 5$ since $x = 5$; The end with $y$ counters dips lower than the end with $x$ counters.

**Determine solutions of inequalities of the form** $x \geq c$ **and** $x \leq c$.

a) Yleana needs at least 7 feet of ribbon for her crafts project. Find the possible lengths of ribbon that would be enough to complete the project. Then represent the possible lengths on a number line.

Let $p$ represent the length, in feet, of the ribbon Yleana needs.

You can write an inequality to show the possible lengths she needs:

$p \geq 7$ $\qquad$ $\geq$ means "is greater than or equal to."

To find the possible lengths of the ribbon, you need to find the values of $p$ that make $p \geq 7$ true.

Since Yleana needs **at least** 7 feet of ribbon, this means that 7 is also a possible value of $p$.

When $p = 7$, $\qquad$ $p \geq 7$ is true.
When $p = 7.4$, $\qquad$ $p \geq 7$ is true.
When $p = 7\frac{4}{9}$, $\qquad$ $p \geq 7$ is true.
When $p = 8$, $\qquad$ $p \geq 7$ is true.
When $p = 8.5$, $\qquad$ $p \geq 7$ is true.
$\vdots$ $\qquad\qquad$ $\vdots$
When $p = 20$, $\qquad$ $p \geq 7$ is true.

The inequality $p \geq 7$ is true for any value of $p$ that is greater than or equal to 7.

Since the inequality has infinitely many solutions, you can represent the solutions of the inequality on a number line as follows:

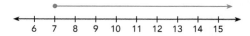

**Math Note**

The shaded circle indicates that the value below the circle is a solution of the inequality.

**Continue on next page**

---

**Determine solutions of inequalities of the form** $x > c$ **and** $x < c$.

a) **Ask** What is the length of the ribbon needed? At least 7 ft What is another way of saying "at least 7 ft?" Greater than or equal to 7 ft If the length is $p$ ft, what can you say about the value of $p$? $p$ is greater or equal to 7. How do you write "$p$ is greater than or equal to 7" in symbols? $p \geq 7$

**Explain** $p \geq 7$ is also an inequality. To solve it, you have to find the values of $p$ that make $p \geq 7$ true.

**Ask** Is $p = 6$ a solution of the inequality? No, because $6 \geq 7$ is not a true statement. Is $p = 7$ a solution? Yes, because $7 \geq 7$ is a true statement.

Can you name another number that is a solution? Yes; possible answer: 8

**Explain** Any value of $p$ that is equal to or greater than 7 will make the inequality $p \geq 7$ true. You can use a graph to show all the solutions.

**Ask** How does the graph show that 7 is a solution of the inequality? A filled circle is shown at $x = 7$. How does the graph show that all numbers more than 7 are solutions? The arrow points to the right of 7.

**Explain** Point out to students that the solutions of $p \geq 7$ are also infinite in number.

**b)** On one winter day, Helena, Montana, had a maximum temperature of −4°C. Find the possible temperatures in Helena that day. Then represent the possible temperatures on a number line.

Let $y$ represent the possible temperatures, in °C, of Helena that day.

Since you know the maximum temperature is −4°C, you can write an inequality

$y \leq -4$                    $\leq$ means "is less than or equal to."

To find the possible temperatures, you need to find the values of $y$ that make $y \leq -4$ true.

When $y = -4$,      $y \leq -4$ is true.
When $y = -4.2$,      $y \leq -4$ is true.
When $y = -4.7$,      $y \leq -4$ is true.
When $y = -5$,      $y \leq -4$ is true.
When $y = -6.7$,      $y \leq -4$ is true.
When $y = -8$,      $y \leq -4$ is true.

The inequality $y \leq -4$ is true for any value of $y$ that is less than or equal to −4.

The solutions can be represented on a number line as shown:

**7** Answers vary.
Sample: $q$ = 3, 4, or 5

**8** Answers vary.
Sample: $d$ = 10, 11, or 12

**9** Answers vary.
Sample: $k$ = 23, 24, or 25

**8** Answers vary.
Sample: $m$ = −28, −27, or −26

## Guided Practice

**7** to **14** Students should note that the solutions of each inequality are given by the inequality.

### Guided Practice

Use substitution to find three solutions of each inequality. Then represent the **7** – **10** solutions of each inequality on a number line. See margin for samples.

**7** $q \geq 3$

**8** $d \leq 12$

**9** $k \leq 25$

**10** $m \geq -28$

**Match each inequality to its graph.**

a) $x < 10$          b) $x \leq 10$          c) $x > 10$          d) $x \geq 10$

**11** 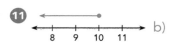 b)

**12** 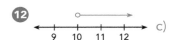 c)

**13** 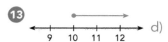 d)

**14** 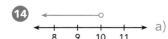 a)

---

**Learn continued**

**b)** **Ask** What is the maximum temperature of the city in winter? −4°C What is another way of saying "The maximum temperature is −4°C"? The temperature is less than or equal to −4°C. If you let the temperature be $y$°C, what can you say about the value of $y$? $y$ is less than or equal to −4. How do you write "$y$ is less than or equal to −4" in symbols? $y \leq -4$

**Explain** $y \leq -4$ is another inequality. To solve this inequality, you have to find the values of $y$ that make $y \leq 4$ true.

**Ask** Is $y = -3$ a solution of the inequality? No, because $-3 \leq -4$ is not a true statement. Is

$y = -4$ a solution? Yes, because $-4 \leq -4$ is a true statement. Can you name another number that is a solution? Yes; possible answer: −5

**Explain** Any value of $y$ that is equal to or less than −4 will make the inequality $y \leq -4$ true. You can use a graph to show all the solutions.

**Ask** How does the graph show that −4 is a solution of the inequality? A filled circle is shown at $y = -4$. How does the graph show that all numbers less than −4 are solutions? The arrow points to the left of −4.

**Explain** Point out that the solutions of $y \leq -4$ are also infinite in number.

## Practice 8.3

Basic ①–⑭
Intermediate ⑮–⑳
Advanced ㉑–㉚

**Rewrite each statement using >, <, ≥, or ≤.**

**①** $k$ is less than 12. $k < 12$

**②** $d$ is greater than 10. $d > 10$

**③** $w$ is greater than or equal to 17. $w \geq 17$

**④** $p$ is less than or equal to 36. $p \leq 36$

**⑤** A sack of potatoes weighs at least 20 pounds. Write an inequality to represent the weight of the sack of potatoes. $x \geq 20$

**⑥** The maximum number of shirts Amanda can buy is 9. Write an inequality to represent the number of shirts that she can buy. $x \leq 9$

**Represent the solutions of each inequality on a number line.**

**⑦** $x > 5$
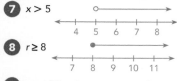

**⑧** $r \geq 8$

**⑨** $m < 22$

**⑩** $q \leq 13$

**Write an inequality for each graph on a number line.**

**⑪**
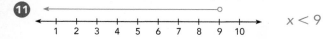
$x < 9$

**⑫**

$x > 14$

**⑬**
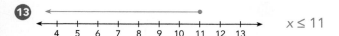
$x \leq 11$

**⑭**

$x \geq 7$

### Assignment Guide

**DAY 1** All students should complete ①–⑩.

**DAY 2** All students should complete ⑪–⑳.

㉑–㉚ provide additional challenge.

Optional: *Extra Practice 8.3*

### RtI Lesson Check

| Before assigning homework, use the following ... | to make sure students ... | Intervene with ... |
|---|---|---|
| Exercises ⑦ and ⑨ | • can represent the solution of an inequality on a number line | Reteach 8.3 |
| **EXIT** Ticket Out the Door | • can write an inequality for a number line | |

**Lesson 8.3** Solving Simple Inequalities    **27**

**EXIT**

## Ticket Out the Door

Write an inequality for the number line below. Then give 4 possible solutions of the inequality: one whole number, one fraction, one mixed number, and one decimal.

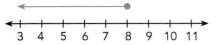

3  4  5  6  7  8  9  10  11

Possible inequality: $x \leq 8$; Possible

solutions: 7, $\frac{1}{3}$, $3\frac{5}{6}$, 4.3

🖱 Also available on Teacher One Stop.

---

**Represent the solutions of each inequality on a number line. Then give three possible integer solutions of each inequality.** ⑮ – ㉒ See margin.

⑮ $p < 9\frac{1}{2}$

⑯ $y > \frac{37}{5}$

⑰ $b \leq \frac{23}{4}$

⑱ $s \geq 6\frac{3}{7}$

⑲ $g > 1.5$

⑳ $m \geq 4.8$

㉑ $z \leq 9.2$

㉒ $r < 16.6$

**Solve.**

㉓ In the inequality $x > 9$, $x$ represents the number of restaurants along a street.

   a) Is 9 a possible value of $x$? Explain. No. $x$ is more than 9.

   b) Is $9\frac{2}{5}$ a possible value of $x$? Explain. No. $x$ is an integer.

   c) Use a number line to represent the solution set of the inequality. Then state the least possible number of restaurants on the street.  ; 10

㉔ In the inequality $q \leq 24.3$, $q$ represents the possible weights, in pounds, of a package.

   a) Is 24.4 a possible value of $q$? Explain. No. $q$ has a maximum value of 24.3.

   b) Is $20\frac{7}{10}$ a possible value of $q$? Explain. Yes. When $q = 20\frac{7}{10}$, $q \leq 24.3$ is true.

   c) Use a number line to represent the solution set of the inequality. Then state the greatest possible weight of the package.  ; 24.3 lb

**Each inequality has the variable on the right side of the inequality symbol. Graph each solution set on a number line.**

㉕ $11 \leq d$

㉖ $7\frac{3}{4} > q$

㉗ $2.5 < h$

㉘ $-6 \geq w$

㉙ $5.7 < m$

㉚ $8.1 \geq n$

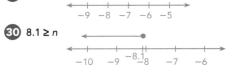

---

⑮

1  2  3  4  5  6  7  8  9  10  11

Answers vary. Sample: $p$ = 5, 6, or 7

⑯
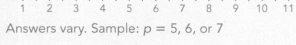

7  $\frac{37}{5}$  8  9  10  11

Answers vary. Sample: $y$ = 8, 9, or 10

⑰
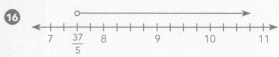

1  2  3  4  5  $\frac{23}{4}$ 6

Answers vary. Sample: $b$ = 3, 4, or 5

⑱

6  $6\frac{3}{7}$  7  8

Answers vary. Sample: $s$ = 7, 8, or 9

⑲
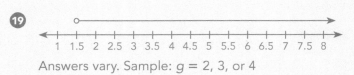

1  1.5  2  2.5  3  3.5  4  4.5  5  5.5  6  6.5  7  7.5  8

Answers vary. Sample: $g$ = 2, 3, or 4

⑳
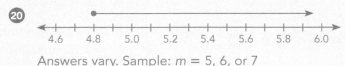

4.6  4.8  5.0  5.2  5.4  5.6  5.8  6.0

Answers vary. Sample: $m$ = 5, 6, or 7

㉑
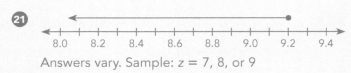

8.0  8.2  8.4  8.6  8.8  9.0  9.2  9.4

Answers vary. Sample: $z$ = 7, 8, or 9

㉒
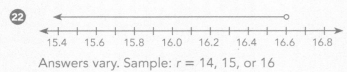

15.4  15.6  15.8  16.0  16.2  16.4  16.6  16.8

Answers vary. Sample: $r$ = 14, 15, or 16

# 8.4 Real-World Problems: Equations and Inequalities

## Lesson Objectives

- Solve real-world problems by writing equations.
- Solve real-world problems by writing inequalities.

**Write algebraic equations to solve real-world problems.**

a) Yesterday Kyle had some stamps. Today his father gave him 12 more stamps. Now he has 27 stamps altogether. How many stamps did Kyle have yesterday?

Let $x$ represent the number of stamps Kyle had yesterday.

Kyle had some stamps. Today he has 12 more stamps. Now he has 27 stamps.

$$x \qquad +12 \qquad =27$$

The equation is $x + 12 = 27$.

To find how many stamps Kyle had yesterday, solve the equation.

$$x + 12 = 27$$
$$x + 12 - 12 = 27 - 12 \qquad \text{Subtract 12 from}$$
$$x = 15 \qquad\qquad\qquad \text{both sides.}$$

Kyle had 15 stamps yesterday.

b) In a pond, there are 3 times as many koi as goldfish. If there are 48 koi, find the number of goldfish in the pond.

Let $g$ represent the number of goldfish in the pond.

There are some goldfish. There are 3 times as many koi. There are 48 koi.

$$g \qquad\qquad \times 3 \qquad\qquad = 48$$

The equation is $3g = 48$.

**Continue on next page**

### KEY CONCEPT

- The process of problem solving involves the application of concepts, skills, and strategies.

### PACING

**DAY 1** Pages 29–30

**DAY 2** Pages 31–34

**Materials:** TRT1

**5-minute Warm Up**

Translate each answer into an algebraic expression.

1. John has x baseball cards. He exchanged 5 of his cards for 10 new ones. How many cards does he have now? $x + 10 - 5 = x + 5$

2. The height of a rectangular box is $\frac{2}{3}$ its length. If the length is $y$ cm, what is the height of the box? $\frac{2y}{3}$ cm

 Also available on Teacher One Stop.

---

**DAY 1**

**Write algebraic equations to solve real-world problems.**

**Demonstrate** Work through example a) to illustrate the problem solving process.

**Step 1** Understand the problem.

**Ask** What information is given? Kyle's father gave him 12 stamps. So he has a total of 27. **What are you asked to find?** How many stamps Kyle had yesterday

**Step 2** Think of a strategy.

**Ask** How can you find the number of stamps Kyle had at first? Write an equation or draw a model.

**Model** To write an equation, use a letter to represent

what you want to find. So, let x be the number of stamps Kyle had. Then, add to it the 12 stamps his father gave him, to get the total 27. The equation is $x + 12 = 27$. You can also draw the model shown in the text.

**Step 3** Solve the problem.

**Ask** How do you solve the equation? Subtract 12 from both sides of the equation.

**Model** Solve the equation or, if preferred, ask a student to do it. Solve example b) using the same process applied to example a).

To find the number of goldfish in the pond, solve the equation.

$3g = 48$

$3g \div 3 = 48 \div 3$      Divide both sides by 3.

$g = 16$

There are 16 goldfish in the pond.

## Best Practices

For **b)**, be sure to connect the bar model shown to the equation. Label the bar representing the number of goldfish g. Then tell students that the equation $3g = 48$ indicates that there are three times as many koi as goldfish and that the total number of koi is 48. Then also label each of the 3 equal parts of the bar representing the number of koi as g.

## Guided Practice

**1** to **5** Students who have difficulty in writing the equations can draw the models for the problems first. Remind students to check each answer against the context of each problem to make sure that the answer is reasonable.

## Guided Practice

**Complete.**

**1** On Monday, Wendy had some leaves in a collection she was making for biology class. After she collected 23 more leaves on Tuesday, she had 41 leaves. Find the number of leaves Wendy had on Monday.

Let r represent the number of leaves Wendy had on Monday.

$r + 23 = \underline{\ ?\ }$   41

$r + 23 - \underline{\ ?\ } = \underline{\ ?\ } - \underline{\ ?\ }$   23; 41; 23

$r = \underline{\ ?\ }$   18

Wendy had $\underline{\ ?\ }$ leaves on Monday.   18

**Write an algebraic equation for each problem. Then solve.**

**2** Carlos thinks of a number. When he adds 17 to it, the result is 45. What is the number that Carlos thought of?   28

**3** Sylvia bought some blouses and T-shirts. She paid a total of $63. The T-shirts cost $29. How much did the blouses cost?   $34

**4** Felicia used 153 yellow beads and some green beads for her art project. She used 9 times as many yellow beads as green beads. How many green beads did she use for the project?   17 green beads

**5** Ivan had saved some quarters. He spent 50 quarters, which was $\frac{2}{5}$ of the quarters he started out with. How many quarters did he start out with?   125 quarters

**Learn continued**

**Step 1** Understand the problem.

**Ask** Looking at the previous page, what information is given in the problem? There are 3 times as many koi as goldfish in a pond. **What are you asked to find?** The number of goldfish in the pond if there are 48 koi

**Step 2** Think of a strategy.

**Ask** How can you find the number of goldfish in the pond? Write an equation or draw a model.

**Model** To write an equation, you use a letter to represent what you want to find. So, let g be the number of goldfish.

**Ask** What is the equation connecting 3, g, and 48 you can write? $3g = 48$

**Step 3** Solve the problem.

**Ask** How do you solve this equation? Divide both sides of the equation by 3.

**Model** Solve the equation or, if preferred, ask a student to do it.

**Write algebraic inequalities to solve real-world problems.**

a) Jamal sees the sign shown in a store window.

Write an inequality to represent the situation. Use a number line to represent the inequality. Then give the greatest possible cost of a T-shirt.

Let c represent the cost of a T-shirt.

All T-shirts cost less than $16.

$$c \quad < \quad 16$$

The inequality $c < 16$ represents the situation.

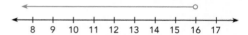

The greatest possible cost of a T-shirt is $15.99.

b) A ski club is organizing a trip. At least 20 club members have to sign up for the trip to cover the cost of the bus. Write an inequality to represent this situation. Use a number line to represent the inequality.

Let w represent the number of members who sign up for the trip.

The number of members who sign up must be at least 20.

$$w \qquad \geq \quad 20$$

The inequality $w \geq 20$ represents the situation.

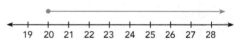

The graph shows that the least number of members who have to sign up is 20.

> **Caution** /////////
>
> **b)** Some students might have trouble identifying the correct inequality to use in real-world problems. Encourage students to review the meanings of the terms that correspond to each type of inequality. For example: "at least 20" club members corresponds to ≥ 20.

Learn **Write algebraic inequalities to solve real-world problems.**

**Model** Work through examples a) and b) to illustrate how to translate a statement of inequality into symbolic form.

a) **Ask** How much does a T-shirt cost? Less than $16 If you let the cost of a T-shirt be $c, what can you say about the value of c? c is less than 16. How do you write "c is less than 16" in symbols? $c < 16$ What are the solutions of this inequality? All numbers less than 16 How do you represent these values on a number line? (See Student Book) Since prices are given to the nearest cent, what is the greatest cost of a T-shirt? $15.99

b) **Ask** How many members have to sign up for the trip? At least 20 How can you express "at least 20" as an inequality? Greater than or equal to 20 members If you let the number of members be w, what can you say about the value of w? w is greater than or equal to 20. How can you write this in symbols? $w \geq 20$

## Guided Practice

 to ⑩ Remind students how to interpret:

At most or not more than: less than or equal to

At least or not less than: greater than or equal to

### 👥 DIFFERENTIATED INSTRUCTION

**Through Enrichment**

Use the Guided Practice exercises to show students that the solutions to real-world problems are often more limited than they would be for an inequality unrelated to the real world. For example, in ⑧ **Ask:** Can the number of words written be a fraction, mixed number, or decimal? *(No, the number of words must be a whole number.)* Can the number of words be a negative integer? *(No)* Point out that the inequality that best describes the situation is $1 \le w \le 50$, with $w$ limited to integers only. This can be read as "$w$ is between 1 and 50, including 1 and 50."

## Guided Practice

**Complete.**

⑥ The figure shows a speed limit sign on a highway.

a) Let $x$ represent the speed in miles per hour.

Write an inequality to represent the situation.

The inequality is __?__. $x \le 55$

b) Give the maximum legal driving speed on the highway.

The maximum legal driving speed is __?__ miles per hour. 55

**Solve.**

⑦ More than 35 guests came to Katrina's birthday party last Sunday.

a) Write an inequality to represent the number of guests who turned up for the birthday party. $x > 35$ or $x \ge 36$

b) What is the least possible number of guests who could have come to the party? 36 guests

⑧ In Mr. Boyle's class, the students are required to summarize a passage in less than 50 words.

a) Write an inequality to represent the number of words that the students can use to summarize the passage. $x < 50$

b) What is the maximum number of words that a student can use? 49 words

⑨ A cargo elevator has a load limit of 240 tons.

a) Write an inequality to represent the load limit of the cargo elevator. $x \le 240$

b) What is the greatest possible load the cargo elevator can carry? 240 tons

⑩ To get a discount coupon at a bookstore, you need to spend at least $50 at the store.

a) Write an inequality to represent the amount of money that you must spend in order to get a discount coupon. $x \ge 50$

b) Andrea has spent $45 at the store, and her friend Alex has spent $55. Which person can get a discount coupon? Alex

## Practice 8.4

Basic ①–⑥
Intermediate ⑦–⑪
Advanced ⑫–⑬

**Write and solve an algebraic equation for each problem. Show your work.**

① Damien thinks of a number. When he adds 32 to it, the sum is 97. What is the number that Damien thought of? 65

② A baker made some bagels in the morning. After selling 85 bagels, there were 64 left. How many bagels did the baker make in the morning?
149 bagels

③ Claudia can text 3 times as fast as Fiona. Claudia can text 78 words per minute. How many words per minute can Fiona text?
26 words per minute

④ Eric spent $\frac{2}{5}$ of his allowance on a jacket. The jacket cost him $12. How much was his allowance? $30

**Write and solve an algebraic inequality for each problem.**

⑤ In a science competition, students have to score more than 40 points in order to move on to the next round.

   a) Write an inequality to represent this situation. Use a number line to represent the inequality. $x > 40$;

   39  40  41  42  43

   b) What is the least number of points a student needs to score in order to move on to the next round? Only whole numbers of points are awarded to students. 41 points

⑥ A stadium has a seating capacity of 65,000 spectators.

   a) What is the maximum number of spectators the stadium can hold? 65,000 spectators

   b) Write an inequality to represent this situation. Then use a number line to represent the inequality. $x \leq 65{,}000$;

   63,000  64,000  65,000  66,000

**Write and solve an algebraic equation or inequality for each problem. Show your work.**

⑦ A bicycle store sells $\frac{4}{7}$ of the mountain bikes in the store. Then only 24 mountain bikes are left. How many mountain bikes were there originally? $\frac{3}{7}x = 24$; 56 mountain bikes

⑧ Mabel has a total of 54 decorative beads. Some are black and some are white. The ratio of the number of black beads to the number of white beads is 7 : 2. How many more black beads than white beads are there? $9x = 54$; 30 more black beads

---

### Practice 8.4

**Assignment Guide**

**DAY 1** All students should complete ①–④, ⑨ and ⑪.

**DAY 2** All students should complete ⑤–⑧ and ⑩.

⑫–⑬ provide additional challenge.

Optional: *Extra Practice 8.4*

**Caution** ///////

In the course of solving a problem, students may forget what each expression they write represents. Have students label each expression as they work on a problem. For example in ③, after they write 3w for the number of words Claudia can text, have them label it "3w: number of words Claudia can text."

---

### RtI Lesson Check

| Before assigning homework, use the following ... | to make sure students ... | Intervene with ... |
| --- | --- | --- |
| Exercises ① and ③ | • can use algebraic equations to solve real-world problems | Reteach 8.4 |
| EXIT Ticket Out the Door | • can draw a number line to represent an inequality | |

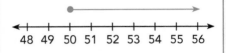
## Ticket Out the Door

In your own words, describe a simple real-world math situation that involves one variable. Write an inequality to correctly describe the situation. Then draw a number line to represent the inequality. Possible answer: A bank requires a deposit of at least $50 to open a savings account. This can be described by the inequality $a \geq 50$.

```
←—+——+——●——+——+——+——+——+——+——→
  48  49  50  51  52  53  54  55  56
```

 Also available on Teacher One Stop.

## Brain @ Work

For students who have difficulty solving the problem, guide them to write an equation using $x$ to represent what they need to find: let the width of the border be $x$ cm, then find the difference between the two perimeters in terms of $x$.

---

9. Gary has a collection of comic books. After selling 70% of his comic books, he has 42 comic books left. How many comic books did he start with?
$0.3x = 42$; 140 comic books

10. There are 30 students in the gym. If there are at least 16 girls, write an inequality to represent the number of boys in the gym. $x \leq 14$

11. The marbles in a box are repackaged in equal numbers into 6 smaller bags. If each bag has more than 8 marbles, what is the least possible number of marbles that could have been in the box? 54 marbles

12. Mr. Edwards is now 3 times as old as his daughter. In 15 years' time, the sum of their ages will be 86.

   a) Find their ages now. $4x + 30 = 86$; Mr. Edwards: 42 years old; His daughter: 14 years old

   b) How old was Mr. Edwards when his daughter was born? 28 years old

13. In a competition, each school is allowed to send a team with at least 5 members, but not more than 8 members. 12 schools participated in the competition.

   a) Find the least possible number of participants in the competition. 60 participants

   b) Find the greatest possible number of participants in the competition. 96 participants

## Brain @ Work

A rectangular photograph is mounted on a rectangular card. There is a border of equal width around the photograph. The perimeter of the card is 40 centimeters longer than that of the photograph. Find the width of the border in centimeters.

5 cm

---

### 👥 DIFFERENTIATED INSTRUCTION

**Through Enrichment**

Because all students should be challenged, have all students try the Brain@Work exercise on this page.

For additional challenging practice and problem solving, see *Enrichment, Course 1*, Chapter 8.

# Chapter Wrap Up

## Concept Map

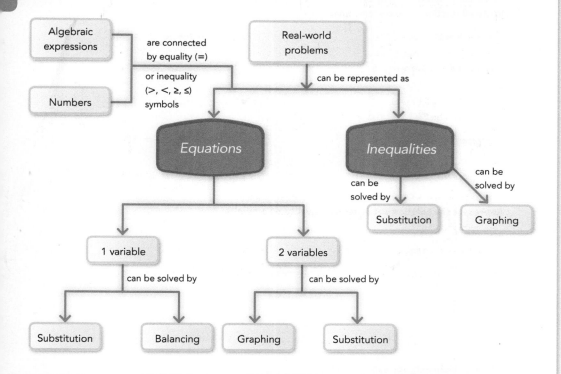

Algebraic expressions → are connected by equality (=) or inequality (>, <, ≥, ≤) symbols

Numbers

Real-world problems → can be represented as

Equations

Inequalities
- can be solved by → Substitution
- can be solved by → Graphing

Equations:
- 1 variable → can be solved by → Substitution, Balancing
- 2 variables → can be solved by → Graphing, Substitution

### Key Concepts

▶ Equations can be solved by substitution, or by adding, subtracting, multiplying, and dividing each side of the equation by the same nonzero number.

▶ The solution of an equation is a value, or values, that makes the equation true.

▶ A linear equation has a dependent and an independent variable.

▶ The solutions of an inequality are all the values that makes the inequality true.

▶ An inequality can be solved by substitution or by graphing on a number line.

## CHAPTER WRAP UP

Use the notes and the examples in the concept map to review solving equations by adding the same number to both sides, by subtracting the same number from both sides, and by multiplying or dividing both sides by the same non-zero number; and to review drawing number lines to represent the solutions of inequalities.

## CHAPTER PROJECT

To widen student's mathematical horizons and to encourage them to think beyond the concepts taught in this chapter, you may want to assign the Chapter 8 project, Planning a Healthy Meal, available in *Activity Book, Course 1*.

## Vocabulary Review

Use these questions to review chapter vocabulary with students.

1. $x + 3 = 9$ is an example of a(n) __?__. equation

2. $y > 7$ is an example of a(n) __?__. inequality

3. $y = 5x$ is called a(n) __?__ equation. linear

4. The value of x that makes $4x = 9$ true is the __?__ of the equation. solution

5. In the linear equation $y = x − 6$, x is the _____ variable and y is the __?__ variable. independent; dependent

 Also available on Teacher One Stop.

# Chapter Review/Test

## Chapter Assessment

Use the Chapter 8 Test A or B in *Assessments, Course 1* to assess how well students have learned the material in this chapter. These assessments are appropriate for reporting results to adults at home and administrators. Test A is shown on page 37A.

## TEST PREPARATION

For additional test prep

- ExamView® Assessment Suite Course 1
- Online Assessment System
  my.hrw.com

11 – 18 See Additional Answers.

# Chapter Review/Test

## Concepts and Skills

**Solve each equation using the concept of balancing. Write all fraction answers in simplest form.**

1. $x + 8 = 27$ $\quad x = 19$

2. $\frac{10}{11} = a + \frac{4}{11}$ $\quad a = \frac{6}{11}$

3. $f + 3.8 = 9.2$ $\quad f = 5.4$

4. $42 = y - 14$ $\quad y = 56$

5. $k - \frac{7}{8} = 2\frac{11}{24}$ $\quad k = 3\frac{1}{3}$

6. $n - 2.7 = 13.4$ $\quad n = 16.1$

7. $6h = 84$ $\quad h = 14$

8. $75.6 = 7.2r$ $\quad r = 10.5$

9. $\frac{4}{5}p = 10$ $\quad p = 12\frac{1}{2}$

10. $9 \cdot \frac{3}{5} = \frac{8}{11}w$ $\quad w = 7\frac{17}{40}$

**Represent the solution set of each inequality on a number line.** 11 – 18 See margin.

11. $b < 7$

12. $b > 13$

13. $m \geq 24$

14. $m \leq 38$

15. $g > \frac{2}{3}$

16. $g \leq 5\frac{3}{5}$

17. $z < 7.1$

18. $z \geq 10.4$

**Write an inequality for each number line.**

19. 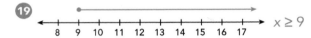 $x \geq 9$

20. 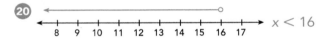 $x < 16$

21. 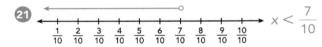 $x < \frac{7}{10}$

22. 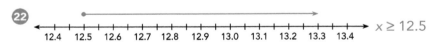 $x \geq 12.5$

## RtI Intervention and Reteaching Recommendations

| Student Book B Review/Test Items | Assessments Chapter 8 Items | Chapter 8 Objectives | Reteach B Chapter 8 |
|---|---|---|---|
| 1 to 10 | Test A: 1–3 Test B: 1–2 | **Objective 1.** Solve equations in one variable. | Lesson 8.1 |
| 11 to 22 | Test A: 4–5 Test B: 3–4 | **Objective 5.** Represent the solutions of an inequality on a number line. | Lesson 8.3 |

**Write an equation for each of the following.**

Patrick is *x* years old. His brother is 9 years older than he is. If his brother is *y* years old, express *y* in terms of *x*. $y = x + 9$

The length of a house is three times its width. The width of the house is *f* yards. If the perimeter of the house is *h* yards, express *h* in terms of *f*. $h = 8f$

## Problem Solving

**Use an algebraic equation or algebraic inequality to solve. Show your work.**

Mrs. Lewis makes some orange juice. After making another 850 milliliters of juice, she now has 4,880 milliliters of orange juice. How much orange juice did Mrs. Lewis make at first? 4,030 mL

Adrian has 5 times as many stickers as Derrick. If Adrian has 325 stickers, how many stickers does Derrick have? 65 stickers

A printer prints fewer than 18 pages per minute. What is the maximum number of pages the printer can print in 7 minutes? 119 pages

If a number is multiplied by 4, it gives the same result as $\frac{2}{7}$ of 504. What is the number? 36

Keane has a total of 96 counters. Some are green and some are red. The ratio of the number of red counters to the number of green counters is 3 : 5. How many more green counters than red counters are there? 24 more green counters

A grocer bought 8 boxes of apples. Each box contains 35 apples and fewer than 40% of the apples in each box are green apples. Find the greatest possible number of green apples in all the 8 boxes. 104 green apples

A rectangular lunch tray has a length of *x* centimeters and a width of 15 cm. The tray's length is at least 20% greater than its width.

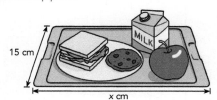

a)   Write an inequality to represent this situation. $x \geq 18$

b)   Suppose *x* is a whole number. Find the least possible perimeter, and the least possible area of the lunch tray.
Perimeter: 66 cm; Area: 270 cm²

### ⚠ RtI Intervention and Reteaching Recommendations

| Student Book B Review/Test Items | Assessments Chapter 8 Items | Chapter 8 Objectives | Reteach B Chapter 8 |
|---|---|---|---|
| 23 to 24 | Test A: 6–8<br>Test B: 5–8 | **Objective 6.** Write a linear equation to relate two real-world quantities. | Lesson 8.2 |
| 25 to 31 | Test A: 9–10<br>Test B: 9–10 | **Objective 7.** Solve real-world problems by writing inequalities. | Lessons 8.1, 8.3 |

## Chapter 8 Tests A and B

Answer key appears in the *Assessments, Course 1*

**Test B, Assessments p. 85**

**Test A, Assessments p. 83**

Name: _____ Date: _____

**CHAPTER TEST A**

**(8)** **Equations and Inequalities**

$\boxed{\begin{array}{c}25\end{array}}$
Suggested Time:
30 min

**Concepts and Skills** (5 × 2 points = 10 points)

**Solve each equation.**

1. $a + 6 = 11$

2. $y - 3.8 = 14.7$

3. $\frac{2}{3}p = 16$

**Represent the solution set of each inequality on a number line.**

4. $m > 8$

5. $w \leq 4.9$

© Marshall Cavendish International (Singapore) Private Limited.

Assessments Course 1    **83**

**Test B, Assessments p. 86**

**Test A, Assessments p. 84**

Name: _____ Date: _____

**Problem Solving** (5 × 3 points = 15 points)

**Use an algebraic equation or algebraic inequality to solve.**
**Show your work.**

6. Sharon has some almonds. After buying another 350 grams of almonds, she now has 1,230 grams of almonds. How many grams of almonds did Sharon have at first?

7. The ratio of the number of dogs to the number of cats at an animal shelter is 5 : 4. If there is a total of 153 cats and dogs, how many cats are in the shelter?

8. Mrs. Roberts is 3 times as old as her son. The sum of their ages is 48 years. How old was Mrs. Roberts when her son was born?

9. Theo gets 2 stars for every 5 correct answers he gives. What is the minimum number of correct answers Theo must give if he wants to get 12 stars?

10. Mark sold $x$ pens for $2 each. He received less than $80 from the sale. Find the greatest possible number of pens he sold.

© Marshall Cavendish International (Singapore) Private Limited.

**84**    Chapter 8   Test A

**TEACHER NOTES**

# Chapter at a Glance

| | | CHAPTER OPENER<br>The Coordinate Plane<br>Recall Prior Knowledge | LESSON 9.1<br>Points on the Coordinate Plane<br>Pages 42–49 | LESSON 9.2<br>Length of Line Segments<br>Pages 50–61 |
|---|---|---|---|---|
| **LESSON AT A GLANCE** | Pacing | 2 days | 2 days | 2 days |
| | Objectives | Every point on the coordinate plane can be represented by a pair of coordinates. | • Name and locate points on the coordinate plane.<br>• Draw and identify polygons on the coordinate plane. | • Find lengths of horizontal and vertical line segments on the coordinate plane.<br>• Solve real-world problems involving coordinates and a coordinate plane. |
| | Vocabulary | | coordinates, coordinate plane, x-axis, y-axis, quadrants | |
| **RESOURCES** | Materials | | TRT12*, TRT18* | TRT12*, TRT18* |
| | Lesson Resources | Student Book B,<br>pp. 38–41<br>*Assessments Course 1*,<br>Chapter 9 Pre-Test<br>*Transition Guide*,<br>Course 1, Skills 35–38 | Student Book B, pp. 42–49<br>*Extra Practice B*, Lesson 9.1<br>*Reteach B*, Lesson 9.1<br>*Activity Book*, Lesson 9.1 | Student Book B, pp. 50–61<br>*Extra Practice B*, Lesson 9.2<br>*Reteach B*, Lesson 9.2 |
| | **Common Core** Standards for Mathematical Content | **6.NS.6, 6.NS.7c**<br>Foundational for **6.NS.6c, 6.G.3, 6.NS.8** | **6.NS.6** Extend number line diagrams... to represent points with negative number coordinates.<br>**6.NS.6c** Find and position... numbers on a coordinate plane.<br>**6.G.3** Draw polygons on the coordinate plane.... | **6.NS.8** Include... absolute value to find distances between points...<br>**6.EE.2c** Evaluate ...formulas used in real-world problems....<br>**6.G.3** Draw polygons on the coordinate plane...; use coordinates to find lengths.... |
| | **Mathematical Practices** | **5.** Use tools strategically. **7.** Look for and use structure. | **4.** Model mathematics. **6.** Attend to precision. **7.** Look for and use structure. | **2.** Reason. **4.** Model mathematics. **5.** Use tools strategically. |

*Teacher Resource Tools (TRT) are available on the Teacher One Stop.*

# Concepts and Skills Across the Courses

| GRADE 5 | COURSE 1 | COURSE 2 |
|---|---|---|
| • Form ordered pairs from patterns, analyze patterns and relationships, and graph the ordered pairs on a coordinate plane. (5.OA.3)<br>• Use a pair of number lines to define a coordinate system. (5.G.1)<br>• Represent real-world and mathematical problems by graphing points in the first quadrant of the coordinate plane. (5.G.2) | • Use a pair of positive and negative number lines to define a coordinate system. (6.NS.6, 6.NS.6b, 6.NS.6c)<br>• Represent real-world and mathematical problems by graphing points in the all four quadrants of the coordinate plane. (6.RP.3a, 6.RP.3b, 6.NS.8, 6.EE.2c, 6.EE.9)<br>• Draw polygons on the coordinate plane to solve problems. (6.NS.8, 6.G.3) | • Recognize a proportional relationship by graphing on a coordinate plane. (7.RP.2a, 7.RP.2b)<br>• Explain what a point (x, y) on a graph means in terms of the situation. (7.RP.2d)<br>• Solve real-life and mathematical problems with positive and negative numbers. (7.EE.3, 7.G.6)<br>• Draw geometric shapes with given conditions. (7.G.2) |

| LESSON 9.3<br>Real-World Problems:<br>Graphing<br>Pages 62–66 | CHAPTER<br>WRAP UP/REVIEW/TEST<br><br>Brain@Work<br>Pages 66–71 |
|---|---|
| 1 day | 2 days |
| • Solve real-world problems involving equations and a coordinate plane. | Reinforce, consolidate, and extend chapter skills and concepts. |
| linear graph | |
| TRT12*, TRT18* | |
| Student Book B, pp. 62–66<br>*Extra Practice B*, Lesson 9.3<br>*Reteach B*, Lesson 9.3 | Student Book B pp. 66–71<br>*Activity Book*, Chapter 9 Project<br>*Enrichment*, Chapter 9<br>*Assessments*, Chapter 9 Test<br> ExamView® Assessment Suite Course 1 |
| **6.RP.3a** Make tables... and plot pairs of values .... **6.RP.3b** Solve unit rate problems.... **6.NS.8** Solve ...problems by graphing points.<br>**6.G.3** Draw polygons in the coordinate plane...in the context of solving...problems. | |
| **1.** Solve problems/persevere.<br>**2.** Reason. **4.** Model mathematics. | **1.** Solve problems/persevere.<br>**5.** Choose tools strategically. |

# Additional Chapter Resources

## TECHNOLOGY

 • Online Student eBook

 • Interactive Whiteboard Lessons

 • Virtual Manipulatives

 • Teacher One Stop

 • ExamView® Assessment Suite Course 1

 • Online Professional Development Videos

## Every Day Counts®
## ALGEBRA READINESS

**The February activities in the Pacing Chart provide:**
- **Review** of standard linear measures and unit conversions (**Ch. 4: 6.RP.3d**)
- **Review and Practice** of writing variable expressions for linear relationships (**Ch. 7–9: 6.EE.2, 6.EE.6, 6.EE.9**)
- **Preview** of data analysis and graphs (**Ch. 13: 6.SP.4, 6.SP.5**)

**Additional Teaching Support**

Online Transition Guide

Online Professional Development Videos

# Chapter 9 The Coordinate Plane

## Points, Figures, and Dimensions

- In this chapter, students identify and plot points on the coordinate plane, and calculate lengths of line segments, including sides of polygons.

### Points, coordinates, and quadrants

- Students identify and plot points on the coordinate plane and identify their quadrants. They also identify the coordinates of points reflected about each axis.

### Points as vertices of polygons

- On the coordinate plane, students plot and connect points to form polygons, which they identify. Given the coordinates of two or more vertices, they use properties of polygons to locate unknown vertices.

### Length of line segments

- Students use absolute value to calculate lengths of segments on the coordinate plane, first along each axis, then parallel to them. Students find lengths of sides of polygons on the coordinate plane, including planes where the grid interval is greater than 1. They solve real-world problems involving polygons.

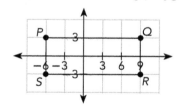

A plan for a patio is shown. Give the coordinates for points P, Q, R, and S. Find the area of the patio in square feet.

**Solution**
The coordinates are $P(-6, 3)$, $Q(9, 3)$, $R(9, -3)$, and $S(-6, -3)$.

$$Area = Length \cdot Width$$
$$= PQ \cdot PS$$
$$= (|-6| + |9|) \cdot (|3| + |-3|)$$
$$= 15 \cdot 6 = 90 \text{ ft}^2$$

- Students also use length to calculate perimeter, and can locate a point in the interior of a polygon if given its distance from two sides of the polygon.

## Data, Graphs, and Relationships

- Students are introduced to linear graphs as a tool for visualizing the relationship between two variables.

### Linear graphs and real-world problems

- Students relate variables by graphing and using linear graphs to solve real-world problems.

  A hose fills a fish tank. The amount of water $w$ in the tank after $t$ minutes is given by $w = 8t$. Graph the relationship between $w$ and $t$. How much water is in the tank in 2.5 minutes? What is the rate at which the tank is filled?

**Solution**
To graph the data, create a table of values.

| t (min) | 0 | 1 | 2 | 3 | 4 |
|---------|---|---|----|----|----|
| w (gal) | 0 | 8 | 16 | 24 | 32 |

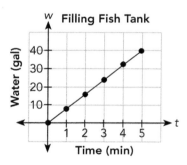

From the graph, you can see that at 2.5 minutes, the tank holds 20 gallons of water.

Since the graph is linear, the tank is being filled at a constant rate. To find the rate, divide the amount of water in the tank at any time by the amount of time it took to fill it with that amount.

$$Rate = \frac{Water}{Time} = \frac{32}{4} = 8 \text{ gal/min}$$

- Students also write inequalities to describe such situations, as well as identify the independent and dependent variables.

# Differentiated Instruction

## Assessment and Intervention

| | ASSESSMENT |  RtI STRUGGLING LEARNERS |
|---|---|---|
| **DIAGNOSTIC** | • Quick Check in Recall Prior Knowledge in Student Book B, pp. 39–41<br>• Chapter 9 Pre-Test in *Assessments* | • Skills 35–38 in *Transition Guide*, *Course 1* |
| **ON-GOING** | • Guided Practice<br>• Lesson Check<br>• Ticket Out the Door | • Reteach worksheets<br>• Extra Practice worksheets<br>• *Activity Book*, Chapter 9 |
| **END-OF-CHAPTER** | • Chapter Review/Test<br>• Chapter 9 Test in *Assessments*<br> • ExamView® Assessment Suite Course 1 | • Reteach worksheets |

### ELL ENGLISH LANGUAGE LEARNERS

Review the terms *coordinate plane*, *x*-axis, *y*-axis, *origin*, and *coordinates*.

**Model** Show a coordinate plane. Plot point *P* at (4, −3).

**Say** A *coordinate plane* is a grid that has an *x*-axis and a *y*-axis. The x-*axis* and y-*axis* cross to form four 90° angles. (Label each angle "90°".) The point where the x-axis and y-axis cross is called the *origin*.

**Model** Label point *P* with its coordinates, (4, −3).

**Say** The *coordinates* of a point tell where to find the point on the coordinate plane. *(Point to the 4.)* The first number is the *x*-coordinate. It tells the distance of the point from the *y*-axis. *(Count the units from the y-axis to P. Then point to the −3.)* The second number is the *y*-coordinate. It tells the distance of the point from the *x*-axis. *(Count the units from the x-axis to P.)*

For definitions, see Glossary, page 301, and Online Multilingual Glossary.

### ADVANCED LEARNERS

• Students can explore the Cartesian coordinate system in three dimensions. Explain that the system is expanded into three dimensions by the addition of a third axis, the *z*-axis, which rises above the coordinate plane through the origin.

• Have students do research to find diagrams of a Cartesian coordinate system in three dimensions. Tell them to observe the notation used to mark the location of a point in three dimensions: (*x*, *y*, *z*). Have students make posters to share what they have learned with the class.

• As needed, provide direction for students, such as suggesting that they use diagrams to show the progression from a number line to a coordinate plane to a system with three axes, as well as how the location of a point is recorded in each.

**To provide additional challenges use:**
• *Enrichment*, Chapter 9
• Student Book B, Brain@Work problem

# CHAPTER 9

# The Coordinate Plane

## Chapter Vocabulary

Vocabulary terms are used in context in the student text. For definitions, see the Glossary at the end of the Student Book and the online Multilingual Glossary.

**coordinates** An ordered pair of numbers that gives the location of a point on a coordinate plane

**coordinate plane** A grid formed by a horizontal number line, called the x-axis, and a vertical number line, called the y-axis, that intersect at right angles

**linear graph** A straight line graph

**quadrants of a coordinate plane** The four sections of a coordinate plane formed by the axes. They are named Quadrant I, Quadrant II, Quadrant III, and Quadrant IV.

**x-axis** The horizontal axis on a coordinate plane

**y-axis** The vertical axis on a coordinate plane

---

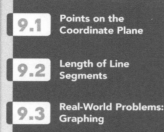

**9.1** Points on the Coordinate Plane

**9.2** Length of Line Segments

**9.3** Real-World Problems: Graphing

**BIG IDEA**

▶ Every point on the coordinate plane can be represented by a pair of coordinates.

---

## Have you ever used a street directory?

A street directory is useful for locating a street in an unfamiliar area. The maps in the directory use a system of coordinates to help you locate the streets easily.

When using a directory, you can look for a street name in the index. The index gives you the correct map to look at and also gives a pair of coordinates so that you can locate the street.

For example, in the map below, Fort Hill Road can be found on map 87, section B2. B2 is a pair of coordinates that tells you the location of the street on the map.

In this chapter, you will use numerical coordinates to locate points on a coordinate plane.

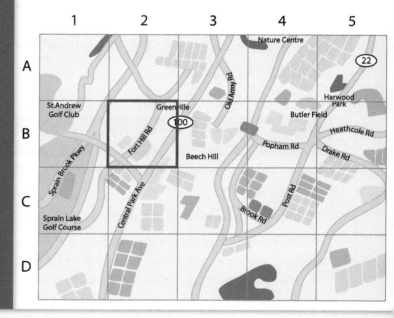

---

## CHAPTER OPENER

**Ask** Has anyone seen a street directory? Do you know what it is for? Possible answer: Yes. It is used to locate unfamiliar streets in a particular area.

**Explain** The maps in a street directory enable you to locate streets that you may not be familiar with. Each street on a map has a pair of coordinates that tell you the part of the map in which the street can be found. For example, the coordinates C, 4 tell you that the street is located in row C and column 4 of the map.

In this chapter, you will learn how to identify the coordinates of points and to plot them on a coordinate plane, as summarized in the **Big Idea**.

# Recall Prior Knowledge

### Identifying and plotting coordinates

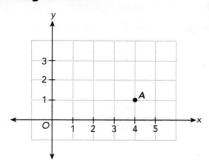

The coordinates of O, the origin, are (0, 0).

To find the location of point A, move 4 units to the right on the x-axis and 1 unit up on the y-axis.

The coordinates of A are (4, 1).

## ✓ Quick Check

**Use the coordinate plane below.**

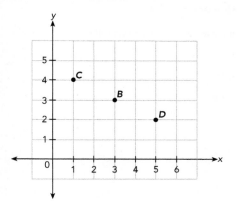

1️⃣ Give the coordinates of points B, C, and D. B (3, 3), C (1, 4), and D (5, 2)

**Use graph paper. Plot the points on a coordinate plane.**

2️⃣ P (3, 2), Q (2, 3), and R (0, 4) See margin.

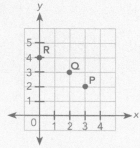

## RECALL PRIOR KNOWLEDGE

Use the ✓ **Quick Check** exercises or Chapter Pre-Test in *Assessments, Course 1*, to assess chapter readiness. For intervention suggestions see the chart below and on the following pages.

🖱 Additional online Reteach and Extra Practice worksheets from previous grades are also available. See the *Transition Guide*, Resource Planner for more information.

| 🔺 **RtI** Assessing Prior Knowledge | | | | Intervene with | |
|---|---|---|---|---|---|
| ✓ Quick Check | *Assessments Course 1, Ch. 9* Pre-Test Items | Skill Objective | Transition Guide | 🖱 Online Resources Grades 4 and 5 | |
| 1️⃣ and 2️⃣ | 1–2 | Identify and plot coordinates. | Skill 35 | Reteach 5B, pp. 103–106; Extra Practice 5B, Lesson 11.2 | |

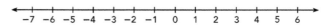

**Representing negative numbers on the number line**

Negative numbers are numbers less than zero.

−2, −10, −23, and −134 are examples of negative numbers.

Negative numbers are found to the left of 0 on the number line.

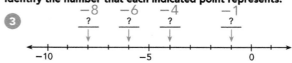

✓ **Quick Check**

**Identify the number that each indicated point represents.**

**3**

| | −8 | −6 | −4 | | −1 |
|---|---|---|---|---|---|

**Draw a horizontal number line to represent each set of numbers.**

**4** −3, 0, 1, 5, 8

**5** −15, −11, −9, −7, −2

**Recognizing and writing the absolute value of a number**

The absolute value of a number is the distance from itself to 0 on the number line. It is always positive or zero.

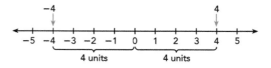

4 units          4 units

−4 is 4 units away from 0. Its absolute value is 4.
Similarly, the absolute value of 4 is also 4.
You can write |−4| = 4, and |4| = 4.

✓ **Quick Check**

**Use the symbol | | to write the absolute values of the following numbers.**

**6** 11  |11| = 11          **7** −16  |−16| = 16          **8** −21  |−21| = 21

---

| ⚠ **RtI** Assessing Prior Knowledge | | | Intervene with | |
|---|---|---|---|---|
| ✓ Quick Check | *Assessments Course 1, Ch. 9 Pre-Test Items* | Skill Objective | Transition Guide | 🖱 Online Resources Grades 4 and 5 |
| **3** to **5** | 3 | Represent negative numbers on the number line. | Skill 36 | |
| **6** to **8** | 4–7 | Identify the absolute value of a number. | Skill 37 | |

## Finding the perimeter of a polygon

The perimeter of a polygon is the distance around it.

Figure *ABCDE* has 5 sides — $\overline{AB}$, $\overline{BC}$, $\overline{CD}$, $\overline{DE}$, and $\overline{EA}$.

The perimeter of figure *ABCDE* is equal to the sum of the lengths of its 5 sides:

$AB + BC + CD + DE + EA$
$= 9 + 7 + 7 + 7 + 9$
$= 39$ cm

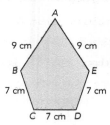

## ✓ Quick Check

**Find the perimeter of each polygon.**

**9** Figure *ABC* is an isosceles triangle.

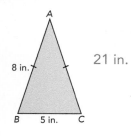

21 in.

**10** Figure *DEF* is an equilateral triangle.

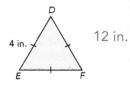

12 in.

**11** Figure *PQRS* is a trapezoid.

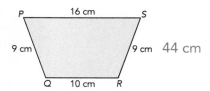

44 cm

**12** Figure *WXYZ* is a parallelogram.

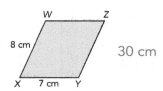

30 cm

**13** Figure *JKLM* is a rhombus.

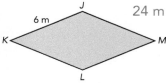

24 m

**9.1** **Points on the Coordinate Plane**

## KEY CONCEPT

• The location of any point on the coordinate plane is given by an ordered pair of numbers called its coordinates.

## PACING

DAY **1** Pages 42–44

DAY **2** Pages 45–49

**Materials:** TRT12, TRT18

 **5-minute Warm Up**

Mark these numbers on a horizontal axis: −3 and 3. Mark these numbers on a vertical axis : 6 and −6.
See Additional Answers.

Also available on Teacher One Stop.

### Lesson Objectives

• Name and locate points on the coordinate plane.
• Draw and identify polygons on the coordinate plane.

**Learn** **Find the coordinates of points on a coordinate plane.**

The coordinate plane is made up of two number lines that intersect at right angles. The horizontal line is called the **x-axis** and the vertical line is called the **y-axis**. The point of intersection, usually labeled O, is the origin.

The x-axis and y-axis divide the coordinate plane into four parts called **quadrants**. Moving counterclockwise around the origin, the quadrants are named Quadrant I, Quadrant II, Quadrant III, and Quadrant IV.

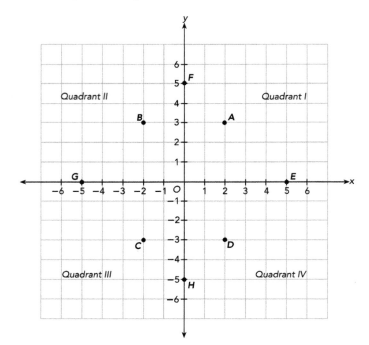

DAY **1**

**Learn** **Find the coordinates of points on a coordinate plane.**

Show students the coordinate plane.

**Ask** What is the horizontal line called? x-axis What is the vertical line called? y-axis What is the point of intersection called? Origin

**Explain** The coordinate plane is made up of the x-axis and the y-axis. They divide the coordinate plane into four parts called quadrants. These quadrants are named Quadrant I, Quadrant II, Quadrant III, and Quadrant IV, counterclockwise from the upper right.

Point *A* is in the first quadrant.
Point *A* is 2 units to the right of the origin,
so its *x*-coordinate is 2. It is 3 units up from the origin,
so its *y*-coordinate is 3.
The coordinates of *A* are (2, 3).
(2, 3) is called an ordered pair.
You can write *A* (2, 3) to represent the location of *A*.

Point *B* is in the second quadrant.
Point *B* is 2 units to the left of the origin, so its *x*-coordinate is −2. It is 3 units up from the origin, so its *y*-coordinate is 3.
The coordinates of *B* are (−2, 3).

Points *A* and *B* are symmetrical about the *y*-axis. Point *A* is said to be the reflection of point *B* across the *y*-axis.

You can also say point *B* is the reflection of point *A* across the *y*-axis.

Point *C* is in the third quadrant.
Point *C* is 2 units to the left of the origin, so its *x*-coordinate is −2. It is 3 units down from the origin, so its *y*-coordinate is −3.
The coordinates of *C* are (−2, −3).

Points *B* and *C* are reflections of each other across the *x*-axis.

Point *D* is in the fourth quadrant.
Point *D* is 2 units to the right of the origin, so its *x*-coordinate is 2.
It is 3 units down from the origin, so its *y*-coordinate is −3.
The coordinates of *D* are (2, −3).

Points *C* and *D* are reflections of each other across the *y*-axis.

Points *E* lies on the *x*-axis. It lies between Quadrant I and Quadrant IV.
Similarly, point *F* lies on the *y*-axis. It lies between Quadrant I and Quadrant II.

Point *G* lies on the *x*-axis. It is between Quadrant II and Quadrant III.

Point *H* lies on the *y*-axis. It is between Quadrant III and Quadrant IV.

**ELL Vocabulary Highlight**

Explain to students that Quadrant I is often referred to as the first **quadrant**, Quadrant II as the second quadrant, etc.

**👥 DIFFERENTIATED INSTRUCTION**

**Through Language Support**

Help students to understand the mathematical meaning of the word *origin* by asking how the word *origin* is used in everyday English. *(Possible answers: the origin of a product, type of food or music, species, or idea)* Explain that the origin of something is where it began. The origin of a coordinate grid is the point at which you begin counting along the *x*-axis or the *y*-axis. The origin is zero on both axes.

---

**Learn continued**

**Ask** Which quadrant is point *A* located in? Quadrant I How many units to the right of the origin is *A*? 2 How many units up from the origin is *A*? 3

**Explain** Since *A* is 2 units to the right of the origin, its *x*-coordinate is 2, and since it is 3 units up from the origin, its *y*-coordinate is 3. So, the coordinates of *A* are (2, 3).

**Ask** Which quadrant is point *B* located in? Quadrant II How many units to the left of the origin is *B*? 2 How many units up from the origin is *B*? 3

**Explain** Since *B* is 2 units to the left of the origin, its *x*-coordinate is −2, and since it is 3 units up from the

origin, its *y*-coordinate is 3. So, the coordinates of *B* are (−2, 3).

**Explain** Explain that points *A* and *B* are symmetrical about the *y*-axis. You can also say that *A* is the reflection of *B*, or *B* is the reflection of *A*, about the *y*-axis.

**Ask** Can you find two other points that are symmetrical about the *y*-axis? Yes; points *C* and *D*, or *E* and *G* What point is a reflection across the *x*-axis of point *B*? Point *C*

**Explain** Make sure students are able to find the coordinates of points *C* and *D*, and that they are also able to locate points *E*, *F*, and *G* on the coordinate plane.

## Guided Practice

**1** Remind students that points to the left of the y-axis have negative x-coordinates and points below the x-axis have negative y-coordinates.

**2** to **4** Emphasize to students that in reading or writing a pair of coordinates, the x-coordinate always comes first. (3, 4) is not the same point as (4, 3).

## Guided Practice

**Use the coordinate plane below.**

**1** Give the coordinates of points P, Q, R, S, T, U, and V. In which quadrant is each point located?

$P$ (3, 0), $Q$ (−3, 3), $R$ (−5, 1), $S$ (−6, −4), $T$ (−4, −7), $U$ (4, −5), and $V$ (3, −2)

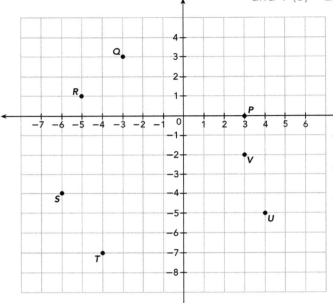

Quadrant II:
Points Q and R
Quadrant III:
Points S and T
Quadrant IV:
Points V and U
Point P lies on the x-axis. It is between Quadrant I and Quadrant IV.

**Use graph paper.** **2** – **4** See margin.

**2** Plot points A (−4, 3), B (3, −4), C (5, 0), D (0, −5), E (−2, −1), and F (2, −1) on a coordinate plane.

**3** Points P and Q are reflections of each other about the x-axis. Give the coordinates of point Q if the coordinates of point P are the following:

a) (−6, 2)

b) (−2, −4)

c) (4, 5)

d) (7, −3)

**4** Points R and S are reflections of each other about the y-axis. Give the coordinates of point S if the coordinates of point R are the following:

a) (−6, 2)

b) (−2, −4)

c) (4, 5)

d) (7, −3)

**2**

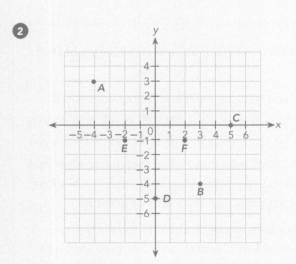

**3** a)

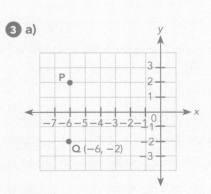

**3** b) – **4** d) See Additional Answers.

**Draw and identify polygons on a coordinate plane.**

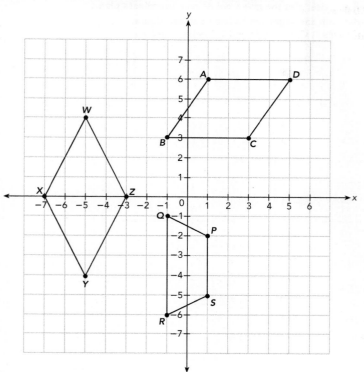

You can join points on a coordinate plane to form geometric figures.

Points A (1, 6), B (−1, 3), C (3, 3), and D (5, 6) are joined to form a parallelogram.

Points P (1, −2), Q (−1, −1), R (−1, −6), and S (1, −5) are joined to form a trapezoid.

Points W (−5, 4), X (−7, 0), Y (−5, −4), and Z (−3, 0) are joined to form a rhombus.

The opposite sides of a parallelogram are parallel.

DAY 2

Learn **Draw and identify polygons on a coordinate plane.**

**Model** Mark points A (1, 6), B (−1, 3), C (3, 3) and D (5, 6) on a coordinate plane. Then join the points to form figure ABCD.

**Ask** What is the figure formed? A parallelogram How do you know that it is a parallelogram? Its opposite sides are parallel.

**Model** Mark points P (1, −2), Q (−1, −1), R (−1, −6) and S (1, −5) on the coordinate plane. Then join the points to form figure PQRS.

**Ask** What is the figure formed? A trapezoid How do you know that it is a trapezoid? One pair of opposite sides are parallel.

**Model** Mark points W (−5, 4), X (−7, 0), Y (−5, −4) and Z (−3, 0) on the coordinate plane. Then join the points to form figure WXYZ.

**Ask** What is the figure formed? A rhombus How do you know that it is a rhombus? Its opposite sides are parallel and the four side lengths are equal.

## Guided Practice

In ⑤, students should copy and complete the grid shown on graph paper. Ask them to describe the figure formed in this exercise and in ⑥ to ⑭. You may want to distribute graph paper or blank coordinate grids for ⑤ to ⑭. See TRT12 or TRT18.

**⑤**

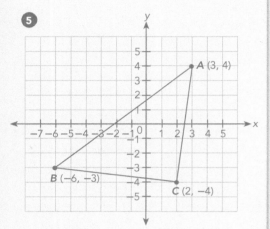

triangle

**⑥**

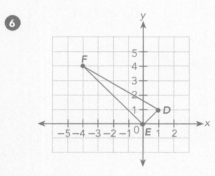

triangle

**⑦**

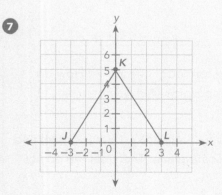

triangle

⑨ – ⑭ See Additional Answers.

## Guided Practice

**Use graph paper. For each exercise, plot the given points on a coordinate plane. Then join the points in order with line segments to form a closed figure. Name each figure formed.**

**⑤** A (3, 4), B (−6, −3), and C (2, −4)

⑤ – ⑭ See margin.

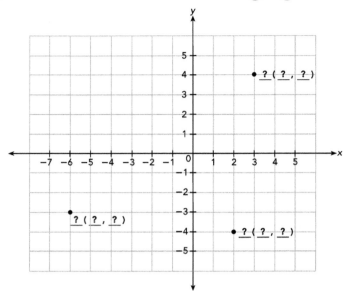

**⑥** D (1, 1), E (0, 0), and F (−4, 4)

**⑦** J (−3, 0), K (0, 5), and L (3, 0)

**⑧** P (3, 2), Q (−1, 2), R (−1, −2), and S (3, −2)

**⑨** W (−3, 2), X (1, −2), Y (3, 0), and Z (−1, 4)

**⑩** A (−5, 2), B (−5, −1), C (−1, −1), and D (1, 2)

**⑪** E (−2, −2), F (−5, −5), G (−2, −5), and H (1, −2)

**⑫** J (−4, 1), K (−3, −1), L (0, −1), and M (2, 1)

**⑬** P (4, 0), Q (0, 4), R (−4, 0), and S (0, −4)

**⑭** W (−2, 0), X (−3, −3), Y (1, 1), and Z (2, 4)

**⑧**

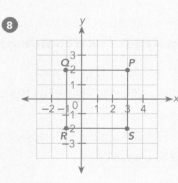

square

# Hands-On Activity

**Materials:**

• graph paper

Work in pairs.

 **STEP 1** Plot four points on a coordinate plane and connect them to form a special quadrilateral such as a parallelogram, a rectangle, or a rhombus. Do not let your partner see your quadrilateral.

 **STEP 2** Tell your partner the coordinates of three out of the four coordinates of the points you plotted in **STEP 1**. Also tell your partner the type of quadrilateral you plotted, and in which quadrant the fourth point is located. Have your partner guess the coordinates of the fourth point.

**Example**

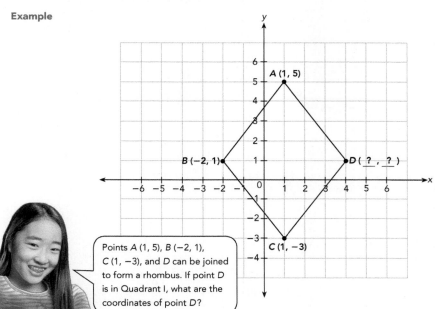

Points A (1, 5), B (−2, 1), C (1, −3), and D can be joined to form a rhombus. If point D is in Quadrant I, what are the coordinates of point D?

**STEP 3** Switch roles with your partner and repeat the activity with other quadrilaterals.

 ## Hands-On Activity

This activity reinforces the plotting of points on a coordinate plane as well as drawing and identifying geometric figures that students have learned.

**Material:** TRT12

**ELL Vocabulary Highlight**

This activity provides a good opportunity to reinforce the meaning of **quadrant**. **Ask:** What is a quadrilateral? (*A figure that has four sides*) Point out that both *quadrant* and *quadrilateral* share the Latin root *quad-*, meaning "four." Ask students for examples of other words that include the root *quad-*. (*Possible answers: quadrangle, quadruple*) Point out that the x- and y-axes divide the coordinate plane into four equal sections called *quadrants*.

## Practice 9.1

Basic ①–⑬
Intermediate ⑭–⑮
Advanced ⑯–⑰

### Assignment Guide

**DAY 1** All students should complete ① – ⑩.

**DAY 2** All students should complete ⑪ – ⑮.

⑯ – ⑰ provide additional challenge.

Optional: *Extra Practice 9.1, Activity Book 9.1*

### 👥 DIFFERENTIATED INSTRUCTION

**Through Kinesthetic Experience**

② For students having trouble, use masking (or colored) tape to create a coordinate plane on the floor that extends 5 units from the origin in every direction. Use index cards to label units −5 to 5 along each axis. Have a student select an ordered pair, for example (2, −1). Ask the student to "plot" the point by walking the correct number of units (steps) along the x-axis and then up or down to the point.

② See Additional Answers.

**Use the coordinate plane below.**

① Give the coordinates of each point. In which quadrant is each point located?

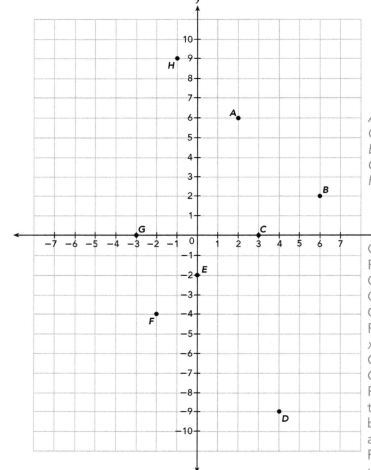

A (2, 6), B (6, 2), C (3, 0), D (4, −9), E (0, −2), F (−2, −4), G (−3, 0), and H (−1, 9)

Quadrant I: Points A and B
Quadrant II: Point H
Quadrant III: Point F
Quadrant IV: Point D
Point C lies on the x-axis. It lies between Quadrant I and Quadrant IV.
Point G lies on the x-axis. It lies between Quadrant II and Quadrant III.
Point E lies on the y-axis. It lies between Quadrant III and Quadrant IV.

**Use graph paper. Plot the points on a coordinate plane. In which quadrant is each point located?**

② A (3, 7), B (2, 0), C (8, −1), D (0, −6), E (−3, −5), and F (−6, 7) See margin.

### ⚠ RtI Lesson Check

| Before assigning homework, use the following ... | to make sure students ... | Intervene with ... |
|---|---|---|
| Exercises ③ and ⑤ | • can locate points on the coordinate plane | |
| Exercise ⑪ | • can draw and identify polygons on the coordinate plane | Reteach 9.1 |
| 🎟 EXIT Ticket Out the Door | • can draw a polygon on a coordinate plane and describe its location using coordinates | |

Use graph paper. Points *A* and *B* are reflections of each other about the *x*-axis. Give the coordinates of point *B* if the coordinates of point *A* are the following:

③ – ⑰ See margin.

**3** (4, 1)  **4** (−2, 3)  **5** (2, −2)  **6** (−1, −3)

Use graph paper. Points *C* and *D* are reflections of each other about the *y*-axis. Give the coordinates of point *D* if the coordinates of point *C* are the following:

**7** (4, 1)  **8** (−2, 3)  **9** (2, −2)  **10** (−1, −3)

Use graph paper. For each exercise, plot the given points on a coordinate plane. Then join the points in order with line segments to form a closed figure. Name each figure formed.

**11** *H* (−5, 1), *J* (−3, −1), *K* (−1, 1), and *L* (−3, 3)

**12** *R* (2, 1), *S* (−1, −3), *T* (4, −3), and *U* (7, 1)

**13** *W* (−5, −2), *X* (−6, −5), *Y* (−1, −5), and *Z* (−3, −2)

Use graph paper. Plot the points on a coordinate plane and answer each question.

**14 a)** Plot points *A* (−6, 5), *C* (5, 1), and *D* (5, 5) on a coordinate plane.

**b)** Figure *ABCD* is a rectangle. Plot point *B* and give its coordinates.

**c)** Figure *ACDE* is a parallelogram. Plot point *E* above $\overline{AD}$ and give its coordinates.

**15 a)** Plot points *A* (−3, 2) and *B* (−3, −2) on a coordinate plane.

**b)** Join points *A* and *B* with a line segment.

**c)** $\overline{AB}$ is a side of square *ABCD*. Name two possible sets of coordinates that could be the coordinates of points *C* and *D*.

**16** Plot points *A* (2, 5) and *B* (2, −3) on a coordinate plane. Figure *ABC* is a right isosceles triangle. If point *C* is in Quadrant III, give the coordinates of point *C*.

**17** Plot points *A* (0, 4), *B* (−4, 0), and *C* (0, −4) on a coordinate plane.

**a)** What kind of triangle is triangle *ABC*?

**b)** Figure *ABCD* is a square. Plot point *D* on the coordinate plane and give its coordinates.

**3**

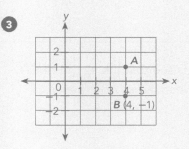

**4**

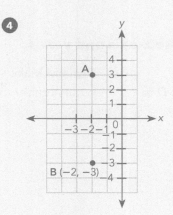

**⑤ – ⑰** See Additional Answers.

# 9.2 | Length of Line Segments

## KEY CONCEPT

- Length is a positive quantity.

## PACING

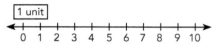

DAY **1** Pages 50–53

DAY **2** Pages 54–61

**Materials:** TRT12, TRT18

### 5-minute Warm Up

Find the number of units between these points on the number line:

1 unit

0 1 2 3 4 5 6 7 8 9 10

a) 0 and 3 3 units

b) 3 and 10 7 units

c) 2 and 7 5 units

d) 5 and 9 4 units

Also available on Teacher One Stop.

## Lesson Objectives

- Find lengths of horizontal and vertical line segments on the coordinate plane.

- Solve real-world problems involving coordinates and a coordinate plane.

**Learn** **Find the lengths of line segments on the x-axis and y-axis.**

Find the lengths of the line segments $\overline{AB}$, $\overline{CD}$, $\overline{EF}$, and $\overline{GH}$.

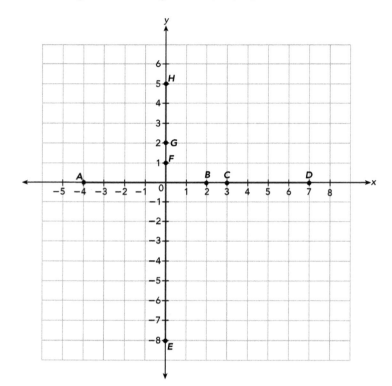

The coordinates of C and D are C (3, 0) and D (7, 0). By counting the number of units from 3 to 7, you can see that the length of $\overline{CD}$ is 4 units.

DAY **1**

**Learn** **Find the lengths of line segments on the x-axis and y-axis.**

**Model** Mark points C (3, 0) and D (7, 0) on the coordinate plane. Then draw a line between C and D to form line segment CD.

**Ask** What is the length of $\overline{CD}$? 4 units

**Explain** Make sure students see that the length of $\overline{CD}$ is the number of units between 3 and 7 on the x-axis.

The coordinates of A and B are A (−4, 0) and B (2, 0). By counting the number of units from −4 to 2, you can see that the length of $\overline{AB}$ is 6 units.

You can also find the length of $\overline{AB}$ this way.

$AB = AO + OB$
$= |{-4}| + |2|$
$= 4 + 2$
$= 6$ units

The length AO is the absolute value of −4, that is, AO = |−4| = 4 units.

**Math Note**

Length is a non-negative quantity. It can be zero or positive.

The coordinates of G and H are G (0, 2) and H (0, 5). By counting the number of units from 2 to 5, you can see that the length of $\overline{GH}$ is 3 units.

The coordinates of E and F are E (0, −8) and F (0, 1). By counting the number of units from −8 to 1, you can see that the length of $\overline{EF}$ is 9 units.

Similarly,

$EF = EO + OF$
$= |{-8}| + |1|$
$= 8 + 1$
$= 9$ units

So, the length of $\overline{EF}$ is 9 units.

## Guided Practice

**Use graph paper. Plot each pair of points on a coordinate plane. Connect the points to form a line segment and find its length.** ① – ⑥ See margin.

① C (3, 0) and D (8, 0)

② E (−6, 0) and F (−2, 0)

③ G (−7, 0) and H (1, 0)

④ J (0, 5) and K (0, 2)

⑤ M (0, −6) and N (0, −3)

⑥ P (0, −3) and Q (0, 5)

## DIFFERENTIATED INSTRUCTION

**Through Home Connection**

On a coordinate grid, plot a point at (−2, 0) and label it with both the ordered pair and "Keisha's House." Plot a second point at (3, 0) and label it with both the ordered pair and "Asa's House." **Ask:** How many blocks is the walk from Keisha's house to Asa's house? *(5 blocks)* How many blocks is the walk from Asa's house to Keisha's house? *(5 blocks)* Point out that, regardless of which location we start at, we always identify the length of the walk as a non-negative number. Repeat with other pairs of locations.

## Guided Practice

① to ⑥ Ask students to find the lengths of the line segments using the two methods they have learned. Students can use the graphs of the line segments to check their calculations.

You may want to distribute graph paper or blank coordinate grids for ① to ⑥. See TRT12 or TRT18.

① – ⑥ See Additional Answers.

**Learn continued**

**Explain** Given that the coordinates of points A and B are (−4, 0) and (2, 0), the length of $\overline{AB}$ is the number of units from −4 to 2 on the x-axis.

**Ask** What is the length of $\overline{AB}$? 6 units

**Explain** Tell students that they can also use this method to find the length of $\overline{AB}$: AB = AO + OB = |−4| + |2| = 4 + 2 = 6 units. AO is the absolute value of −4 and OB is the absolute value of 2. Emphasize that length is a non-negative quantity. It can be zero or positive.

**Ask** What are the absolute values of −4 and 2? 4 and 2

**Model** Connect points G (0, 2) and H (0, 5) to form $\overline{GH}$.

**Explain** The length of $\overline{GH}$ is the number of units from 2 to 5.

**Ask** What is the length of $\overline{GH}$? 3 units

**Model** Connect points E (0, −8) and F (0, 1) to form $\overline{EF}$.

**Explain** The length of $\overline{EF}$ is the number of units between −8 and 1 on the y-axis.

**Ask** What is the length of $\overline{EF}$? 9 units

**Explain** Remind students that to find the length of $\overline{EF}$, they can also use this method: EF = EO + OF = |−8| + |1| = 8 + 1 = 9 units

## DIFFERENTIATED INSTRUCTION

**Through Language Support**

Some students may confuse the terms *horizontal* and *vertical*. Direct their attention to the root word *horizon* in *horizontal*. **Ask:** What is a horizon? *(The line that forms the apparent boundary between Earth and the sky)* Point out that horizontal lines are called that because they are parallel to the horizon.

### Best Practices

You may want to reinforce the concept that points that have the same *y*-coordinate are the endpoints of a horizontal line segment and that points that have the same *x*-coordinate are the endpoints of a vertical line segment. Have students name the coordinates of other points in each of the line segments shown on the coordinate plane and then identify the pattern.

<sup>L</sup>earn **Find lengths of line segments parallel to the *x*-axis and *y*-axis.**

Find the lengths of the line segments $\overline{RS}$, $\overline{MN}$, and $\overline{PQ}$.

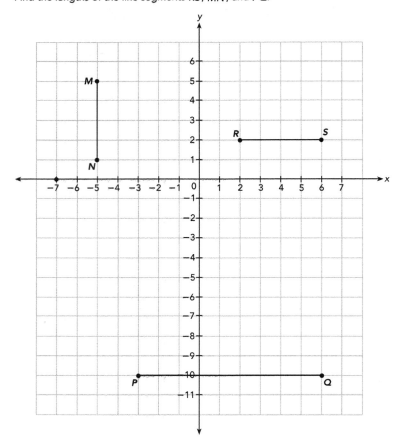

The line segment $\overline{RS}$ joins points R (2, 2) and S (6, 2). The *y*-coordinates of points R and S are the same, so $\overline{RS}$ is a horizontal line segment.

$\overline{RS}$ is parallel to the *x*-axis.

Using the *x*-coordinates of R (2, 2) and S (6, 2),

$RS = |\text{x-coordinate of } S| - |\text{x-coordinate of } R|$
$\quad = |6| - |2|$
$\quad = 4 \text{ units}$

So, the length of $\overline{RS}$ is 4 units.

<sup>L</sup>earn **Find the lengths of line segments parallel to the *x*-axis and *y*-axis.**

**Model** Connect points R (2, 2) and S (6, 2) to form $\overline{RS}$.

**Ask** Which axis is $\overline{RS}$ parallel to? The x-axis How can you find the length of $\overline{RS}$? Count the number of units from 2 to 6 along the x-axis.

**Explain** Tell students that they can also find the length

of $\overline{RS}$ using this method:

$RS = |\text{x-coordinate of } S| - |\text{x-coordinate of } R|$
$\quad = |6| - |2|$
$\quad = 6 - 2$
$\quad = 4 \text{ units}$

The line segment $\overline{MN}$ joins points $M$ $(-5, 5)$ and $N$ $(-5, 1)$. The x-coordinates of points $M$ and $N$ are the same, so $\overline{MN}$ is a vertical line segment.

Using the y-coordinates of $M$ $(-5, 5)$ and $N$ $(-5, 1)$,

$MN = |\text{y-coordinate of } M| - |\text{y-coordinate of } N|$
$= |5| - |1|$
$= 4$ units

So, the length of $\overline{MN}$ is 4 units.

$\overline{MN}$ is parallel to the y-axis.

The line segment $\overline{PQ}$ joins points $P$ $(-3, -10)$ and $Q$ $(6, -10)$. The y-coordinates of points $P$ and $Q$ are the same, so $\overline{PQ}$ is a horizontal line segment.

Using the x-coordinates of $P$ $(-3, -10)$ and $Q$ $(6, -10)$,

$PQ = |\text{x-coordinate of } P| + |\text{x-coordinate of } Q|$
$= |-3| + |6|$
$= 9$ units

So, the length of $\overline{PQ}$ is 9 units.

$\overline{PQ}$ is parallel to the x-axis.

## Guided Practice

**Use graph paper. Plot each pair of points on a coordinate plane. Connect the points to form a line segment and find its length.** **7** – **12** See margin.

**7** $A$ $(1, -2)$ and $B$ $(6, -2)$

**8** $C$ $(-1, 3)$ and $D$ $(5, 3)$

**9** $E$ $(-3, 4)$ and $F$ $(1, 4)$

**10** $G$ $(-3, 2)$ and $H$ $(-3, 6)$

**11** $J$ $(-1, -6)$ and $K$ $(-1, 4)$

**12** $L$ $(5, 6)$ and $M$ $(5, 1)$

**7**
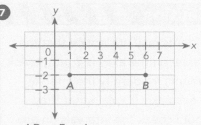
$AB = 5$ units

**8**
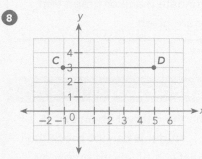
$CD = 6$ units

**9** – **12** See Additional Answers.

## Guided Practice

**7** to **12** Ask students to find the lengths of the line segments using the two methods they have learned. Students can use the graphs of the line segments to check their calculations. You may want to distribute graph paper or blank coordinate grids for **7** to **12**. See TRT12 or TRT18.

---

**Learn continued**

**Model** Connect points $M$ $(-5, 5)$ and $N$ $(-5, 1)$ to form $\overline{MN}$.

**Ask** Which axis is $\overline{MN}$ parallel to? The y-axis How can you find the length of $\overline{MN}$? Count the number of units from 1 to 5.

**Explain** Tell students that they can also find the length of $\overline{MN}$ using this method:

$\overline{MN} = |\text{y-coordinate of } M| - |\text{y-coordinate of } N|$
$= |5| - |1|$
$= 5 - 1$
$= 4$ units

**Model** Connect points $P$ $(-3, -10)$ and $Q$ $(6, -10)$ to form $\overline{PQ}$.

**Ask** Which axis is $\overline{PQ}$ parallel to? The x-axis How can you find the length of $\overline{PQ}$? Count the number of units from $P$ to $Q$.

**Explain** Tell students that they can also find the length of $\overline{PQ}$ using this method:

$PQ = |\text{x-coordinate of } P| + |\text{x-coordinate of } Q|$
$= |-3| + |6|$
$= 3 + 6$
$= 9$ units

## Learn  Plot points on a coordinate plane for a real-world problem and solve it.

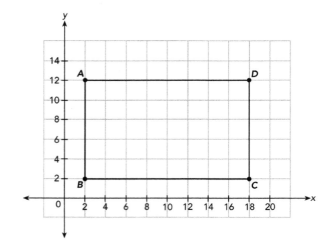

A plan of a rectangular garden is shown. The side length of each grid square is 2 meters.

a) Give the coordinates of points $A$, $B$, $C$, and $D$.

   The coordinates are $A$ (2, 12), $B$ (2, 2), $C$ (18, 2), and $D$ (18, 12).

b) Find the length and width of the garden in meters.

   Length = $AD$
   = 18 − 2
   =16 m

   The length of the garden is 16 meters.

   Width = $AB$
   = 12 − 2
   = 10 m

   The width of the garden is 10 meters.

c) Find the area of the garden in square meters.

   Area = $\ell w$         Write formula.
   = 16 · 10        Substitute.
   = 160 m²         Multiply.

   The area of the garden is 160 square meters.

---

## DAY 2

## Learn  Plot points on a coordinate plane for a real-world problem and solve it.

**Model**  Draw rectangle $ABCD$, given in the text, on a coordinate plane.

**Explain**  Explain to students that rectangle $ABCD$ is the plan of a rectangular garden.

a) **Ask**  What are the coordinates of point $A$? (2, 12) What are the coordinates of point $B$, $C$, and $D$? (2, 2), (18, 2) and (18, 12)

   **Explain**  Point out to students that the side length of each grid square represents a distance of 2 meters.

b) **Ask**  How can you find the length, in meters, of the garden? Find length of $\overline{AD}$. $\overline{AD}$ is 8 grid squares long, and each square = 2 meters, so 8 × 2 = 16 m. How can you find the width? Find length of $\overline{AB}$. $\overline{AB}$ is 5 grid squares long, and each square = 2 meters, so 5 × 2 = 10 m.

c) **Ask**  How can you find the area of the garden in square meters? Use the formula $A = \ell w$: 16 × 10 = 160 m².

**d)** Find the perimeter of the garden *ABCD* in meters.

Perimeter = 2 · (ℓ + w)
            = 2 · (16 + 10)
            = 2 · 26
            = 52 m

The perimeter of the garden is 52 meters.

**e)** There is a palm tree planted at point *E* in the garden at a distance of 12 meters from $\overline{AB}$ and 4 meters from $\overline{AD}$. Give the coordinates of point *E* and plot it on the coordinate plane.

First find how many grid squares from $\overline{AB}$ point *E* is.

1 grid square represents 2 meters.
12 m = 12 ÷ 2
       = 6 grid squares

For point *E* to be in the garden, the *x*-coordinate has to be 6 units to the right of $\overline{AB}$. So, point *E* is 1 + 6 = 7 grid squares to the right of the *y*-axis. The *x*-coordinate of point *E* is 7 × 2 = 14.

Then find how many grid squares from $\overline{AD}$ point *E* is.

4 m = 4 ÷ 2
      = 2 grid squares

For point *E* to be in the garden, the *y*-coordinate has to be 2 units below $\overline{AD}$. So, point *E* is 6 − 2 = 4 grid squares above the *x*-axis. The *y*-coordinate of point *E* is 4 × 2 = 8.

The coordinates of *E* are (14, 8).

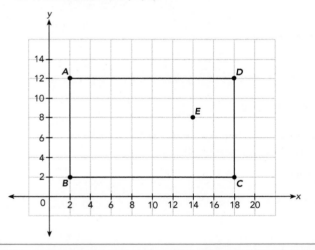

**DIFFERENTIATED INSTRUCTION**

**Through Modeling**

When locating the palm tree at point *E*, you may want to model the process on the coordinate grid. Skip count 12 meters (6 units) to the right of $\overline{AB}$ and draw a vertical line segment within the rectangle along *x* = 14. Then skip count 4 meters (2 units) down from $\overline{AD}$ and draw a horizontal line segment within the rectangle along *y* = 8. Plot point *E* at the intersection of these two segments.

**Learn continued**

**d)** **Ask** How can you find the perimeter of the garden in meters? Use the formula Perimeter = 2 · (ℓ + w): 2 · (16 + 10) = 2 · 26 = 52 m

**Ask** Given that each grid square is 2 meters, how can you locate a point in the garden that is 12 meters from $\overline{AB}$? Start at *AB* and count 6 grid squares to the right, because 6 × 2 = 12 m. What is the *x*-coordinate of point *E*? 14

**Model** Show students that point *E* lies somewhere on the vertical line that goes through (0, 14).

**Ask** Given that *E* is 4 meters from $\overline{AD}$ and is in the garden, how can you find the *y*-coordinate of point *E*? Count 2 grid squares (4 meters) down from $\overline{AD}$. The *y*-coordinate is 8.

**Model** Show students how to plot point *E* on the coordinate plane, and how to read that the coordinates are (14, 8).

## Guided Practice

**13** to **15** You may want to distribute graph paper. See TRT12. Note that the length of $\overline{BC}$ is given in **14**. Students do not need to calculate this length.

**DIFFERENTIATED INSTRUCTION**

**Through Enrichment**

**14** After students find the perimeter, challenge them to estimate the area of triangle *ABC*. If necessary, explain that they need to calculate the area of a unit square (25 square units), estimate the number of unit squares within the triangle (about 5), and multiply (5 · 25 = 125 square units).

## Guided Practice

**In the diagram, triangle *ABC* represents a plot of land. The side length of each grid square is 5 meters. Use the diagram to answer questions 13 to 15.**

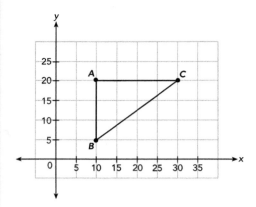

**13** Give the coordinates of points *A, B,* and *C.*  A (10, 20), B (10, 5), and C (30, 20)

**14** Mr. Manning wants to build a fence around the plot of land. If *BC* is 25 meters, how many meters of fencing does he need?

$AB = \underline{\ ?\ } - \underline{\ ?\ }$  20; 5

$= \underline{\ ?\ }$ m  15

$AC = \underline{\ ?\ } - \underline{\ ?\ }$  30; 10

$= \underline{\ ?\ }$ m  20

Perimeter of triangle $ABC = AB + BC + AC$

$= \underline{\ ?\ } + \underline{\ ?\ } + \underline{\ ?\ }$  15; 25; 20

$= \underline{\ ?\ }$ m  60

Mr. Manning needs $\underline{\ ?\ }$ meters of fencing.  60

**15** A pole is located at point *D* on the plot of land at a distance of 10 meters from $\overline{AB}$ and 5 meters from $\overline{AC}$. Give the coordinates of point *D*.

1 grid square represents 5 meters.

$10\ m = \underline{\ ?\ } \div 5$  10

$= \underline{\ ?\ }$ grid squares  2

For point D to be on the plot of land, the x-coordinate has to be
  ?  grid squares to the right of $\overline{AB}$. So, point D is  ?  +  ?  =  ?  2; 2; 2; 4
grid squares to the right of the y-axis. The x-coordinate of point D is
  ?  ×  ?  =  ? . 4; 5; 20

For point D to be on the plot of land, the y-coordinate has to be
  ?  grid square below $\overline{AC}$. So, point D is  ?  −  ?  =  ?  1; 4; 1; 3
grid squares above the x-axis. The y-coordinate of point D is
  ?  ×  ?  =  ? . 3; 5; 15

The coordinates of D are (  ? ,  ? ). 20; 15

**In the diagram, rectangle PQRS represents a parking lot of a supermarket.
The side length of each grid square is 4 meters. Use the diagram to answer
questions 16 to 18.**

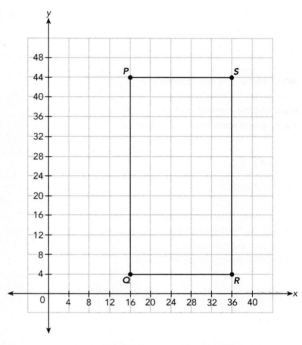

**16** Give the coordinates of points P, Q, R, and S. P (16, 44), Q (16, 4), R (36, 4), and S (36, 44)

**17** The manager of the supermarket wants to build a concrete wall around the
parking lot. What is the perimeter of the wall?  120 m

**18** The entrance of the supermarket is at point T. It lies on $\overline{PQ}$, and point T is
8 meters from point P. Give the coordinates of point T.  T (16, 36)

## Guided Practice

In 16 to 18, remind students to think
about the scale on the axes.

### Assignment Guide

**DAY 1** All students should complete **1** – **6**.

**DAY 2** All students should complete **7** – **14**.

**15** – **22** provide additional challenge.

Optional: *Extra Practice 9.2*

**1**

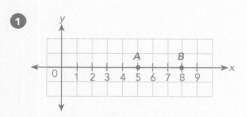

*AB* = 3 units

**2**

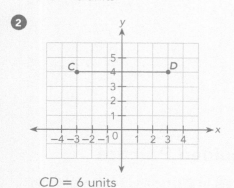

*CD* = 6 units

**3** – **9** See Additional Answers.

## Practice 9.2

Basic **1**–**6**
Intermediate **7**–**14**
Advanced **15**–**22**

**Use graph paper. Plot each pair of points on a coordinate plane. Connect the points to form a line segment and find its length. 1** – **9** See margin.

**1** *A* (5, 0) and *B* (8, 0)

**2** *C* (−3, 4) and *D* (3, 4)

**3** *E* (−5, −2) and *F* (8, −2)

**4** *G* (0, −5) and *H* (0, 2)

**5** *J* (−5, −3) and *K* (−5, −8)

**6** *M* (1, 7) and *N* (1, −8)

**Use graph paper. Find the coordinates.**

**7** Rectangle *PQRS* is plotted on a coordinate plane. The coordinates of *P* are (−1, −3) and the coordinates of *Q* are (−1, 2). Each unit on the coordinate plane represents 1 centimeter, and the perimeter of rectangle *PQRS* is 20 centimeters. Find the coordinates of points *R* and *S* given these conditions:

    **a)** Points *R* and *S* are to the left of points *P* and *Q*.

    **b)** Points *R* and *S* are to the right of points *P* and *Q*.

**8** Rectangle *ABCD* is plotted on a coordinate plane. The coordinates of *A* are (2, 3) and the coordinates of *B* are (−2, 3). Each unit on the coordinate plane represents 3 centimeters, and the perimeter of rectangle *ABCD* is 48 centimeters. Find the coordinates of points *C* and *D* given these conditions:

    **a)** Points *C* and *D* are below points *A* and *B*.

    **b)** Points *C* and *D* are above points *A* and *B*.

**9** Rectangle *PQRS* is plotted on a coordinate plane. The coordinates of *P* are (−1, 4) and the coordinates of *Q* are (−1, −4). Each unit on the coordinate plane represents 1 centimeter, and the area of rectangle *PQRS* is 64 square centimeters. Find the coordinates of points *R* and *S* given these conditions:

    **a)** Points *R* and *S* are to the left of points *P* and *Q*.

    **b)** Points *R* and *S* are to the right of points *P* and *Q*.

### RtI Lesson Check

| Before assigning homework, use the following ... | to make sure students ... | Intervene with ... |
|---|---|---|
| Exercises **1** and **3** | • can plot points and find lengths of segments on a coordinate plane | |
| Exercises **7** and **13** | • can plot points on a coordinate plane to solve real-world problems | Reteach 9.2 |
| **EXIT** Ticket Out the Door | • can solve problems involving figures drawn on a coordinate plane | |

In the diagram, rectangle *ABCD* represents a shopping plaza. The side length of each grid square is 10 meters. Use the diagram to answer questions **10** to **14**.

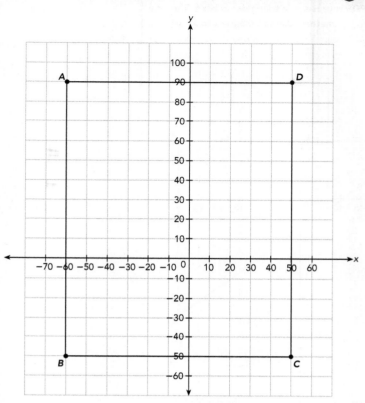

**10** Give the coordinates of points *A, B, C,* and *D*.
A (−60, 90), B (−60, −50), C (50, −50), and D (50, 90)

**11** Write down the shortest distance of points *A, B, C,* and *D* from the *y*-axis.
A: 60 m, B: 60 m, C: 50 m, and D: 50 m

**12** Write down the shortest distance of points *A, B, C,* and *D* from the *x*-axis.
A: 90 m, B: 50 m, C: 50 m, and D: 90 m

**13** Find the area and perimeter of the shopping plaza.
Area: 15,400 m²; Perimeter: 500 m

**14** A man at the shopping plaza is standing 50 meters from $\overline{AD}$, and 40 meters from $\overline{DC}$.

   a)   Find the coordinates of the point representing the man's location.  (10, 40)

   b)   Find the shortest distance in meters from the man's location to the side $\overline{BC}$.  90 m

## DIFFERENTIATED INSTRUCTION

### Through Communication

**15** Some students may have difficulty locating point *B*. Distribute blank coordinate grids and have students copy the diagram. **Ask:** Since *ABCR* is a rectangle, what do we know about the side opposite $\overline{AR}$? *(It must be parallel to $\overline{AR}$.)* Tell students to draw a line through point *C* that is parallel to $\overline{AR}$. Ask: What do we know about the side opposite *RC*? *(It must be parallel to $\overline{RC}$.)* Tell students to draw a line through point *A* that is parallel to $\overline{RC}$. **Ask:** Where is point *B*? *(It is at (5, −5).)*

In the diagram, triangle *PQR* represents a triangular garden. The side length of each grid square is 5 meters. Use the diagram to answer questions **15** to **19**.

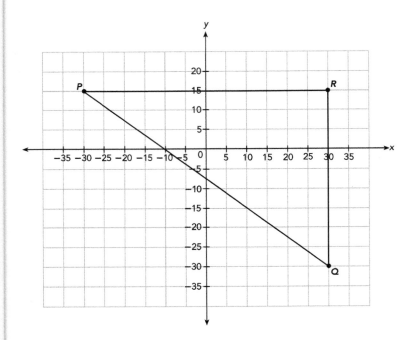

**15** Use graph paper. A rectangular region *ABCR* in the garden is to be fenced in. Point *A* lies on $\overline{PR}$, and is 35 meters away from point *P*. Point *C* lies below $\overline{PR}$, and is 20 meters away from point *R*. Plot and label points *A*, *B*, and *C* on the coordinate plane. Write the coordinates of points *A*, *B*, and *C*. See margin.

**16** If *PQ* is 75 meters, what is the perimeter of the triangular garden in meters? 180 m

**17** Find the area of the enclosed region *ABCR* in square meters. 500 m²

**18** Find the perimeter of the enclosed region *ABCR* in meters. 90 m

**19** If *PQ* is 75 meters, what is the perimeter of the garden that is not enclosed? 180 m

**15**

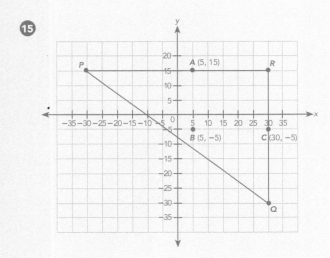

The diagram shows the outline of a park. The side length of each grid square is 10 meters. Use the diagram to answer questions 20 to 22.

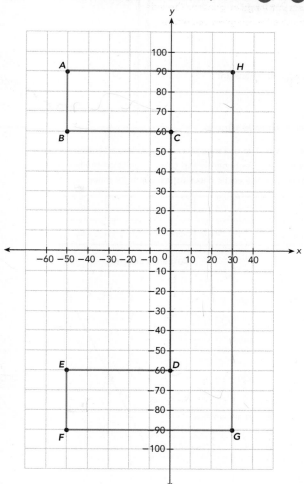

20 Find the area of the park in square meters. 8,400 m²

21 Brandon starts at point A and walks all the way around the perimeter of the park. If he walks at 1.5 meters per second, about how many seconds pass before he returns to point A? Round your answer to the nearest second. 413 s

22 A picnic table in the park is 20 meters from $\overline{BC}$, and is closer to point B than it is to point C. Write down two possible pairs of coordinates for the location of the picnic table. Answers vary. Sample: (−40, 80) and (−30, 80)

# KEY CONCEPT

- Data can be represented by tables and graphs.

# PACING

**DAY 1** Pages 62–66

**Materials:** TRT12, TRT18

## 5-minute Warm Up

A granola bar costs $1.50. Ask students to complete the table.

| Granola bar (number) | 1 | 2 | 3 | 4 | 5 |
|---|---|---|---|---|---|
| Cost ($) | | | | | |

See Additional Answers.

Also available on Teacher One Stop.

## ELL Vocabulary Highlight

Make sure that students understand the meaning of the term **linear graph**. Point out that the root of the word *linear* is *line*.

---

# 9.3 Real-World Problems: Graphing

## Lesson Objective

- Solve real-world problems involving equations and a coordinate plane.

**Vocabulary**
linear graph

### Learn Graph an equation on a coordinate plane.

Angela is driving to the Raccoon River. The distance traveled, *d* miles, after *t* hours, is given by $d = 40t$. Graph the relationship between *d* and *t*. Use 2 units on the horizontal axis to represent 1 hour and 2 units on the vertical axis to represent 20 miles.

| Time (t hours) | 0 | 1 | 2 | 3 | 4 |
|---|---|---|---|---|---|
| Distance Traveled (d miles) | 0 | 40 | 80 | 120 | 160 |

a) What type of graph is it?

It is a straight line graph. This is also called a **linear graph**.

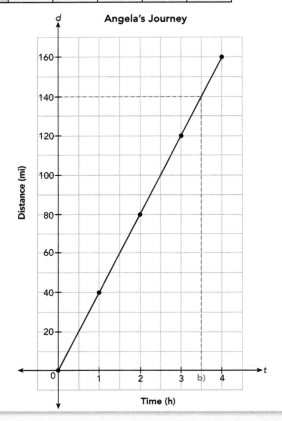

Angela's Journey

---

**DAY 1**

### Learn Graph an equation on a coordinate plane.

**Model** Plot the points given in the table on a coordinate plane.

a) **Ask** What type of graph will you get if you connect the points? A linear graph

**Explain** Tell students that the graph is a linear graph because it is a straight line graph.

**b)** How far did Angela drive in 3.5 hours?

From the graph, Angela drove 140 miles.

**c)** What is the speed at which Angela is driving?

$$\text{Speed} = \frac{\text{total distance}}{\text{total time}}$$
$$= \frac{160}{4}$$
$$= 40 \text{ mi/h}$$

Angela is driving at 40 miles per hour.

**d)** Angela has driven for 4 hours. If she drives for another hour at this constant speed, how far will she drive in all?

$$\text{Distance} = \text{speed} \times \text{time}$$
$$= 40 \times 5$$
$$= 200 \text{ mi}$$

She will drive 200 miles.

**e)** If Angela wants to drive at least 120 miles, how many hours will she need to drive? Express your answer in the form of an inequality in terms of $t$, where $t$ stands for the number of hours.

$t \geq 3$

**f)** Name the dependent and independent variables.

$d$ is the dependent variable, and $t$ is the independent variable.

## Guided Practice
**Use graph paper. Solve.**

**1** A car uses 1 gallon of gas for every 20 miles traveled. The amount of gas left in the gas tank, $x$ gallons, after traveling $y$ miles is given by $y = 240 - 20x$. Copy and complete the table. Graph the relationship between $x$ and $y$. Use 1 unit on the horizontal axis to represent 1 gallon and 1 unit on the vertical axis to represent 20 miles. See margin.

**a)**

| Amount of Gas (x gallons) | 12 | 10 | ? | 6 | ? | 8; 4 |
|---|---|---|---|---|---|---|
| Distance Traveled (y miles) | 0 | 40 | 80 | 120 | 160 | |

**b)** What type of graph is it?

It is a __?__ graph. straight line or linear

**Caution**

Students may not be accustomed to seeing coordinate planes in which the x-axis and the y-axis feature different intervals. Explain that the intervals along the two axes of a coordinate plane or a graph often differ, and that it is important to check the intervals on both axes before working with a coordinate plane or reading a graph.

## Guided Practice

**1** Watch to make sure that students understand how to set up the scales on the axes of their graphs.

**1**

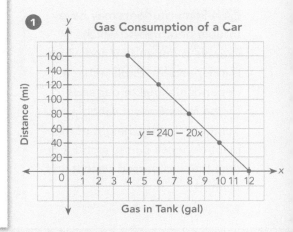

Gas Consumption of a Car

$y = 240 - 20x$

Distance (mi)

Gas in Tank (gal)

---

**Learn continued**

**b) Ask** How can you use the graph to find how far Angela drove? First, locate 3.5 on the time axis. Next, note the point where the vertical line through 3.5 meets the graph. Then, read the value where the horizontal line through this point meets the distance axis: 140 miles.

**c) Ask** How can you use the speed formula to find the speed at which Angela is driving?
$\text{Speed} = \frac{\text{total distance}}{\text{total time}} = \frac{160}{4} = 40 \text{ mi/h}$; 40 miles per hour

**d) Ask** Angela has driven at a constant speed for 4 hours. If she drives at this constant speed for another hour, how can you find how far she will drive? You can use the distance formula to find the distance that Angela will drive in 5 hours. Distance = speed × time = 40 × 5 = 200 mi; 200 miles.

**e) Ask** How many hours will Angela need to drive 120 miles? $\frac{120}{40} = 3$ h How can this be expressed in the form of an inequality in terms of $t$, where $t$ stands for the number of hours? $t \geq 3$

**f) Ask** What is the dependent variable? $d$ What is the independent variable? $t$

**1 e)** Help students to see how their line graph makes the distance at which the car runs out of gas obvious. **Ask:** How much gas does a car have in its tank when it runs out of gas? *(No gas, 0 gallons)* What happens to the line you have graphed when the number of gallons of gas in the tank, the x-value, equals zero? *(The line intersects the y-axis at (0, 240).)* What does that tell you about the situation? *(If you travel 240 miles, you will use up all the gas and have 0 gallons in the tank.)*

### DIFFERENTIATED INSTRUCTION

**Through Language Support**

**2 f)** Some students may have trouble determining which variable is dependent and which is independent. Explain that a dependent variable *depends* on the independent variable. Point out that the height of the plant *depends* on the amount of time that has passed since it was planted.

c) How many gallons of gas will be left in the tank after the car has traveled 60 miles?
From the graph, there will be __?__ gallons of gas left. 9

d) How many gallons of gas will be left in the tank after the car has traveled 100 miles?
From the graph, there will be __?__ gallons of gas left. 7

e) After the car has traveled 160 miles, how much farther can the car travel before it runs out of gas?

After 160 miles, __?__ gallons of gas were left. 4

The car uses 1 gallon for every __?__ miles traveled. 20

Distance = number of gallons × mileage

$$= \underline{\ ?\ } \times \underline{\ ?\ } \quad 4; 20$$

$$= \underline{\ ?\ } \text{ mi} \quad 80$$

The car can travel another __?__ miles. 80

f) If the car travels more than 40 miles, how much gas is left in the tank? Express your answer in the form of an inequality in terms of x, where x stands for the amount of gas left in the gas tank.
If the distance traveled is more than 40 miles, then __?__ . $x < 10$

g) Name the dependent and independent variables. Dependent: $y$, Independent: $x$

2 Sarah plants a seed. After $t$ weeks, the height of the plant, $h$ centimeters, is given by $h = 2t$. Copy and complete the table. Graph the relationship between $t$ and $h$. Use 1 unit on the horizontal axis to represent 1 week and 1 unit on the vertical axis to represent 2 centimeters. See margin.

a)

| Time (t weeks) | 0 | 1 | 2 | 3 | 4 | 5 |
|---|---|---|---|---|---|---|
| Height (h centimeters) | ? | 2 | 4 | 6 | ? | ? |

0; 8; 10

b) What type of graph is it? straight line graph or linear graph

c) What is the height of the plant after 3 weeks? 6 cm

d) What is the height of the plant after 5 weeks? 10 cm

e) What is the height of the plant if less than 4 weeks have passed? Express your answer in the form of an inequality in terms of $h$, where $h$ stands for the height of the plant in centimeters. $h < 8$

f) Name the dependent and independent variables. Dependent: $h$, Independent: $t$

2
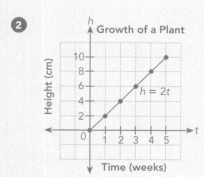

**Use graph paper. Solve.**

**①** A cyclist took part in a competition. The distance traveled, *d* meters, after *t* minutes, is given by $d = 700t$. Graph the relationship between *t* and *d*. Use 2 units on the horizontal axis to represent 1 minute and 1 unit on the vertical axis to represent 350 meters. See margin.

| Time (*t* minutes) | 0 | 1 | 2 | 3 | 4 |
|---|---|---|---|---|---|
| Distance Traveled (*d* meters) | 0 | 700 | 1,400 | 2,100 | 2,800 |

a) What type of graph is it? straight line graph or linear graph

b) What is the distance traveled in 2.5 minutes? 1,750 m

c) What is the distance traveled in 3.5 minutes? 2,450 m

d) What is the average speed of the cyclist? 700 m/min

e) Assuming that the cyclist travels at a constant speed throughout the competition, what distance will he travel in 7 minutes? 4,900 m

f) If the cyclist needs to cycle for at least 2.1 kilometers, how many minutes will he need to cycle? Express your answer in the form of an inequality in terms of *t*, where *t* stands for the number of minutes. $t \geq 3$

g) Name the dependent and independent variables. Dependent: *d*, Independent: *t*

**②** A bus uses 1 gallon of diesel for every 7 miles traveled. The amount of diesel left in the gas tank, *p* gallons, after traveling *q* miles, is given by $q = 112 - 7p$. Copy and complete the table. Graph the relationship between *p* and *q*. Use 1 unit on the horizontal axis to represent 1 gallon and 1 unit on the vertical axis to represent 7 miles. See margin.

a)

| Amount of Diesel (*p* gallons) | 16 | 14 | 12 | 10 | 8 | |
|---|---|---|---|---|---|---|
| Distance Traveled (*q* miles) | 0 | ? | 28 | 42 | ? | 14; 56 |

b) How many gallons of diesel were left after the bus has traveled 49 miles? 9 gal

c) After the bus has traveled for 56 miles, how much farther can the bus travel before it runs out of diesel? 56 mi

d) If the bus travels more than 28 miles, how much diesel is left? Express your answer in the form of an inequality in terms of *p*, where *p* stands for the amount of diesel left. $p < 12$

**Practice 9.3**

**Assignment Guide**

DAY **1** All students should complete ①–③.
Optional: *Extra Practice 9.3*

 **DIFFERENTIATED INSTRUCTION**

**Through Communication**

**①** f) Some students may need to be reminded of how to convert metric measurements. **Ask:** How many meters are in 1 kilometer? *(1 km = 1,000 m)* So, how do we find how many meters are in 2.1 kilometers? *(2.1 · 1,000 = 2,100 meters)*

①–② See Additional Answers.

**RtI Lesson Check**

| Before assigning homework, use the following ... | to make sure students ... | Intervene with ... |
|---|---|---|
| Exercise **①** | • can represent data in tables and graphs | |
| EXIT **Ticket Out the Door** | • can graph and analyze a relationship between a dependent and an independent variable | Reteach 9.3 |

③ See Additional Answers.

**EXIT**

## Ticket Out the Door

A water tank has 10 gal of water in it. A hose is placed in the tank. Every min, 20 gal of water flows out of hose and into the tank. The number of gal of water $g$ in the tank after $m$ min is given by $g = 20m + 10$. Graph the relationship between $m$ and $g$. Use 1 unit on the horizontal axis to represent 1 min and 1 unit on the vertical axis to represent 20 gal. How much water is in the tank at 1 min, 3 min, and 5 min? See Additional Answers.

 Also available on Teacher One Stop.

## Brain @ Work

Students discover that when they draw line segments connecting the midpoints of the sides of any quadrilateral, the line segments will always form a parallelogram.

① – ③ See Additional Answers.

---

③ A kettle of water is heated and the temperature of the water, $j°C$, after $k$ minutes, is given by $j = 5k + 30$. Copy and complete the table. Graph the relationship between $k$ and $j$. Use 1 unit on the horizontal axis to represent 1 minute and 1 unit on the vertical axis to represent 5°C. See margin.

a)

| Time ($k$ minutes) | 0 | 2 | 4 | 6 | ? | 8 |
|---|---|---|---|---|---|---|
| Temperature ($j°C$) | ? | 40 | ? | 60 | 70 | 30; 50 |

b) What is the temperature of the water after 5 minutes? 55°C

c) What is the average rate of the heating? 5°C/min

d) Assuming the temperature of the water rises at a constant rate, what is the temperature of the water after 10 minutes? 80°C

e) The kettle of water needs to be heated till the water boils. For how many minutes does the kettle need to be heated? Express your answer in terms of $k$, where $k$ stands for the number of minutes. (Hint: Water boils at 100°C.) $k \geq 14$

## Brain @ Work

Use graph paper. For each exercise, plot the points on a coordinate plane.

① $A(-5, 1)$, $B(-3, -3)$, $C(3, 1)$, and $D(-1, 5)$    ① – ③ See margin.

② $J(4, 2)$, $K(-2, 4)$, $L(-4, 0)$, and $M(0, -2)$

③ $S(-1, 3)$, $T(-3, -1)$, $U(1, -1)$, and $V(5, 3)$

④ In questions ① to ③, what is the figure formed? The figure formed is a quadrilateral.

⑤ a) For each figure in questions ① to ③, mark the middle of each side and connect the points in order. See margin.

b) What are the figures formed? Explain your answers. See below.

b) Parallelograms. Both pairs of opposite sides are equal in length. Both pairs of opposite sides are parallel.

---

## DIFFERENTIATED INSTRUCTION

**Through Enrichment**

Because all students should be challenged, have all students try the Brain@Work exercises on this page.

For additional challenging practice and problem solving, see *Enrichment, Course 1*, Chapter 9.

# Chapter Wrap Up

## Concept Map

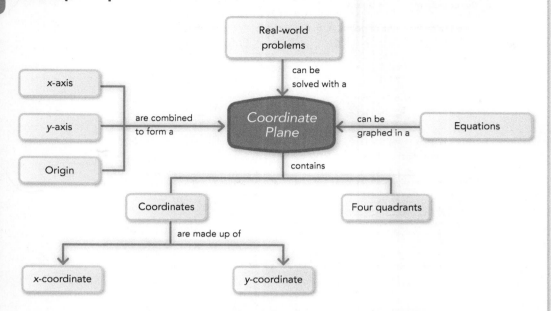

## Key Concepts

▶ The x-axis and y-axis divide the coordinate plane into four quadrants. The quadrants are called Quadrant I, Quadrant II, Quadrant III, and Quadrant IV.

▶ Each point on a coordinate plane can be located by using an ordered pair (x, y).

▶ For any point,
- the x-coordinate tells how far to the left or right of the origin the point is relative to the x-axis.
- the y-coordinate tells how far up or down from the origin the point is relative to the y-axis.

▶ Points to the left of the y-axis have negative x-coordinates. Points below the x-axis have negative y-coordinates.

▶ A straight line graph is also called a linear graph. A linear equation has a straight line graph.

## CHAPTER WRAP UP

Use the notes and the examples in the concept map to review finding the coordinates of points, plotting points on the coordinate plane, finding the lengths of line segments parallel to the coordinate axes, and interpreting linear graphs.

## CHAPTER PROJECT

To widen student's mathematical horizons and to encourage them to think beyond the concepts taught in this chapter, you may want to assign the Chapter 9 project, Graphing Rubber Band Data, available in *Activity Book, Course 1.*

## Vocabulary Review

Use these questions to review chapter vocabulary with students.

1. The horizontal axis on a coordinate plane is called the __?__. x-axis

2. The vertical axis on a coordinate plane is called the __?__. y-axis

3. Ordered pairs of numbers that give the location of points on a coordinate plane are called __?__. coordinates

4. The x-axis and the y-axis divide the coordinate plane into four __?__. quadrants

 Also available on Teacher One Stop.

## Chapter Assessment

Use the Chapter 9 Test A or B in *Assessments, Course 1* to assess how well students have learned the material in this chapter. These assessments are appropriate for reporting results to adults at home and administrators. Test A is shown on page 71A.

## TEST PREPARATION

For additional test prep

- **ExamView® Assessment Suite Course 1**

- **Online Assessment System** my.hrw.com

**2** – **10** See Additional Answers.

# Chapter Review/Test

## Concepts and Skills
Use the coordinate plane below.

**1** Give the coordinates of points A, B, C, D, and E. A (−4, −3), B (0, −6), C (2, −4), D (6, 3), and E (−2, 3)

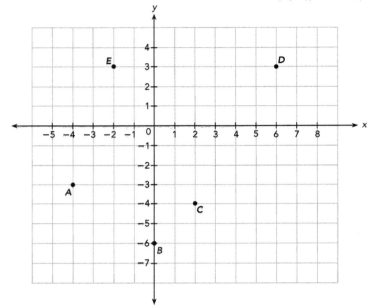

Use graph paper. Plot the points on a coordinate plane. In which quadrant is each point located?

**2** A (3, 5), B (−2, 0), C (7, −2), D (0, −5), and E (−3, −8)      **2** – **10** See margin.

Use graph paper. Points A and B are reflections of each other about the x-axis. Give the coordinates of point B if the coordinates of point A are the following:

**3** (3, 6)          **4** (−6, 2)          **5** (5, −4)          **6** (−3, −5)

Use graph paper. Points C and D are reflections of each other about the y-axis. Give the coordinates of point D if the coordinates of point C are the following:

**7** (3, 6)          **8** (−6, 2)          **9** (5, −4)          **10** (−3, −5)

## RtI Intervention and Reteaching Recommendations

| Student Book B Review/Test Items | Assessments Chapter 9 Items | Chapter 9 Objectives | Reteach B Chapter 9 |
| --- | --- | --- | --- |
| **1** to **10** | 1–4 | **Objective 1.** Locate points on the coordinate plane. | Lesson 9.1 |

Use graph paper. For each exercise, plot the given points on a coordinate plane. Then connect the points in order with line segments to form a closed figure. Name each figure formed.

**11** A (2, −4), B (2, 4), C (−6, 4), and D (−6, −4)

**11** – **26** See margin.

**12** E (0, −2), F (−3, 1), G (−5, −1), and H (−2, −4)

**13** J (0, 1), K (1, 4), and L (−4, 3)

**14** M (6, 5), N (3, 5), P (3, −3), and Q (6, −3)

**15** A (6, −3), B (4, 2), C (−1, 2), and D (0, −3)

**16** E (−1, 6), F (−3, 3), G (3, 3), and H (5, 6)

**17** J (6, 1), K (8, −2), L (2, −2), and M (0, 1)

**18** P (2, 7), Q (−1, 7), R (−5, 4), and S (4, 4)

**19** T (−2, 1), U (−6, 1), V (−6, −3), and W (−2, −3)

Use graph paper. Plot the points on a coordinate plane and answer the question.

**20** a) Plot points A (1, −1) and B (7, −1) on a coordinate plane. Connect the two points to form a line segment.

b) Point C lies above $\overline{AB}$, and is 2 units away from the x-axis. If triangle ABC is an isosceles triangle with base $\overline{AB}$, find the coordinates of point C.

c) Points D and E lie below $\overline{AB}$ such that ABDE is a rectangle. If BD is 5 units, find the coordinates of points D and E.

Use graph paper. Plot each pair of points on a coordinate plane. Connect the points to form a line segment and find its length.

**21** A (−1, 0) and B (8, 0)

**22** C (−2, 4) and D (6, 4)

**23** E (−6, −2) and F (−6, −6)

**24** G (−5, −4) and H (2, −4)

**25** J (0, −3) and K (0, −8)

**26** M (5, 2) and N (5, −5)

**11**

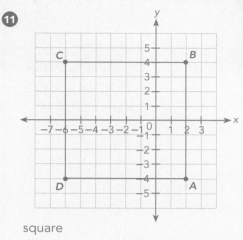

square

**12**

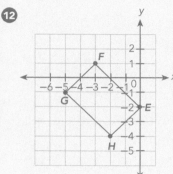

rectangle

**13**

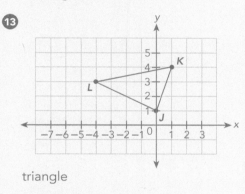

triangle

**14** – **26** See Additional Answers.

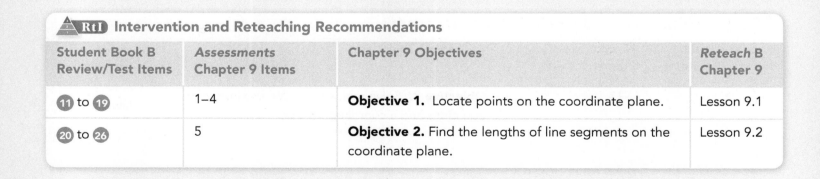

**RtI** Intervention and Reteaching Recommendations

| Student Book B Review/Test Items | Assessments Chapter 9 Items | Chapter 9 Objectives | Reteach B Chapter 9 |
|---|---|---|---|
| **11** to **19** | 1–4 | **Objective 1.** Locate points on the coordinate plane. | Lesson 9.1 |
| **20** to **26** | 5 | **Objective 2.** Find the lengths of line segments on the coordinate plane. | Lesson 9.2 |

## Problem Solving

The diagram shows the plan of a room. The side length of each grid square is 10 feet.
Use the diagram to answer questions 27 to 30.

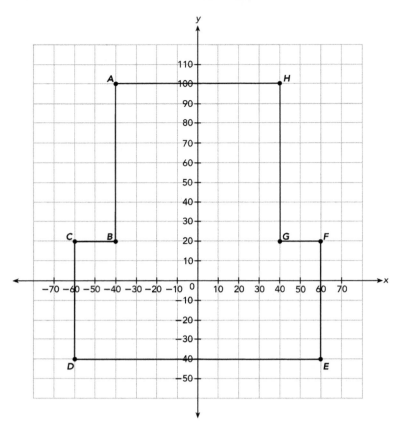

27. The eight corners of the room are labeled points *A* to *H*. Give the coordinates of each of these corners. *A* (−40, 100), *B* (−40, 20), *C* (−60, 20), *D* (−60, −40), *E* (60, −40), *F* (60, 20), *G* (40, 20), and *H* (40,100)

28. The entrance of the room is situated along $\overline{AH}$. What is the shortest possible distance in feet between the entrance and $\overline{DE}$ of the room?  140 ft

29. Diana walks across the room from point *G* to point *G*, and then walks from point *G* to point *H*. Find the total distance, in feet, that Diana walks.  160 ft

30. Calculate the floor area of the room in square feet.  13,600 ft²

**Use graph paper. Solve.**

**31** An athlete took part in a race. The distance the athlete ran, v meters, after t minutes, is given by v = 300t. Graph the relationship between t and v. Use 2 units on the horizontal axis to represent 1 minute and 1 unit on the vertical axis to represent 150 meters. See margin.

| Time (t minutes) | 0 | 1 | 2 | 3 | 4 |
|---|---|---|---|---|---|
| Distance Traveled (v meters) | 0 | 300 | 600 | 900 | 1,200 |

a) What type of graph is it? straight line graph or linear graph

b) What is the distance the athlete ran in 3.5 minutes? 1,050 m

c) What is the average speed of the athlete? 300 m/min

d) Assuming the athlete runs at a constant speed, what is the distance she will run in 8 minutes? 2,400 m

e) Name the dependent and independent variables. Dependent: v, Independent: t

**32** A truck uses 1 gallon of diesel for every 12 miles traveled. The amount of diesel left in the gas tank, r gallons, after traveling s miles is given by s = 300 − 12r. Copy and complete the table. Graph the relationship between r and s. Use 1 unit on the horizontal axis to represent 1 gallon and 1 unit on the vertical axis to represent 12 miles. Start your horizontal axis at 17 gallons. See margin.

a)

| Amount of Diesel (r gallons) | 25 | ? 23 | 21 | 19 | 17 |
|---|---|---|---|---|---|
| Distance Traveled (s miles) | 0 | 24 | 48 | 72 | ? 96 |

b) How many gallons of diesel are left after the truck has traveled 60 miles? 20 gal

c) After the truck has traveled for 72 miles, how much farther can the truck travel before it runs out of diesel? 228 mi

d) If the truck travels more than 48 miles, how much diesel is left in the gas tank? Express your answer in the form of an inequality in terms of r, where r stands for the amount of diesel left. r < 21

**31**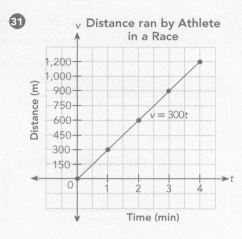

v Distance ran by Athlete in a Race

v = 300t

Distance (m) / Time (min)

**32**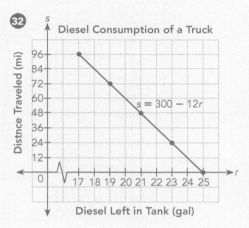

s Diesel Consumption of a Truck

s = 300 − 12r

Distnce Traveled (mi) / Diesel Left in Tank (gal)

# Chapter 9 Tests A and B

Answer key appears in the *Assessments, Course 1*

Test B, Assessments p. 92

Test A, Assessments p. 89

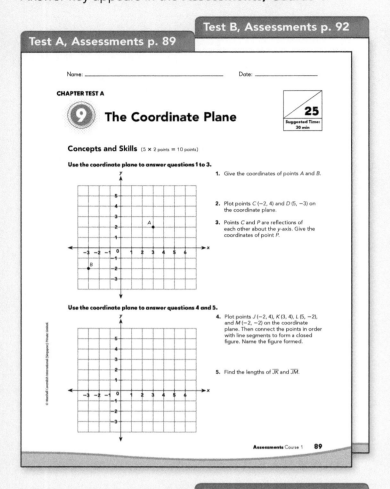

Test B, Assessments p. 93

Test A, Assessments p. 90

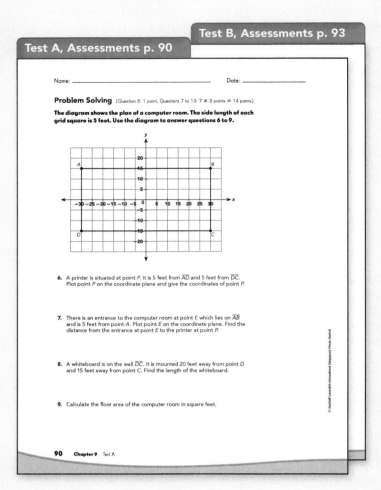

Test B, Assessments p. 94

Test A, Assessments p. 91

Name: _____     Date: _____

A swimmer participated in a competition. The distance swam, $d$ meters, after $t$ seconds, is given by the equation $d = 1.5t$. Use the data in the table to answer questions 10 to 13.

| Time ($t$ seconds) | 0 | 10 | 20 | 30 | 40 |
|---|---|---|---|---|---|
| Distance Swam ($d$ meters) | 0 | 15 | 30 | 45 | 60 |

10. Graph the relationship between $t$ and $d$. Use 1 unit on the horizontal axis to represent 5 seconds and 1 unit on the vertical axis to represent 4 meters.

11. What was the distance swam in 25 seconds?

12. What was the average speed of the swimmer?

13. Assuming the swimmer swam at a constant speed, what was the distance he swam in 2 minutes?

Assessments Course 1  **91**

# Chapter at a Glance

| | | CHAPTER OPENER<br>Area of Polygons<br>Recall Prior Knowledge | LESSON 10.1<br>Area of Triangles<br>Pages 75–87 | LESSON 10.2<br>Area of Parallelograms<br>and Trapezoids<br>Pages 88–98 |
|---|---|---|---|---|
| **LESSON AT A GLANCE** | Pacing | 2 days | 2 days | 3 days |
| | Objectives | The area of a polygon can be found by dividing it into smaller shapes, and then adding the areas of those shapes. | • Use a formula to find the area of a triangle. | • Use a formula to find the area of a parallelogram, given its base and height.<br>• Use a formula to find the area of a trapezoid, given its bases and height. |
| | Vocabulary | | formula, height, base | |
| **RESOURCES** | Materials | | scissors, TRT12*, TR21–23* | scissors, TRT24–25* |
| | Lesson Resources | Student Book B, pp. 72–74<br>*Assessments Course 1,* Chapter 10 Pre-Test<br>*Transition Guide, Course 1,* Skills 39–41 | Student Book B, pp. 75–87<br>*Extra Practice B,* Lesson 10.1<br>*Reteach B,* Lesson 10.1<br>*Activity Book,* Lessons 10.1–10.3 | Student Book B, pp. 88–98<br>*Extra Practice B,* Lesson 10.2<br>*Reteach B,* Lesson 10.2<br>*Activity Book,* Lessons 10.1–10.3 |
| | **Common Core**<br>Standards for Mathematical Content | **6.EE.2c**<br>Foundational for **6.G.1, 6.G.3** | **6.EE.2c** Evaluate ...expressions that arise from formulas used in real-world problems.<br>**6.G.1** Find the area of right triangles, other triangles, ... | **6.G.1** Find the area of ...special quadrilaterals, ...by decomposing into triangles and other shapes....<br>**6.G.3** Draw polygons in the coordinate plane.... |
| | **Mathematical Practices** | **6.** Attend to precision. **7.** Look for and use structure. | **4.** Model mathematics. **7.** Look for and use structure. **8.** Express regularity in reasoning. | **4.** Model mathematics. **7.** Look for and use structure. **8.** Express regularity in reasoning. |

*Teacher Resource Tools (TRT) are available on the Teacher One Stop.

# Concepts and Skills Across the Courses

| GRADE 5 | COURSE 1 | COURSE 2 |
|---|---|---|
| • Apply and extend understandings of multiplication of fractions and decimals to find the area of a rectangle. (5.NBT.7, 5.NF.4b)<br>• Graph points in the coordinate plane to solve problems. (5.G.1, 5.G.2)<br>• Understand the attributes of two-dimensional figures. (5.G.3) | • Evaluate expressions that arise from formulas used in real-world problems. (6.EE.2c.)<br>• Solve real-world or mathematical problems involving area of triangles, quadrilaterals, and other polygons. (6.G.1)<br>• Draw polygons in the coordinate plane to solve problems. (6.G.3) | • Use variables to represent quantities in real-world or mathematical problems. (7.EE.4, 7.EE.4a)<br>• Know the relationship among the formulas for the area and circumference of a circle. (7.G.4)<br>• Solve real-world and mathematical problems involving circumference and area of circles. (7.G.6) |

| LESSON 10.3<br>Area of Other Polygons<br>Pages 99–103 | LESSON 10.4<br>Area of Composite Figures<br>Pages 104–112 | CHAPTER<br>WRAP UP/REVIEW/TEST<br>Brain@Work<br>Pages 113–117 |
|---|---|---|
| 1 day | 2 days | 2 days |
| • Divide polygons into triangles.<br>• Find the area of a regular polygon by dividing it into smaller shapes. | • Recognize that a plane figure is made up of polygons.<br>• Solve problems involving areas of composite figures. | Reinforce, consolidate, and extend chapter skills and concepts. |
| regular polygon | | |
| TRT26* | TRT26* | |
| Student Book B, pp. 99–103<br>*Extra Practice B,* Lesson 10.3<br>*Reteach B,* Lesson 10.3<br>*Activity Book,* Lessons 10.1–10.3 | Student Book B, pp. 104–112<br>*Extra Practice B,* Lesson 10.4<br>*Reteach B,* Lesson 10.4 | Student Book B, pp. 113–117<br>*Activity Book,* Chapter 10 Project<br>*Enrichment,* Chapter 10<br>*Assessments,* Chapter 10 Test<br>ExamView® Assessment Suite Course 1 |
| **6.G.1** Find the area of... polygons by composing into rectangles or decomposing into triangles and other shapes; ... | **6.G.1** ...apply these techniques (composing or decomposing) in the context of solving real-world and mathematical problems. | |
| **1.** Solve problems/persevere. **3.** Construct arguments. **6.** Attend to precision. | **1.** Solve problems/persevere. **6.** Attend to precision. **8.** Express regularity in reasoning. | **1.** Solve problems/persevere. **6.** Attend to precision. **7.** Look for and use structure. |

# Additional Chapter Resources

## TECHNOLOGY

 • Online Student eBook

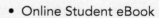 • Interactive Whiteboard Lessons

 • Virtual Manipulatives

 • Teacher One Stop

 • ExamView® Assessment Suite Course 1

 • Online Professional Development Videos

## Every Day Counts®
## ALGEBRA READINESS

The March activities in the Pacing Chart provide:

• **Review** of metric linear measures and decimal multiplication (**Ch. 3: 6.NS.3; Ch. 4: 6.RP.3d**)

• **Review** of patterns, triangles, and triangle categories (**Ch. 10: 6.G.1**)

• **Practice** evaluating variable expressions (**Ch. 10: 6.EE.2c**)

# Math Background

# Chapter 10  Area of Polygons

## Deriving Area Formulas

- In this chapter, students derive formulas for areas of triangles, parallelograms, trapezoids, and regular polygons. They use the formulas to find areas and, given an area, identify unknown dimensions.

### From rectangle to triangles

- Students use a diagonal to divide a rectangle into two right triangles. Seeing that the two triangles are congruent, they realize that the area of each triangle is half the area of the rectangle.

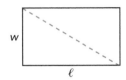

Area of rectangle $= \ell \cdot w$

Area of triangle $= \dfrac{1}{2}(\ell \cdot w)$

- Through a Hands-On Activity, students prove the formula also applies to non-right triangles.

### Understanding base and height

- Students learn that the terms *length* and *width*, appropriate for discussing rectangles, do not apply to other polygons. They explore the geometric meaning of *base*, and learn that any side of a triangle can be considered its base, not just a side at the bottom.

- Students learn that a *height* of a triangle is a perpendicular segment that extends from the base to the opposite vertex. Through work with a variety of examples, they see that the height may be a side of the triangle or may be represented by a dashed line segment drawn inside or outside of it.

### From rectangle to other parallelograms

- By drawing a height, students divide a parallelogram into a trapezoid and a triangle. Rearranging these figures into a rectangle, students derive the formula for the area of a parallelogram: $A = bh$.

## Triangles as Building Blocks

- Students will learn that the formula for the area of a triangle is the basis for deriving other area formulas as well as for finding the areas of composite figures.

### Triangles within trapezoids

- Students derive the formula for the area of a trapezoid by using a diagonal to divide a trapezoid into two triangles.

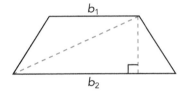

The diagonal divides the trapezoid into two triangles that have the same height, $h$.

Area of top triangle $= \dfrac{1}{2}(h \cdot b_1)$

Area of bottom triangle $= \dfrac{1}{2}(h \cdot b_2)$

The area of the trapezoid is equal to the combined area of the triangles.

Area of trapezoid $= \dfrac{1}{2}(h \cdot b_1) + \dfrac{1}{2}(h \cdot b_2)$

$\qquad\qquad = \dfrac{1}{2}h(b_1 + b_2)$

### Triangles within regular polygons

- Students learn that any regular polygon can be divided into a minimum number of identical triangles by drawing line segments from each vertex to the center. Given the length of one side of a regular polygon and the height of one of the identical triangles, students can then find the area of the polygon.

### Finding areas of composite figures

- Students learn that plane figures are made up of polygons. They divide composite figures into triangles, rectangles, parallelograms, and trapezoids, apply the area formulas they have learned, and add the areas to find the total area of a figure.

## Assessment and Intervention

| | ASSESSMENT |  RtI STRUGGLING LEARNERS |
|---|---|---|
| **DIAGNOSTIC** | • Quick Check in Recall Prior Knowledge in Student Book B, pp. 73–74<br>• Chapter 10 Pre-Test in *Assessments* | • Skills 39–41 in *Transition Guide*, *Course 1* |
| **ON-GOING** | • Guided Practice<br>• Lesson Check<br>• Ticket Out the Door | • Reteach worksheets<br>• Extra Practice worksheets<br>• *Activity Book*, Chapter 10 |
| **END-OF-CHAPTER** | • Chapter Review/Test<br>• Chapter 10 Test in *Assessments*<br>• ExamView® Assessment Suite Course 1 | • Reteach worksheets |

### ELL ENGLISH LANGUAGE LEARNERS

Review the term *base*.

**Say** In everyday English, the word *base* means the bottom piece of something. The top of a table sits on its base. A statue of a man or woman often stands on a stone base. In geometry, *base* has a special meaning.

**Model** Draw a triangle and a parallelogram.

**Say** Any side of a triangle can be its base, Any side of a parallelogram can be its base. The base of a triangle or parallelogram does not have to be on the bottom.

**Model** Draw two trapezoids, one with its bases at bottom and top, the other with bases left and right.

**Say** A trapezoid has two bases. The bases of a trapezoid are the two sides that are parallel. The bases of a trapezoid do not have to be its top and bottom.

For definitions, see Glossary, on page 301, and Online Multilingual Glossary.

### ADVANCED LEARNERS

• On page 91 of Student Book B, students derive the formula for the area of a trapezoid by dividing a trapezoid into two triangles. There are other means of arriving at this formula. Have students derive the formula by using one or both of two other methods: by dividing the trapezoid into two trapezoids, or by dividing it into a rectangle and two right triangles.

• As needed, provide direction for students. Have them begin with trapezoid *ABDE* on page 91. To use two trapezoids, suggest students divide *ABDE* by drawing a horizontal segment across the midpoints of the nonparallel sides, then flipping the top trapezoid clockwise to form one long parallelogram.

• To divide trapezoid *ABDE* into a rectangle and two right triangles, suggest students draw line segments from points *A* and *E* perpendicular to $\overline{BD}$.

**To provide additional challenges use:**
• *Enrichment*, Chapter 10
• Student Book A, Brain@Work problem

# CHAPTER

# 10

## CHAPTER

## 10

# Area of Polygons

## Chapter Vocabulary

Vocabulary terms are used in context in the student text. For definitions, see the Glossary at the end of the Student Book and the Online Multilingual Glossary.

**base (of a triangle)** Any side of a triangle from which the height of a triangle is measured

**formula** A general mathematical equation or rule

**height (of a triangle)** The perpendicular distance from the base to the opposite vertex of a triangle

**regular polygon** A polygon whose sides are all the same length, and whose angles are all the same measure

**10.1** Area of Triangles

**10.2** Area of Parallelograms and Trapezoids

**10.3** Area of Other Polygons

**10.4** Area of Composite Figures

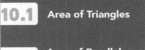

BIG IDEA

▶ The area of a polygon can be found by dividing it into smaller shapes, and then adding the areas of those shapes.

## Have you ever made a quilt?

Quilted fabrics have been used throughout the world for thousands of years. A needle and thread are used to combine the layers of fabric that make up a quilt.

The top of a quilt may be made of bits of fabric pieced together into "blocks." To decide how much fabric is needed, a quilter needs to know the size and shape of each block and the size and shape of all the pieces.

In this chapter, you'll learn how to find areas of various geometric shapes like those shown in the quilt block below.

## CHAPTER OPENER

Use the chapter opener to talk about shapes and area of polygons in a real-life situation.

**Ask** Have you ever seen a quilt? Possible answer: Yes What is it made of? It is made of blocks of fabric in the shape of polygons.

**Explain** Each block is made up of smaller pieces of fabric that are sewn together.

**Ask** How much fabric is needed to make a quilt? Possible answer: A quilter needs to know the shape and size of each block, and the shape and size of all the smaller pieces that make up each block, in order to figure out how much fabric is needed for the quilt.

In this chapter, you will learn about areas of polygons, which can be found by dividing a polygon into smaller pieces, and then adding the areas of these shapes as stated in the **Big Idea.**

## Recall Prior Knowledge

### Finding the area of a rectangle using a formula

The longer side of a rectangle is called the length.
The shorter side is called the width.

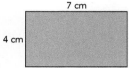
7 cm

4 cm

The opposite sides of a rectangle have the same length. If $\ell$ is the length and $w$ is the width, the formula for area is Area = $\ell w$.

Area of rectangle = $\ell w$
$= 7 \cdot 4$
$= 28$ cm$^2$

The area of the rectangle is 28 square centimeters.

#### ✓ Quick Check

**Solve.**

1. The length of a rectangle is 15 meters and its width is 8 meters. Find the area of the rectangle. 120 m$^2$

### Finding the area of a square using a formula

A side length of a square is 12 meters. Find the area of the square.

12 m

Area of square = $\ell^2$
$= 12^2$
$= 144$ m$^2$

The side lengths of a square are all equal. If $\ell$ represents the side length, the formula for area is Area = $\ell^2$.

The area of the square is 144 square meters.

#### ✓ Quick Check

**Solve.**

2. A side length of a square is 10 centimeters. Find the area of the square.
100 cm$^2$

### RECALL PRIOR KNOWLEDGE

Use the ✓ Quick Check exercises or the Chapter Pre-Test in *Assessments, Course 1*, to assess chapter readiness. For intervention suggestions, see the chart below and on the next page.

Additional online Reteach and Extra Practice worksheets from previous grades are also available. See the *Transition Guide*, Resource Planner for more information.

### ▲ RtI Assessing Prior Knowledge

| ✓ Quick Check | Assessments Course 1, Ch. 10 Pre-Test Items | Skill Objective | Intervene with | |
| --- | --- | --- | --- | --- |
| | | | Transition Guide | Online Resources Grades 4 and 5 |
| 1 | 1 | Find the area of a rectangle using a formula. | Skill 39 | Reteach 4B, pp. 121–128; Extra Practice 4B, Lesson 12.1 |
| 2 | 2 | Find the area of a square using a formula. | Skill 40 | Reteach 4B, pp. 135–138; Extra Practice 4B, Lesson 12.2 |

**Chapter 10** Area of Polygons    **73**

---
**Identifying parallelograms, trapezoids, and rhombuses**

Figure *ABCD* is a parallelogram. There are two pairs of parallel sides. $\overline{AB}$ is parallel to $\overline{DC}$. $\overline{AD}$ is parallel to $\overline{BC}$.

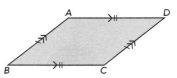

Figure *PQRS* is a trapezoid. There is one pair of parallel sides. $\overline{PS}$ is parallel to $\overline{QR}$.

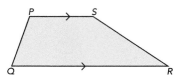

Figure *WXYZ* is a rhombus. The side lengths of a rhombus are equal, and the opposite sides are parallel. $\overline{WX}$ is parallel to $\overline{ZY}$. $\overline{XY}$ is parallel to $\overline{WZ}$.

☑ **Quick Check** ③ – ⑤ See margin.

**Name each figure and identify the pairs of parallel lines.**

③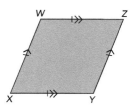

④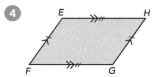

⑤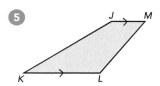

---

③ Rhombus; $\overline{RU} \parallel \overline{ST}$ ; $\overline{SR} \parallel \overline{TU}$

④ Parallelogram; $\overline{EF} \parallel \overline{HG}$; $\overline{EH} \parallel \overline{FG}$

⑤ Trapezoid; $\overline{JM} \parallel \overline{KL}$

---

**Lesson Objective**

- Use a formula to find the area of a triangle.

**Vocabulary**

formula    base

height

### Learn — Derive the **formula** for the area of a triangle.

Area of rectangle = $\ell w$

The diagonal of a rectangle divides it into two congruent triangles.

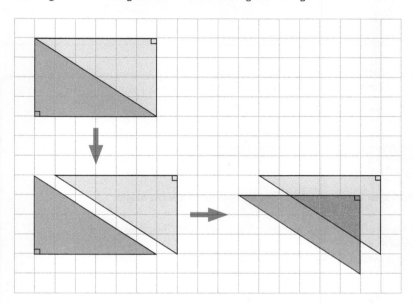

The area of the yellow triangle is half the area of the rectangle.

Area of the triangle

$= \frac{1}{2} \cdot$ area of the rectangle

$= \frac{1}{2} \cdot \ell w$

Continue on next page

## KEY CONCEPTS

- You can use this formula to find the area of a triangle:
  Area of triangle $= \frac{1}{2} bh$

- You can find the height of a triangle given its area and base.

- You can find the base of a triangle given its area and height.

## PACING

DAY **1**   Pages 75–80

DAY **2**   Pages 80–87

**Materials:** scissors, TRT12, TRT21–TRT23

### 5-minute Warm Up

Find the area of this triangle:

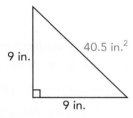

9 in.

40.5 in.²

9 in.

Also available on Teacher One Stop.

---

DAY **1**

### Learn — Derive the formula for the area of a triangle.

**Explain** Remind students about the formula for area of a rectangle: Area of rectangle $= \ell w$

**Model** Draw the rectangle shown in the text.

**Ask** How can the rectangle be divided into two congruent triangles? By drawing a diagonal across the rectangle

**Explain** The diagonal divides the rectangle into two congruent triangles.

**Ask** What is the area of the yellow triangle? Half the area of the rectangle What is the area of the blue triangle? Half the area of the rectangle What formula can be derived to find the area of the yellow or blue triangle? Area of triangle $= \frac{1}{2} \cdot$ area of the rectangle or $\frac{1}{2} \cdot \ell w$

Any side of a triangle can be called its **base**. The perpendicular distance from the base to the opposite vertex of the triangle is called the **height** of the triangle.

$$\text{Area of triangle} = \frac{1}{2} \cdot \ell w$$
$$= \frac{1}{2} \cdot \text{base} \cdot \text{height}$$

Using *b* for base and *h* for height, you can write the formula as

Area of triangle = $\frac{1}{2}bh$

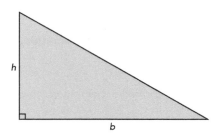

## Hands-On Activity

**Materials:**
• scissors
• graph paper

**PROVE THE FORMULA FOR FINDING THE AREA OF A TRIANGLE**

Work in pairs.

**Triangle *PQR* is an acute triangle. $\overline{QR}$ is the base and *PX* is the height.**

**STEP 1** Draw triangle *PQR* on a piece of graph paper as shown. Then draw and label rectangle *AQRD*.

**Example**

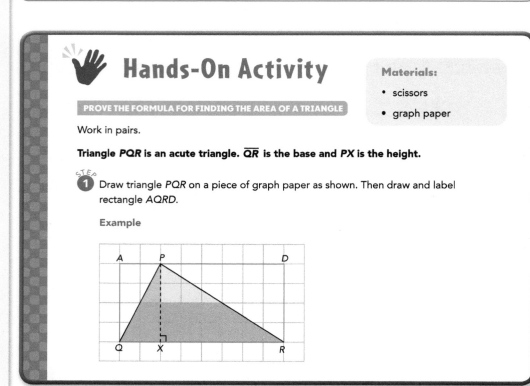

**Learn continued**

**Ask** Which side of a triangle is its base? Any side What do you call the perpendicular distance from the base to the opposite vertex of the triangle? The triangle's height

**Explain** The length of the rectangle has now become the base of the triangle. The width of the rectangle has now become the height of the triangle. Using *b* for base and *h* for height, you can write the formula for area of triangle as Area of triangle = $\frac{1}{2}bh$.

**Ask** Will this formula work for any right triangle? Explain. Yes, because any right triangle can be combined with a copy of it to form a rectangle. The length of the rectangle will be the base of the triangle and the width of the rectangle will be the height of the triangle.

**STEP 2** Cut up triangle *PQR* into smaller triangles. Rearrange the triangles to form rectangle *EQRF*, as shown below.

**Example**

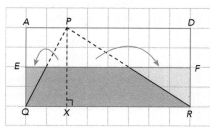

The orange, blue, and yellow figures form a rectangle.

**STEP 3** Find the area of rectangle *EQRF*. How does its area compare to the area of rectangle *AQRD*? See margin.

How does the area of triangle *PQR* compare to the area of rectangle *EQRF*?

How does the area of triangle *PQR* compare to the area of rectangle *AQRD*?

**Triangle *MNP* is an obtuse triangle. $\overline{NP}$ is the base and *MF* is the height.**

**STEP 1** Draw triangle *MNP* on a piece of graph paper as shown. Then draw and label rectangle *ANPD*.

**Example**

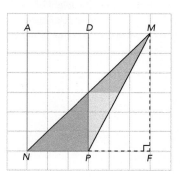

**Continue on next page**

Area of rectangle *EQRF* = 16 units$^2$

Area of rectangle *AQRD* = 32 units$^2$

The area of rectangle *EQRF* is half the area of rectangle *AQRD*.

The area of triangle *PQR* is equal to the area of rectangle *EQRF*.

The area of triangle *PQR* is half the area of rectangle *AQRD*.

Area of triangle *PQR* = 16 units$^2$

**Hands-On Activity**

**3** Tell students that the formula for the area of triangle applies to all types of triangles (acute, obtuse, right angle) Remind them also that:

- An acute triangle has all angles measuring less than 90°.
- An obtuse triangle has one Angle measuring greater than 90°.

STEP **2** Cut up triangle MNP into smaller triangles. Rearrange the triangles to form rectangle ENPF, as shown below.

See margin.

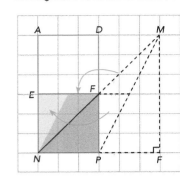

STEP **3** Find the area of rectangle ENPF. How does its area compare to the area of rectangle ANPD?

How does the area of triangle MNP compare to the area of rectangle ENPF?

How does the area of triangle MNP compare to the area of rectangle ANPD?

$^{earn}$ **Find the area of a triangle.**

a) In triangle ABC, $\overline{AX}$ is perpendicular to $\overline{BC}$.

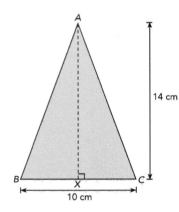

14 cm

10 cm

**Math Note**

Any side of a triangle can be called the base. The height of the triangle is the perpendicular distance from the opposite vertex to the base.

Base = BC = 10 cm
Height = AX = 14 cm

Area of triangle ABC = $\frac{1}{2}$ bh        Write formula.

= $\frac{1}{2}$ · 10 · 14        Substitute.

= 70 cm²        Multiply.

The area of triangle ABC is 70 square centimeters.

$^{earn}$ **Find the area of a triangle.**

a) **Explain** For triangle ABC, a dotted line segment $\overline{AX}$ is drawn from A to the base. If $\overline{AX}$ is perpendicular to $\overline{BC}$, then $\overline{BC}$ is the base and $\overline{AX}$ is the height of the triangle.

**Ask** What are the base and height of triangle ABC? 10 cm; 14 cm How do you find the area of triangle

ABC? By using the formula Area of triangle = $\frac{1}{2}$ bh

What is the area of triangle ABC? $\frac{1}{2}$ · 10 · 14

= 70 cm²

**3** Area of rectangle ENPF = 9 units²

The area of rectangle ENPF is half the area of rectangle ANPD.

Area of rectangle ANPD = 18 units²

The area of triangle MNP is equal to the area of rectangle ENPF.

The area of triangle MNP is half the area of rectangle ANPD.

Area of triangle MNP = 9 units²

**b)** In triangle *PQR*, $\overline{PX}$ is perpendicular to $\overline{QR}$.

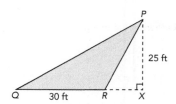

25 ft

30 ft

Q        30 ft        R        X

**Caution** ///////

*PR* is **not** the height of the triangle. *PX* is the height because it is the perpendicular distance from *P* to the base.

Base = *QR* = 30 ft
Height = *PX* = 25 ft

Area of triangle *PQR* = $\frac{1}{2}$ *bh*          Write formula.

$= \frac{1}{2} \cdot 30 \cdot 25$          Substitute.

$= 375\ ft^2$          Multiply.

The area of triangle *PQR* is 375 square feet.

## Guided Practice

**Complete to find the base, height, and area of each triangle. Each square measures 1 unit by 1 unit.**

**1**

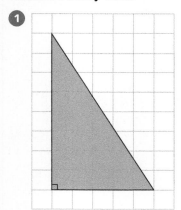

**2**

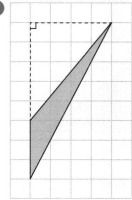

**1** Answers vary. Sample:

Base = __?__ units  5

Height = __?__ units  8

Area = $\frac{1}{2}$ *bh*

$= \underline{?} \cdot \underline{?} \cdot \underline{?}\ \frac{1}{2}; 5; 8$

$= \underline{?}\ units^2\ 20$

Base = __?__ units  3

Height = __?__ units  4

Area = $\frac{1}{2}$ *bh*

$= \underline{?} \cdot \underline{?} \cdot \underline{?}\ \frac{1}{2}; 3; 4$

$= \underline{?}\ units^2\ 6$

---

**Learn continued**

**b) Model** Use the example in the text to illustrate that the height of a triangle may lie outside the triangle itself.

**Ask** Is $\overline{PR}$ the height of triangle *PQR*? No

**Explain** $\overline{PR}$ is not the height of triangle *PQR* because $\overline{PR}$ is not perpendicular to the base $\overline{QR}$. The dotted line segment *PX* represents the height because it is the perpendicular distance from *P* to the base. The height of a triangle must always be perpendicular to its base.

**Ask** What are the base and height of triangle *PQR*? 30 ft; 25 ft How do you find the area of triangle *PQR*? By using the formula Area of triangle = $\frac{1}{2}$ *bh* What is the area of triangle *PQR*? $\frac{1}{2} \cdot 30 \cdot 25 =$ 375 ft$^2$

**DIFFERENTIATED INSTRUCTION**

**Through Concrete Manipulatives**

You may want to distribute paper cut-outs of triangle *ABC* in **a)** to help students identify all three bases and height pairs. Label the vertices of the triangle as shown. Then have students identify all three base/height pairs. ($\overline{BC}$ and a perpendicular segment from $\overline{BC}$ to vertex *A*; $\overline{AB}$ and a perpendicular segment from $\overline{AB}$ to vertex *C*; $\overline{AC}$ and a perpendicular segment from $\overline{AC}$ to vertex *B*)

## Guided Practice

**1** and **2** Have students identify the base and height of the triangles using the grid squares as a guide. Explain that the base of triangle is not always at the bottom, and the height is not always a vertical distance.

**3**

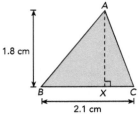

**4**

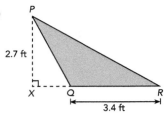

Base = __?__ cm  2.1

Height = __?__ cm  1.8

Area of triangle ABC

$= \frac{1}{2} bh$

$= \underline{?} \cdot \underline{?} \cdot \underline{?}$  $\frac{1}{2}$; 2.1; 1.8

$= \underline{?}$ cm²  1.89

Base = __?__ ft  3.4

Height = __?__ ft  2.7

Area of triangle PQR

$= \frac{1}{2} bh$

$= \underline{?} \cdot \underline{?} \cdot \underline{?}$  $\frac{1}{2}$; 3.4; 2.7

$= \underline{?}$ ft²  4.59

**Learn** **Find the height of a triangle given its area and base.**

The area of triangle FGH is 46 square inches. Find the height of the triangle.

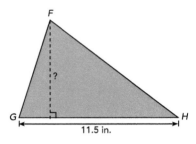

11.5 in.

Area of triangle $FGH = \frac{1}{2} bh$          Write formula.

$46 = \frac{1}{2} \cdot 11.5 \cdot h$          Substitute.

$46 = 5.75 \cdot h$          Simplify.

$46 \div 5.75 = 5.75h \div 5.75$          Divide each side by 5.75.

$8 = h$          Simplify.

The height of triangle FGH is 8 inches.

**DAY 2**

**Learn** **Find the height of a triangle given its area and base.**

**Model** Use the example in the text to demonstrate how to find the height of a triangle given its area and base.

**Ask** What is the formula for area of triangle? Area of triangle $= \frac{1}{2} bh$ What are you given in the problem? The area and base of the triangle Since Area of triangle $= \frac{1}{2} bh$, what equation can you write? $46 = \frac{1}{2} \cdot 11.5 \cdot h$

**Explain** The equation $46 = \frac{1}{2} \cdot 11.5 \cdot h$ can be simplified and written as $46 = 5.75 \cdot h$.

**Ask** How do you solve this equation? Divide both sides by 5.75. So, what is h equal to? $h = 8$

**Summarize** The height of triangle FGH is 8 inches.

## Guided Practice

**Complete to find the height of triangle *JKL*.**

**5** The area of triangle *JKL* is 35 square meters. Find the height of triangle *JKL*.

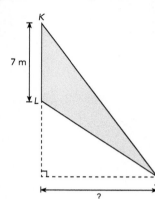

Area of triangle $JKL = \frac{1}{2}bh$

$$\underline{\ ?\ } = \underline{\ ?\ } \cdot \underline{\ ?\ } \cdot h \quad 35;\ \frac{1}{2};\ 7$$

$$\underline{\ ?\ } = \underline{\ ?\ } \cdot h \quad 35;\ 3.5$$

$$\underline{\ ?\ } \div \underline{\ ?\ } = \underline{\ ?\ }\,h \div \underline{\ ?\ } \quad 35;\ 3.5;\ 3.5;\ 3.5$$

$$\underline{\ ?\ } = h \quad 10$$

The height of triangle *JKL* is $\underline{\ ?\ }$ meters.  10

---

**Learn  Find the base of a triangle given its area and height.**

The area of triangle *XYZ* is 36.5 square centimeters. Find the base of the triangle.

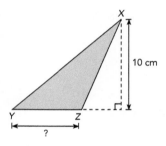

| | |
|---|---|
| Area of triangle $XYZ = \frac{1}{2}bh$ | Write formula. |
| $36.5 = \frac{1}{2} \cdot b \cdot 10$ | Substitute. |
| $36.5 = \frac{1}{2} \cdot 10 \cdot b$ | Commutative property. |
| $36.5 = 5 \cdot b$ | Simplify. |
| $36.5 \div 5 = 5b \div 5$ | Divide each side by 5. |
| $7.3 = b$ | Simplify. |

The base of triangle *XYZ* is 7.3 centimeters.

---

## Guided Practice

 Let students identify the height and the base of the triangle. Remind them that the base is not always at the bottom of the triangle.

### 👥 DIFFERENTIATED INSTRUCTION

**Through Communication**

Point out that when using the formula for the area of a triangle to identify an unknown base or height, students can multiply both sides of the equation by 2 to get rid of the $\frac{1}{2}$ in the formula.

**Ask:** Will multiplying both sides of the equation by 2 change the value for *b* or *h*? (*No*) Why not? (*Because when you multiply both sides of the equation by the same number, the two sides of the equation remain equal.*) What property states that? (*Multiplication property of equality*) To show that this is true, work through the calculation in **5** again, this time multiplying both sides of the equation by 2 right after you substitute the values for *A* and *b*.

---

**Learn  Find the base of a triangle given its area and height.**

**Model** Use the example in the text to demonstrate how to find the base of a triangle given its area and height.

**Ask** What is the formula for area of a triangle? Area of triangle $= \frac{1}{2}bh$ What are you given in the problem? Area and height of the triangle Since Area of triangle $= \frac{1}{2}bh$, what equation can you write? $36.5 = \frac{1}{2} \cdot b \cdot 10$

**Explain** Using the commutative property of multiplication, the equation can be written as $36.5 = \frac{1}{2} \cdot 10 \cdot b$ which simplifies to $36.5 = 5 \cdot b$.

**Ask** How do you solve this equation? Divide both sides by 5. So, what is *b* equal to? $b = 7.3$

**Summarize** The base of triangle *XYZ* is 7.3 centimeters.

## Guided Practice

**Complete to find the base of each triangle.**

**6** The area of triangle *LMN* is 36 square inches. Find the base of triangle *LMN*.

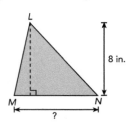

Area of triangle *LMN* $= \frac{1}{2}bh$

$$\underline{\ \ ?\ \ } = \underline{\ \ ?\ \ } \cdot b \cdot \underline{\ \ ?\ \ } \qquad 36; \frac{1}{2}; 8$$

$$= \underline{\ \ ?\ \ } \cdot \underline{\ \ ?\ \ } \cdot b \qquad \frac{1}{2}; 8$$

$$\underline{\ \ ?\ \ } = \underline{\ \ ?\ \ } \cdot b \qquad 36; 4$$

$$\underline{\ \ ?\ \ } \div \underline{\ \ ?\ \ } = \underline{\ \ ?\ \ } b \div \underline{\ \ ?\ \ } \qquad 36; 4; 4; 4$$

$$\underline{\ \ ?\ \ } = b \qquad 9$$

The base of triangle *LMN* is $\underline{\ \ ?\ \ }$ inches. 9

**7** The area of triangle *PQR* is 19.2 square centimeters. Find the base of triangle *PQR*.

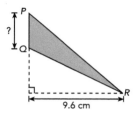

Area of triangle *PQR* $= \frac{1}{2}bh$

$$\underline{\ \ ?\ \ } = \underline{\ \ ?\ \ } \cdot b \cdot \underline{\ \ ?\ \ } \qquad 19.2; \frac{1}{2}; 9.6$$

$$= \underline{\ \ ?\ \ } \cdot \underline{\ \ ?\ \ } \cdot b \qquad \frac{1}{2}; 9.6$$

$$\underline{\ \ ?\ \ } = \underline{\ \ ?\ \ } \cdot b \qquad 19.2; 4.8$$

$$\underline{\ \ ?\ \ } \div \underline{\ \ ?\ \ } = \underline{\ \ ?\ \ } b \div \underline{\ \ ?\ \ } \qquad 19.2; 4.8; 4.8; 4.8$$

$$\underline{\ \ ?\ \ } = b \qquad 4$$

The base of triangle *PQR* is $\underline{\ \ ?\ \ }$ centimeters. 4

## Practice 10.1

Basic ①–⑭
Intermediate ⑮–㉓
Advanced ㉔–㉙

**Identify a base and a height of each triangle.** ①–⑥ Answers vary. Sample:

**①**

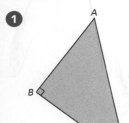

$b : BC$ ; $h : AB$

**②**

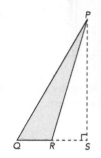

$b : QR$; $h : PS$

**Copy each triangle. Label a base with the letter _b_ and a height with the letter _h_.**

**③**

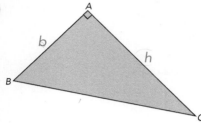

**④**

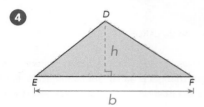

**⑤**

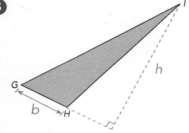

**⑥**

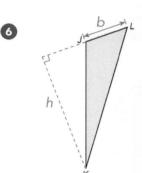

---

## Practice 10.1

### Assignment Guide

**DAY 1** All students should complete ①–⑧, ⑮–⑰.

**DAY 2** All students should complete ⑨–⑭, ⑱–㉓.

㉔–㉙ provide additional challenge.

Optional: *Extra Practice 10.1, Activity Book 10.1–10.3*

### Best Practices

Point out that there are three possible answers. For example: in ③, the possible base/height pairs are $\overline{AC}$ and $\overline{AB}$; $\overline{AB}$ and $\overline{AC}$; and $\overline{BC}$ and a perpendicular dashed line segment drawn from $\overline{BC}$ to vertex *A*.

### Best Practices

③ to ⑥ TRT23 includes diagrams of the triangles in these exercises. Students can label a base and height for each triangle on the Teacher Resource page.

### RtI Lesson Check

| Before assigning homework, use the following ... | to make sure students ... | Intervene with ... |
| --- | --- | --- |
| Exercises ① and ⑦ | • can use a formula to find the area of a triangle | Reteach 10.1 |
| EXIT Ticket Out the Door | • can find the base of a triangle, given its height and its area | |

**Find the area of each triangle.**

**7**

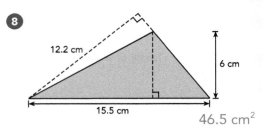

25 cm

15 cm

4 cm

50 cm²

**8**

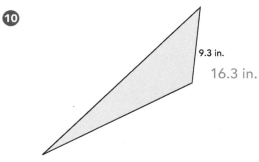

12.2 cm

6 cm

15.5 cm

46.5 cm²

**Best Practices**

**9** to **14** A calculator is suggested for these exercises. You may choose to have students complete the exercises without a calculator so that they may practice dividing with decimals.

The area of each triangle is 76 square inches. Find the height and round your answer to the nearest tenth of an inch.

**9**

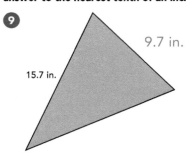

15.7 in.

9.7 in.

**10**

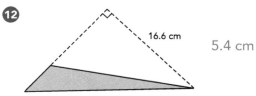

9.3 in.

16.3 in.

The area of each triangle is 45 square centimeters. Find the base and round your answer to the nearest tenth of a centimeter if necessary.

**11**

7.2 cm

12.5 cm

**12**

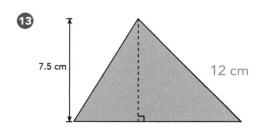

16.6 cm

5.4 cm

**13**

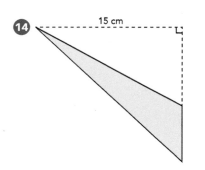

7.5 cm

12 cm

**14**

15 cm

6 cm

**Find the area of the shaded region.**

15
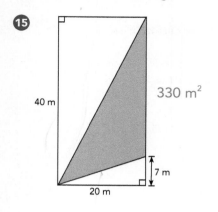

40 m

330 m²

7 m

20 m

16
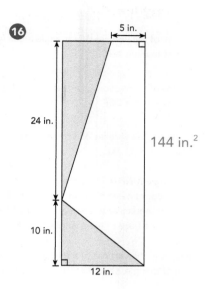

5 in.

24 in.

144 in.²

10 in.

12 in.

17
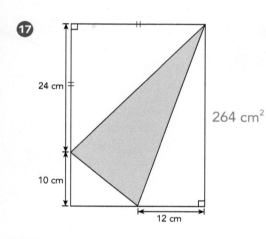

24 cm

264 cm²

10 cm

12 cm

18
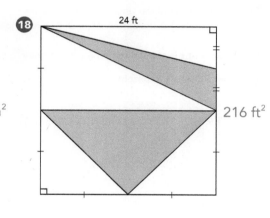

24 ft

216 ft²

19
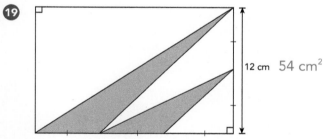

12 cm   54 cm²

## DIFFERENTIATED INSTRUCTION

**Through Visual Cues**

To solve ㉖, suggest that students draw a large rectangle by extending $\overline{JH}$ to a length equal to $\overline{DG}$ and then draw two horizontal sides. **Ask:** What is the area of the new rectangle? ($56 \cdot 28 = 1{,}568$ ft²) What is the area of unshaded rectangle *EFHJ*? ($28 \cdot 24 = 672$ ft²) So, what is the combined area of the two smaller rectangles, the one above the unshaded rectangle and the one below it? ($1{,}568 - 672 = 896$ ft²) Point out that the purple areas are triangles formed by dividing each of the two smaller rectangles by a diagonal. **Ask:** How are the areas of the two purple triangles related to the areas of the two rectangles? *(Half the areas of the rectangles)* What is the combined area of the purple triangles? ($\frac{1}{2} \cdot 896 = 448$ ft²)

**Use graph paper. Solve.** ㉕ – ㉕ See margin.

㉕ The coordinates of the vertices of a triangle are *A* (4, 7), *B* (4, 1), and *C* (8, 1). Find the area of triangle *ABC*.

㉑ The coordinates of the vertices of a triangle are *D* (1, 7), *E* (−3, 2), and *F* (6, 2). Find the area of triangle *DEF*.

㉒ The coordinates of the vertices of a triangle are *J* (−5, 2), *K* (1, −2), and *L* (5, −2). Find the area of triangle *JKL*.

㉓ The area of triangle *MNP* is 17.5 square units. The coordinates of *M* are (−9, 5), and the coordinates of *N* are (−2, 0). The height of triangle *MNP* is 5 units and is perpendicular to the *x*-axis. Point *P* lies to the right of point *N*. Given that $\overline{NP}$ is the base of the triangle, find the coordinates of point *P*.

㉔ The coordinates of the vertices of a triangle are *X* (1, 2), *Y* (−6, −2), and *Z* (1, −4). Find the area of triangle *XYZ*. (Hint: Use the vertical side as the base.)

㉕ The coordinates of the vertices of a triangle are *P* (−2, 6), *Q* (−4, 2), and *R* (5, 1). Find the area of triangle *PQR*. (Hint: Draw a rectangle around triangle *PQR*.)

**Find the area of the shaded region for questions ㉖ to ㉙.**

㉖ Figure *DGHJ* is a trapezoid.

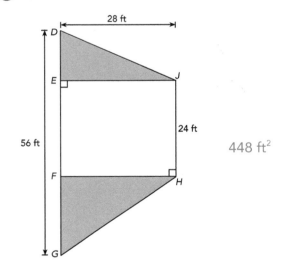

448 ft²

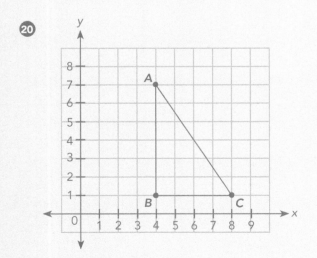

Area of triangle *ABC* = 12 units²

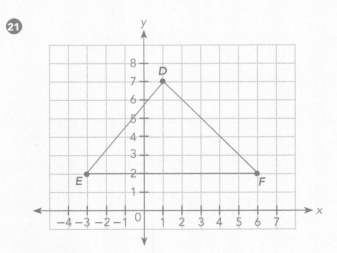

Area of triangle *DEF* = 22.5 units²

㉒ – ㉕ See Additional Answers.

**27** Figure *ABCD* is a rectangle. The length of $\overline{ZB}$ is $\frac{3}{7}$ the length of $\overline{AB}$.

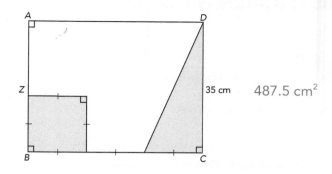

35 cm    487.5 cm²

**28** The area of triangle *PQS* is $\frac{7}{12}$ of the area of trapezoid *PRST*.

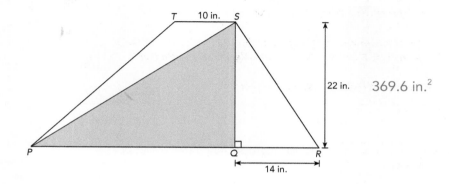

22 in.    369.6 in.²

10 in.

14 in.

**29** Figure *EFHL* is a parallelogram. The length of $\overline{FG}$ is $\frac{5}{8}$ the length of $\overline{FH}$.

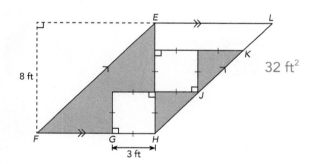

8 ft

3 ft

32 ft²

## KEY CONCEPTS

- You can use a formula to find the area of a parallelogram: Area of parallelogram = $bh$

- You can use a formula to find the area of a trapezoid: Area of trapezoid = $\frac{1}{2}h(b_1 + b_2)$

## PACING

DAY **1** Pages 88–90

DAY **2** Pages 91–93

DAY **3** Pages 94–98

**Materials:** scissors, TRT24–25

### 5-minute Warm Up

Draw a rectangle, a trapezoid, and a parallelogram. Compare your drawings with a partner's, and describe how the three types of figures are different from each other. Check students' work.

 Also available on Teacher One Stop.

---

# 10.2 Area of Parallelograms and Trapezoids

**Lesson Objectives**

- Use a formula to find the area of a parallelogram, given its base and height.
- Use a formula to find the area of a trapezoid, given its bases and height.

### Learn — Derive the formula for the area of a parallelogram.

Figure $ABCD$ is a parallelogram with base $\overline{BC}$ and height $AX$.

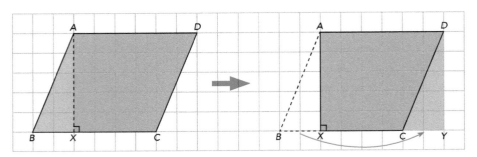

Triangle $ABX$ is cut and moved to the side, where $\overline{AB}$ is placed against $\overline{DC}$. Rectangle $AXYD$ is formed.

Since the area of the parallelogram is the same as the rectangle,
Area of parallelogram = area of rectangle $AXYD$
$$= XY \cdot AX$$

Notice that $\overline{XY}$ has the same length as the base $\overline{BC}$ of the parallelogram. $AX$ is the width of the rectangle and is also the height of the parallelogram. Using $b$ for base, and $h$ for height, you can write this formula for the area of a parallelogram:

Area of parallelogram = $bh$

> Any side of a parallelogram can be considered the base. The height is the perpendicular distance from the opposite side to the base.

---

DAY **1**

### Learn — Derive the formula for the area of a parallelogram.

**Model** Use the illustration in the text to demonstrate how to find the area of a parallelogram.

**Ask** What triangle is formed when a line segment, $\overline{AX}$, is drawn from $A$ to the base of the parallelogram? Triangle $ABX$ What figure is formed when you move triangle $ABX$ so that side $\overline{AB}$ is placed against $\overline{DC}$? Rectangle $AXYD$ Since the area of parallelogram is the same as the area of the rectangle, what equation can you write? Area of parallelogram = area of rectangle $= XY \cdot AX$

**Explain** $\overline{XY}$ has the same length as the base $BC$ of the parallelogram. $AX$ is the width of the rectangle and is also the height of the parallelogram.

**Ask** If $b$ is base, and $h$ is height, what formula can you write for the area of a parallelogram? Area of parallelogram = $bh$

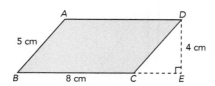

## Learn Find the area of a parallelogram.

In the figure, *ABCD* is a parallelogram and $\overline{BE}$ is straight.

5 cm

4 cm

A D

B 8 cm C E

**Caution** //////

The height of the parallelogram is *DE*. *DC* is **not** the height of the parallelogram, because $\overline{DC}$ is **not** perpendicular to the base.

Base = *BC* = 8 cm
Height = *DE* = 4 cm

Area of *ABCD* = *bh*          Write formula.
          = *BC* · *DE*          Substitute.
          = 8 · 4          Multiply.
          = 32 cm²

The area of parallelogram *ABCD* is 32 square centimeters.

### Guided Practice

**Complete to find the base, height, and area of each parallelogram.**
**Each square measures 1 unit by 1 unit.**

**1**

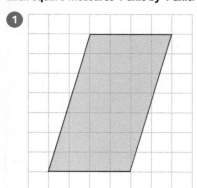

Base = _?_ units  4

Height = _?_ units  7

Area = *bh*

= _?_ · _?_  4; 7

= _?_ units²  28

**2**

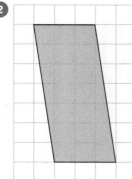

Base = _?_ units  3

Height = _?_ units  7

Area = *bh*

= _?_ · _?_  3; 7

= _?_ units²  21

### Guided Practice

**1** and **2** Some students may identify a base that may not lead to the solution given the situation. Guide them to check if a side has a corresponding height they can use. If the side selected as base does not give you a perpendicular height then choose another base.

### Best Practices

You may want to review the properties of a parallelogram before working with them. A parallelogram is a quadrilateral that
1) has two pairs of parallel, congruent sides,
2) has opposite angles congruent, and
3) has two diagonals, each of which divides the figure into two congruent triangles.

## Learn Find the area of a parallelogram.

**Model** Use the example in the text to demonstrate how to find the area of a parallelogram.

**Explain** Remind students about the formula for area of a parallelogram: Area of parallelogram = *bh*.

**Ask** What are the base and height of parallelogram *ABCD*? Base: 8 cm; height: 4 cm

**Explain** Explain to students that since *DC* is not perpendicular to the base, it is not the height of the parallelogram. *DE* is the height of the parallelogram.

**Ask** What is the area of parallelogram *ABCD*?

Area of parallelogram *ABCD* = *bh*
          = *BC* · *DE*
          = 8 · 4
          = 32 cm²

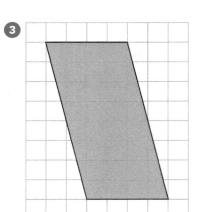

**3** Base = __?__ units  4

Height = __?__ units  8

Area = $bh$

= __?__ · __?__  4; 8

= __?__ units²  32

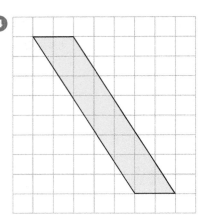

**4** Base = __?__ units  2

Height = __?__ units  8

Area = $bh$

= __?__ · __?__  2; 8

= __?__ units²  16

**Complete to find the area of each parallelogram.**

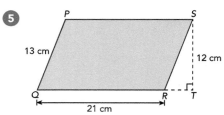

**5**

Base = __?__ cm  21

Height = __?__ cm  12

Area = $bh$

= __?__ · __?__  21; 12

= __?__ cm²  252

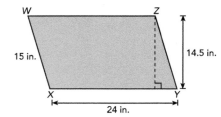

**6**

Base = __?__ in.  24

Height = __?__ in.  14.5

Area = $bh$

= __?__ · __?__  24; 14.5

= __?__ in.²  348

## Guided Practice

**5** Watch for students who mistakenly multiply 21 centimeters by 13 centimeters, thinking that the height of the parallelogram is 13 centimeters. Remind them that *PQ* is not the height of the parallelogram because it is not perpendicular to the base. Point out that the right angle symbol is a clue that *ST* is the height of the parallelogram.

earn

**Derive the formula for the area of a trapezoid.**

Figure *ABDE* is a trapezoid with bases $\overline{AE}$ and $\overline{BD}$ and height *EC*. $\overline{AE}$ is parallel to $\overline{BD}$.

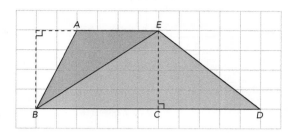

The diagonal $\overline{BE}$ of the trapezoid divides it into two triangles. Both triangles have the same height.

Area of trapezoid = area of blue triangle + area of orange triangle

$$= \frac{1}{2} \cdot AE \cdot height + \frac{1}{2} \cdot BD \cdot height$$

$$= \frac{1}{2} \cdot height \cdot \underbrace{(AE + BD)}$$
sum of the lengths of the parallel sides of the trapezoid

Area of trapezoid $= \frac{1}{2} \cdot height \cdot$ sum of the lengths of the parallel sides

The parallel sides in a trapezoid are called its bases. One base is usually labeled $b_1$, and the other is labeled $b_2$. The perpendicular distance between the bases is the height of the trapezoid. Using *h* for height, you can write a formula for the area of a trapezoid.

Area of trapezoid

$= \frac{1}{2} h$(sum of the lengths of the parallel sides)

$= \frac{1}{2} h$(sum of the bases)

**Math Note**

$b_1$ and $b_2$ are read as "b sub 1" and "b sub 2."

Area of trapezoid $= \frac{1}{2} h(b_1 + b_2)$

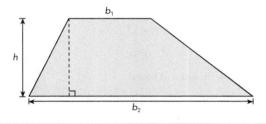

**Best Practices**

You may want to review what trapezoids are before working with them. A trapezoid is a quadrilateral that has two parallel, noncongruent bases. The other two sides may or may not be congruent, and it may or may not have two right angles.

**DIFFERENTIATED INSTRUCTION**

**Through Multiple Representation**

The subscript notation will be new to most students. Explain that writing $b_1$ and $b_2$ is the easiest way to write Base 1 and Base 2 in formulas. The subscripts are in no way related to the lengths of these sides.

DAY **2**

earn
**Derive the formula for the area of a trapezoid.**

**Model** Use the example in the text to show students how to find the area of a trapezoid.

**Explain** Point out that in the trapezoid, the diagonal $\overline{BE}$ divides it into two triangles: triangles *ABE* and *BDE*.

**Ask** What can you say about the heights of the two triangles? They are the same. How could you use the area of a triangle formula to find the area of the trapezoid? Find the areas of the triangles and add them together.

**Explain** Explain that Area of trapezoid =

$\frac{1}{2} \cdot AE \cdot height + \frac{1}{2} \cdot BD \cdot height$. Show students that the equation can be simplified and rewritten using the distribution property: Area of trapezoid = $\frac{1}{2} \cdot height \cdot (AE + BD)$, where $(AE + BD)$ is the sum of the lengths of the two bases of the trapezoid.

**Ask** One of the bases is labeled $b_1$ and the other one, $b_2$. How about the perpendicular distance between the bases? *h* for height What formula can you write for the area of trapezoid when you know its height and the length of its bases? Area of trapezoid = $\frac{1}{2} h$(sum of the bases)

**Lesson 10.2** Area of Parallelograms and Trapezoids    **91**

## Learn — Find the area of a trapezoid.

In the figure, *TUVW* is a trapezoid. $\overline{TW}$ is parallel to $\overline{UV}$. Find the area of trapezoid *TUVW*.

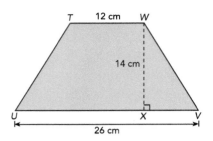

$\overline{TW}$ and $\overline{UV}$ are parallel, so they are the bases of the trapezoid.

Height = *WX* = 14 cm

Sum of the bases = *TW* + *UV*

$= 12 + 26$

$= 38$ cm

Area of trapezoid $= \frac{1}{2}h$(sum of the bases)  — Write formula.

$= \frac{1}{2} \cdot 14 \cdot 38$  — Substitute.

$= 266$ cm²  — Multiply.

The area of *TUVW* is 266 square centimeters.

### Caution

Based on their work finding the areas of other polygons, some students may mistakenly believe that any side of a trapezoid can be a base. Point out to students that the bases of a trapezoid are always the two parallel sides. Trapezoids are not like triangles and parallelograms, where any side can be considered a base.

## Guided Practice

**Complete to find the sum of the bases, height, and area of each trapezoid. Each square measures 1 unit by 1 unit.**

**7**
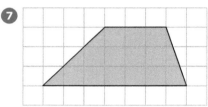

Height = __?__ units  3

Sum of bases = __?__ + __?__  3; 7

$= $ __?__ units  10

Area $= \frac{1}{2}h$(sum of bases)

$= $ __?__ $\cdot$ __?__ $\cdot$ __?__ $\frac{1}{2}$; 3; 10

$= $ __?__ units²  15

**8**
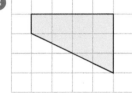

Height = __?__ units  4

Sum of bases = __?__ + __?__  1; 3

$= $ __?__ units  4

Area $= \frac{1}{2}h$(sum of bases)

$= $ __?__ $\cdot$ __?__ $\cdot$ __?__ $\frac{1}{2}$; 4; 4

$= $ __?__ units²  8

## Learn — Find the area of a trapezoid.

**Model** Use the example to demonstrate how to find the area of a trapezoid.

**Ask** What is the formula for area of a trapezoid? Area of trapezoid $= \frac{1}{2}h$(sum of the bases) What are you given in the problem? Height of figure *TUVW*: 14 cm; length of bases: 12 cm and 26 cm What are you asked to find? The area of trapezoid *TUVW* Since area of trapezoid $= \frac{1}{2}h$(sum of the bases), what equation can you write? Area of trapezoid $= \frac{1}{2} \cdot 14 \cdot (12 + 26) = \frac{1}{2} \cdot 14 \cdot 38 = 266$ cm² So, what is the area of trapezoid *TUVW*? 266 cm²

**9**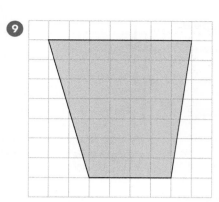

Height = __?__ units  7

Sum of bases = __?__ + __?__  7; 4

    = __?__ units  11

Area = $\frac{1}{2}$ h(sum of bases)

    = __?__ · __?__ · __?__  $\frac{1}{2}$; 7; 11

    = __?__ units²  38.5

**10**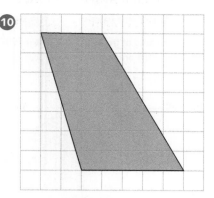

Height = __?__ units  7

Sum of bases = __?__ + __?__  3; 5

    = __?__ units  8

Area = $\frac{1}{2}$ h(sum of bases)

    = __?__ · __?__ · __?__  $\frac{1}{2}$; 7; 8

    = __?__ units²  28

**Complete to find the area of each trapezoid.**

**11**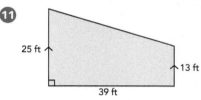

25 ft

13 ft

39 ft

Height = __?__ ft  39

Sum of bases = __?__ + __?__  25; 13

    = __?__ ft  38

Area = $\frac{1}{2}$ h(sum of bases)

    = __?__ · __?__ · __?__  $\frac{1}{2}$; 39; 38

    = __?__ ft²  741

**12**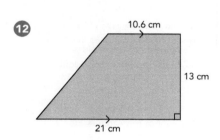

10.6 cm

13 cm

21 cm

Height = __?__ cm  13

Sum of bases = __?__ + __?__  10.6; 21

    = __?__ cm  31.6

Area = $\frac{1}{2}$ h(sum of bases)

    = __?__ · __?__ · __?__  $\frac{1}{2}$; 13; 31.6

    = __?__ cm²  205.4

## DIFFERENTIATED INSTRUCTION

**Through Communication**

You may want to help students see the strategy voiced by the student in the text. **Ask:** What are we trying to find? *(The area of triangle ADC)* What dimension of triangle *ADC* do we already know? *(AD = 56 m)* Explain that since you already know the length of *AD*, use that as the base of the triangle. **Ask:** If $\overline{AD}$ is the base of triangle *ADC*, which segment is its height? *($\overline{EC}$)* And what is $\overline{EC}$ in relation to trapezoid *ABCD*? *($\overline{EC}$ is also the height of trapezoid ABCD.)* Explain that, since you know the area of trapezoid *ABCD*, you can use the area formula to find the height of the trapezoid.

---

### Apply the formula for the area of a trapezoid.

The area of trapezoid *ABCD* is 4,196.5 square meters. $\overline{AD}$ is parallel to $\overline{BC}$. Find the area of triangle *ADC*.

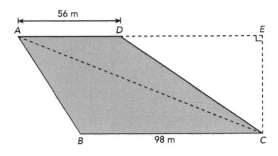

> To find the area of triangle *ADC*, you need to know the height of the triangle. If you use $\overline{AD}$ as the base of the triangle, then its height is the same as the height of trapezoid *ABCD*.

First use the trapezoid area formula to find the height of the trapezoid.

| | |
|---|---|
| Area of trapezoid $= \frac{1}{2}h(b_1 + b_2)$ | Write formula. |
| $= \frac{1}{2} \cdot EC \cdot (AD + BC)$ | Substitute. |
| $= \frac{1}{2} \cdot EC \cdot (56 + 98)$ | |
| $= \frac{1}{2} \cdot EC \cdot (154)$ | Add inside parentheses. |
| $= \frac{1}{2} \cdot 154 \cdot EC$ | Apply commutative property. |
| $= 77 \cdot EC$ | Simplify. |

Since area of trapezoid = 4,196.5 m², 
$77 \cdot EC$ = area of trapezoid 
$77 \cdot EC = 4{,}196.5$ 
$\quad EC = 4{,}196.5 \div 77$ 
$\quad\quad = 54.5$ m 
Height of trapezoid = EC 
$\quad\quad\quad\quad\quad\quad = 54.5$ m

Then use the fact that *EC* is also the height of the triangle to find the area of the triangle.

| | |
|---|---|
| Area of triangle $ADC = \frac{1}{2}bh$ | Write formula. |
| $= \frac{1}{2} \cdot 56 \cdot 54.5$ | Substitute. |
| $= 1{,}526$ m² | Multiply. |

The area of triangle *ADC* is 1,526 square meters.

---

 **DAY 3**

### Apply the formula for the area of a trapezoid.

**Model** Use the example to demonstrate how to solve multi-step area problems.

**Ask** What are you given in the problem? Area of trapezoid *ABCD*: 4,196.5 m²; length of $b_1$: 56 m and length of $b_2$: 98 m What are you asked to find? Area of triangle *ADC*

**Explain** Emphasize that to find the area of the triangle, the height must be known first. If *AD* is the base of the triangle, then its height is the same as the height of trapezoid *ABCD*.

**Ask** How can you find the area of the triangle? First,

find the height of the trapezoid by using the trapezoid area formula. Substitute *EC* for *h*, and substitute the values of $b_1$ and $b_2$ into the formula and evaluate. Area of trapezoid $= \frac{1}{2}h(b_1 + b_2) = \frac{1}{2} \cdot EC \cdot (56 + 98) = 77 \cdot EC$ Since the area of the trapezoid is 4,196.5 m², how can you find the height of the trapezoid? Write and solve an equation:

$$\text{Area of trapezoid} = 77 \cdot EC$$
$$4{,}196.5 \div 77 = EC$$
$$54.5 \text{ m} = EC$$

So, what is the area of triangle *ADC*? 1,526 m²

## Guided Practice

**Complete to find the area of triangle *ABD*.**

**13** The area of trapezoid *ABCD* is 1,248 square centimeters.

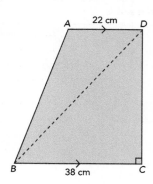

Area of trapezoid $ABCD = \frac{1}{2}h(b_1 + b_2)$

$$= \frac{1}{2} \cdot h \cdot (\underline{\;?\;} + \underline{\;?\;}) \quad 22; 38$$

$$= \frac{1}{2} \cdot h \cdot \underline{\;?\;} \quad 60$$

$$= \frac{1}{2} \cdot \underline{\;?\;} \cdot h \quad 60$$

$$= \underline{\;?\;} \cdot h \quad 30$$

Since area of trapezoid $= \underline{\;?\;}$ cm², 1,248

$\underline{\;?\;} \cdot h =$ area of trapezoid  30

$\underline{\;?\;} \cdot h = \underline{\;?\;}$  30; 1,248

$h = \underline{\;?\;} \boxed{?} \underline{\;?\;}$  1,248; ÷; 30

$\quad = \underline{\;?\;}$ cm  41.6

Height of trapezoid $= \underline{\;?\;}$  *DC*

$\qquad = \underline{\;?\;}$ cm  41.6

Area of triangle $ABD = \frac{1}{2}bh$

$$= \frac{1}{2} \cdot \underline{\;?\;} \cdot \underline{\;?\;} \quad 22; 41.6$$

$$= \underline{\;?\;} \text{ cm}^2 \quad 457.6$$

The area of triangle *ABD* is $\underline{\;?\;}$ square centimeters.  457.6

## Guided Practice

**13** Remind students to read the problem carefully. They should identify what information is given in the problem and in the diagram, and what they are being asked to find. They should also think about how the dimensions of trapezoid *ABCD* are related to the dimensions of triangle *ABD*.

## Practice 10.2

Basic ① – ⑯
Intermediate ⑰ – ㉒
Advanced ㉓

### Assignment Guide

**DAY 1** All students should complete ① – ⑥, ⑲ and ⑳.

**DAY 2** All students should complete ⑦ – ⑫, ㉑ and ㉒.

**DAY 3** All students should complete ⑬ – ⑱.

㉓ provides additional challenge.
Optional: *Extra Practice 10.2,*
*Activity Book 10.1–10.3*

### Best Practices

① to ④ Teacher Resource page (TRT24) includes diagrams of the parallelograms in these exercises. Students can label a base and height for each parallelogram on the Teacher Resource page.

⑦ to ⑩ TRT25 includes diagrams of the trapezoids in these exercises. Students can label the bases and height for each trapezoid on the Teacher Resource page.

① – ④ Answers vary. Sample:

**Copy each parallelogram. Label a base and a height for each. Use *b* and *h.***

①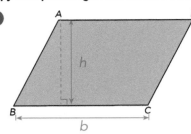

②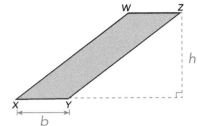

③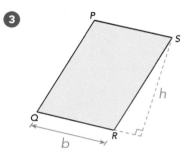

④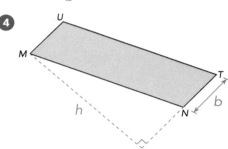

**Find the area of each parallelogram.**

⑤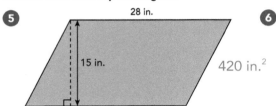
28 in.
15 in.
420 in.²

⑥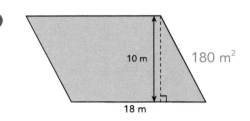
10 m
18 m
180 m²

**Copy each trapezoid. Label the height and bases. Use *h*, $b_1$, and $b_2$.**

⑦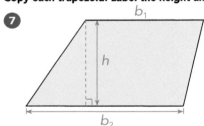

⑧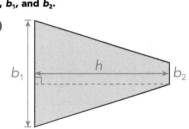

### RtI Lesson Check

| Before assigning homework, use the following ... | to make sure students ... | Intervene with ... |
|---|---|---|
| Exercise ⑤ | • can use a formula to find the area of a parallelogram, given its base and height | |
| Exercise ⑪ | • can use a formula to find the area of a trapezoid, given its base and height | Reteach 10.2 |
| EXIT **Ticket Out the Door** | • can find an unknown dimension of a trapezoid, given its area and two other dimensions | |

**9**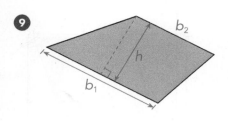

**10**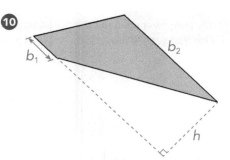

**Find the area of each trapezoid.**

**11**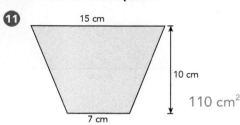

110 cm²

**12**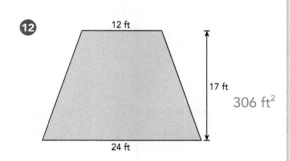

306 ft²

The area of each parallelogram is 64 square inches. Find the height.
Round your answer to the nearest tenth of an inch.

**13**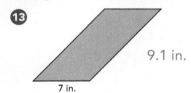

9.1 in.

**14**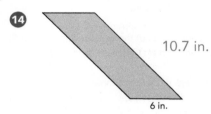

10.7 in.

**Best Practices**

**13** to **16** A calculator is suggested for these exercises. You may choose to have students complete the exercises without a calculator so that they may practice dividing with decimals.

The area of each trapezoid is 42 square centimeters. Find the height.
Round your answer to the nearest tenth of a centimeter.

**15**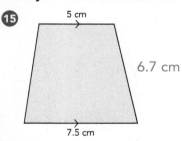

6.7 cm

**16**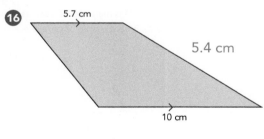

5.4 cm

**19**

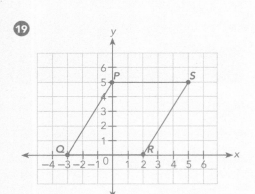

Area of parallelogram *PQRS*
= 25 units²

**Solve.**

**17** The area of trapezoid *ABCD* is 503.25 square centimeters.
Find the length of $\overline{BC}$. 21 cm

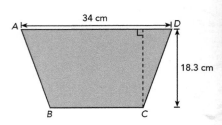

**18** The area of trapezoid *EFGH* is 273 square centimeters.
Find the area of triangle *EGH*. 98 cm²

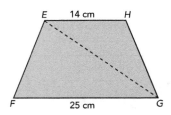

**Solve. Use graph paper.** **19** – **22** See margin.

**19** The coordinates of the vertices of a parallelogram are *P* (0, 5), *Q* (−3, 0),
*R* (2, 0), and *S* (5, 5). Find the area of parallelogram *PQRS*.

**20** Three out of the four coordinates of the vertices of parallelogram *WXYZ* are
*W* (0, 1), *X* (−4, −4), and *Y* (−1, −4). Find the coordinates of *Z*. Then find the
area of the parallelogram.

**21** The coordinates of the vertices of trapezoid *EFGH* are *E* (−3, 3), *F* (−3, 0),
*G* (1, −4), and *H* (1, 4). Find the area of the trapezoid.

**22** Three out of the four coordinates of the vertices of trapezoid *ABCD* are
*A* (0, 1), *B* (−4, −4), and *C* (−1, −4). $\overline{AD}$ is parallel to $\overline{BC}$. AD is 6 units.
The point *D* lies to the right of point *A*. Find the coordinates of point *D*.
Then find the area of the trapezoid.

**Solve.**

**23** Parallelogram *PQRT* is made up of isosceles triangle *PST* and
trapezoid *PQRS*. Find the area of parallelogram *PQRT*.

290 cm²

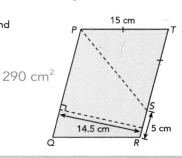

**20**

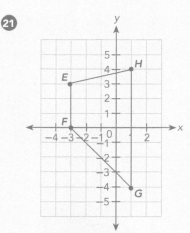

Area of parallelogram *WXYZ*
= 15 units²

**21**

Area of trapezoid *EFGH*
= 22 units²

**22** See Additional Answers.

**Lesson Objectives**

- Divide polygons into triangles.
- Find the area of a regular polygon by dividing it into smaller shapes.

**Vocabulary**

regular polygon

## KEY CONCEPTS

- Polygons can be divided into triangles.

- You can find the area of a regular polygon by dividing it into smaller shapes.

## PACING

**DAY 1** Pages 99–103

**Materials:** TRT26

**5-minute Warm Up**

Draw a polygon of your choice. Then divide it into triangles. Compare your drawing with a partner's Check students' work.

Also available on Teacher One Stop.

**Learn** **Find the areas of regular polygons.**

a) Patrick drew a regular pentagon with side lengths of 16 centimeters. He divided the pentagon into 5 identical triangles, and measured the height of one of the triangles to be 11 centimeters. Find the area of the pentagon.

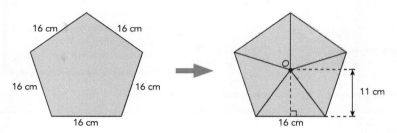

The line segments from O to each vertex of the pentagon divide it into 5 identical triangles. These triangles are isosceles triangles.

Area of each triangle $= \frac{1}{2} bh$

$\qquad = \frac{1}{2} \cdot 16 \cdot 11$

$\qquad = 88$ cm²

Area of pentagon $= 5 \cdot 88$

$\qquad = 440$ cm²

The area of the pentagon is 440 square centimeters.

**Continue on next page**

**DAY 1**

**Learn** **Find the areas of regular polygons.**

**Model** Use the problem to illustrate how to find the areas of regular polygons.

a) **Ask** What are you given in the problem? Side lengths of the pentagon: 16 cm; pentagon divided into 5 identical triangles; height of each triangle: 11 cm What are you asked to find? Area of the pentagon

**Explain** The sum of the areas of the 5 identical triangles is the area of the pentagon.

**Ask** How can you find the area of each triangle? By using the formula Area of triangle $= \frac{1}{2} bh$ So, what is the area of each triangle? Area of triangle $= \frac{1}{2} bh$ $= \frac{1}{2} \cdot 16 \cdot 11 = 88$ cm² What is the area of the pentagon? $5 \cdot 88 = 440$ cm²

## ELL Vocabulary Highlight

Make sure that students understand the meaning of the term *regular polygon*. Remind them that a regular polygon is a polygon in which all sides have the same length and all angles have the same measure.

## Caution ///////

Seeing that a regular hexagon divides into six equilateral triangles, some students may mistakenly assume that all regular polygons can be divided into equilateral triangles. Point out that the regular pentagon divided into five identical triangles in a) produced five *isosceles* triangles. A regular hexagon is the only regular polygon that, when divided into identical triangles determined by the number of its sides, produces equilateral triangles. When any other regular polygon is divided this way, the triangles will be isosceles triangles.

b)   Johanna has a hexagonal placemat. She measured the sides and found that they were all 9.3 inches long. She then divided the hexagon into 6 identical triangles. She measured the height of one triangle and found that it was 8 inches. Find the area of the placemat.

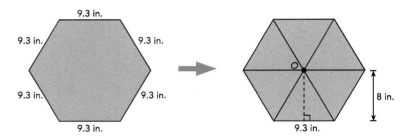

Area of each triangle $= \frac{1}{2}bh$

$= \frac{1}{2} \cdot 9.3 \cdot 8$

$= 37.2$ in.$^2$

Area of placemat $= 6 \cdot 37.2$

$= 223.2$ in.$^2$

The area of the placemat is 223.2 square inches.

### Math Note

The line segments from the center to each vertex of a regular hexagon divide it into 6 identical triangles. These triangles are equilateral triangles.

### Guided Practice

**Give the minimum number of identical triangles you could divide each regular polygon into so that you could find the area of the polygon.**

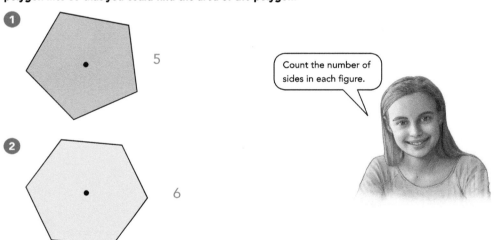

Count the number of sides in each figure.

**Learn continued**

b) **Ask** What are you given in the problem? Side lengths of hexagonal placemat: 9.3 in.; hexagon divided into 6 identical triangles; height of each triangle: 8 in. What are you asked to find? Area of the placemat

**Explain** The sum of the areas of the 6 identical triangles is the area of the pentagon.

**Ask** How can you find the area of each triangle? By using the formula Area of triangle $= \frac{1}{2}bh$ So, what is the area of each triangle? Area of triangle $= \frac{1}{2}bh = \frac{1}{2} \cdot 9.3 \cdot 8 = 37.2$ in.$^2$ What is the area of the pentagon? $6 \cdot 37.2 = 223.2$ in.$^2$

**Complete.**

**3** Blake drew a regular pentagon with side lengths of 6 inches. He divided the pentagon into 5 identical triangles, and measured the height of one of the triangles to be 4.1 inches. Find the area of the pentagon.

Area of triangle $= \frac{1}{2}bh$

$= \underline{\ ?\ } \cdot \underline{\ ?\ } \cdot \underline{\ ?\ } \quad \frac{1}{2};\ 6;\ 4.1$

$= \underline{\ ?\ }$ in.$^2$  12.3

Area of pentagon $= \underline{\ ?\ } \cdot$ area of triangle  5

$= \underline{\ ?\ } \cdot \underline{\ ?\ } \quad$ 5; 12.3

$= \underline{\ ?\ }$ in.$^2$  61.5

The area of the pentagon is $\underline{\ ?\ }$ square inches.  61.5

**4** Melanie drew a regular hexagon with side lengths of 28 centimeters. She divided the hexagon into 6 identical triangles, and measured the height of one of the triangles to be 24.2 centimeters. Find the area of the hexagon.

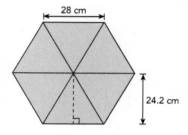

28 cm

24.2 cm

Area of triangle $= \frac{1}{2}bh$

$= \underline{\ ?\ } \cdot \underline{\ ?\ } \cdot \underline{\ ?\ } \quad \frac{1}{2};\ 28;\ 24.2$

$= \underline{\ ?\ }$ cm$^2$  338.8

Area of hexagon $= \underline{\ ?\ } \cdot$ area of triangle  6

$= \underline{\ ?\ } \cdot \underline{\ ?\ } \quad$ 6; 338.8

$= \underline{\ ?\ }$ cm$^2$  2,032.8

The area of the hexagon is $\underline{\ ?\ }$ square centimeters.  2,032.8

## Guided Practice

**3** and **4**  Make sure students have understood the strategy and procedures to find the area of a hexagon given the side length of the hexagon and height of one of the identical triangles.

### DIFFERENTIATED INSTRUCTION

**Through Visual Cues**

**3**  Suggest that students draw a diagram of the pentagon and label the given dimensions.

### DIFFERENTIATED INSTRUCTION

**Through Enrichment**

Show students a simple formula for the area of any regular polygon. Draw hexagon *ABCDEF* on the board with center at *O*. Label the distance from *O* to one side as *a*. Show students that the area of the hexagon can be written as

$\frac{1}{2}a \cdot AB + \frac{1}{2} \cdot BC + \cdots \frac{1}{2}a \cdot FA$

$= \frac{1}{2}a \cdot (AB + BC + \cdots FA)$

$= \frac{1}{2}a \cdot P$, where *P* is the perimeter of the hexagon.

## Assignment Guide

**DAY 1** All students should complete **1** – **8**, **9** – **10** provide additional challenge.

Optional: *Extra Practice 10.3*

## Best Practices

After students have completed **1** and **2**, **Ask:** What do you notice about the minimum number of identical triangles any polygon can be divided into? *(The number of identical triangles is equal to the number of sides each polygon has.)* Point out that when a regular polygon is divided into a minimal number of identical triangles, each side of the regular polygon becomes a base of one of the triangles. **Ask:** What is the minimum number of identical triangles a square can be divided into? *(4)* A regular pentagon? *(5)* A regular hexagon? *(6)* A regular octagon? *(8)*

---

# Practice 10.3

Basic **1**–**3**
Intermediate **4**–**8**
Advanced **9**–**10**

**Give the minimum number of identical triangles you could divide each regular polygon into so that you could find the area of the polygon.**

**1**
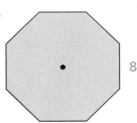
8

**2**
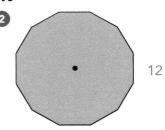
12

**Solve.**

**3** Derrick drew a regular pentagon with side lengths of 8 centimeters. He divided the pentagon into 5 identical triangles, and measured the height of one of the triangles to be 5.5 centimeters. Find the area of the pentagon. 110 cm²

**4** Lydia drew a regular hexagon. She divided it into 6 identical triangles, and measured the height of one of the triangles to be 4 inches. The area of the hexagon is 55.2 square inches. Find the length of each side of the hexagon.

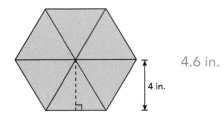
4.6 in.
4 in.

**5** A floor tile is in the shape of a regular hexagon. Greg uses 187.5 floor tiles for a room. The area of the room is 450 square feet. Find the length of each side of the hexagon.

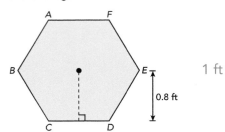
1 ft
0.8 ft

---

## ⚠ RtI Lesson Check

| Before assigning homework, use the following ... | to make sure students ... | Intervene with ... |
| --- | --- | --- |
| Exercise **1** | • divide polygons into triangles | |
| Exercise **3** | • find the area of a regular polygon by dividing it into isosceles triangles | Reteach 10.3 |
| **EXIT** Ticket Out the Door | • use triangles to find the area of a regular pentagon | |

**Use the given information to find the area of each regular polygon.**

**6** The shaded area is 9.7 square inches.

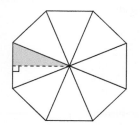 155.2 in²

**7** The shaded area is 12.8 square centimeters.

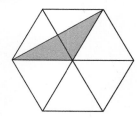 76.8 cm²

**8** Suppose you have three identical equilateral triangles. Use a sketch to show how you can make each of the following from two or more of the triangles. Identify the quadrilateral.

**a)** a quadrilateral whose area is two times as great as an equilateral triangle. parallelogram

**b)** a quadrilateral whose area is three times as great as an equilateral triangle. trapezoid

**Each figure is made from a regular polygon surrounded by identical triangles. Find the area of each figure.**

**9**
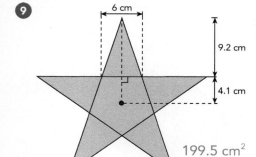 199.5 cm²

**10**
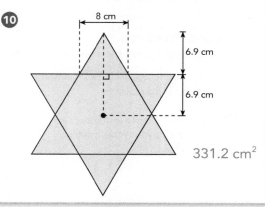 331.2 cm²

## 10.4 Area of Composite Figures

## KEY CONCEPTS

- A plane figure is made up of polygons.
- You can solve problems involving areas of composite figures.

## PACING

DAY **1** Pages 104–106

DAY **2** Pages 107–112

**Materials:** TRT26

### 5-minute Warm Up

Draw a polygon of your choice. Then divide it into other polygons. Identify the other polygons formed, and compare your drawing with a partner's.
Check students' work.

 Also available on Teacher One Stop.

 **1** – **2** See Additional Answers.

### Lesson Objectives

- Recognize that a plane figure is made up of polygons.
- Solve problems involving areas of composite figures.

**Learn Recognize that a plane figure can be divided into other polygons.**

Trapezoid *PQRS* can be divided into many polygons.
It can be divided into a rectangle and a triangle.

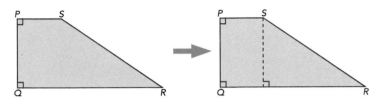

It can also be divided into three triangles.

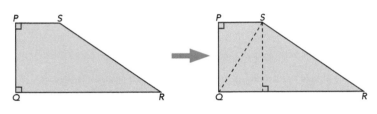

There are many other ways to divide trapezoid *PQRS*.

### Guided Practice

**Use graph paper. Copy the hexagon and solve.**  See margin.

**1** Divide the hexagon into two identical triangles and a rectangle.

**2** Divide the hexagon in another way. Name the polygons that make up the hexagon.

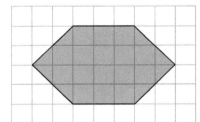

DAY **1**

**Learn Recognize that a plane figure can be divided into other polygons.**

**Model** Use the illustration of the trapezoid to discuss that a plane figure can be divided into other polygons. You may also want to have a trapezoid cut-out that can be folded.

**Ask** What shapes are formed when the trapezoid is divided as shown in the text? At first, a rectangle and a triangle are formed. When the rectangle is folded, three triangles are formed.

**Summarize** Lead students to conclude that there are many other ways to divide a trapezoid.

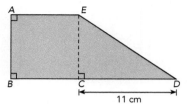

## Learn Solve problems involving rectangles and triangles.

Trapezoid *ABDE* is made up of square *ABCE* and triangle *ECD*. The area of square *ABCE* is 64 square centimeters. The length of $\overline{CD}$ is 11 centimeters. Find the area of triangle *ECD*, and trapezoid *ABDE*.

A diagram shows trapezoid with vertices A, E on top and B, C, D on bottom, with 11 cm marked for CD.

Area of square *ABCE* = 64 cm²

$\ell^2 = 64$, so
$\ell = \sqrt{64}$
$\ell = 8$

To find the side length of a square, find the square root of the area.

Use the fact that *EC* = 8 and is also the height of triangle *ECD*.

Area of triangle *ECD* = $\frac{1}{2}bh$      Write formula.

                = $\frac{1}{2} \cdot CD \cdot EC$      Substitute.

                = $\frac{1}{2} \cdot 11 \cdot 8$      Multiply.

                = 44 cm²

The area of triangle *ECD* is 44 square centimeters.

Area of trapezoid *ABDE*
= area of square *ABCE* + area of triangle *ECD*
= 64 + 44
= 108 cm²

The area of trapezoid *ABDE* is 108 square centimeters.

## Learn Solve problems involving rectangles and triangles.

**Model** Use the example to demonstrate how to solve problems involving rectangles and triangles.

**Ask** What are you given in the problem? Shapes that make up trapezoid *ABDE*: square *ABCE* and triangle *ECD*; area of square *ABCE*: 64 in.²; length of $\overline{CD}$: 11 cm What are you asked to find? The area of triangle *ECD* and trapezoid *ABDE* What information do you need to know in order to find the area of triangle *ECD*? The height, *EC* How can you use the area of square *ABCE* find *EC*? Find $\sqrt{64} = 8$.

**Ask** How can you find the area of the triangle? By using the formula Area of a triangle = $\frac{1}{2}bh$ = $\frac{1}{2} \cdot CD \cdot EC = \frac{1}{2} \cdot 11 \cdot 8 = 44$ cm² How can you find the area of trapezoid *ABDE*? By using the equation Area of trapezoid = area of square *ABCE* + area of triangle *ECD* = 64 + 44 = 108 cm² Is there another way you could use to find the area of the trapezoid? Explain. Yes; the area of a trapezoid formula, $A = \frac{1}{2}h(b_1 + b_2)$ can be used. Why was this not the first choice of methods? Because it is easier just to add the two areas that are known.

## Guided Practice

 Have students work in pairs to discuss the strategy they can use to solve the problem. If necessary, guide the students how to determine the unknown values from the given values.

### DIFFERENTIATED INSTRUCTION

**Through Communication**

③ It may be helpful to some students for you to guide them through the reasoning behind the process of solving this problem. Point out that they already know the area of the triangle but not of the square that together make up the trapezoid. **Ask:** Do you know any of the dimensions of square *ABCE*? *(No)* Direct students to the dashed segment $\overline{EC}$, its length labeled with a question mark. **Ask:** What is $\overline{EC}$ in terms of square *ABCE*? *(1 side)* What is $\overline{EC}$ in terms of triangle *ECD*? *(1 side, its height)* Can you use any of the information you do know to calculate the length of $\overline{EC}$? *(Yes, you can substitute the area of the triangle ECD and the length of $\overline{CD}$, its base, into the formula for the area of a triangle to identify $\overline{EC}$, the height of the triangle.)*

## Guided Practice

**Complete.**

③ Trapezoid *ABDE* is made up of square *ABCE* and triangle *ECD*. The area of triangle *ECD* is 60 square inches. The length of $\overline{CD}$ is 12 inches.

a) Find the height of triangle *ECD*.

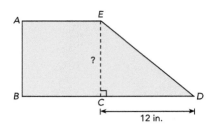

Area of triangle *ECD* = \_\_?\_\_ in.²   60

Area of triangle *ECD* = $\frac{1}{2}$ *bh*

$\qquad = \frac{1}{2} \cdot \underline{\ \ ?\ \ } \cdot EC$   12

$\qquad \underline{\ \ ?\ \ } = \underline{\ \ ?\ \ } \cdot EC$   60; 6

$\qquad \underline{\ \ ?\ \ } \div \underline{\ \ ?\ \ } = \underline{\ \ ?\ \ } \cdot EC \div \underline{\ \ ?\ \ }$   60; 6; 6; 6

$\qquad \underline{\ \ ?\ \ } = EC$   10

The height of triangle *ECD* is \_\_?\_\_ inches.   10

b) Find the area of square *ABCE*.

Area of square *ABCE* = $\ell^2$

$\qquad = \underline{\ \ ?\ \ }^2$   10

$\qquad = \underline{\ \ ?\ \ }$ in.²   100

The area of square *ABCE* is \_\_?\_\_ square inches.   100

c) Find the area of trapezoid *ABDE*.

Area of the trapezoid *ABDE*

= area of square *ABCE* + area of triangle *ECD*

= \_\_?\_\_ + \_\_?\_\_   100; 60

= \_\_?\_\_ in.²   160

The area of trapezoid *ABDE* is \_\_?\_\_ square inches.   160

### Learn Solve problems involving parallelograms, triangles, and rectangles.

Trapezoid PQTU is made up of parallelogram PQRV, triangle VRS, and square VSTU. The area of trapezoid PQSV is 99 square inches. Find the area of trapezoid PQTU.

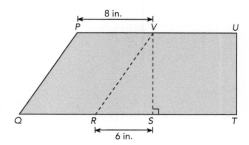

Apply the formula for the area of a trapezoid to find VS.
Area of trapezoid PQSV

$$= \frac{1}{2} h(b_1 + b_2)$$

$$= \frac{1}{2} \cdot VS \cdot (PV + QS)$$

$$= \frac{1}{2} \cdot VS \cdot (8 + 8 + 6)$$

$$= \frac{1}{2} \cdot VS \cdot 22$$

$$= 11 \cdot VS$$

Since area of trapezoid PQSV = 99 in.²,

| Area of trapezoid PQSV = 11 · VS | Write formula. |
| $99 = 11 \cdot VS$ | Substitute. |
| $99 \div 11 = 11 \cdot VS \div 11$ | Divide each side by 11. |
| $9 = VS$ | Simplify. |

Then find the area of square VSTU.

Area of square VSTU = $VS^2$
$= 9^2$
$= 81$ in.²

Then find the area of trapezoid PQTU.

Area of trapezoid PQTU = area of trapezoid PQSV + area of square VSTU
$= 99 + 81$
$= 180$ in.²

The area of trapezoid PQTU is 180 square inches.

### Best Practices

You may want to suggest that students check their answer by using the formula for area of a trapezoid. They should recognize that PV = QR, and VS = ST = VU, which will enable them to find the lengths of the bases of the trapezoid:

$$A = \frac{1}{2} h(b_1 + b_2)$$

$$= \frac{1}{2} \cdot 9(8 + 9 + 8 + 6 + 9)$$

$$= \frac{1}{2} \cdot 9(40)$$

$$= \frac{1}{2} \cdot 360$$

$$= 180 \text{ in.}^2$$

---

## DAY 2

### Learn Solve problems involving parallelograms, triangles, and rectangles.

**Ask** What are given in the problem? Shapes that make up trapezoid PQTU: parallelogram PQRV, triangle VRS, and square VSTU; area of trapezoid PQSV = 99 in.²; length of $\overline{PV}$ = 8 in.; length of $\overline{RS}$ = 6 in. **What are you asked to find?** The area of trapezoid PQTU

**Ask** What formula can be applied for the area of a trapezoid to find VS? Area of the trapezoid
$= \frac{1}{2} h(b_1 + b_2) = \frac{1}{2} \cdot VS \cdot (PV + QS) = \frac{1}{2} \cdot VS \cdot (8 + 8 + 6)$

$= \frac{1}{2} \cdot VS \cdot (22) = 11 \cdot VS$ Since area of trapezoid PQSV
= 99 in.², what equation can be written to solve for VS?

Area of trapezoid PQSV = 11 · VS
$99 = 11 \cdot VS$
**How do you solve this equation?** Divide each side by 11.
So, $99 \div 11 = 11 \cdot VS \div 11$
$9 = VS$

Since VS = 9 in., how can you find the area of square VSTU? By using the equation Area of square VSTU = $VS^2 = 9^2 = 81$ in.² After finding all the required values, how can you find the area of trapezoid PQTU? By using the equation Area of trapezoid PQTU = area of trapezoid PQSV + area of square VSTU = 99 + 81 = 180 in.²

## Guided Practice

**4** Before students start solving this problem, ask them to think first about what information they are given in the problem (the area of the parallelogram), and what related information is given in the diagram (the length of the base of the parallelogram). Then ask them to think about what information they can find out from these "clues." This act of "previewing" is a helpful problem-solving strategy.

**DIFFERENTIATED INSTRUCTION**

**Through Visual Cues**

A difficult part of this problem is deciding which side of parallelogram *ABEF* should be its base. Rotating the figure 90° should help students see $\overline{AB}$ as the base of the parallelogram. So, the height of the parallelogram is the same as the height of triangle *BDE*.

**Complete.**

**4** The area of parallelogram *ABEF* is 84 square meters.

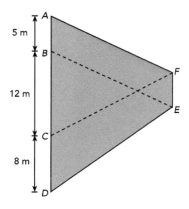

a) Find the area of triangle *BDE*.

Area of parallelogram *ABEF* = *bh*

$$\underline{\quad?\quad} = \underline{\quad?\quad} \cdot h \quad 84; 5$$

$$\underline{\quad?\quad} \div \underline{\quad?\quad} = \underline{\quad?\quad} h \div \underline{\quad?\quad} \quad 84; 5; 5; 5$$

$$\underline{\quad?\quad} = h \quad 16.8$$

The height of parallelogram *ABEF* is also the height of triangle *BDE*.

Area of triangle *BDE* = $\frac{1}{2}bh$

$$= \frac{1}{2} \cdot BD \cdot h$$

$$= \frac{1}{2} \cdot (\underline{\quad?\quad} + \underline{\quad?\quad}) \cdot \underline{\quad?\quad} \quad 12; 8; 16.8$$

$$= \underline{\quad?\quad} \text{ m}^2 \quad 168$$

The area of triangle *BDE* is $\underline{\quad?\quad}$ square meters. 168

b) Find the area of trapezoid *CDEF*.

Parallelogram *ABEF* and trapezoid *CDEF* have the same height.

Area of trapezoid *CDEF* = $\frac{1}{2}h(b_1 + b_2)$

$$= \underline{\quad?\quad} \cdot \underline{\quad?\quad} \cdot (\underline{\quad?\quad} + \underline{\quad?\quad}) \quad \frac{1}{2}; 16.8; 5; 8$$

$$= \underline{\quad?\quad} \text{ m}^2 \quad 109.2$$

The area of trapezoid *CDEF* is $\underline{\quad?\quad}$ square meters. 109.2

Basic **1** – **7**
Intermediate **8** – **9**
Advanced **10** – **14**

**Copy each figure and draw straight lines to divide. Describe two ways to find the area of each figure.**

**1** Divide the figure into a rectangle and two right triangles.

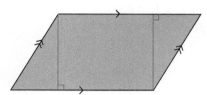

$bh$; sum of areas of the two right triangles and the rectangle

**2** Divide the figure into a rectangle and two right triangles.

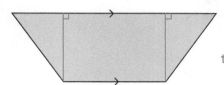

$\frac{1}{2}h(b_1 + b_2)$; sum of areas of the two right triangles and the rectangle

**3** Divide the figure into a rectangle and a right triangle.

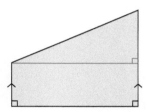

$\frac{1}{2}h(b_1 + b_2)$; sum of areas of the right triangle and the rectangle

**Copy each figure and draw straight lines to divide. Describe a way to find the area.**

 **4**

Sum of areas of the triangle and rectangle

**5**

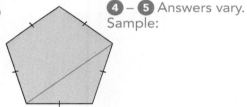

Sum of areas of the trapezoid and triangle

**4** – **5** Answers vary.
Sample:

**RtI Lesson Check**

| Before assigning homework, use the following ... | to make sure students ... | Intervene with ... |
| --- | --- | --- |
| Exercise **1** | • can recognize that a plane figure is made up of polygons | Reteach 10.4 |
| Exercise **9** | • can solve problems involving areas of composite figures | |
| EXIT Ticket Out the Door | • understand how to divide up a polygon into smaller shapes to find its area | |

**7** Teacher Resource page (TRT26) includes diagrams of the polygons in this exercise. Note that some students may be confused because no dimensions of the figure are identified in the diagram or in the question statement. Tell students that they should first name and label the vertices of the figure. Next, they should decide how to divide the figure into smaller polygons, naming and labeling additional points as necessary. Finally, they should identify by name which sides or line segments they would need to measure in order to calculate the areas of the polygons they have constructed.

**DIFFERENTIATED INSTRUCTION**

**Through Visual Cues**

**8** Make sure students see that the height of trapezoid *ABDE* is also the height of parallelogram *ABCE*, and the height of triangle *EBC*.

---

**Find the area of each figure.**

**6** Parallelogram *ABDE* is made up of square *ACDF*, triangle *ABC*, and triangle *FDE*. Triangle *ABC* and triangle *FDE* are identical. The area of square *ACDF* is 36 square meters. Find the area of triangle *ABC*. Then find the area of parallelogram *ABDE*.

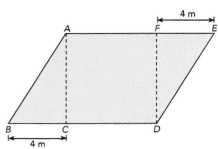

Area of triangle *ABC*: 12 m²;
Area of parallelogram *ABDE*: 60 m²

**7** *Math Journal* Describe how you would divide the figure with straight lines. Which sides of the figure would you measure to find its area? Explain your answer.

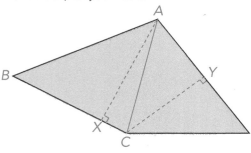

Answers vary. Sample:
I would divide it into two triangles.
I would measure the lengths of $\overline{BC}$, $\overline{AX}$, $\overline{AD}$, and $\overline{CY}$, so that I can find the area of the two triangles.

**Find the area of triangle EBC.**

**8** In the figure below, trapezoid *ABDE* is made up of three triangles, and figure *ABCE* is a parallelogram. Find the area of triangle *EBC* if the area of trapezoid *ABDE* is 180 square centimeters.

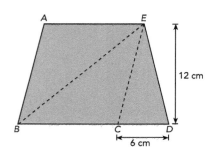

72 cm²

**Solve. Use graph paper.** See margin.

**9** **a)** Plot the points $P(-2, 2)$, $Q(-2, -2)$, $R(-4, -5)$, $S(1, -5)$, and $T(3, -2)$ on a coordinate plane. Connect the points in order to form figure $PQRST$.

**b)** Find the area of figure $PQRST$.

**c)** Point $V$ lies on along $\overline{QT}$. The area of triangle $PQV$ is $\frac{2}{5}$ the area of triangle $PQT$. Give the coordinates of point $V$. Plot point $V$ on the coordinate plane.

**Find the area of trapezoid MNRS.**

**10** In the figure below, trapezoid $MNRS$ is made up of trapezoid $MNPT$, triangle $TPQ$, and parallelogram $TQRS$. The area of triangle $TPQ$ is 84 square feet. The lengths of $\overline{NP}$, $\overline{PQ}$, and $\overline{QR}$ are in the ratio 2 : 1.5 : 1. Find the area of trapezoid $MNRS$.

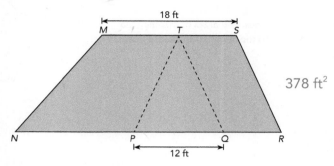

378 ft²

**Find the area of triangle BDE.**

**11** The figure below is made up of two trapezoids $ABEF$ and $BCDE$. The area of triangle $FGE$ is 26 square inches, and the area of trapezoid $BCDE$ is 82.5 square inches. $BG$ is equal to $GE$. Find the area of triangle $BDE$.

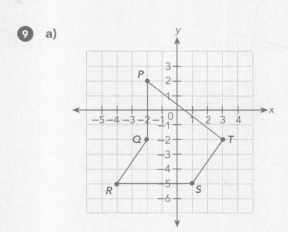

71.5 in.²

**9** **a)**

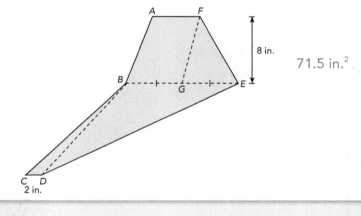

**9** **b)** Area of figure $PQRST$ = 25 units²

**9** **c)**

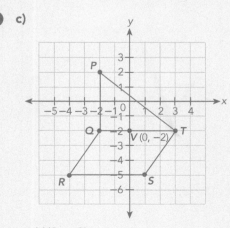

$V(0, -2)$

**Find the area of the shaded region.**

**12** $\frac{3}{8}$ of the triangle is shaded.

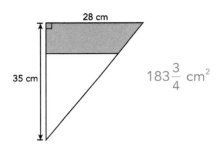

$183\frac{3}{4}$ cm²

**Find the height of trapezoid PQRS.**

**13** Trapezoid *PQRS* is made up of isosceles triangle *PQS* and triangle *SQR*. The area of triangle *PQS* is 16.5 square inches. The areas of triangle *PQS* and triangle *SQR* are in the ratio 2 : 3. Find the height of trapezoid *PQRS*.

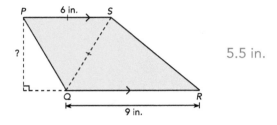

5.5 in.

**Find the area of each figure.**

 **14** In the figure below, trapezoid *ABCD* is made up of square *BCDE* and triangles *ABF* and *AFE*. The area of square *BCDE* is 576 square feet. The ratio of *BF* to *FE* is 2 : 1. Find the area of triangle *ABF*.

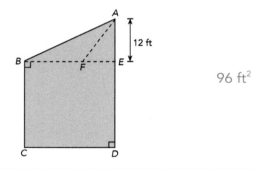

96 ft²

 **Ticket Out the Door**

Identify three possible combinations of polygons that the figure below can be divided into in order to find its area.

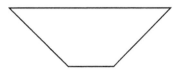

Possible answers: 1 rectangle and 2 right triangles; 1 parallelogram and 1 triangle; 2 triangles; 3 triangles; 4 triangles; 1 triangle and 1 trapezoid; 2 trapezoids

 Also available on Teacher One Stop.

# Brain @ Work

**1** Figure *ABCD* is made up of square *PQRS* and four identical triangles. The area of triangle *APD* is 49 square feet. The lengths of $\overline{AP}$ and $\overline{PD}$ are in the ratio 1 : 2. Find the area of figure *ABCD*. 245 ft²

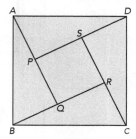

**2** The figure is made up of squares *BCDE* and *AEFH*. The length of $\overline{DE}$ is 6 centimeters, and the length of $\overline{EF}$ is 12 centimeters.

a) Write the length of $\overline{FG}$ in terms of *x*. $(12 - x)$ centimeters

b) Find the area of the shaded region in terms of *x*.
$(36 + 6x)$ square centimeters

c) Give the value of *x* for which the shaded region has the greatest area. What is the shape of the shaded region for the value of *x* you have given?

12; triangle

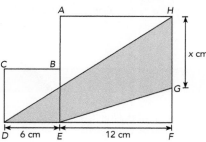

**3** Figure *ABCD* is a square. Point *S* is in the middle of $\overline{AD}$, and point *T* is in the middle of and $\overline{CD}$. What fraction of the square is shaded? $\dfrac{3}{8}$

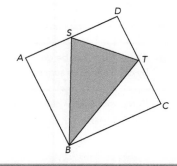

# Brain @ Work

**1** If students need a hint, suggest they consider a rectangle formed by two of the triangles. **Ask:** How does the area of this rectangle compare to the area of the square? *(It is twice the area of the square.)* How does the area of the square compare to the area of one triangle? *(The areas are equal.)* So how can you find the area of the entire figure? *(Multiply the area of one triangle by 5: 5 · 49 = 245 square units.)*

**2** Give students a hint that when *x* is the maximum, its value is 12 centimeters. The area of the shaded part is the difference between the two right triangles.

 **DIFFERENTIATED INSTRUCTION**

**Through Enrichment**

Because all students should be challenged, have all students try the Brain@Work exercise on this page.

For additional challenging practice and problem solving, see *Enrichment, Course 1*, Chapter 10.

Use the notes and the examples in the concept map to review shapes of polygons; formulas for areas of triangles, rectangles, parallelograms; forming proportion statements based on comparing quantities; forming linear algebraic equations.

## CHAPTER PROJECT

To widen students' mathematical horizons and to encourage them to think beyond the concepts taught in this chapter, you may want to assign the Chapter 10 project, Area Puzzle, available in *Activity Book, Course 1*.

# Chapter Wrap Up

## Concept Map

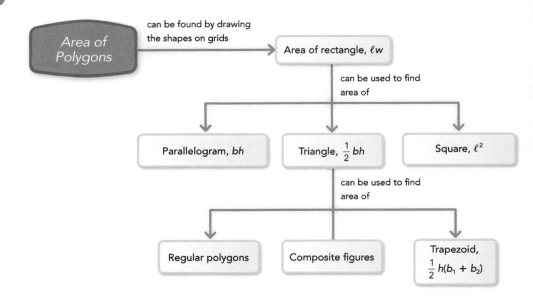

## Key Concepts

▶ The area of a triangle is $\frac{1}{2}bh$.

▶ The area of a parallelogram is $bh$.

▶ The area of a trapezoid is $\frac{1}{2}h(b_1 + b_2)$.

▶ Any polygon can be divided into triangles. You can find the area of the polygon by calculating the sum of the areas of all the triangles that make up the figure.

▶ Composite figures can be divided into shapes such as triangles, parallelograms, and trapezoids.

## Vocabulary Review

Use these questions to review chapter vocabulary with students.

1.  A general mathematical equation or rule is called a(n) __?__. formula

2.  The distance from the base to the opposite vertex of a triangle is called a(n) __?__ height

3.  A(n) __?__ is a polygon whose sides are all the same length, and whose angles are all the same measure. regular polygon

4.  Any side of a triangle from which the height of a triangle is measured is called a(n) __?__. base

Also available on Teacher One Stop.

# Chapter Review/Test

## Concepts and Skills

**Identify a base and a height of each triangle.** ①–② Answers vary. Sample:

①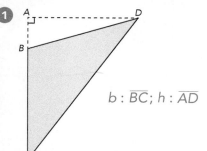

$b : \overline{BC}; h : \overline{AD}$

②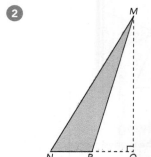

$b : \overline{NP}; h : \overline{MQ}$

**Find the area of each figure.**

③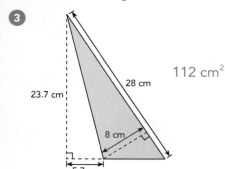

112 cm²

④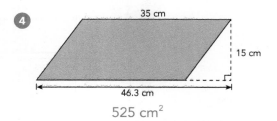

35 cm

15 cm

46.3 cm

525 cm²

⑤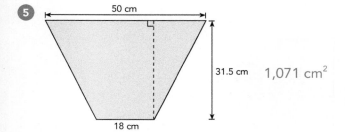

50 cm

31.5 cm    1,071 cm²

18 cm

### Chapter Assessment

Use the Chapter 10 Test A or B in *Assessments, Course 1* to assess how well students have learned the material in this chapter. These assessments are appropriate for reporting results to adults at home and administrators. Test A is shown on page 117A.

## TEST PREPARATION

For additional test prep

- **ExamView® Assessment Suite Course 1**
- **Online Assessment System** my.hrw.com

### Rtl Intervention and Reteaching Recommendations

| Student Book B Review/Test Items | Assessments Chapter 10 Items | Chapter 10 Objectives | Reteach B Chapter 10 |
|---|---|---|---|
| ① to ③ | Test A: 1–2 Test B: 1–2 | **Objective 1.** Use a formula to find the area of a triangle. | Lesson 10.1 |
| ④ | Test A: 4 Test B: 4 | **Objective 2.** Use a formula to find the area of a parallelogram, given its base and height. | Lesson 10.2 |
| ⑤ | Test A: 3 Test B: 3 | **Objective 3.** Use a formula to find the area of a trapezoid, given its base and height. | Lesson 10.2 |

**Find the area of the shaded region.**

6. The area of the regular octagon below is 560 square inches.

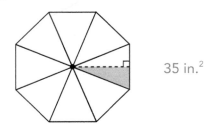

35 in.²

## Problem Solving

**Find the area of the shaded region.**

7.

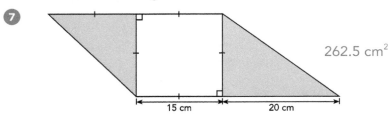

262.5 cm²

15 cm   20 cm

**Solve.**

8. Figure *ABCD* is a parallelogram. *BC* is 16 centimeters, *CD* is 12 centimeters, and *AH* is 10 centimeters.

   a) Find the area of parallelogram *ABCD*. 160 cm²

   b) Find the length of $\overline{AK}$. Round your answer to the nearest tenth of a centimeter. 13.3 cm²

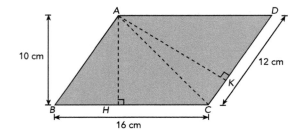

10 cm          12 cm

B   H          C

16 cm

**RtI Intervention and Reteaching Recommendations**

| Student Book B Review/Test Items | Assessments Chapter 10 Items | Chapter 10 Objectives | Reteach B Chapter 10 |
|---|---|---|---|
| 6 | Test A: 5 <br> Test B: 5 | **Objective 4.** Find the area of a regular polygon by dividing it into smaller shapes. | Lesson 10.3 |
| 7 and 26 | Test A: 6–9 <br> Test B: 6–9 | **Objective 5.** Solve problems involving areas of composite figures. | Lesson 10.4 |

**9** Figure ABCD is a trapezoid. The length of $\overline{BC}$ is 36 centimeters. The areas of triangles ABC and ACD are in the ratio 1.5 : 1. Find the length of $\overline{AD}$.

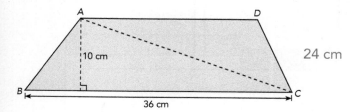

24 cm

**10** Parallelogram PRTV is made up of triangle PQV, triangle QUV, and trapezoid QRTU. The area of parallelogram PRTV is 96 square feet. The lengths of $\overline{TU}$ and $\overline{UV}$ are equal. Find the area of triangle QUV.

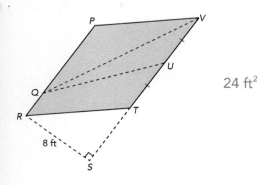

24 ft²

**11** Charles drew a regular hexagon and divided it into two identical trapezoids. The side length of the hexagon is 16 centimeters, and the length of the diagonal shown is 32 centimeters. Charles measured the height of one of the trapezoids and found that the height was 13.9 centimeters. Find the area of the hexagon.

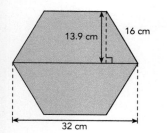

667.2 cm²

**RtI Intervention and Reteaching Recommendations**

| Student Book B Review/Test Items | Assessments Chapter 10 Items | Chapter 10 Objectives | Reteach B Chapter 10 |
|---|---|---|---|
| **9** to **11** | Test A: 6−9 <br> Test B: 6−9 | **Objective 5.** Solve problems involving areas of composite figures. | Lesson 10.4 |

# ASSESSMENT PAGES FOR CHAPTER 10

## Chapter 10 Tests A and B

Answer key appears in the *Assessments, Course 1*

**Test B, Assessments p. 99**

**Test A, Assessments p. 96**

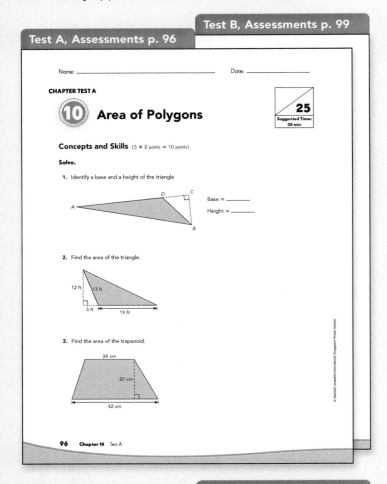

Name: _____ Date: _____

CHAPTER TEST A

**10** **Area of Polygons**

☐ **25**
Suggested Time: 30 min

**Concepts and Skills** (5 × 2 points = 10 points)

**Solve.**

1. Identify a base and a height of the triangle

   Base = _____
   Height = _____

2. Find the area of the triangle.

3. Find the area of the trapezoid.

96    Chapter 10  Test A

**Test B, Assessments p. 100**

**Test A, Assessments p. 97**

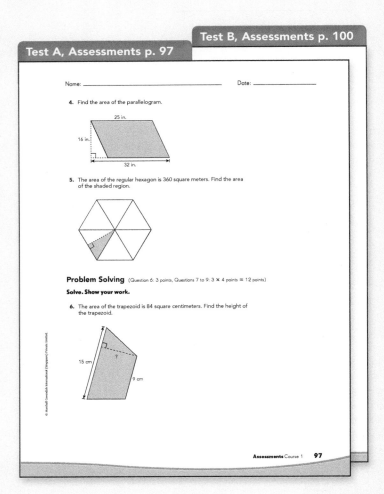

Name: _____ Date: _____

4. Find the area of the parallelogram.

5. The area of the regular hexagon is 360 square meters. Find the area of the shaded region.

**Problem Solving** (Question 6: 3 points, Questions 7 to 9: 3 × 4 points = 12 points)

**Solve. Show your work.**

6. The area of the trapezoid is 84 square centimeters. Find the height of the trapezoid.

Assessments Course 1    97

**Test B, Assessments p. 101**

**Test A, Assessments p. 98**

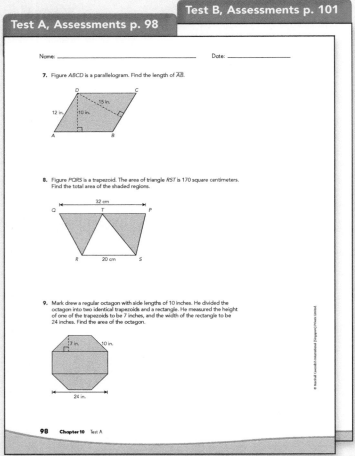

Name: _____ Date: _____

7. Figure *ABCD* is a parallelogram. Find the length of $\overline{AB}$.

8. Figure *PQRS* is a trapezoid. The area of triangle *RST* is 170 square centimeters. Find the total area of the shaded regions.

9. Mark drew a regular octagon with side lengths of 10 inches. He divided the octagon into two identical trapezoids and a rectangle. He measured the height of one of the trapezoids to be 7 inches, and the width of the rectangle to be 24 inches. Find the area of the octagon.

98    Chapter 10  Test A

# Chapter at a Glance

| | | CHAPTER OPENER<br>Circumference and Area of a Circle<br><br>Recall Prior Knowledge | LESSON 11.1<br>Radius, Diameter, and Circumference of a Circle<br>Pages 122–135 | LESSON 11.2<br>Area of a Circle<br>Pages 136–142 |
|---|---|---|---|---|
| **LESSON AT A GLANCE** | Pacing | 2 days | 2 days | 2 days |
| | Objectives | 💡 A circle is a geometric figure that has many useful applications in the real world. | • Identify parts of a circle.<br>• Recognize that a circle's diameter is twice its radius.<br>• Use the formula for the circumference of a circle.<br>• Identify semicircles and quarter circles and find the distance around them. | • Use the formula to calculate the areas of circles, semicircles, and quadrants. |
| | Vocabulary | | center, radius, radii, diameter, circumference, arc, semicircle, quadrant | |
| **RESOURCES** | Materials | | compass, ruler, protractor, TRT27*, circle cut-outs, drawing triangle (or set square) | compass, circle cut-outs |
| | Lesson Resources | Student Book B, pp. 181–121<br>*Assessments Course 1,* Chapter 11 Pre-Test<br>*Transition Guide, Course 1,* Skills 42–47 | Student Book B, pp. 122–135<br>*Extra Practice B,* Lesson 11.1<br>*Reteach B,* Lesson 11.1 | Student Book B, pp. 136–142<br>*Extra Practice B,* Lesson 11.2<br>*Reteach B,* Lesson 11.2<br>*Activity Book,* Lesson 11.2 |
| **Common Core**<br>Standards for Mathematical Content | | 6.NS.3 | 7.G.1. Know the formulas for the area and circumference of a circle and use them to solve problems... | 6.EE.1 Write and evaluate numerical expressions involving whole-number exponents.<br>7.G.4. Know the formulas for the area... of a circle... |
| **Mathematical Practices** | | 6. Attend to precision.<br>7. Look for and use structure. | 2. Reason. 3. Construct arguments.<br>5. Use tools strategically. | 3. Construct arguments. 4. Model mathematics. 8. Express regularity in reasoning. |

*Teacher Resource Tools (TRT) are available on the Teacher One Stop.*

# Concepts and Skills Across the Courses

| GRADE 5 | COURSE 1 | COURSE 2 |
|---|---|---|
| • Evaluate numerical expressions with grouping symbols (5.OA.1)<br>• Apply multiplication of fractions and decimals to find the area of a rectangle. (5.NBT.7, 5.NF.4b)<br>• Understand the attributes of two-dimensional figures. (5.G.3) | • Evaluate numerical expressions with whole-number exponents. (6.EE.1)<br>• Evaluate formulas used in real-world problems. (6.EE.2c.)<br>• Solve problems involving area. (6.G.1, 7.G.4) | • Use variables to represent quantities in real-world. (7.EE.4, 7.EE.4a)<br>• Know the relationship among the formulas for the area and circumference of a circle. (7.G.4)<br>• Solve problems involving circumference and area. (7.G.6) |

| LESSON 11.3<br>Real-World Problems: Circles<br>Pages 143–158 | CHAPTER<br>WRAP UP/REVIEW/TEST<br>CUMULATIVE REVIEW<br><br>Brain@Work<br>Pages 158–167 |
|---|---|
| 2 days | 3 days |
| • Solve real-world problems involving area and circumference of circles.<br>• Solve real-world problems involving semicircles, quadrants, and composite figures. | Reinforce, consolidate, and extend chapter skills and concepts. |
| | |
| Student Book B, pp. 143–158<br>*Extra Practice B*, Lesson 11.3<br>*Reteach B*, Lesson 11.3 | Student Book B pp. 158–167<br>*Activity Book*, Chapter 11 Project<br>*Enrichment*, Chapter 11<br>*Assessments*, Chapter 11 Test<br>Chapters 8–11 Benchmark Test<br>ExamView® Assessment Suite Course 1 |
| **6.EE.2c.** Evaluate expressions ... that arise from formulas used in real-world problems.<br>**7.G.4.** Know the formulas for the area and circumference of a circle... | |
| **1.** Solve problems/persevere.<br>**2.** Reason. **6.** Attend to precision. | **1.** Solve problems/persevere. **5.** Use tools strategically. **7.** Look for and use structure. |

# Additional Chapter Resources

## TECHNOLOGY

• Online Student eBook

• Interactive Whiteboard Lessons

• Virtual Manipulatives

• Teacher One Stop

• ExamView® Assessment Suite Course 1

• Online Professional Development Videos

## Every Day Counts®
## ALGEBRA READINESS

**The March activities in the Pacing Chart provide:**

• **Review** of decimal multiplication (**Ch. 3, 6.NS.3**)
• **Review** of graphs of linear relationships (**Ch. 8 and 9; 6.EE.9**)
• **Practice** evaluating variable expressions (**Ch. 11, 6.EE.1, 6.EE.2c**)

# Chapter 11  Circumference and Area of a Circle

## A Plane Figure but Not a Polygon

- In this chapter, students learn to identify parts of a circle: radius, diameter, circumference, semicircles, and quadrants. They use formulas to find area and circumference of circles and the area of and the distance around figures that involve circular parts.

### Comparisons to polygons

- While a circle is a plane figure, it is not a polygon because it has no sides. Instead of being defined by the number, positions, or relative length of sides, a circle is defined by the fact that every point on it is equidistant from a center point.

- Like polygons, a circle consists only of points on the circumference. Points in the interior of this set form a circular disk. These points are within the circle, but not part of it.

- In previous courses, students worked with polygons, using formulas to calculate unknown lengths, perimeter, and area. Building on those skills, students learn to find circumference and area of circles.

### Radius, diameter, and circumference

- Using manipulatives, students find that each circle has an infinite number of radii and diameters, and that any diameter of a circle is twice the length of any of its radii.

- Students discover that the circumference of a circle is about 3 times its diameter. They learn that the ratio of circumference to diameter is a constant, that this constant is written as $\pi$, and that 3.14 and $\frac{22}{7}$ are commonly used as approximations for $\pi$.

### Deriving the area formula

- Students cut a circle into sectors and rearrange the sectors to form a near-rectangle with a width that is the radius $r$ of the circle and a length that is $\frac{1}{2}$ the circumference $C$ of the circle. They substitute those values into the formula for the area of a rectangle to derive the formula for the area of a circle.

For a rectangle: $A = \ell w$

$$A = \frac{1}{2} C \cdot r$$

$$= \frac{1}{2} \cdot 2\pi r \cdot r = \pi r^2$$

The near-rectangle used to approximate a rectangle is an introductory exercise in the methods of calculus. By imagining the circle being cut into smaller and smaller wedges, the near rectangles become closer and closer to being a rectangle.

## Finding Dimensions of Circles

### Circumference and distance around

- Students use the circumference formula, $C = 2\pi r$, to find the distance around circles and parts of circles.

Find the distance around the semicircle. Use $\pi \approx \frac{22}{7}$.

Length of arc $= \frac{1}{2} \cdot 2\pi r = \pi r$

$\approx \frac{22}{7} \cdot 14 = 44$

Distance around $= 44 + 28 = 72$

28 cm

The distance around the semicircle is approximately 72 centimeters.

### Area

- Students use the area formula, $A = \pi r^2$ to find the area of circles, semicircles, and quadrants.

One of 4 panes of glass in a circular window is missing. How many square feet of glass are needed to replace the missing pane? Use $\pi \approx 3.14$.

Area of quadrant $= \frac{1}{4} \cdot \pi r^2$

$\approx \frac{1}{4} \cdot 3.14(3)^2$

$= \frac{1}{4} \cdot 3.14(9)$

$= \frac{1}{4} \cdot 28.26$

$= 7.07$

6 ft

About 7.07 square feet of glass are needed to replace the missing pane.

# Differentiated Instruction

## Assessment and Intervention

| | ASSESSMENT | RtI STRUGGLING LEARNERS |
|---|---|---|
| **DIAGNOSTIC** | • Quick Check in Recall Prior Knowledge in Student Book B, pp. 119–120<br>• Chapter 11 Pre-Test in *Assessments* | • Skills 42–47 in *Transition Guide, Course 1* |
| **ON-GOING** | • Guided Practice<br>• Lesson Check<br>• Ticket Out the Door | • Reteach worksheets<br>• Extra Practice worksheets, Ch 8–11 Cumulative Practice worksheets<br>• *Activity Book*, Chapter 11 |
| **END-OF-CHAPTER** | • Chapter Review/Test<br>• Chapter 11 Test, Chapters 8–11 Benchmark Test in *Assessments*<br>• ExamView® Assessment Suite Course 1 | • Reteach worksheets |

### ELL ENGLISH LANGUAGE LEARNERS

Review the terms *radius, diameter,* and *circumference.*

**Model** Draw a circle. Mark and identify its center point. As you describe each part of the circle, draw an example on the circle.

**Say** A *radius* is a line segment with one endpoint at the center of a circle and the other endpoint on the circle. A *diameter* is a line segment that passes through the center of a circle and has both endpoints on the circle. The distance around the circle is called the *circumference.*

**Model** After you have drawn each part, label it with its name so that the name spans the part. Write *radius* along the entire length of the radius. Write *diameter* along the entire length of the diameter. Write *circumference* so that the word spans the entire circumference of the circle.

For definitions, see Glossary, page 301, and  Online Multilingual Glossary.

### ADVANCED LEARNERS

• Students can create posters that define the terms *circle, radius, diameter, circumference,* and $\pi$, and that also demonstrate the relationships among the various parts of circles. Tell students they should rely as much as possible on using visual methods to convey the information. For example, a poster might explain that $\pi$ is the value of the ratio of a circle's circumference to its diameter and show the written ratio of those two part names, $\dfrac{\text{circumference}}{\text{diameter}}$, with each name written in a different color. Next to the ratio, a diagram of a circle would show the circumference and diameter, each part drawn, labeled, or highlighted in the same color as the term.

• As needed, provide direction for students. Suggest they rely on interrelated diagrams, formulas, labels, and colors to visually explain and connect the terms.

**To provide additional challenges use:**
• *Enrichment*, Chapter 11
• Student Book A, Brain@Work problem

**CHAPTER**

**11**

# Circumference and Area of a Circle

## Chapter Vocabulary

Vocabulary terms are used in context in the student text. For definitions, see the Glossary at the end of the Student Book and the Online Multilingual Glossary.

**arc** A portion of a circle

**center** A point within a circle that is the same distance from all points on a circle

**circumference** The distance around a circle

**diameter** A line segment that connects two points on a circle and passes through its center; also the length of this segment

**quadrant** A quarter of a circle

**radii** Plural of *radius*

**radius (*r*)** A line segment connecting the center and a point on the circle; also the length of this segment

**semicircle** A half of a circle

**BIG IDEA**

▶ A circle is a geometric figure that has many useful applications in the real world.

## Have you ever seen a rainbow?

A rainbow is an optical effect that occurs when light shines on water droplets suspended in the air. A good time to look for a rainbow is after a rain shower in the late afternoon or early evening. Stand with the sun behind you and look towards the horizon. If conditions are right, you might see a rainbow.

The shape of a rainbow is part of a circle. In fact, if you are flying in an airplane, you might see the whole circle of a rainbow out the window.

Under the right conditions, you can also make your own rainbow. Stand outdoors with the sun behind you and use a garden hose to spray water out in all directions. You might even see a circular rainbow.

## CHAPTER OPENER

Use the chapter opener to talk about circumference and area of a circle in a real-life situation.

**Ask** Have you ever seen a rainbow? Yes

**Explain** What you often see is only a part of the rainbow. The rainbow is actually a full circle that can be seen if you are high up in an airplane. The circle is a shape that has many useful applications in the real world, none more important than the invention of the wheel.

In this chapter, you will learn some properties of the circle and how to apply them to solve real-world problems as stated in the **Big idea**.

## Recall Prior Knowledge

### Adding decimals

Find the value of 0.8 + 4.53.

**STEP 1**
Add the hundredths.

```
    0 . 8
+   4 . 5 3
          3
```

**STEP 2**
Add the tenths.

```
      1
    0 . 8
+   4 . 5 3
        3 3
```

**STEP 3**
Add the ones.

```
    1
    0 . 8
+   4 . 5 3
    5 . 3 3
```

The value of 0.8 + 4.53 is 5.33.

#### ✔ Quick Check

Add.

**1** 0.451 + 3.12  3.571

**2** 0.861 + 6.95  7.811

**3** 13.74 + 3.791  17.531

### Subtracting decimals

Find the value of 6.12 − 3.56.

**STEP 1**
Substract the hundredths.

```
      0  1
    6 . 1̶ 2
−   3 . 5 6
          6
```

**STEP 2**
Subtract the tenths.

```
    5  10  1
    6̶ . 1̶  2
−   3 . 5  6
        5  6
```

**STEP 3**
Subtract the ones.

```
    5  10  1
    6̶ . 1̶  2
−   3 . 5  6
    2 . 5  6
```

The value of 6.12 − 3.56 is 2.56.

#### ✔ Quick Check

Subtract.

**4** 5.45 − 1.78  3.67

**5** 12.795 − 0.816  11.979

**6** 42.781 − 36.19  6.591

### RECALL PRIOR KNOWLEDGE

Use the ✔ Quick Check exercises or the Chapter Pre-Test in *Assessments, Course 1*, to assess chapter readiness. For intervention suggestions, see the chart below and on the following pages.

🖱 Additional online Reteach and Extra Practice worksheets from previous grades are also available. See the *Transition Guide*, Resource Planner for more information.

### ⚠ RtI Assessing Prior Knowledge

| ✔ Quick Check | *Assessments Course 1*, Ch. 11 Pre-Test Items | Skill Objective | Intervene with | |
|---|---|---|---|---|
| | | | Transition Guide | 🖱 Online Resources Grades 4 and 5 |
| **1** to **3** | 1−3 | Add decimals. | Skill 42 | Reteach 4B, pp. 57−74; Extra Practice 4B, Lesson 8.1 |
| **4** to **6** | 4−6 | Subtract decimals. | Skill 43 | Reteach 4B, pp. 75−90; Extra Practice 4B, Lesson 8.2 |

## Multiplying decimals

Find the value of 2.45 × 6.

**STEP 1**
Multiply the hundredths.

$$\begin{array}{r} 2 \,.\, 4 \,\overset{3}{5} \\ \times \qquad 6 \\ \hline 0 \end{array}$$

**STEP 2**
Multiply the tenths.

$$\begin{array}{r} 2 \,.\, \overset{2}{4} \,\overset{3}{5} \\ \times \qquad 6 \\ \hline 7 \; 0 \end{array}$$

**STEP 3**
Multiply the ones.

$$\begin{array}{r} \overset{2}{2} \,.\, 4 \; 5 \\ \times \qquad 6 \\ \hline 14 \,.\, 7 \; 0 \end{array}$$

The value of 2.45 × 6 is 14.7.

### ✔ Quick Check

**Multiply.**

**7** 1.34 × 9  12.06

**8** 4.246 × 2  8.492

**9** 7.487 × 8  59.896

## Dividing decimals

Find the value of 0.75 ÷ 6.

$$\begin{array}{r} 0\,.\,1\,2\,5 \\ 6\overline{)0\,.\,7\,5} \\ \underline{6\phantom{0000}} \\ 1\,5 \\ \underline{1\,2} \\ 3\,0 \\ \underline{3\,0} \\ 0 \end{array}$$

7 tenths ÷ 6 = 1 tenth R 1 tenth

Regroup the remainder 1 tenth.
1 tenth = 10 hundredths
10 hundredths + 5 hundredths = 15 hundredths
15 hundredths ÷ 6 = 2 hundreds R 3 hundredths

Regroup the remainder 3 hundredths.
3 hundredths = 30 thousandths
30 thousandths ÷ 6 = 5 thousandths

The value of 0.75 ÷ 6 is 0.125.

### ✔ Quick Check

**Divide.**

**10** 2.56 ÷ 5  0.512

**11** 2.429 ÷ 7  0.347

**12** 1.143 ÷ 9  0.127

**13** 4.671 ÷ 9  0.519

**14** 0.656 ÷ 8  0.082

**15** 0.867 ÷ 3  0.289

## ▲ RtI  Assessing Prior Knowledge

| ✔ Quick Check | Assessments Course 1, Ch. 11 Pre-Test Items | Skill Objective | Intervene with | |
|---|---|---|---|---|
| | | | Transition Guide | 🖱 Online Resources Grades 4 and 5 |
| **7** to **9** | 7–9 | Multiply decimals. | Skill 44 | Reteach 5B, pp. 19–30; Extra Practice 5B, Lesson 9.1 |
| **10** to **15** | 10–12 | Divide decimals. | Skill 45 | Reteach 5B, pp. 39–56; Extra Practice 5B, Lesson 9.3 |

## Rounding numbers to the nearest whole number

Round 3.14 to the nearest whole number.

To round to the nearest whole number, look at the tenths digit.
Round up if the tenths digit is 5 or greater.
Round down if the tenths digit is less than 5.

In 3.14, the tenths digit is 1.
Because 1 is less than 5, 3.14 rounded to the nearest whole number is 3.

### ✓ Quick Check

**Round to the nearest whole number.**

| | | |
|---|---|---|
| 16 4.56 5 | 17 12.05 12 | 18 26.48 26 |
| 19 6.50 7 | 20 14.15 14 | 21 46.59 47 |

## Rounding numbers to the nearest tenth

Round 10.58 to the nearest tenth.

To round to the nearest tenth, look at the hundredths digit.
Round up if the hundredths digit is 5 or greater.
Round down if the hundredths digit is less than 5.

In 10.58, the hundredths digit is 8.
Because 8 is greater than 5, 10.58 rounded to the nearest tenth is 10.6.

### ✓ Quick Check

**Round to the nearest tenth.**

| | | |
|---|---|---|
| 22 7.68 7.7 | 23 3.05 3.1 | 24 19.92 19.9 |
| 25 5.55 5.6 | 26 8.17 8.2 | 27 2.44 2.4 |
| 28 43.65 43.7 | 29 23.73 23.7 | 30 17.51 17.5 |

## RtI Assessing Prior Knowledge

| Quick Check | Assessments Course 1, Ch. 11 Pre-Test Items | Skill Objective | Intervene with | |
|---|---|---|---|---|
| | | | Transition Guide | Online Resources Grades 4 and 5 |
| 16 to 21 | 13 – 15 | Round numbers to the nearest whole number. | Skill 46 | Reteach 4B, pp. 47 – 48; Extra Practice 4B, Lesson 7.4 |
| 22 to 30 | 16 – 18 | Round numbers to the nearest tenth. | Skill 47 | Reteach 4B, pp. 49 – 50; Extra Practice 4B, Lesson 7.4 |

## KEY CONCEPTS

- The radius of a circle is a line segment connecting the center and a point on the circle.

- The diameter of a circle is a line segment that connects two points on a circle and passes through its center.

- The circumference of a circle is the distance around the circle.

- The ratio of the circumference of a circle to its diameter is the constant $\pi$.

## PACING

DAY **1** Pages 122–126

DAY **2** Pages 127–135

**Materials:** compass, ruler, protractor, TRT27, circle cut-outs, drawing triangle (or set square)

 **5-minute Warm Up**

Simplify.

**1.** $\frac{12}{5} \times 5$  12  **2.** $\frac{22}{7} \times 14$  44

 Also available on Teacher One Stop.

**Lesson Objectives**
- Identify parts of a circle.
- Recognize that a circle's diameter is twice its radius.
- Use formulas to find the circumference of a circle.
- Identify semicircles and quarter circles, and find the distance around them.

**Vocabulary**

| center | radius, radii |
| diameter | circumference |
| arc | semicircle |
| quadrant | |

Learn **Identify the center and radius of a circle.**

These are circles.

You can use a compass to draw a circle. Notice that all points on the circle are the same distance from the center.

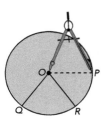

$O$ is the center of the circle.

$\overline{OP}$ is a radius of the circle.

$\overline{OQ}$ and $\overline{OR}$ are also **radii** of the circle.

$OP = OQ = OR$

The plural of radius is radii. In a given circle, all radii have the same length.

A radius is a line segment connecting the center and a point on the circle.

DAY **1**

Learn **Identify the center and radius of a circle.**

**Model** With a compass, draw a circle of radius 8 inches on the board. Label the center of the circle $O$ and any 3 points on the circumference $P$, $Q$ and $R$. Draw line segments $OP$, $OQ$, and $OR$.

**Explain** $O$ is the center of the circle. $\overline{OP}$ is a radius of the circle. $\overline{OQ}$ and $\overline{OR}$ are also radii of the circle. You can see that $OP = OQ = OR = 8$ inches.

**Ask** If you label another point on the circumference $S$, what do you call $\overline{OS}$ and what is its length? A radius; 8 in. What can you say about the radii of a circle? They all have the same length.

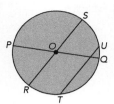

## Learn — Identify the diameter of a circle.

In the circle below, $O$ is the center. The line segments $\overline{PQ}$ and $\overline{RS}$ pass through the center $O$. $\overline{PQ}$ is a diameter of the circle. $\overline{RS}$ is another diameter of the circle. $\overline{TU}$ is not a diameter.

A diameter of a circle is a line segment that connects two points on the circle and passes through its center.

All diameters of a given circle have the same length.

$\overline{OP}$, $\overline{OQ}$, $\overline{OR}$, and $\overline{OS}$ are radii of the circle.

$OP = OQ = OR = OS$

So $PQ = 2 \cdot OP$
   $= 2 \cdot OQ$
   $= 2 \cdot OR$
   $= 2 \cdot OS$

**Math Note**

Diameter $= 2 \cdot$ radius
Radius $=$ Diameter $\div 2$

## Guided Practice

**Complete.**

**1** In the figure, $O$ is the center of the circle with $\overline{AB}$, $\overline{CD}$, and $\overline{ED}$ as shown.

a) Name all the diameters that are drawn in the circle. $\overline{AB}$ and $\overline{CD}$

b) Which line segment that joins two points on the circle is not a diameter? Explain why it is not a diameter. $\overline{ED}$. The line segment $\overline{ED}$ does not pass through the center, $O$.

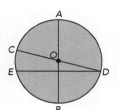

**2** The radius of a circle is 6 centimeters. What is the length of its diameter?

Diameter $= 2 \cdot$ radius

$= \underline{?} \; \boxed{?} \; \underline{?} \quad 2; \cdot; 6$

$= \underline{?} \;$ cm $\quad 12$

The diameter of the circle is $\underline{?}$ centimeters. $\quad 12$

**3** The diameter of a circle is 15 inches. What is the length of its radius?

Radius $=$ diameter $\div 2$

$= \underline{?} \; \boxed{?} \; \underline{?} \quad 15; \div; 2$

$= \underline{?} \;$ in. $\quad 7.5$

The radius of the circle is $\underline{?}$ inches. $\quad 7.5$

## Learn — Identify the diameter of a circle.

## 👋 Hands-On Activity

Students should note that the distance between the tips of the arms of the compass is the radius of the circle. Help students who may have difficulty using a compass by demonstrating how to hold the compass properly.

### ELL Vocabulary Highlight

To help students understand the meaning of *circumference*, compare it to *perimeter*. The circumference of a circle is the distance around the circle, while the distance around a polygon is called its *perimeter*. Both terms describe the distance around a plane figure: *circumference* for circles and *perimeter* for polygons.

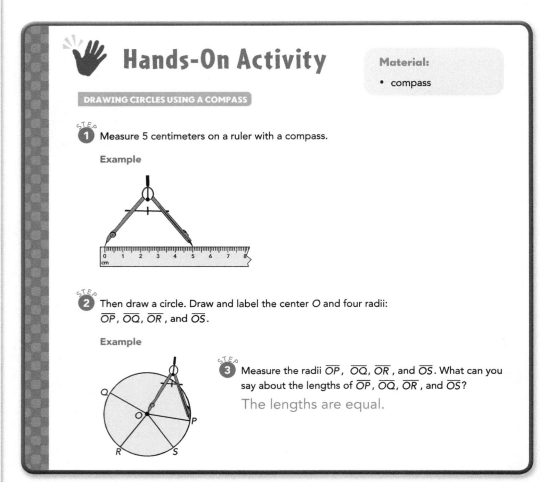

## 👋 Hands-On Activity

**Material:**
• compass

**DRAWING CIRCLES USING A COMPASS**

**STEP 1** Measure 5 centimeters on a ruler with a compass.

**Example**

**STEP 2** Then draw a circle. Draw and label the center $O$ and four radii: $\overline{OP}$, $\overline{OQ}$, $\overline{OR}$, and $\overline{OS}$.

**Example**

**STEP 3** Measure the radii $\overline{OP}$, $\overline{OQ}$, $\overline{OR}$, and $\overline{OS}$. What can you say about the lengths of $\overline{OP}$, $\overline{OQ}$, $\overline{OR}$, and $\overline{OS}$?

The lengths are equal.

**Learn Identify the circumference of a circle.**

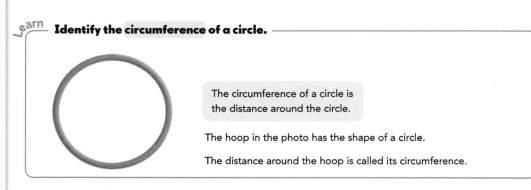

The circumference of a circle is the distance around the circle.

The hoop in the photo has the shape of a circle.

The distance around the hoop is called its circumference.

---

**Learn Identify the circumference of a circle.**

**Model** Use the picture in the text to show students how to identify the circumference of a circle.

**Ask** Look at the hoop. What is its shape? Circle
What do you call the distance around the hoop?
Circumference

**Summarize** Lead students to conclude that the distance around a circle is called its circumference.

# Hands-On Activity

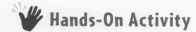

**INVESTIGATING THE RELATIONSHIP BETWEEN THE CIRCUMFERENCE AND DIAMETER OF A CIRCLE**

 **STEP 1** Lisa uses a string to measure the circumference of each circle to the nearest tenth of a centimeter and records it in a table.

  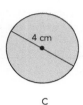 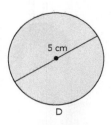

A          B            C           D

Copy the table. Divide the circumference of each circle by its diameter. Round your answers to the nearest tenth. Record your results.

| Circle | Diameter (cm) | Circumference (cm) | Circumference ÷ diameter |
|--------|---------------|---------------------|--------------------------|
| A | 2 | 6.2 | ? |
| B | 3 | 9.4 | ? |
| C | 4 | 12.5 | ? |
| D | 5 | 15.6 | ? |

3.1
3.1
3.1
3.1

What do you notice about the quotients in the last column?

The circumference of any circle divided by its diameter always gives the same value.

The Greek letter $\pi$ is used to represent this value.

 The letter $\pi$ is pronounced "pie."

**Continue on next page** ➡

---

# Hands-On Activity

This activity allows students to discover that the ratio of the circumference of a circle to its diameter is constant. Students should work individually. You may want to use TRT27 to record the results.

**1** Make sure that the quotients have been rounded to the nearest tenth or 1 decimal place. Tell students that the circumference of any circle divided by its diameter always results in the same number. The Greek letter $\pi$ (pi) is used to represent this number.

 **DIFFERENTIATED INSTRUCTION**

**Through Concrete Manipulatives**

You may want students to take measurements from actual objects such as a variety of sizes of plastic lids from containers and compiling their own tables like the one here. This will help students to see that the relationship between diameter and circumference is an actual physical property, not just a mathematical abstraction.

2 Ask students to press [π] and [ENTER] on their calculators to see the value of $\pi$ up to 9 decimal places. The value of $\pi$ when it is rounded to the

a) nearest tenth is 3.1
b) nearest hundredth is 3.14
c) nearest thousandth is 3.142

Emphasize that $\pi$ has no exact fraction or decimal value. Explain that the value of $\pi$ is often approximated as 3.14 or $\frac{22}{7}$. Since $\pi$ = circumference ÷ diameter, then circumference = $\pi \cdot$ diameter. If $C$ is the circumference and the diameter is $d$, the formula for the circumference of a circle can be written as $C = \pi d$.

3 Make sure students understand that if $r$ is the radius of the circle, the formula for diameter can be written as $d = 2r$. So, the circumference formula can be written as $C = \pi \times 2r = 2\pi r$.

STEP 2 To see the value of $\pi$ up to 9 decimal places, press [π] [ENTER] on your calculator. Round the value of $\pi$ to

a) the nearest tenth. 3.1
b) the nearest hundredth. 3.14
c) the nearest thousandth. 3.142

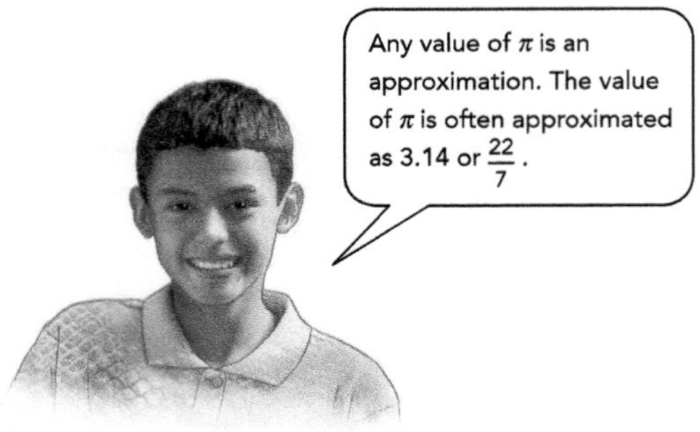


STEP 3 In STEP 1, you learned that the circumference of any circle divided by its diameter is equal to $\pi$. You can use this fact to write a formula for the circumference of a circle. Complete the following statement.

Since circumference ÷ diameter = $\pi$,

Circumference = $\pi \cdot$ __?__ diameter

You also know that the diameter of a circle is 2 times its radius. You can use this fact to write a related formula for the circumference of a circle. Complete the following statement.

Circumference = $\pi \cdot$ diameter
= $\pi \cdot 2 \cdot$ __?__ radius
= $2 \cdot \pi \cdot$ __?__ radius

Using $C$ for circumference, $d$ for diameter, and $r$ for radius, you can write these formulas as

$C = \pi d$
$C = 2\pi r$

**Math Note**

$\pi d$ means $\pi \cdot d$ and $2\pi r$ means $2 \cdot \pi \cdot r$.

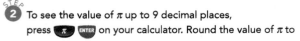

arn

## Find the circumference of a circle.

a) Find the circumference of the plate shown. Use $\frac{22}{7}$ as an approximation for $\pi$.

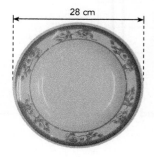

28 cm

| | |
|---|---|
| Circumference = $\pi d$ | Write formula. |
| $\approx \frac{22}{7} \cdot 28$ | Substitute. |
| $= \frac{22}{{}_1 7} \cdot \frac{28^4}{1}$ | Divide by the common factor, 7. |
| $= 22 \cdot 4$ | Simplify. |
| $= 88$ cm | Multiply. |

> **Math Note**
>
> The symbol $\approx$ means "approximately equal to."

The circumference of the plate is approximately 88 centimeters.

b) The radius of a bicycle wheel is 10.5 inches. Find the circumference of the wheel. Use 3.14 as an approximation for $\pi$.

| | |
|---|---|
| Circumference = $2\pi r$ | Write formula. |
| $\approx 2 \cdot 3.14 \cdot 10.5$ | Substitute. |
| $= 65.94$ in. | Multiply. |

The circumference of the bicycle wheel is approximately 65.94 inches.

## Guided Practice

Copy and complete the table. Use $\frac{22}{7}$ as an approximation for $\pi$.

**4**

| Circle | Radius (cm) | Diameter (cm) | Circumference (cm) | |
|---|---|---|---|---|
| A | ? | 14 | ? | 7; 44 |
| B | 21 | ? | ? | 42; 132 |
| C | 10.5 | ? | ? | 21; 66 |

---

**DAY 2**

earn **Find the circumference of a circle.**

a) **Model** Use the example to demonstrate how to find the circumference of a circle given its diameter.

**Ask** What is the formula for circumference of a circle? $C = \pi d$ What are you given in the problem? The value of $\pi$: $\frac{22}{7}$; the diameter of the plate: 28 cm Since $C = \pi d$, what equation can you write? $C = \frac{22}{7} \cdot 28$ How do you evaluate this product? Divide 7 out of both the factor 28 and the denominator.

**Explain** Then, the equation can be simplified and written as $C = 22 \cdot 4$.

**Ask** So, what is the circumference of the plate? 88 cm

b) **Ask** What are you given in the problem? The radius of the wheel: 10.5 in.; the value of $\pi$: 3.14 How can you find the circumference of the wheel? By using the formula $C = 2\pi r$ So, what is the circumference of the wheel? $2 \cdot 3.14 \cdot 10.5 = 65.94$ in.

**Summarize** The circumference of the bicycle wheel is approximately 65.94 inches.

**Lesson 11.1** Radius, Diameter, and Circumference of a Circle **127**

Help students understand the meanings of *semicircle* and *quadrant* through their etymologies. The prefix *semi-* means "half," so a semicircle is a half circle. Other words that begin with *semi-* include *semifinal*, *semiconductor*, and *semicolon*. The root *quad* in the word *quadrant* means "four," so a quadrant of a circle is one fourth of a circle. Other words that feature the root *quad* include *quadrangle*, *quadrilateral*, and *quadruplet*.

**Caution**

Some students may confuse semicircles and quadrants with the arcs that form a portion of them. Explain that semicircles and quadrants are plane shapes. A semicircle consists of an arc that is half the circumference of a circle and the diameter joining the endpoints of that arc. A quadrant consists of an arc that is a quarter of the circumference of a circle and the radius to each endpoint of that arc.

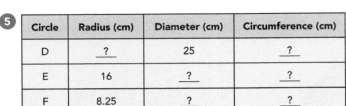
Copy and complete the table. Use 3.14 as an approximation for π.

**5**

| Circle | Radius (cm) | Diameter (cm) | Circumference (cm) | |
|--------|-------------|---------------|--------------------|--|
| D | ? | 25 | ? | 12.5; 78.5 |
| E | 16 | ? | ? | 32; 100.48 |
| F | 8.25 | ? | ? | 16.5; 51.81 |

**Learn** **Recognize that half of a circle is a semicircle and a quarter of a circle is a quadrant.**

You can divide a circle into halves. Each half circle is called a semicircle.

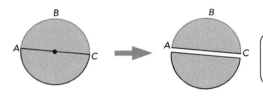

*ABC* is an **arc** of the circle. It is a semicircular arc.

The length of the semicircular arc *ABC* is half the circumference of the circle.

You can divide a circle into quarters. Each quarter circle is called a quadrant.

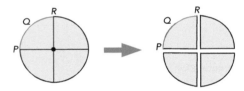

*PQR* is also an arc. It is the arc of a quadrant.

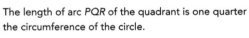

The length of arc *PQR* of the quadrant is one quarter the circumference of the circle.

**Learn** **Recognize that half of a circle is a semicircle and a quarter of a circle is a quadrant.**

**Model** Fold a circle cut-out along the diameter to show students that a circle can be divided into halves as shown in the text.

**Explain** Each half circle has an arc that is half the circumference of the circle. A semicircle consists of this arc together with the diameter joining the endpoints of the arc. A semicircle is a closed figure.

**Model** Fold the circle into quarters.

**Explain** Each quarter circle has an arc that is one fourth the circumference of the circle. A quadrant consists of this arc together with the two radii that make a closed, plane figure.

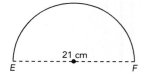

**Find the lengths of a semicircular arc and the arc of a quadrant.**

a)  A length of wire is bent into a semicircular arc. The length of $\overline{EF}$ is 21 centimeters.

Find the length of the wire. Use $\frac{22}{7}$ as an approximation for $\pi$.

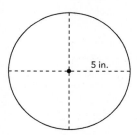

$$\text{Circumference} = \pi d \qquad\qquad \text{Write formula.}$$
$$\approx \frac{22}{7} \cdot 21 \qquad\qquad \text{Substitute.}$$
$$= 66 \text{ cm} \qquad\qquad \text{Multiply.}$$

$$\text{Length of semicircular arc} = \frac{1}{2} \times 66$$
$$= 33 \text{ cm}$$

Length of wire = Length of semicircular arc
= 33 cm

The length of the wire is approximately 33 centimeters.

b)  A circular ring of radius 5 inches is cut into four equal parts. Find the length of each arc of a quadrant. Use 3.14 as an approximation for $\pi$.

$$\text{Circumference} = 2\pi r \qquad\qquad \text{Write formula.}$$
$$\approx 2 \cdot 3.14 \cdot 5 \qquad\qquad \text{Substitute.}$$
$$= 31.4 \text{ in.} \qquad\qquad \text{Multiply.}$$

$$\text{Length of each arc of the quadrant} = \frac{1}{4} \times 31.4$$
$$= 7.85 \text{ in.}$$

The length of each arc of a quadrant is approximately 7.85 inches.

**Find the lengths of a semicircular arc and the arc of a quadrant.**

a)  **Model** Use the example to show students how to find the length of a semicircular arc.

**Ask** What are you given in the problem? The length of $\overline{EF}$, which is also the diameter: 21 cm; the value of $\pi$: $\frac{22}{7}$ So, what is the circumference of the whole circle? $C = \pi d \approx \frac{22}{7} \cdot 21 = 66$ cm

**Explain** The length of a semicircular arc is half of the circumference.

**Ask** So, what is the length of the semicircular wire? $\frac{1}{2} \times 66 = 33$ cm

b)  **Model** Use the example to show students how to find the length of an arc of a quadrant.

**Ask** What are you given in the problem? The radius of the ring: 5 in.; the value of $\pi$: 3.14 **What are you asked to find?** The length of an arc of a quadrant How can you find the length of this arc in terms of the circumference? By using the formula $C = 2\pi r$ and then multiplying by $\frac{1}{4}$. So, what is the length of each arc of the quadrant? $\frac{1}{4} \cdot 3.14 \cdot 10 = 7.85$ in.

**Summarize** The length of each arc of a quadrant is approximately 7.85 inches.

## Guided Practice

**6** and **7** Remind students that when asked to find the distance around a figure or object that is semicircular, the diameter has to be included. Similarly, with a figure or object that is a quadrant, the distance around the shape or object will include the two radii.

 **DIFFERENTIATED INSTRUCTION**

**Through Communication**

**7** You may want to guide students through the solution steps. First, have students copy the diagram on paper. **Ask:** According to the problem, what is cut from a square? *(A quadrant)* What is a quadrant? *(One fourth of a circle)* Next, have students draw the rest of the circle. **Ask:** What part of the circle is each of the straight sides that outline part of the quadrant? *(A radius)* What is the length of the radius? *(10 cm)* How do we know that length? *(One side of the square is labeled "10 cm.")* Now, students can use the circumference formula to calculate the length of the arc of the quadrant.

## Guided Practice

**Complete.**

**6** A circular hoop is cut into two equal parts. Its diameter is 35 inches. Find the length of each semicircular arc. Use $\frac{22}{7}$ as an approximation for $\pi$.

Circumference of hoop = $\pi d$

$$\approx \underline{\ ?\ } \ \text{?} \ \underline{\ ?\ } \quad \frac{22}{7}; \cdot; 35$$

$$= \underline{\ ?\ } \text{ in.} \quad 110$$

Length of each semicircular arc = $\frac{1}{2}$ · circumference of hoop

$$= \underline{\ ?\ } \ \text{?} \ \underline{\ ?\ } \quad \frac{1}{2}; \cdot; 110$$

$$= \underline{\ ?\ } \text{ in.} \quad 55$$

The length of each semicircular arc is approximately $\underline{\ ?\ }$ inches. 55

**7** A quadrant is cut from a square. The side of the square is 10 centimeters. Find the length of the arc of the quadrant. Use 3.14 as an approximation for $\pi$.

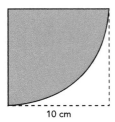

10 cm

Circumference of circle = $2\pi r$

$$\approx 2 \cdot \underline{\ ?\ } \cdot \underline{\ ?\ } \quad 3.14; 10$$

$$= \underline{\ ?\ } \text{ cm} \quad 62.8$$

Length of the arc of the quadrant = circumference ÷ 4

$$= \underline{\ ?\ } \div \underline{\ ?\ } \quad 62.8; 4$$

$$= \underline{\ ?\ } \text{ cm} \quad 15.7$$

The length of the arc of the quadrant is approximately $\underline{\ ?\ }$ centimeters. 15.7

# Hands-On Activity

**Materials:**
- compass
- drawing triangles
- ruler
- protractor

 **STEP 1** Use a compass to draw a circle of radius 2 inches. Label the center *O*.

**STEP 2** Draw and label a diameter of the circle $\overline{PQ}$. What do you notice?

A diameter of a circle divides it into __?__ semicircles.  2

This figure is one of the semicircles.

Find the distance around the semicircle.
Use 3.14 as an approximation for $\pi$.  10.28 in.

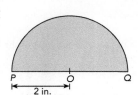

**STEP 3** In your circle, draw a second diameter perpendicular to $\overline{PQ}$ using a ruler and protractor, or a drawing triangle. Label it $\overline{RS}$. What do you notice?

a)  Two perpendicular diameters of a circle divide it into __?__ quadrants.  4

This figure is one of the quadrants.

Find the distance around the quadrant.
Use 3.14 as an approximation for $\pi$.  7.14 in.

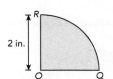

b)  This figure is made up of the semicircular arc, the arc of a quadrant, and the radii $\overline{OR}$ and $\overline{OQ}$. Find the distance around the figure. Use 3.14 as an approximation for $\pi$.  13.42 in.

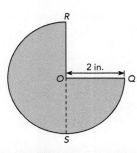

 **Hands-On Activity**

This activity enables students to discover that any diameter of a circle cuts it into two semicircles, and two perpendicular diameters cut it into four quadrants.

**3** You may also want to review with students how to use a drawing triangle (or a set square) to draw the second diameter.

## Best Practices

Point out that the distance around a semicircle consists of the sum of the lengths of a diameter and an arc of a semicircle. Then point out that the distance around a quadrant consists of the sum of two radii and the length of an arc of a quadrant.

### Assignment Guide

DAY **1** All students should complete **1** – **5**.

DAY **2** All students should complete **6** – **28**.

**29** – **31** provide additional challenge.

Optional: *Extra Practice 11.1*

## Practice 11.1

Basic **1**–**26**
Intermediate **27**–**28**
Advanced **29**–**31**

**Use the figure to complete. In the figure, O is the center of the circle and $\overline{XY}$ is a straight line.**

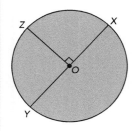

**1** $\overline{OX}$, $\overline{OY}$, and $\overline{OZ}$ are __?__ of the circle.  radii

**2** $\overline{XY}$ is a __?__ of the circle.  diameter

**3** OX = __?__ = __?__  OZ; OY

**4** XY = __?__ · OZ  2

**5** Circumference of the circle = $\pi$ · __?__  diameter or XY

**Find the circumference of each circle. Use $\frac{22}{7}$ as an approximation for $\pi$.**

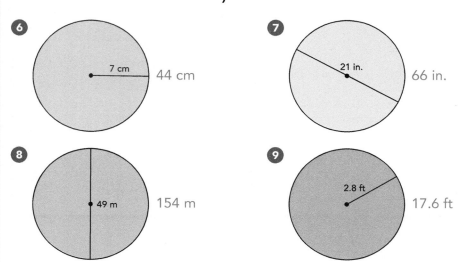

**6** 7 cm    44 cm

**7** 21 in.    66 in.

**8** 49 m    154 m

**9** 2.8 ft    17.6 ft

### RtI Lesson Check

| Before assigning homework, use the following ... | to make sure students ... | Intervene with ... |
| --- | --- | --- |
| Exercise **1** | • can identify parts of a circle | |
| Exercise **7** | • can use formula to find the circumference of a circle | Reteach 11.1 |
| **EXIT** Ticket Out the Door | • can define and relate the terms radius, diameter, and circumference | |

**Find the length of each arc. Use $\frac{22}{7}$ as an approximation for π.**

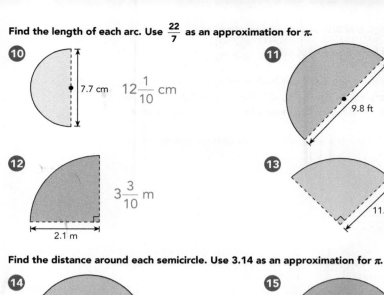

10. 7.7 cm    $12\frac{1}{10}$ cm

11. 9.8 ft    $15\frac{2}{5}$ ft

12. 2.1 m    $3\frac{3}{10}$ m

13. 11.2 cm    $17\frac{3}{5}$ cm

**Find the distance around each semicircle. Use 3.14 as an approximation for π.**

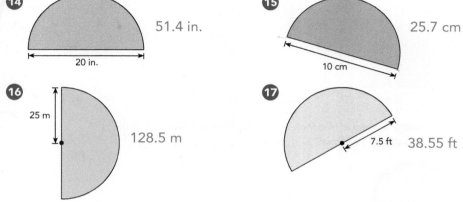

14. 20 in.    51.4 in.

15. 10 cm    25.7 cm

16. 25 m    128.5 m

17. 7.5 ft    38.55 ft

**Find the distance around each quadrant. Use $\frac{22}{7}$ as an approximation for π.**

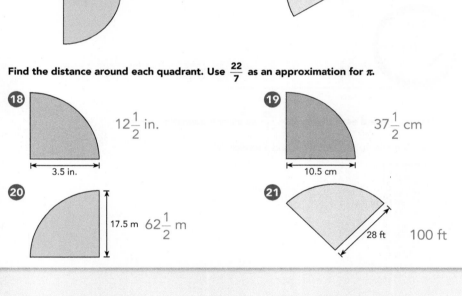

18. 3.5 in.    $12\frac{1}{2}$ in.

19. 10.5 cm    $37\frac{1}{2}$ cm

20. 17.5 m    $62\frac{1}{2}$ m

21. 28 ft    100 ft

**Solve. Show your work. Use 3.14 as an approximation for π.**

**22** A circular garden has a diameter of 120 feet. Find its circumference. 376.8 ft

**23** A circular coaster has a radius of 4 centimeters. Find its circumference. 25.12 cm

**24** The diameter of a roll of tape is $5\frac{1}{2}$ centimeters. Find its circumference. 17.27 cm

**25** The shape of a floor mat is a semicircle. Find the distance around the mat.

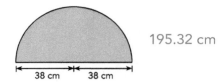

195.32 cm

38 cm   38 cm

**26** A small playground is shaped like a quadrant, as shown. Find the distance around the playground.

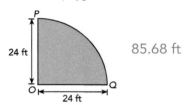

85.68 ft

P

24 ft

O   24 ft   Q

**27** If the radius of a wheel is 14 inches, what is the distance traveled when the wheel turns around 100 times?

14 in.

8,792 in.

**Find the distance around each figure. Use $\frac{22}{7}$ as an approximation for π.**

**28** The figure is made up of a rectangle and a semicircle.

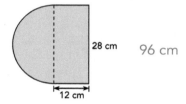

28 cm   96 cm

12 cm

**29** The figure is made up of an equilateral triangle and a semicircle.

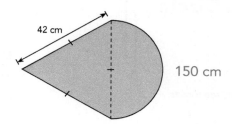

42 cm

150 cm

**Find the distance around each figure. Use 3.14 as an approximation for π.**

**30** The figure is made up of a rectangle and two identical semicircles.

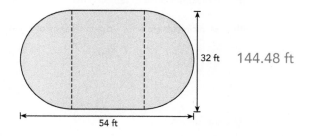

32 ft     144.48 ft

54 ft

**31** The figure is made up of two identical quadrants, a semicircle, and an equilateral triangle.

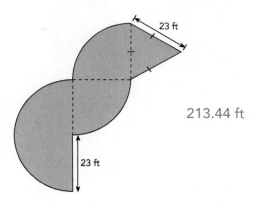

23 ft

213.44 ft

23 ft

**EXIT**

**Ticket Out the Door**

In your own words, define *radius*, *diameter*, and *circumference*. Then explain how radius, diameter, and circumference are mathematically related. Possible answer: A radius is a line segment from the center to any point on the circle. A diameter is a segment across a circle through its center. Circumference is the distance around a circle. The length of a diameter is twice the length of a radius. The circumference is equal to π times the diameter or 2 times π times the radius.

 Also available on Teacher One Stop.

## KEY CONCEPT

- The area of a circle can be found by using the formula Area of a circle $= \pi r^2$.

## PACING

DAY **1** Pages 136–139

DAY **2** Pages 139–142

**Materials:** compass, circle cut-outs

 **5-minute Warm Up**

Find the lengths of semicircles with the following circumferences:

1. 24 cm  12 cm
2. 19 in.  9.5 in.
3. 27.4 cm  13.7 cm
4. 2y in.  y in.

Also available on Teacher One Stop.

---

**11.2** **Area of a Circle**

### Lesson Objective

- Use formulas to calculate the areas of circles, semicircles, and quadrants.

**Learn** **Derive the formula for the area of a circle.**

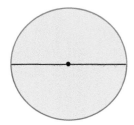

A diameter divides a circle of radius r into 2 semicircles.

Length of semicircular arc $= \frac{1}{2} \cdot$ circumference of circle

$$= \frac{1}{2} \cdot 2\pi r$$

$$= \pi r$$

Suppose you cut a circle of radius r into 16 equal pieces.

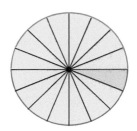

The cuts all go through the center of the circle.

You can cut one of the pieces into 2 equal parts.

---

DAY **1**

**Learn** **Derive the formula for the area of a circle.**

Review with students that the length of a semicircle is half the circumference.

**Ask** What is the circumference of a circle of radius r? $2\pi r$ What is the length of each semicircular arc? $\pi r$

**Model** Show the circle cut-out and the one cut into 16 equal pieces. Rearrange the cut circle to match the figure shown in the text.

---

Arrange all the pieces to form the figure shown below. You can also label the dimensions of the figure.

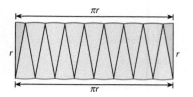

The semicircular arcs form the top and bottom of the figure.

Area of circle = area of the figure

Now suppose you cut the circle into as many equal pieces as possible. You can form the figure shown at the right.

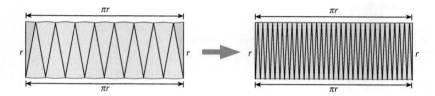

As the number of pieces keeps increasing, the top and bottom of the figure gradually become straight lines. Then the figure gradually becomes a rectangle of length $\pi r$ and width $r$. You can write an expression for its area in terms of $r$. Because the rectangle is made up of the same pieces as the original circle, the area of the circle is equal to the area of the rectangle.

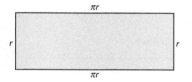

Area of circle = area of rectangle

$\quad = \pi r \cdot r$

$\quad = \pi \cdot r \cdot r$

$\quad = \pi r^2$

$r \cdot r$ is written as $r^2$.

Your can write the formula as

Area of circle = $\pi r^2$

### Learn continued

**Explain** You can see that the circle has been rearranged into the figure in the text.

**Ask** How many arcs form the bottom of the figure? 8 How many arcs of this length form the top of the figure? $7 + 1 = 8$ What is the length of the top and bottom of the figure? Half the circumference or the length of a semicircular arc What is this length in terms of the radius $r$ of the circle? $\pi r$ What is the height of this figure? $r$

**Explain** The area of the circle is the area of this figure. If you cut the circle into more and more pieces, the top and bottom of the figure will become more and more like straight lines.

**Ask** What figure is formed then? A rectangle What is the length of this rectangle? $\pi r$ What is its width? $r$ What is the area of the rectangle? $\pi r \times r = \pi r^2$ Does the rectangle cover as much area as the original circle? Yes What can you say about the area of the circle then? The area of the circle is equal to the area of the rectangle.

**Explain** So, the formula for area of a circle can be written as Area = $\pi r^2$.

## Caution

Some students may try to evaluate $\pi \cdot 7^2$ by multiplying $\pi$ times 7 and then squaring. Be sure they understand that the exponent applies only to the radius, and not to $\pi$. Have them recall the order of operations: all exponents are to be evaluated before any multiplication.

### DIFFERENTIATED INSTRUCTION

**Through Enrichment**

Remind students that when substituting 3.14 or $\frac{22}{7}$ for $\pi$ in a calculation, they are using an approximation. Suggest that students recalculate their answers for ❶ through ❸ first by substituting $\frac{22}{7}$ and then by using the button on their calculators. Ask students to compare how each of the three methods of computation affected their answers.

---

### Learn Find the area of a circle.

a) The radius of a circular disc is 7 inches. Find its area. Use $\frac{22}{7}$ as an approximation for $\pi$.

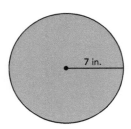

7 in.

| | | |
|---|---|---|
| Area | $= \pi r^2$ | Write formula. |
| | $\approx \frac{22}{7} \cdot 7^2$ | Substitute. |
| | $= \frac{22}{\cancel{7}} \cdot 7 \cdot 7^1$ | Divide by the common factor, 7. |
| | $= 22 \cdot 7$ | Simplify. |
| | $= 154 \text{ in.}^2$ | Multiply. |

The area of the disc is approximately 154 square inches.

b) The diameter of a circle is 24 centimeters. Find its area. Use 3.14 as an approximation for $\pi$.

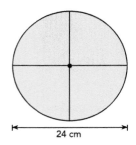

24 cm

Radius of circle = diameter ÷ 2
= 24 ÷ 2
= 12 cm

| | | |
|---|---|---|
| Area | $= \pi r^2$ | Write formula. |
| | $\approx 3.14 \cdot 12^2$ | Substitute. |
| | $= 3.14 \cdot 144$ | Simplify. |
| | $= 452.16 \text{ cm}^2$ | Multiply. |

The area of the circle is approximately 452.16 square centimeters.

### Guided Practice
**Complete. Use 3.14 as an approximation for $\pi$.**

❶ Find the area of a circle that has a radius of 18 centimeters.

Area $= \pi r^2$

$\approx \underline{\ ?\ } \cdot \underline{\ ?\ }^2$  3.14; 18

$= \underline{\ ?\ } \cdot \underline{\ ?\ }$  3.14; 324

$= \underline{\ ?\ } \text{ cm}^2$  1,017.36

The area of the circle is approximately $\underline{\ ?\ }$ square centimeters.  1,017.36

---

### Learn Find the area of a circle.

a) **Model** Use the problem to illustrate how to find the area of a circular disc given its radius.

**Ask** What are you given in the problem? The radius of the disc: 7 in.; the value of $\pi$: $\frac{22}{7}$ What are you asked to find? Area of the disc

**Explain** To find the area of the disc, substitute the values of $\pi$ and $r$ into the formula for area of a circle and evaluate. Area of disc $= \pi r^2 \approx \frac{22}{7} \times 7 \times 7$ $= 22 \times 7 = 154 \text{ in.}^2$

**Summarize** The area of the disc is approximately 154 square inches.

b) **Model** Use the problem to illustrate how to find the area of a circle given its diameter.

**Ask** What are you given in the problem? The diameter of the circle: 24 cm; the value of $\pi$: 3.14 What are you asked to find? Area of the circle What is the formula for the area of a circle? $A = \pi r^2$ How can you find the radius of the circle? By dividing the diameter by 2

**Explain** So, radius of the circle $= \frac{24}{2} = 12$ cm. Area of circle $= \pi r^2 \approx 3.14 \times 12 \times 12 = 452.16 \text{ cm}^2$

**Summarize** The area of the circle is approximately 452.16 square centimeters.

**2** Find the area of a circle that has a radius of 15 inches.

Area = $\pi r^2$

$\approx$ ___?___ · ___?___ ²    3.14; 15

= ___?___ · ___?___    3.14; 225

= ___?___ in.²    706.5

The area of the circle is approximately ___?___ square inches.   706.5

**3** Find the area of a circle that has a diameter of 26 centimeters.

Radius = diameter ÷ 2

= ___?___ ÷ ___?___    26; 2

= ___?___ cm    13

Area = $\pi r^2$

$\approx$ ___?___ · ___?___ ²    3.14; 13

= ___?___ · ___?___    3.14; 169

= ___?___ cm²    530.66

The area of the circle is approximately ___?___ square centimeters.   530.66

**Learn** **Find the area of a semicircle.**

The diameter of a circle is 14 feet. Find the area of a semicircle. Use $\frac{22}{7}$ as an approximation for $\pi$.

Radius = diameter ÷ 2
      = 14 ÷ 2
      = 7 ft

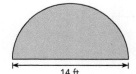
14 ft

Area of semicircle = $\frac{1}{2}$ · area of circle

     = $\frac{1}{2}$ · $\pi r^2$       Write formula.

     $\approx$ $\frac{1}{2}$ · $\frac{22}{7}$ · $7^2$       Substitute.

     = $\frac{1}{{}_1 2}$ · $\frac{22^{11}}{{}_1 7}$ · 7 · $7^1$       Divide by the common factors, 2 and 7.

     = 11 · 7       Simplify.

     = 77 ft²       Multiply.

The area of a semicircle is approximately 77 square feet.

**DAY 2**

**Learn** **Find the area of a semicircle.**

**Model** Use the example to demonstrate how to find the area of a semicircle.

**Ask** What are you given in the problem? The diameter of the circle: 14 ft; the value of $\pi$: $\frac{22}{7}$ What is the radius of the circle? Radius = diameter ÷ 2 = 14 ÷ 2 = 7 ft Since the area of the semicircle is half the area of a circle, what formula can you use to find the area of the semicircle? $\frac{1}{2}$ · $\pi r^2$ What equation can you write

for the area of a semicircle? Area of semicircle = $\frac{1}{2}$ · $\frac{22}{7}$ · $7^2$ How do you solve this equation? Divide out the common factors from the numerators and denominators of $\frac{1}{2}$, $\frac{22}{7}$, and 7, which are 2 and 7.

**Explain** The equation can be simplified and written as Area of semicircle = 11 · 7 = 77 ft²

**Ask** So, what is the area of the semicircle? Approximately 77 ft²

**Caution** ///////

When using the formula for area, some students may multiply the radius by 2 instead of squaring it. Suggest that students who are having this problem rewrite the area formula as $A = \pi \cdot r \cdot r$.

**Best Practices**

Now that students are finding areas of semicircles and quadrants, reinforce the difference between semicircles and quadrant and arcs of semicircles or quadrants. Remind students that semicircles and quadrants are plane figures. Plane figures have areas, which are measured in square units. The arc of a semicircle or quadrant has a length, which is measured in linear units.

## Guided Practice

**4** Remind students that the area of a quadrant is one fourth the area of the circle.

---

## Guided Practice

**Complete. Use** $\frac{22}{7}$ **as an approximation for π.**  See margin.

**4** Find the area of a quadrant.

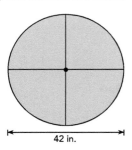

14 ft

Area of quadrant = $\underline{\quad?\quad}$ · area of circle

$\quad\quad\quad\quad = \underline{\quad?\quad} \cdot \pi r^2$

$\quad\quad\quad\quad \approx \underline{\quad?\quad} \cdot \underline{\quad?\quad} \cdot \underline{\quad?\quad}^2$

$\quad\quad\quad\quad = \underline{\quad?\quad} \cdot \underline{\quad?\quad} \cdot \underline{\quad?\quad} \cdot \underline{\quad?\quad}$

$\quad\quad\quad\quad = \underline{\quad?\quad}\ ft^2$

The area of a quadrant is approximately $\underline{\quad?\quad}$ square feet.

**5** The diameter of a circle is 42 inches. Find the area of a quadrant.

42 in.

Radius = diameter ÷ 2

$\quad\quad\quad = \underline{\quad?\quad} \div 2$

$\quad\quad\quad = \underline{\quad?\quad}\ in.$

Area of quadrant = $\underline{\quad?\quad}$ · area of circle

$\quad\quad\quad\quad = \underline{\quad?\quad} \cdot \pi r^2$

$\quad\quad\quad\quad \approx \underline{\quad?\quad} \cdot \underline{\quad?\quad} \cdot \underline{\quad?\quad}^2$

$\quad\quad\quad\quad = \underline{\quad?\quad} \cdot \underline{\quad?\quad} \cdot \underline{\quad?\quad} \cdot \underline{\quad?\quad}$

$\quad\quad\quad\quad = \underline{\quad?\quad}\ in.^2$

The area of a quadrant is approximately $\underline{\quad?\quad}$ square inches.

---

**4** $\frac{1}{4}$; $\frac{1}{4}$; $\frac{1}{4}$; $\frac{22}{7}$; 14; $\frac{1}{4}$; $\frac{22}{7}$; 14; 14; 154; 154

**5** 42; 21; $\frac{1}{4}$; $\frac{1}{4}$; $\frac{1}{4}$; $\frac{22}{7}$; 21; $\frac{1}{4}$; $\frac{22}{7}$; 21; 21; $346\frac{1}{2}$; $346\frac{1}{2}$

## Practice 11.2

Basic ①–⑨
Intermediate ⑩–⑪
Advanced ⑫

**Find the area of each circle. Use 3.14 as an approximation for π.**

**①**

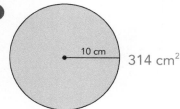

10 cm

314 cm²

**②**

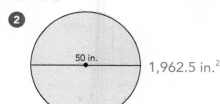

50 in.

1,962.5 in.²

**Find the area of each semicircle. Use $\frac{22}{7}$ as an approximation for π.**

**③**

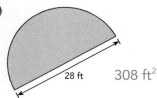

28 ft

308 ft²

**④**

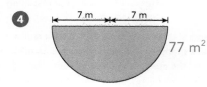

7 m    7 m

77 m²

**Find the area of each quadrant to the nearest tenth. Use 3.14 as an approximation for π.**

**⑤**

113.0 in.²

12 in.

**⑥**

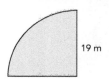

19 m

283.4 m²

**Solve. Show your work.**

**⑦** A circular pendant has a diameter of 7 centimeters. Find its area. Use $\frac{22}{7}$ as an approximation for π. $38\frac{1}{2}$ cm²

**⑧** The shape of the stage of a lecture theater is a semicircle. Find the area of the stage. Use 3.14 as an approximation for π.

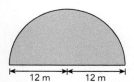

226.08 m²

12 m    12 m

**Practice 11.2**

### Assignment Guide

DAY **1** All students should complete ①, ②, ⑦, and ⑩.

DAY **2** All students should complete ③ – ⑥, ⑧, ⑨ and ⑪.

⑫ provides additional challenge.

Optional: *Extra Practice 11.2, Activity Book 11.2*

### RtI Lesson Check

| Before assigning homework, use the following ... | to make sure students ... | Intervene with ... |
|---|---|---|
| Exercises ①, ③ and ⑤ | • can use formulas to calculate the areas of circles, semicircles, and quadrants | Reteach 11.2 |
| **EXIT** Ticket Out the Door | • can compare the area of a semicircle to a given area | |

**DIFFERENTIATED INSTRUCTION**

**Through Visual Cues**

**11** Some students may need help getting started. **Ask:** What shape is formed by the dashed radii of the 4 drinking glasses? *(Square)* What makes up 1 side of the square? *(Radii of 2 drinking glasses)* What is the length of each side of the square? *(10 cm)* What is its area? *(100 cm²)* How does the area of the shaded portion relate to the area of the square? *(The shaded area is equal to the area of the square minus the area of 4 quadrants of the circles.)*

**EXIT**

## Ticket Out the Door

Trina's class plans to make a banner. The banner will be semicircle with a diameter of 4 yards. Is 6 square yards of fabric enough to make the banner? Explain your answer. No. $\pi r^2 =$ 3.14 · 2 · 2 = 12.56. The area of the semicircle is half that area: 12.56 ÷ 2 = 6.28. 6.28 > 6, so 6 square yards of fabric is not enough.

Also available on Teacher One Stop.

---

**9** The shape of a balcony floor is a quadrant. Find the area of the balcony floor. Use 3.14 as an approximation for π.

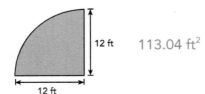

12 ft    113.04 ft²

12 ft

**10** The cost of an 8-inch pizza is $4. The cost of a 16-inch pizza is $13. Use 3.14 as an approximation for π.

**a)** How much greater is the area of the 16-inch pizza than the area of the 8-inch pizza? 150.72 in.²

**b)** Which is a better deal? Explain your reasoning.
16-inch pizza, because it costs less per square inch than the 8-inch pizza.

**11** Four identical drinking glasses each have a radius of 5 centimeters. The glasses are arranged so that they touch each other as shown in the figure below. Find the area of the green portion. Use 3.14 as an approximation for π.

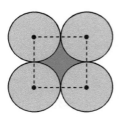

21.5 cm²

**12** The figure is made up of trapezoid ABCD and a semicircle. The height of trapezoid ABCD is $\frac{5}{6}$ the length of $\overline{BC}$. Find the area of the figure. Use $\frac{22}{7}$ as an approximation for π.

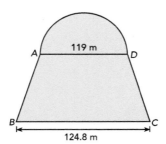

A   119 m   D

18,240.85 m²

B

124.8 m   C

## Lesson Objectives

- Solve real-world problems involving area and circumference of circles.
- Solve real-world problems involving semicircles, quadrants, and composite figures.

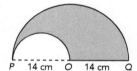

**Use the formula for circumference to solve real-world problems.**

a) A circular mat has a diameter of 53 centimeters. Lily wants to sew a decorative braid around the mat. How many centimeters of braid does she need? Give your answer to the nearest tenth of a centimeter. Use 3.14 as an approximation of $\pi$.

| | |
|---|---|
| Circumference of mat = $\pi d$ | Write formula. |
| $\approx 3.14 \cdot 53$ | Substitute. |
| $= 166.42$ cm | Multiply. |
| $\approx 166.4$ cm | Round to the nearest tenth of a centimeter. |

Lily needs approximately 166.4 centimeters of decorative braid.

b) A metalworker cuts out a large semicircle with a diameter of 28 centimeters. Then the metalworker cuts a smaller semicircle out of the larger one and removes it. The diameter of the semicircular piece that is removed is 14 centimeters. Find the distance around the shape after the smaller semicircle is removed. Use $\frac{22}{7}$ as an approximation for $\pi$.

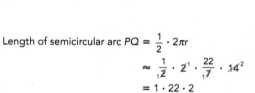

P    14 cm    O    14 cm    Q

> To find the distance around the shape, you need to add up the two arc lengths and OQ.

| | |
|---|---|
| Length of semicircular arc $PQ = \frac{1}{2} \cdot 2\pi r$ | Write formula. |
| $\approx \frac{1}{\not{2}} \cdot \not{2}^1 \cdot \frac{22}{\not{7}} \cdot \not{14}^2$ | Substitute. Divide by the common factors, 2 and 7. |
| $= 1 \cdot 22 \cdot 2$ | Simplify. |
| $= 44$ cm | Multiply. |

**Continue on next page** ➡

## KEY CONCEPT

- The problem solving process involves the application of concepts, skills, and strategies.

## PACING

| DAY 1 | Pages 143–149 |
|---|---|
| DAY 2 | Pages 149–159 |

**Materials:** none

### 5-minute Warm Up

Review how to identify the perimeters and areas of composite figures. Ask students to outline the perimeters and shade the areas of these figures.

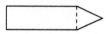 

Check students' work.

 Also available on Teacher One Stop.

---

 **DAY 1**

**Use the formula for circumference to solve real-world problems.**

a) **Model** Use the example to demonstrate the process of solving problems involving the circumference of circles.

b) **Model** Use the example to demonstrate the process of solving problems involving semicircles.

**Step 1** Understand the problem.

**Ask** What is given in the problem? Diameter of the large semicircle: 28 cm, diameter of semicircle cut out: 14 cm; and $\pi$: $\frac{22}{7}$ What are you asked to find? The distance around the figure formed

**Step 2** Think of a strategy.

**Ask** What does the distance around the figure consist of? 2 semicircular arcs PO and OQ, and the radius OQ

**Step 3** Solve the problem.

**Explain** Length of semicircular arc $PQ = \frac{1}{2} \cdot 2\pi r$
$\approx \frac{1}{2} \cdot 2 \cdot \frac{22}{7} \cdot 14$ Then divide out the common factors of the numerators and denominators, 2 and 7 to simplify the equation to $1 \cdot 22 \cdot 2 = 44$ cm.

Length of semicircular arc $PO = \frac{1}{2} \cdot \pi d$          Write formula.

$$\approx \frac{1}{{}_1\cancel{2}} \cdot \frac{\overset{11}{\cancel{22}}}{{}_1\cancel{7}} \cdot \cancel{14}^{2}$$          Substitute. Divide by the common factors, 2 and 7.

$$= 1 \cdot 11 \cdot 2$$          Simplify.

$$= 22 \text{ cm}$$          Multiply.

Distance around the shape
= length of semicircular arc $PQ$ + length of semicircular arc $PO$ + $OQ$
= 44 + 22 + 14
= 80 cm

The distance around the shape is approximately 80 centimeters.

c)  The shape of a table top is made up of a semicircle and a quadrant.
Find the distance around the table top. Use 3.14 as an approximation
for $\pi$.

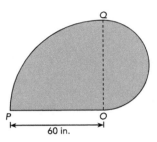

Length of semicircular arc $QO = \frac{1}{2} \cdot \pi d$          Write formula.

$$\approx \frac{1}{2} \cdot 3.14 \cdot 60$$          Substitute.

$$= 94.2 \text{ in.}$$          Multiply.

Length of arc $PQ = \frac{1}{4} \cdot 2\pi r$          Write formula.

$$\approx \frac{1}{{}_1\cancel{4}} \cdot 2 \cdot 3.14 \cdot \cancel{60}^{15}$$          Substitute. Divide by the common factor, 4.

$$= 1 \cdot 2 \cdot 3.14 \cdot 15$$          Simplify.

$$= 94.2 \text{ in.}$$          Multiply.

Distance around the table top
= length of semicircular arc $QO$ + length of arc $PQ$ + $PO$
= 94.2 + 94.2 + 60
= 248.4 in.

The distance around the table top is approximately 248.4 inches.

## Learn continued

**Ask** How can you find the length of semicircular arc
$PO$? Use the formula Length of semicircular arc $PO$
$= \frac{1}{2} \cdot \pi d \approx \frac{1}{2} \cdot \frac{22}{7} \cdot 14$ Then divide out the common
factors of the numerators and denominators, 2 and 7,

to simplify the expression on the right side to
$1 \cdot 11 \cdot 22 = 22$ cm.

**Explain** The length of semicircular arc $PO$ is
22 centimeters.

**Ask** What is the distance around the shape? Distance
around the shape = length of semicircular arc $PQ$ +
length of semicircular arc $PO$ + $OQ$ = 44 + 22 + 14
= 80 cm

c) **Ask** What are you given in the problem? The shape
of the table top: semicircle and quadrant; diameter
of the table top: 60 in.; $\pi$: 3.14 **What are you asked
to find?** The distance around the table top

**Explain** Before finding the distance around the
table top, first find the lengths of semicircular arc
$QO$ and arc $PQ$.

**Ask** What is the length of semicircular arc $QO$?
94.2 in. What is the length of arc $PQ$? 94.2 in. So,
what is the distance around the table top? Distance
around the table top = length of semicircular arc
$QO$ + length of arc $PQ$ + $PO$ = 94.2 + 94.2 + 60
= 248.4 in.

## Guided Practice

**Complete. Use 3.14 as an approximation for π.**

**1** The circumference of the moon is the approximate distance around a circle with radius 1,736 kilometers. Find the circumference of the moon.

a) Round your answer to the nearest 10 kilometers.

Circumference of moon = $2\pi r$

$\approx$ __?__ · __?__ · __?__   2; 3.14; 1,736

= __?__ km   10,902.08

The circumference of the moon to the nearest 10 kilometers is __?__ kilometers.   10,900

b) Round your answer to the nearest 1,000 kilometers.

The circumference of the moon to the nearest 1,000 kilometers is __?__ kilometers.   11,000

**2** A greeting card is made up of three semicircles. O is the center of the large semicircle. Sarah wants to decorate the distance around the card with a ribbon. How much ribbon does Sarah need? Round your answer to the nearest inch.

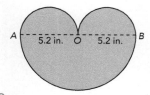

A ---- 5.2 in.  O  5.2 in. ---- B

Length of semicircular arc $AB = \dfrac{1}{2} \cdot 2\pi r$

$\approx$ __?__ · __?__ · __?__ · __?__   $\dfrac{1}{2}$; 2; 3.14; 5.2

= 1 · __?__ · __?__   3.14; 5.2

= __?__ in.   16.328

Semicircular arcs AO and OB have the same length.

Total length of semicircular arcs AO and OB

= $2 \cdot \dfrac{1}{2} \cdot \pi d$

$\approx$ __?__ · __?__ · __?__ · __?__   2; $\dfrac{1}{2}$; 3.14; 5.2

= 1 · __?__ · __?__   3.14; 5.2

= __?__ in.   16.328

Distance around the card

= length of semicircular arc AB + total length of semicircular arcs AO and OB

= __?__ + __?__   16.328; 16.328

= __?__ in.   32.656

$\approx$ __?__ in.   33

Sarah needs approximately __?__ inches of ribbon.   33

## Guided Practice

Remind students that the length of a semicircle is $\dfrac{1}{2}\pi d$ or $\pi r$ and the length of a quadrant is $\dfrac{1}{4}\pi d$ or $\dfrac{1}{2}\pi r$, where d is the diameter of the circle and r the radius.

**2** Students should note that the two semicircles have the same diameter. So, their total length is equal to the circumference of a circle of the same diameter.

# Guided Practice

**3** Students should note that the quadrant and the semicircle have the same radius. So, the length of the quadrant is half that of the semicircle.

**3** As part of her artwork, Sally bends a length of wire into the shape shown. The shape is made up of a semicircle and a quadrant. Find the length of the wire.

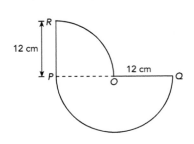

Length of semicircular arc $PQ$

$= \frac{1}{2} \cdot 2\pi r$

$\approx \underline{?} \cdot 2 \cdot \underline{?} \cdot \underline{?}$   $\frac{1}{2}$; 3.14; 12

$= 1 \cdot \underline{?} \cdot \underline{?}$   3.14; 12

$= \underline{?}$ cm   37.68

Length of arc $RO = \frac{1}{4} \cdot 2\pi r$

$\approx \frac{1}{4} \cdot 2 \cdot \underline{?} \cdot \underline{?}$   3.14; 12

$= \underline{?}$ cm   18.84

Distance around the shape

$=$ length of semicircular arc $PQ$ + length of arc $RO$ + $RP$ + $OQ$

$= \underline{?} + \underline{?} + \underline{?} + \underline{?}$   37.68; 18.84; 12; 12

$= \underline{?}$ cm   80.52

The length of the wire is approximately $\underline{?}$ centimeters.   80.52

## ᴸᵉᵃʳⁿ Use the formula for area of a circle to solve real-world problems.

a) A jewelry designer is making a pendant. The pendant will be a circular disc (center $O$) with a circular hole cut out of it, as shown. The radius of the disc is 35 millimeters. Find the area of the pendant. Use $\frac{22}{7}$ as an approximation for $\pi$.

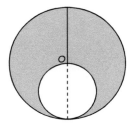

Area of disc $= \pi r^2$

$\approx \frac{22}{7} \cdot 35^2$

$= \frac{22}{{}_1 7} \cdot 35 \cdot 35^{\,5}$

$= 22 \cdot 35 \cdot 5$

$= 3{,}850$ mm²

Radius of hole $=$ diameter $\div 2$

$= 35 \div 2$

$= 17.5$ mm

## ᴸᵉᵃʳⁿ Use formula for area of circle to solve real-world problems.

**Model** Use a) and b) to demonstrate the process of solving problems involving the areas of circles, semicircles, and quadrants.

a) **Step 1** Understand the problem.

**Ask** What are you given in the problem? The radius of the circular disc: 35 mm; the diameter of the hole:

35 mm; and $\pi$: $\frac{22}{7}$ What is the radius of the hole?

$\frac{35}{2} = 17.5$ mm What are you asked to find? The area of the pendant

**Step 2** Think of a strategy.

**Ask** How can you find the area of the pendant? First, find the area of the disc using the formula $A = \pi r^2$. Next, find the radius of the hole: diameter $\div 2$. Then find the area of the hole using the formula $A = \pi r^2$. Finally, to find the area of the pendant, subtract the area of the hole from the area of the disc.

**Step 3** Solve the problem.

**Explain** Area of disc $= \pi r^2 \approx \frac{22}{7} \cdot 35^2 = 3{,}850$ mm²

Radius of hole $=$ diameter $\div 2 = 35 \div 2 = 17.5$ mm

$$\text{Area of hole} = \pi r^2$$
$$\approx \frac{22}{7} \cdot 17.5 \cdot 17.5$$
$$= 962.5 \text{ mm}^2$$

$$\text{Area of pendant} = \text{area of disc} - \text{area of hole}$$
$$= 3,850 - 962.5$$
$$= 2,887.5 \text{ mm}^2$$

The area of the pendant is approximately 2,887.5 square millimeters.

**b)** A graphic designer creates a design for a company logo. The design is a green semicircle with a white quadrant, as shown. Find the area of the green part of the design. Use 3.14 as an approximation for $\pi$.

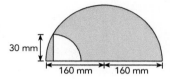

30 mm

160 mm | 160 mm

$$\text{Area of semicircle} = \frac{1}{2} \cdot \pi r^2$$
$$\approx \frac{1}{2} \cdot 3.14 \cdot 160^2$$
$$= \frac{1}{1\cancel{2}} \cdot 3.14 \cdot 160 \cdot \cancel{160}^{80}$$
$$= 1 \cdot 3.14 \cdot 160 \cdot 80$$
$$= 40,192 \text{ mm}^2$$

$$\text{Area of quadrant} = \frac{1}{4} \cdot \pi r^2$$
$$\approx \frac{1}{4} \cdot 3.14 \cdot 30^2$$
$$= \frac{1}{1\cancel{4}} \cdot 3.14 \cdot \cancel{30}^{15} \cdot \cancel{30}^{15}$$
$$= 1 \cdot 3.14 \cdot 15 \cdot 15$$
$$= 706.5 \text{ mm}^2$$

Area of green part
= area of semicircle − area of quadrant
= 40,192 − 706.5
= 39,485.5 mm$^2$

The area of the green part of the design is approximately 39,485.5 square millimeters.

**Learn continued**

$\text{Area of hole} \approx \frac{22}{7} \cdot 17.5 \cdot 17.5 = 962.5 \text{ mm}^2$

$\text{Area of pendant} \approx 3,850 - 962.5 = 2,887.5 \text{ mm}^2$

**b) Step 1** Understand the problem.

**Ask** What are you given in the problem? The radius of the semicircle: 160 mm; the radius of the quadrant: 30 mm; $\pi$: 3.14 **What are you asked to find?** The area of the green part of the design

**Step 2** Think of a strategy.

**Ask** How can you find the area of the green part? First, find the area of the semicircle using the formula $A = \frac{1}{2} \cdot \pi r^2$. Next, find the area of the

quadrant using the formula $A = \frac{1}{2} \cdot \pi r^2$. Finally, to find the area of the green part, subtract the area of the quadrant from the area of the semicircle.

**Step 3** Solve the problem.

**Explain** $\text{Area of semicircle} \approx \frac{1}{2} \cdot 3.14 \cdot 160 \cdot 160$
$$= 40,192 \text{ mm}^2$$

$\text{Area of quadrant} \approx \frac{1}{4} \cdot 3.14 \cdot 30 \cdot 30 = 706.5 \text{ mm}^2$

$\text{Area of green part} \approx 40,192 - 706.5 = 39,485.5 \text{ mm}^2$

**④** Remind students that they can solve the problem by subtracting the area of the missing quadrant from the area of the whole circle.

**⑤** Students should note that the two semicircles have the same radius. So their total area is equal to the area of a circle of the same radius.

**Caution** ▨▨▨▨▨

**⑤** Some students may not notice that the diameter of each semicircle equals the radius of the quadrant. They may substitute 42 for the radius when calculating the area of the quadrant and also, mistakenly, when finding the areas of the semicircles. Point out that the quadrant is part of a circle that is twice the size of the circles the semicircles are part of, so the quadrant and semicircles do not have the same radius.

Guided Practice

**Complete. Use $\frac{22}{7}$ as an approximation for $\pi$.** **④** – **⑤** See margin.

**④** Judy baked a pizza and had part of it for lunch. After the meal, the shape of the remaining pizza is made up of a semicircle and a quadrant. Find the area of the remaining pizza.

Area of quadrant $= \frac{1}{4} \cdot \pi r^2$

$\approx \frac{1}{4} \cdot \underline{?} \cdot \underline{?}^2$

$= \frac{1}{4} \cdot \underline{?} \cdot \underline{?} \cdot \underline{?}$

$= \underline{?}$ cm²

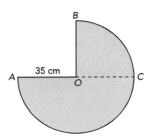

Area of semicircle $= \frac{1}{2} \cdot \pi r^2$

$\approx \frac{1}{2} \cdot \underline{?} \cdot \underline{?}^2$

$= \frac{1}{2} \cdot \underline{?} \cdot \underline{?} \cdot \underline{?}$

$= \underline{?}$ cm²

Area of remaining pizza = area of quadrant + area of semicircle

$= \underline{?} + \underline{?}$

$= \underline{?}$ cm²

The area of the remaining pizza is approximately $\underline{?}$ square centimeters.

**⑤** A rug is made up of a quadrant and two semicircles. Find the area of the rug.

Area of quadrant $= \frac{1}{4} \cdot \pi r^2$

$\approx \frac{1}{4} \cdot \underline{?} \cdot \underline{?}^2$

$= \frac{1}{4} \cdot \underline{?} \cdot \underline{?} \cdot \underline{?}$

$= \underline{?}$ in.²

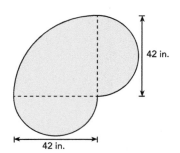

Radius of semicircle = diameter ÷ 2

$= \underline{?} \div \underline{?}$

$= \underline{?}$ in.

**④** $\frac{22}{7}$; 35; $\frac{22}{7}$; 35; 35; 962.5; $\frac{22}{7}$; 35; $\frac{22}{7}$; 35; 35; 1,925; 962.5; 1,925; 2,887.5; 2,887.5

**⑤** $\frac{22}{7}$; 42; $\frac{22}{7}$; 42; 42; 1,386; 42; 2; 21; 2; $\frac{1}{2}$; $\frac{22}{7}$; 21; $\frac{22}{7}$; 21; 21; 1,386; 1,386; 1,386; 2,772; 2,772

Total area of two semicircles $= 2 \cdot \dfrac{1}{2} \cdot \pi r^2$

$$\approx \underline{\ ?\ } \cdot \underline{\ ?\ } \cdot \underline{\ ?\ } \cdot \underline{\ ?\ }^{2}$$

$$= 1 \cdot \underline{\ ?\ } \cdot \underline{\ ?\ } \cdot \underline{\ ?\ }$$

$$= \underline{\ ?\ } \text{ in.}^2$$

Area of figure = area of quadrant + total area of two semicircles

$$= \underline{\ ?\ } + \underline{\ ?\ }$$

$$= \underline{\ ?\ } \text{ in.}^2$$

The area of the rug is approximately $\underline{\ ?\ }$ square inches.

### Learn  Solve real-world problems involving rates and circles.

**1** The tire of a car has a radius of 10.5 inches. How many revolutions does the tire need to make for the car to travel 13,200 inches? Use $\dfrac{22}{7}$ as an approximation for $\pi$.

10.5 in.

Circumference of tire $= 2\pi r$

$$\approx 2 \cdot \dfrac{22}{7} \cdot 10.5$$

$$= \dfrac{22}{\,7} \cdot \overset{3}{\cancel{21}}$$

$$= 66 \text{ in.}$$

The car travels approximately 66 inches with one revolution of the tire.

Number of revolutions = distance ÷ circumference of tire
$$= 13{,}200 \div 66$$
$$= 200$$

The tire needs to make approximately 200 revolutions to travel 13,200 inches.

**Continue on next page** ▶

---

DAY **2**

### Learn  Solve real-world problems involving rates and circles.

**Model** Use **1** and **2** to demonstrate the process of solving problems involving rates and circles.

**1** **Step 1** Understand the problem.

**Ask** What are you given in the problem? The radius of the tire: 10.5 in.; $\pi = \dfrac{22}{7}$ What are you asked to find? The number of revolutions the tire needs to make for it to travel 13,200 inches

**Step 2** Think of a strategy.

**Ask** What is the distance traveled in one revolution of the tire equal to? The circumference of the tire

**Step 3** Solve the problem.

**Explain** So, $2\pi r \approx 2 \cdot \dfrac{22}{7} \cdot 10.5 = 66$ in. How can you find the number of revolutions the tire needs to make for the car to travel 13,200 inches? By dividing the distance to be traveled by the circumference of the tire

**Explain** Number of revolutions
$$= \text{distance} \div \text{circumference of tire}$$
$$\approx 13{,}200 \div 66 = 200$$

**Summarize** The tire needs to make approximately 200 revolutions to travel 13,200 inches.

**2** A field is shaped like the diagram below. It is a rectangle with semicircles at the two ends. There is a running track around the field. Use 3.14 as an approximation for $\pi$.

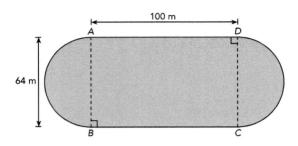

a) Find the length of the running track. Round your answer to the nearest ten meters.

Semicircular arcs AB and DC have the same length.

Total length of semicircular arcs $AB$ and $DC = 2 \cdot \dfrac{1}{2} \cdot \pi d$

$$= 1 \cdot \pi d$$
$$\approx 1 \cdot 3.14 \cdot 64$$
$$= 200.96 \text{ m}$$

Length of running track = total length of semicircular arcs $AB$ and $DC + AD + BC$
$$= 200.96 + 100 + 100$$
$$= 400.96 \text{ m}$$
$$\approx 400 \text{ m} \qquad \text{Round to the nearest ten meters.}$$

The length of the running track is approximately 400 meters.

b) An athlete ran around the track one time at an average speed of 8 meters per second. How many seconds did it take him to run around the track?

Time taken = distance ÷ speed
$$\approx 400 \div 8 \qquad \text{Substitute.}$$
$$= 50 \text{ s} \qquad \text{Divide.}$$

It took the athlete approximately 50 seconds to run one time around the track.

c) A gardener is hired to cut the grass in the field. She cuts the grass at an average rate of 40 square meters per minute. How many hours will she take to finish the entire field? Round your answer to the nearest hour.

---

**Learn continued**

**2 a) Ask** What are you given in the problem?
Length of rectangle: 100 m; diameter of each semicircle: 64 m; and $\pi$: 3.14 **What are you asked to find?** The length of the running track, rounded to the nearest ten meters

**Ask** What does the length of the track consist of? Total lengths of semicircular arcs $AB$ and $DC$ + lengths of $\overline{AD}$ and $\overline{BC}$

**Explain** Total length of semicircular arcs $AB$ and $DC = 2 \cdot \dfrac{1}{2} \cdot \pi d = 1 \cdot 3.14 \cdot 64 = 200.96$ m

Length of running track = 200.96 + 100 + 100
= 400.96 ≈ 400 m

**Summarize** The length of the track is approximately 400 meters.

b) **Ask** What is the speed of the athlete? 8 m/s How many seconds will he take to run 400 meters? 50 seconds

**Explain** To find the approximate time taken by the athlete to run once around the track, use the formula Time taken = distance ÷ speed ≈ 400 ÷ 8
= 50 seconds

c) **Ask** At what rate is the gardener cutting the grass? 40 m² per minute **What are you asked to find?** The approximate time taken by the gardener to finish cutting grass in the entire field

The areas of the two semicircles are equal.

Radius of circle = diameter ÷ 2

$$= 64 \div 2$$
$$= 32 \text{ m}$$

Total area of two semicircles = $2 \cdot \dfrac{1}{2} \cdot \pi r^2$      Write formula.

$$\approx \overset{1}{2} \cdot \dfrac{1}{\underset{1}{2}} \cdot 3.14 \cdot 32^2$$      Substitute. Divide by the common factor, 2.

$$= 1 \cdot 3.14 \cdot 32 \cdot 32$$      Simplify.

$$= 3{,}215.36 \text{ m}^2$$      Multiply.

Area of rectangle $ABCD = \ell w$

$$= 100 \cdot 64$$      Substitute.

$$= 6{,}400 \text{ m}^2$$      Multiply.

Area of field = area of rectangle $ABCD$ + total area of two semicircles

$$= 6{,}400 + 3{,}215.36$$
$$= 9{,}615.36 \text{ m}^2$$

Time taken by gardener = area of field ÷ rate of cutting grass

$$\approx 9{,}615.36 \div 40$$      Substitute.

$$= 240.384 \text{ min}$$      Divide by 60 to convert to hours.

$$= 4.0064 \text{ h}$$

$$\approx 4 \text{ h}$$      Round to the nearest hour.

The gardener will take approximately 4 hours to finish the entire field.

## Guided Practice

Complete. Use $\dfrac{22}{7}$ as an approximation for $\pi$.

**6** The diameter of a bicycle wheel is 60 centimeters. How far does the wheel travel when it makes 35 revolutions? Give your answer in meters.

Circumference of wheel = $\pi d$

$$\approx \underline{\ ?\ } \cdot \underline{\ ?\ } \ \dfrac{22}{7}; 60$$

$$= \underline{\ ?\ } \text{ cm} \ 188\dfrac{4}{7}$$

Distance traveled = circumference of wheel · number of revolutions

$$= \underline{\ ?\ } \cdot \underline{\ ?\ } \ 188\dfrac{4}{7}; 35$$

$$= \underline{\ ?\ } \text{ cm} \ 6{,}600$$

$$= \underline{\ ?\ } \text{ m} \ 66$$      Divide by 100 to convert to meters.

The wheel travels approximately $\underline{\ ?\ }$ meters. 66

## Guided Practice

**6** Remind students that the distance traveled in one revolution of the wheel is equal to the circumference of the wheel.

**Learn continued**

**How do you find the number of hours?** First, find the radius of the circle using the formula Radius = diameter ÷ 2. Next, find the total area of the two semicircles: $2 \cdot \dfrac{1}{2} \cdot \pi r^2$. Then, find the area of rectangle $ABCD$: $\ell w$. Next, find the area of the field: area of rectangle $ABCD$ + area of two semicircles. Finally, to find the time taken by the gardener: area of field ÷ rate of cutting grass

**Explain** Explain to students that —

Radius of circle = $64 \div 2 = 32$ m

Total area of the two semicircles $\approx 2 \cdot \dfrac{1}{2} \cdot 3.14 \cdot 32^2$
$= 3{,}215.36 \text{ m}^2$

Area of rectangle $ABCD = 100 \cdot 64 = 6{,}400 \text{ m}^2$

Area of field $\approx 3{,}215.36 + 6{,}400 = 9{,}615.36 \text{ m}^2$

Time taken by the gardener $\approx 9{,}615.36 \div 40 = 240.384$ min $= 4.006$ h $\approx 4$ h

**Summarize** The gardener will take approximately 4 hours to finish the entire field.

## Guided Practice

**7** Remind students that the total length of the two semicircles is equal to the circumference of a circle of the same diameter, and their total area is equal to the area of the circle. Inform them that they can use direct proportion to solve problems on rates that are constant.

 **7** A park is shaped like the diagram below. It is a rectangle with semicircles at the two ends. There is a running track around the park.

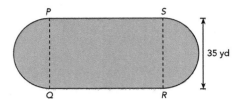

a) The total length of the track is 220 yards. Find the length of $\overline{PS}$.

The track is made up of semicircular arcs $PQ$ and $SR$, and sides $PS$ and $QR$. Semicircular arcs $PQ$ and $SR$ are equal.

Total length of semicircular arcs $PQ$ and $SR$

$= 2 \cdot \frac{1}{2} \cdot \pi d$

$\approx 1 \cdot \underline{\quad?\quad} \cdot \underline{\quad?\quad} \quad \frac{22}{7}; 35$

$= \underline{\quad?\quad}$ yd   110

The length of $\overline{PS}$ and $\overline{QR}$ are equal.

Total length of track $= 220$

$PS + QR +$ total length of semicircular arcs $PQ$ and $SR = 220$

$PS + QR + \underline{\quad?\quad} = 220$   110      Substitute.

$PS + QR = 220 \underbullet{?} \underline{\quad?\quad}$   $-; 110$      Solve equation.

$2 \cdot PS = \underline{\quad?\quad}$   110

$PS = \underline{\quad?\quad} \underbullet{?} \underline{\quad?\quad}$   $110; \div; 2$

$= \underline{\quad?\quad}$ yd   55

The length of $\overline{PS}$ is approximately $\underline{\quad?\quad}$ yards.   55

b) A jogger runs once around the track in 125 seconds. What is his average speed in yards per second?

The jogger runs $\underline{\quad?\quad}$ yards in 125 seconds.   220

125 seconds $\longrightarrow \underline{\quad?\quad}$   220

1 second $\longrightarrow \underline{\quad?\quad} \underbullet{?} \underline{\quad?\quad}$   $220; \div; 125$

$= \underline{\quad?\quad}$ yd   1.76

The average speed of the jogger is $\underline{\quad?\quad}$ yards per second.   1.76

**c)** A gardener is hired to water the grass in the park. Using a machine, he waters 4 square yards per second. How many minutes will he take to water the entire park? Round your answer to the nearest minute.

Radius = diameter ÷ 2

$$= \underline{\quad?\quad} \div 2 \quad 35$$

$$= \underline{\quad?\quad} \text{ yd} \quad 17.5$$

The areas of the two semicircles are equal.

Total area of two semicircles $= 2 \cdot \dfrac{1}{2} \cdot \pi r^2$

$$\approx 2 \cdot \dfrac{1}{2} \cdot \underline{\quad?\quad} \cdot \underline{\quad?\quad}^2 \quad \dfrac{22}{7};\ 17.5$$

$$= 1 \cdot \underline{\quad?\quad} \cdot \underline{\quad?\quad} \cdot \underline{\quad?\quad} \quad \dfrac{22}{7};\ 17.5;\ 17.5$$

$$= \underline{\quad?\quad} \text{ yd}^2 \quad 962\dfrac{1}{2}$$

Area of rectangle PQRS = ℓw

$$= \underline{\quad?\quad} \cdot \underline{\quad?\quad} \quad 55;\ 35$$

$$= \underline{\quad?\quad} \text{ yd}^2 \quad 1,925$$

Area of park = area of rectangle PQRS + total area of two semicircles

$$= \underline{\quad?\quad} + \underline{\quad?\quad} \quad 1,925;\ 962\dfrac{1}{2}$$

$$= \underline{\quad?\quad} \text{ yd}^2 \quad 2,887\dfrac{1}{2}$$

Time taken = area of park ÷ rate of watering park

$$= \underline{\quad?\quad} \div \underline{\quad?\quad} \quad 2,887\dfrac{1}{2};\ 4$$

$$= \underline{\quad?\quad} \text{ s} \quad 721.875$$

$$= \underline{\quad?\quad} \text{ min} \quad 12.03125$$

$$\approx \underline{\quad?\quad} \text{ min} \quad 12 \qquad \text{Round to the nearest minute.}$$

To find the time taken to water the park, think:
Rate of watering = area of park ÷ time taken
You can write this equation as:
Time taken = area of park ÷ rate of watering park
Remember to express the answer in minutes, not seconds.

The gardener will take approximately __?__ minutes to water the entire park.  12

## Practice 11.3

Basic ①–④
Intermediate ⑤–⑨
Advanced ⑩–⑭

**Solve. Show your work.**

① The radius of a circular pond is 8 meters. Find its area and circumference. Use 3.14 as an approximation for $\pi$. Area: 200.96 m²; Circumference: 50.24 m

② The diameter of a metal disc is 26 centimeters. Find its area and circumference. Use 3.14 as an approximation for $\pi$. Area: 530.66 cm²; Circumference: 81.64 cm

③ The shape of a carpet is a semicircle. Use $\frac{22}{7}$ as an approximation for $\pi$.

   a) Find its area. 77 ft²

   b) Janice wants to put a fringed border on all sides of the carpet. How many feet of fringe are needed? 36 ft

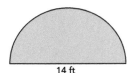

14 ft

④ The circumference of the rim of a wheel is 301.44 centimeters. Find the diameter of the rim. Use 3.14 as an approximation for $\pi$. 96 cm

⑤ A Japanese fan is made out of wood and cloth. The shape of the fan is made up of two overlapping quadrants. What is the area of the portion that is made of cloth? Use $\frac{22}{7}$ as an approximation for $\pi$. 462 cm²

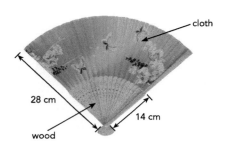

cloth

28 cm

14 cm

wood

---

### RtI Lesson Check

| Before assigning homework, use the following ... | to make sure students ... | Intervene with ... |
| --- | --- | --- |
| Exercises ① and ⑨ | • can solve real-world problems involving area and circumference of circles | |
| Exercises ③ and ⑤ | • can solve real-world problems involving semicircles, quadrants, and composite figures | Reteach 11.3 |
| **EXIT** Ticket Out the Door | • can solve a real-world problem involving area and distance around a semicircle | |

**6** A pancake restaurant serves small silver-dollar pancakes and regular-size pancakes. Use 3.14 as an approximation for $\pi$.

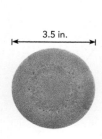 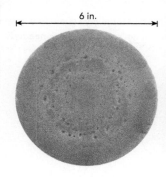

6 in.

3.5 in.

**a)** What is the area of a small silver dollar-pancake? Round your answer to the nearest tenth of an inch. $9.6 \text{ in.}^2$

**b)** What is the area of a regular-size pancake? Round your answer to the nearest tenth of a square inch. $28.3 \text{ in.}^2$

**c)** If the total price of 6 small silver-dollar pancakes is the same as the total price of 3 regular-size pancakes, which is a better deal? 3 regular-size pancakes

**7** A park is shaped like a rectangle with a semicircle on one end, and another semicircle cut out of one side.

**a)** Find the distance around the park. 560 m

**b)** Find the area of the park.
Use $\frac{22}{7}$ as an approximation for $\pi$. $11,900 \text{ m}^2$

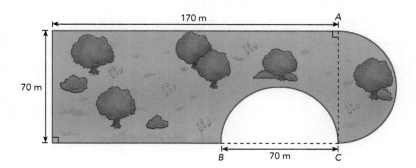

170 m

70 m

A

70 m

B        C

**8** The diameter of a circular fountain in a city park is 28 feet. A sidewalk that is 3.5 feet will be built around the fountain. Use $\frac{22}{7}$ as an approximation for $\pi$.

a) Find the area of the sidewalk. $346\frac{1}{2}$ ft²

b) 0.8 bag of concrete will be needed for every square foot of the new sidewalk. What is the minimum number of bags needed? 278 bags

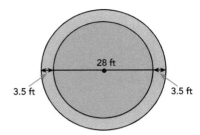

 **9** The diagram shows an athletic field with a track around it. The track is 4 feet wide. The field is a rectangle with semicircles at the two ends. Find the area of the track. Use 3.14 as an approximation for $\pi$.

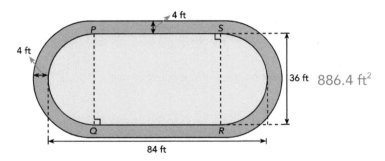

886.4 ft²

**10** The petal of a paper flower is created by cutting along the outlines of two overlapping quadrants within a square. Use 3.14 as an approximation for $\pi$.

a) Find the distance around the shaded part. 31.4 cm

b) Find the area of the shaded part. 57 cm²

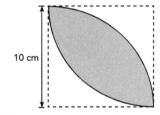

11 Wheels A and B are placed side by side on a straight road. The diameter of wheel A is 56 inches. The diameter of wheel B is 35 inches. Suppose each wheel makes 15 revolutions. Find the distance between the wheels after they have made these 15 revolutions.

Use $\frac{22}{7}$ as an approximation for $\pi$. 990 in.

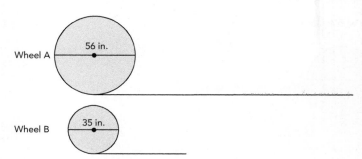

Wheel A    56 in.

Wheel B    35 in.

 12 Nine identical circles are cut from a square sheet of paper whose sides are 36 centimeters long. If the circles are as large as possible, what is the area of the paper that is left after all the circles are cut out? Use 3.14 as an approximation for $\pi$. 278.64 cm$^2$

13 A designer drew an icon as shown below. O is the center of the circle, and $\overline{AB}$ is a diameter. Two semicircles are drawn in the circle. If AB is 28 millimeters, find the area of the shaded part. Use $\frac{22}{7}$ as an approximation for $\pi$. 308 mm$^2$

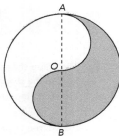

**Use graph paper. Solve.**

14 Mary wants to draw the plan of a circular park on graph paper. The coordinates of the center of the park are A (3, 4). The circle has a radius of 3 units.

a) Use a compass and draw the plan of the circular park on graph paper. See margin.

b) Assume that the y-axis points north and south. A barbecue pit is located at the northernmost part of the park. Plot and label the location of the barbecue pit as point B. Give the coordinates of point B. See margin for graph.; B (3, 7)

c) Connect points A, B, and the origin to form a triangle. Find the area of the triangle. 4.5 units$^2$

**DIFFERENTIATED INSTRUCTION**

**Through Visual Cues**

12 Some students may be put off by the seeming complexity of this problem. Suggest that they draw a diagram (three rows of three circles, all touching, with each row and column extending to the paper's edge). Then, ask them to consider how the area of the nine circles relates to the area of the square of paper and the area of paper left over when the circles are cut out.

14 a) and b)

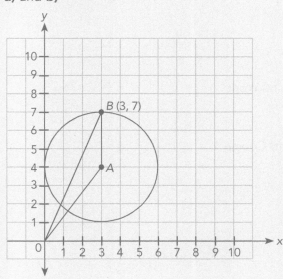

## Ticket Out the Door

A semicircular window has a diameter of 56 inches. To insulate the window for winter, Avi wants to cut out a piece of plastic and tape it over the window. How much plastic does he need? What length of tape does he need to tape along its edge? Show your work. Use $\frac{22}{7}$ for $\pi$. Avi needs approximately 1,232 in.² of plastic to cover the window:

$A = \frac{1}{2}\pi r^2 \approx \frac{1}{2} \cdot \frac{22}{7} \cdot 28^2$
$= 1,232$; and the distance around the semicircle $\approx \frac{1}{2} C + d =$
$(\frac{1}{2} \cdot \frac{22}{7} \cdot 56) + 56 = 88 + 56 = 144$ in.

 Also available on Teacher One Stop.

## Brain @ Work

1 This question requires students to visualize that the two arcs of the shaded part form the arc of a quadrant.

15 A wire is bent to make the shape below. The shape is made up of four identical circles. Each circle intersects two other circles. The four circles meet at a common point *T*, which is the center of square *PQRS*. Use $\frac{22}{7}$ as an approximation for $\pi$.

a) Find the length of the wire. 464 cm

b) Find the area of the whole shape. 2,016 cm²

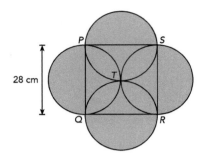

## Brain @ Work

1 The figure shows two identical overlapping quadrants. Find the distance around the shaded part. Use 3.14 as an approximation for $\pi$. Round your answer to the nearest tenth of a centimeter.

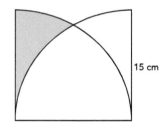

38.6 cm

15 cm

 **DIFFERENTIATED INSTRUCTION**

**Through Enrichment**

Because all students should be challenged, have all students try the Brain@Work exercises on these two pages.

For additional challenging practice and problem solving, see *Enrichment, Course 1*, Chapter 11.

**2** A cushion cover design is created from a circle of radius 7 inches, and 4 quadrants. Find the total area of the shaded parts of the design. Use $\frac{22}{7}$ as an approximation for $\pi$.

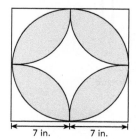

7 in.     7 in.

112 in.²

**3** Two identical wheels are placed along a straight path so that their centers are 9.31 meters apart. The radius of each wheel is 3.5 centimeters. They are pushed towards each other at the same time, each making one revolution per second. How long does it take for them to knock into each other? Use $\frac{22}{7}$ as an approximation for $\pi$. 21 s

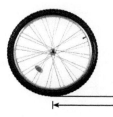 

9.31 m

**4** A stage prop is made up of a semicircle and a quadrant. Its area is 924 square inches. Find the value of x. Use $\frac{22}{7}$ as an approximation for $\pi$.

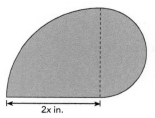

14

2x in.

Use the notes and the examples in the concept map to review these:

Diameter of a circle = 2r

Circumference of a circle = πd or 2πr where d is the diameter and r the radius

Length of a semicircle = $\frac{1}{2}$ πd or πr

Length of a quadrant = $\frac{1}{4}$ πd or $\frac{1}{2}$ πr

Area of a circle = πr²

Area of a semicircle = $\frac{1}{2}$ πr²

Area of a quadrant = $\frac{1}{4}$ πr²

## CHAPTER PROJECT

To widen student's mathematical horizons and to encourage them to think beyond the concepts taught in this chapter, you may want to assign the Chapter 11 project, A Triangle Inscribed in a Semicircle, available in *Activity Book, Course 1.*

# Chapter Wrap Up

## Concept Map

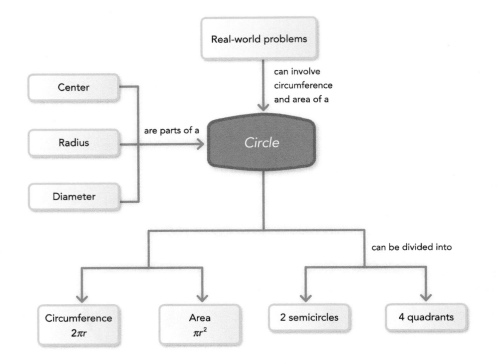

## Key Concepts

▶ All radii of a circle are equal.

▶ A diameter of a circle is twice its radius.

▶ The number π is the ratio of the circumference to the diameter of a circle.

## Vocabulary Review

Use these questions to review chapter vocabulary with students.

1. The distance around a circle is its __?__. circumference

2. A portion of a circle is a(n) __?__ of the circle. arc

3. A line segment connecting the center of a circle to a point on the circle is a(n) __?__ of the circle. radius

4. A line segment that connects two points on a circle and passes through its center is a(n) __?__ of the circle. diameter

5. A half of a circle is a(n) __?__. semicircle

6. A quarter of a circle is a(n) __?__. quadrant

🖱 Also available on Teacher One Stop.

# Chapter Review/Test

## Concepts and Skills

Find the circumference and area of each circle. Use $\frac{22}{7}$ as an approximation for $\pi$.

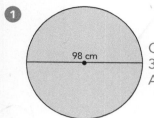

**1**

98 cm

Circumference:
308 cm;
Area: 7,546 cm$^2$

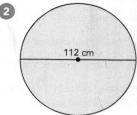

**2**

112 cm

Circumference:
352 cm;
Area: 9,856 cm$^2$

Find the distance around each semicircle. Use $\frac{22}{7}$ as an approximation for $\pi$.

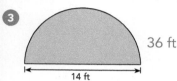

**3**

36 ft

14 ft

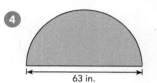

**4**

162 in.

63 in.

Find the distance around each quadrant. Round your answer to the nearest tenth. Use 3.14 as an approximation for $\pi$.

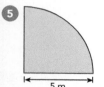

**5**

17.85 m

5 m

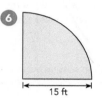

**6**

53.55 ft

15 ft

**Solve. Show your work.**

**7** The diameter of a flying disc is 10 inches. Find the circumference and area of the disc. Use 3.14 as an approximation for $\pi$. Circumference: 31.4 in.; Area: 78.5 in.$^2$

**8** The area of a compact disc is $452\frac{4}{7}$ square centimeters. What is the diameter of the compact disc? Use $\frac{22}{7}$ as an approximation for $\pi$. 24 cm

**9** The circumference of a circular table is 816.4 centimeters. Find the radius of the table. Use 3.14 as an approximation for $\pi$. 130 cm

## Chapter Assessment

Use the Chapter 11 Test A or B in *Assessments, Course 1* to assess how well students have learned the material in this chapter. These assessments are appropriate for reporting results to adults at home and administrators. Test A is shown on page 163A.

## TEST PREPARATION

For additional test prep

🖱 ExamView® Assessment Suite Course 1

🖱 Online Assessment System
my.hrw.com

## ⚠ RtI Intervention and Reteaching Recommendations

| Student Book B Review/Test Items | Assessments Chapter 11 Items | Chapter 11 Objectives | Reteach B Chapter 11 |
|---|---|---|---|
| **1** to **7** and **9** | Test A: 1 Test B: 1 | **Objective 1.** Identify the diameter and radius of a circle, and use them to find the circumferences of circles, semicircles, and quadrants. | Lesson 11.1 |
| **7** to **8** | Test A: 2 Test B: 2 | **Objective 2.** Use formulas to calculate the areas of circles, semicircles, and quadrants. | Lesson 11.2 |

## Problem Solving

 **Solve. Show your work.**

10 A water fountain shoots up a jet of water. The water falls back down onto the ground in the shape of a circle. Michelle wants the circle of water on the ground to be 0.7 meter wider on each side. She gradually increases the strength of the water jet. The area of the circle of water increases at 0.2 square meter per second. Use $\frac{22}{7}$ as an approximation for $\pi$.

a) Find the area of the original circle of water. 13.86 m²

b) Find the area of the larger circle of water. 24.64 m²

c) How long does it take for the original circle of water to become the larger circle of water? Round your answer to the nearest second. 54 s

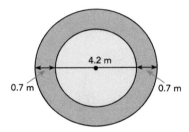

11 A machine in an assembly line stamps pieces of metal. The stamping plate on the machine travels in a path shaped like the arc of a quadrant as the stamping plate opens and closes. It takes the machine 5 seconds to open and close the stamping plate one time. Use $\frac{22}{7}$ as an approximation for $\pi$.

a) Find the total distance the outside edge of the stamping plate travels when the machine opens and closes one time. 121 cm

b) Find the speed of the stamping plate's outside edge in centimeters per second. 24.2 cm/s

c) Assume the machine starts and ends in an open position. How many seconds will it take the machine to stamp 500 pieces of metal? 2,500 s

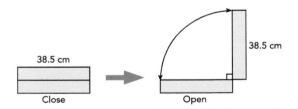

## RtI Intervention and Reteaching Recommendations

| Student Book B Review/Test Items | Assessments Chapter 11 Items | Chapter 11 Objectives | Reteach B Chapter 11 |
|---|---|---|---|
| 10 to 11 | Test A: 3–5<br>Test B: 3–5 | **Objective 3.** Solve real-world problems involving area and circumference of circles. | Lesson 11.3 |

**12** The figure shows four identical quadrants enclosed in a square. The side length of the square is 20 inches. Find the area of the blue part. Use 3.14 as an approximation for π. $86 \text{ in.}^2$

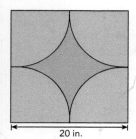

20 in.

**13** The figure shows 3 identical circles. *X*, *Y*, and *Z* are the centers of the circles, and the radius of each circle is 15 feet. $\frac{1}{6}$ of each circle is shaded. What is the total area of the shaded portion? Round your answer to the nearest tenth of a foot. Use 3.14 as an approximation for π. $353.3 \text{ ft}^2$

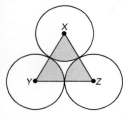

**14** The figure is made up of one semicircle and two quadrants. The distance around the figure is 97.29 inches. Find the value of *k*. Use 3.14 as an approximation for π. $23.5$

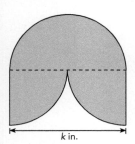

*k* in.

---

# Chapter 11 Tests A and B

Answer key appears in the *Assessments, Course 1*

---

**Test B, Assessments p. 107**

**Test A, Assessments p. 104**

Name: _____     Date: _____

**CHAPTER TEST A**

**⑪ Circumference and Area of a Circle**

```
[  /25  ]
Suggested Time:
30 min
```

**Concepts and Skills** (5 × 2 points = 10 points)

**Solve. Show your work.**

1. Find the circumference of a circle with radius 25 inches. Use 3.14 as an approximation for π.

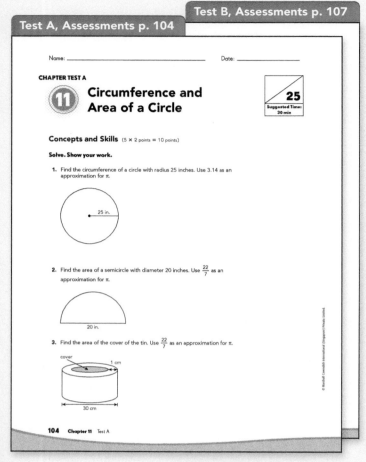

2. Find the area of a semicircle with diameter 20 inches. Use $\frac{22}{7}$ as an approximation for π.

20 in.

3. Find the area of the cover of the tin. Use $\frac{22}{7}$ as an approximation for π.

cover      1 cm

30 cm

---

**Test B, Assessments p. 108**

**Test A, Assessments p. 105**

Name: _____     Date: _____

4. The circumference of a circular plate is 94.2 centimeters. Find the radius of the plate. Use 3.14 as an approximation for π.

5. The diameter of a bicycle wheel is 14 inches. What is the distance travelled in feet when the wheel makes 3 revolutions? Use $\frac{22}{7}$ as an approximation for π.

**Problem Solving** (Question 6: 3 points, Questions 7 to 9: 3 × 4 points = 12 points)

**Solve. Show your work.**

6. The figure is made up of three semicircles. Find the area of the shaded part. Use 3.14 as an approximation for π.

8 cm      8 cm

---

**Test B, Assessments p. 109**

**Test A, Assessments p. 106**

Name: _____     Date: _____

7. The figure is made up of three identical semicircles and another two identical smaller semicircles. Find the perimeter of the figure. Use 3.14 as an approximation for π.

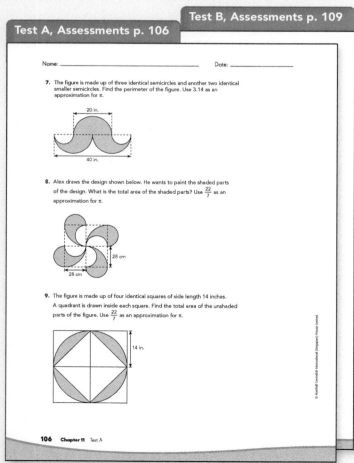

20 in.

40 in.

8. Alex draws the design shown below. He wants to paint the shaded parts of the design. What is the total area of the shaded parts? Use $\frac{22}{7}$ as an approximation for π.

28 cm

28 cm

9. The figure is made up of four identical squares of side length 14 inches. A quadrant is drawn inside each square. Find the total area of the unshaded parts of the figure. Use $\frac{22}{7}$ as an approximation for π.

14 in.

---

## CUMULATIVE REVIEW CHAPTERS 8–11

**1**
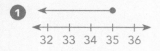
32  33  34  35  36

**2**
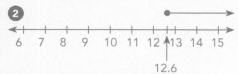
6  7  8  9  10  11  12  13  14  15
12.6

**3**

−2  −1  0  $\frac{41}{5}$  2

**4**
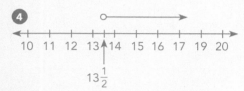
10  11  12  13  14  15  16  17  19  20
$13\frac{1}{2}$

**5  a)**
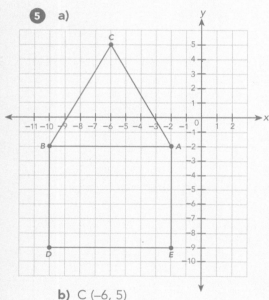

**b)** C (−6, 5)

**c)** D (−10, −9); E (−2, −9)

# Cumulative Review Chapters 8–11

## Concepts and Skills

**1 – 5** See margin.

**Represent the solution set of each inequality on a number line.** (Lesson 8.3)

**1** $p \le 35$

**2** $q \ge 12.6$

**3** $r < \frac{4}{5}$

**4** $s > 13\frac{1}{2}$

**Use graph paper. Plot the points on a coordinate plane and answer the question.** (Lesson 9.1)

**5  a)** Plot points A (−2, −2) and B (−10, −2) on a coordinate plane. Connect the two points to form a line segment.

**b)** Point C lies above $\overline{AB}$, and is 5 units away from the x-axis. If triangle ABC is an isosceles triangle with base $\overline{AB}$, find the coordinates of point C.

**c)** Points D and E lie below $\overline{AB}$ such that ABDE is a rectangle. If BD is 7 units, find the coordinates of points D and E.

**Find the area of each figure.** (Lesson 10.2)

**6**
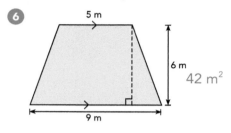
5 m
6 m
9 m
42 m$^2$

**7**
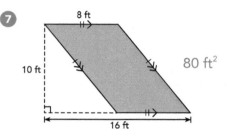
8 ft
10 ft
16 ft
80 ft$^2$

**Solve. Show your work.** (Lessons 8.2, 11.1, 11.2)

**8** The cost of a shirt is p dollars. The cost of a pair of pants is twice the cost of the shirt. If the cost of the pair of pants is t dollars, express t in terms of p. $t = 2p$

**9** A can has a circular base of diameter 8 centimeters. Find the area of this base. Use 3.14 as an approximation for π. 50.24 cm$^2$

**10** The cross section of a bowl is in the shape of a semicircle. The area of the semicircle is 77 square centimeters. Find its radius. Use $\frac{22}{7}$ as an approximation for π. 7 cm

**11** The circumference of a platinum ring is 44 millimeters. Find its radius. Use $\frac{22}{7}$ as an approximation for π. 7 mm

---

## Assessment

Use Benchmark Test A or B for Chapters 8–11 in *Assessments, Course 1* to assess how well students have learned the material taught in these Chapters. These assessments are appropriate for reporting results to adults at home and administrators.

Test B, Assessments p. 117

Test A, Assessments p. 110

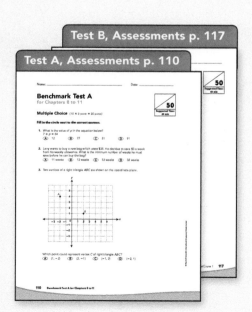

## TEST PREPARATION

For additional test prep

**ExamView® Assessment Suite Course 1**

**Online Assessment System** my.hrw.com

## Problem Solving

**Solve. Show your work.**

**12** Emily weighs *x* pounds. Jonathan weighs 3 times as much as Emily. If Jonathan weighs 81 pounds, write an equation in terms of *x* and solve it. (Chapter 8)  $3x = 81; 27$

**13** Kim has a bag of yo-yos. Some of the yo-yos are red. The rest are yellow. The ratio of the number of red yo-yos to the number of yellow yo-yos is 5 : 9. If Kim has a total of *b* yo-yos, how many more yellow yo-yos than red yo-yos are there? (Chapter 8)  $\frac{2}{7}b$

**14** The length of a rectangle is 4*n* centimeters, and it is twice as long as the width. The perimeter of the rectangle is twice as long as that of an equilateral triangle. Find the side length of the triangle in terms of *n*.  (Chapter 10)  *2n* centimeters

**15** The length of the minute hand of a clock is 6.5 centimeters. How far does the tip of the minute hand travel in an hour? Use 3.14 as an approximation for $\pi$.  40.82 cm  (Chapter 11)

**16** The area of trapezoid *ABCE* is 36 square meters. Find the height of the trapezoid. (Chapter 10)

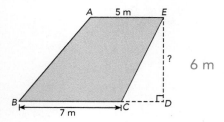

**Find the area of the shaded region.** (Chapter 10)

**17**

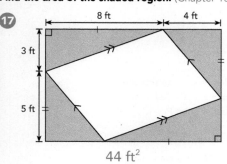

44 ft²

**18**

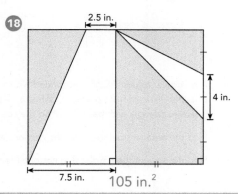

105 in.²

**Find the area of the shaded region. Use 3.14 as an approximation for π.** (Chapters 10, 11)

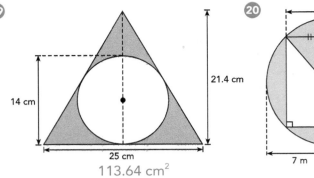

**19**

21.4 cm

14 cm

25 cm

113.64 cm²

**20**

10 m

10 m

7 m

78.86 m²

**Solve.**

**21** The diagram shows the plan of a square garden. The side length of each grid square is **2 meters.** (Chapters 9, 10)

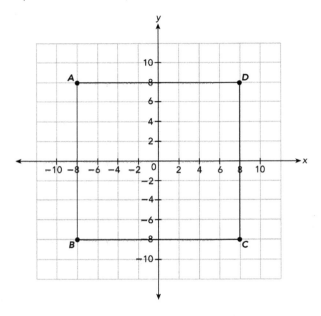

a) A triangular region *ABP* is surrounded with a wooden fence. The shortest possible distance from point *P* to $\overline{AB}$ is 8 meters, and triangle *ABP* is an isosceles triangle with base $\overline{AB}$. Find the coordinates of point *P*. P (0, 0)

b) Find the area and perimeter of the garden. Area: 256 m²; Perimeter: 64 m

c) Find the area of the garden that lies outside triangle *ABP* in square meters. 192 m²

**Solve. Use graph paper to answer the question.**

**22** An aspen tree is 300 centimeters tall. It grows 15 centimeters taller each month. The height of the tree, $h$ centimeters, over $t$ months is given by $h = 300 + 15t$. Copy and complete the table. Graph the relationship between $t$ and $h$. Use 1 unit on the horizontal axis to represent 1 month and 1 unit on the vertical axis to represent 15 centimeters. Start your vertical axis at 300 centimeters. (Chapters 8, 9) See margin.

**22**
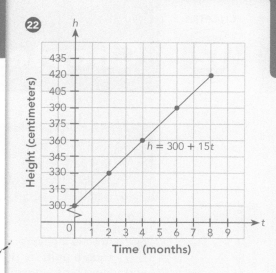

a)

| Time $t$ (months) | 0 | ? | 4 | 6 | 8 | 2 |
|---|---|---|---|---|---|---|
| Height $h$ (centimeters) | 300 | 330 | 360 | ? | ? | 390; 420 |

b) What is the height of the tree after 3 months? 345 cm

c) Assuming the growth of the tree is constant for the next year, what is the height of the tree after 10 months? 450 cm

d) If the tree is at least 360 centimeters tall, how many months have passed? Express your answer in the form of an inequality in terms of $t$, where $t$ stands for the number of months that have passed. $t \geq 4$

e) Name the dependent and independent variables. Dependent: $h$, Independent: $t$

**Solve. Show your work.**

**23** A circular garden is surrounded by a cement path that is 1.5 meters wide. Find the area of the path. Use 3.14 as an approximation for $\pi$. (Chapter 11)

40.035 m²

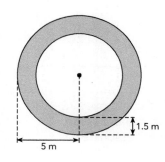

1.5 m

5 m

**24** Figure *PRSV* is a parallelogram. The length of $\overline{VU}$ and $\overline{UT}$ are equal. The area of parallelogram *QRSW* is 30 square inches. The length of $\overline{RS}$ is 6 inches. (Chapter 10)

a) Find the height of parallelogram *QRSW*. 5 in.

b) Find the area of triangle *PRV*. 30 in.²

c) If you did not know the length of $\overline{RS}$, explain how you could find the area of triangle *PRV*.
See margin.

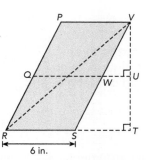

6 in.

**24** c) The area of triangle *PRV* is 30 square inches. Parallelograms *QRSW* and *PQWV* are identical. They have the same base and height. So, the area of parallelogram *PRSV* = 2 · 30 = 60 in.². Parallelogram *PRSV* is divided into 2 identical triangles, *PRV* and *RSV*. So, the area of triangle *PRV* = $\frac{1}{2}$ · 60 = 30 in.².

**CHAPTER**

**(12)**

# Chapter at a Glance

**Additional Teaching Support**

 Online Teacher's Edition

Online Professional Development Videos

| | | **CHAPTER OPENER** Surface Area and Volume of Solids Recall Prior Knowledge | **LESSON 12.1** Nets of Solids Pages 172–180 | **LESSON 12.2** Surface Area of Solids Pages 181–188 |
|---|---|---|---|---|
| **LESSON AT A GLANCE** | Pacing | 2 days | 2 days | 2 days |
| | Objectives | Area is measured in square units, and the surface area of a prism or pyramid is the sum of the areas of its faces. Volume is measured in cubic units, and the volume of a prism is the area of its base times its height. | • Identify the net of a prism and a pyramid. • Identify the solid formed by a given net. | • Find the surface area of a prism and a pyramid. |
| | Vocabulary | | net, pyramid | surface area |
| **RESOURCES** | Materials | | TRT28–TRT33* | |
| | Lesson Resources | Student Book B, pp. 168–171 *Assessments Course 1,* Chapter 12 Pre-Test *Transition Guide, Course 1,* Skills 48–50 | Student Book B, pp. 172–180 *Extra Practice B,* Lesson 12.1 *Reteach B,* Lesson 12.1 | Student Book B, pp. 181–188 *Extra Practice B,* Lesson 12.2 *Reteach B,* Lesson 12.2 |
| **Common Core** Standards for Mathematical Content | | **6.EE.1, 6.EE.2c, 6.G.2** Foundational for **6.G.4** | **6.G.4.** Represent three-dimensional figures using nets made up of triangles and rectangles. | **6.EE.1** Write and evaluate numerical expressions involving whole-number exponents. **6.G.4**...Use nets to find surface area. Apply in the context of solving real-world problems. |
| **Mathematical Practices** | | **4.** Model mathematics. **7.** Look for and use structure. | **3.** Construct arguments. **4.** Model mathematics. **6.** Attend to precision. | **2.** Reason. **8.** Express regularity in reasoning. |

*Teacher Resource Tools (TRT) are available on the Teacher One Stop.*

# Concepts and Skills Across the Courses

| **GRADE 5** | **COURSE 1** | **COURSE 2** |
|---|---|---|
| • Evaluate numerical expressions with grouping symbols. (5.OA.1) • Recognize volume as an attribute of solid figures and understand volume measurement by counting unit cubes. (5.MD.3, 5.MD.4) • Solve problems involving volume of prisms—whole-number edge lengths. (5.MD.5, 5.MD.5A–5. MD.5C) | • Evaluate numerical expressions with whole-number exponents. (6.EE.1) • Evaluate expressions that arise from formulas used in real-world problems. (6.EE.2c.) • Solve problems involving surface area and volume of prisms with fractional edge lengths. (6.G.2, 6.G.4) | • Use variables to represent quantities in problems. (7.EE.4, 7.EE.4a) • Solve problems involving volume and surface area of three-dimensional objects composed of triangles, quadrilaterals, polygons, cubes, and right prisms. (7.G.6) |

| LESSON 12.3<br>Volume of Prisms<br>Pages 189–199 | LESSON 12.4<br>Real-World Problems:<br>Surface Area and Volume<br>Pages 200–208 | CHAPTER<br>WRAP UP/REVIEW/TEST<br><br>Brain@Work<br>Pages 208–213 |
|---|---|---|
| 2 days | 2 days | 2 days |
| • Find the volume of a prism. | • Solve problems involving surface area and volume of prisms. | Reinforce, consolidate, and extend chapter skills and concepts. |
| cross section | | |
| unit cubes | | |
| Student Book B, pp. 189–199<br>*Extra Practice B*, Lesson 12.3<br>*Reteach B*, Lesson 12.3<br>*Activity Book*, Lesson 12.3 | Student Book B, pp. 200–208<br>*Extra Practice B*, Lesson 12.4<br>*Reteach B*, Lesson 12.4 | Student Book B pp. 208–213<br>*Activity Book*, Chapter 12 Project<br>*Enrichment*, Chapter 12<br>*Assessments*, Chapter 12 Test<br> ExamView® Assessment Suite<br>Course 1 |
| **6.EE.1** Write and evaluate numerical expressions involving whole-number exponents.<br>**6.G.2** Find the volume of a right rectangular prism with fractional edge lengths... | **6.EE.2c.** Evaluate expressions ... involving whole number exponents that arise from formulas used in real-world problems...<br>**6.G.2** Apply the volume formulas $V = \ell wh$ and $V = bh$. | |
| **4.** Model mathematics. **6.** Attend to precision. **8.** Express regularity in reasoning. | **1.** Solve problems/persevere.<br>**2.** Reason. **5.** Use tools strategically. | **1.** Solve problems/persevere. **7.** Look for and use structure. |

# Additional Chapter Resources

## TECHNOLOGY

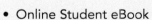
Every Day Counts®
## ALGEBRA READINESS

 • Online Student eBook

 • Interactive Whiteboard Lessons

 • Virtual Manipulatives

 • Teacher One Stop

 • ExamView® Assessment Suite Course 1

 • Online Professional Development Videos

**The April activities in the Pacing Chart provide:**

• **Review** of variable expressions (**Ch. 7 and 8: 6.EE.2**)

• **Review** of graphs of linear relationships (**Ch. 8 and 9: 6.EE.9**)

• **Practice** identifying vertices, faces, and edges of three-dimensional figures (**Ch. 12: 6.G.4**)

# Chapter 12  Surface Area and Volume of Solids

## Visualizing Solids

- In this chapter, students extend their knowledge of plane figures to solids. They relate solids to their nets and use nets to find surface area.

### Relating solids, nets, and diagrams

- Visualizing a solid based on a two-dimensional illustration is difficult for students. The Hands-On Activities in this chapter are useful for helping students relate concrete and pictorial models. Students fold nets into solids, break solids into nets, and draw both nets and solids.

- Color coding can help students relate concrete solids to their nets and to pictorial representations. Shading bases one color, congruent faces a second color, and each incongruent face a separate color, helps students to relate the position of a base or face of a solid to its location in a net, and also helps develop surface area and volume formulas.

- Reinforce the concrete-pictorial connection by having students draw prisms. Isometric dot paper can help students with their first drawings.

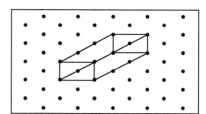

## Formulas and Algebraic Thinking

- Students use formulas and algebraic thinking to solve surface area and volume problems.

### Working with formulas

- Students need to use formulas thoughtfully. For example, in the formula for surface area of a cube with edge $e$, $S = 6e^2$, be sure students understand that the exponent applies only to $e$, not to $6e$.

- Help students see relationships among formulas by making a hierarchy. Use color coding to highlight relationships. For example, start with the formula for the volume of any prism, $V = B \cdot h$. Below that write the formula for the volume of a rectangular prism, $V = \ell \cdot w \cdot h$, and the formula for the volume of a triangular prism, $V = \left(\frac{1}{2} \cdot b \cdot h\right) \cdot h_1$, where $h$ is the height of the triangle and $h_1$ is the height of the prism. Below the formula for a rectangular prism, write the formula for the volume of a square prism, $V = e^2 \cdot h$, and below that write the formula for the volume of a cube, $V = e^2 \cdot e = e^3$.

## Solving real-world problems

- Students solve real-world problems involving the surface area and volume of prisms and pyramids.

A cardboard box in the shape of a rectangular prism is 4 inches long, 2 inches wide, and 3 inches high. How much cardboard was used to make the box?

**Solution**
Draw a net of the rectangular prism.

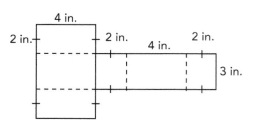

Total area of faces (excluding bases)
= $(4 + 2 + 4 + 2) \cdot 3$
= $12 \cdot 3$
= $36$ in.$^2$

Area of bases = $2 \cdot 4 \cdot 2$
         = $16$ in.$^2$

Surface area = $36 + 16$
         = $52$ in.$^2$

52 inches$^2$ of cardboard was used to make the box.

- It may be helpful for some students to calculate the area of each face and base, then find their sum.

# Differentiated Instruction

## Assessment and Intervention

| | ASSESSMENT | RtI STRUGGLING LEARNERS |
|---|---|---|
| **DIAGNOSTIC** | • Quick Check in Recall Prior Knowledge in Student Book B, pp. 169–171<br>• Chapter 12 Pre-Test in *Assessments* | • Skills 48–50 in *Transition Guide, Course 1* |
| **ON-GOING** | • Guided Practice<br>• Lesson Check<br>• Ticket Out the Door | • Reteach worksheets<br>• Extra Practice worksheets<br>• *Activity Book*, Chapter 12 |
| **END-OF-CHAPTER** | • Chapter Review/Test<br>• Chapter 12 Test in *Assessments*<br>• ExamView® Assessment Suite Course 1 | • Reteach worksheets |

### ELL ENGLISH LANGUAGE LEARNERS

Review the terms *prism, base, face,* and *pyramid.*

**Model** Draw a scalene triangular prism.

**Say** A *prism* is a type of solid. A prism has two *bases*. The bases are the same size and shape, and are parallel. The sides of a prism that are not bases are called *faces*. All the faces of any prism are parallelograms. (Here they are rectangles.) The faces of a prism connect its two bases.

**Model** Draw a square pyramid.

**Say** A *pyramid* is a type of solid. A pyramid has only one *base*. Any polygon can be the base of a pyramid. (Here the base is a square.) The sides of a pyramid are called *faces*. The faces of any pyramid are triangles. Each face of a pyramid begins at one side of the base and ends at the vertex.

For definitions, see Glossary, page 301, and  Online Multilingual Glossary.

### ADVANCED LEARNERS

• Students can explore how surface area and volume change as a prism is scaled up. Draw a rectangular prism 2 units by 2 units by 1 unit. Have students find its surface area and volume. Then have them double each dimension and find the surface area and volume again. Have students repeat the process two more times, recording all their measurements in a table.

• Start with the same rectangular prism. Have students triple its dimensions three times, finding its surface area and volume after each tripling, and recording all measurements in a table.

• Ask students to identify patterns as the dimensions of the prism are increased. (When doubled, surface area increases 4, or $2^2$, times and volume increases 8, or $2^3$, times. When tripled, surface area increases 9, or $3^2$, times and volume increases 27, or $3^3$, times.)

**To provide additional challenges use:**
• *Enrichment*, Chapter 12
• Student Book B, Brain@Work problem

# CHAPTER 12

# Surface Area and Volume of Solids

**12.1** Nets of Solids

**12.2** Surface Area of Solids

**12.3** Volume of Prisms

**12.4** Real-World Problems: Surface Area and Volume

## Chapter Vocabulary

Vocabulary terms are used in context in the student text. For definitions, see the Glossary at the end of the Student Book and the Online Multilingual Glossary

**cross section** A shape formed when a plane slices through a solid

**net** A plane figure that can be folded to make a solid

**pyramid** A solid whose base is a polygon and whose other faces are triangles that share a common vertex

**surface area** The total area of the faces (including the bases) and curved surfaces of a solid

💡 **BIG IDEA**

▶ Area is measured in square units, and the surface area of a prism or pyramid is the sum of the areas of its faces. Volume is measured in cubic units, and the volume of a prism is the area of its base times its height.

## How can math help you make candles?

To make a candle, you need some wax, a mold, and a wick. Then you melt the wax, pour it into the mold, and insert the wick. When the wax has cooled and hardened, you can wrap the candle in plastic.

How much wax will you need? To find out, you can find the volume of the mold. How much plastic wrap will you need? To find out, you can find the surface area of the candle.

## CHAPTER OPENER

Use the chapter opener to talk about volume and surface area in a real-life situation.

**Ask** When you light a candle, have you ever thought about how it was made? Liquid wax is poured into a mold, a wick is inserted into the wax and when the wax has cooled, the candle can be removed from the mold. The candle can then be wrapped in plastic.

**Ask** How can you find how much wax is used to make a candle? Find the volume of the mold. The volume of the wax used is equal to the volume of the mold. How can you find the surface area of a candle? The surface area is the sum of the areas of all of its faces.

In this chapter, you will learn how to measure the surface area and volume of solids in square and cubic units as summarized in the **Big Idea**.

## Recall Prior Knowledge

### Identifying special prisms

A prism is a solid with two parallel congruent bases joined by faces that are parallelograms. A prism is named by the shape of its base.

**Cube**

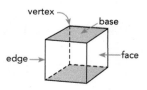

Each base of a cube is a square.

**Rectangular prism**

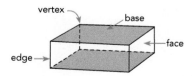

Each base of a rectangular prism is a rectangle.

**Triangular prism**

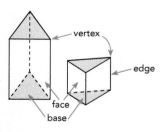

Each base of a triangular prism is a triangle.

### ✔ Quick Check

**Name each prism. In each prism, identify a base, a face, an edge, and a vertex.**

**1** 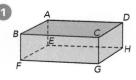  **2** 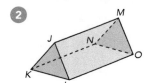  **3**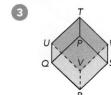

**1** – **3** See margin.

**1** Base: Answers vary. Sample: *ABCD*; *EFGH*
Face: Answers vary. Sample: *ABFE*; *BFGC*; *CDHG*; *AEHD*
Edge: Answers vary. Sample: $\overline{AB}$, $\overline{BC}$, $\overline{BF}$, $\overline{AD}$
Vertex: Answers vary. Sample: *A, B, C, D, E, F, G, H*

**2** Base: Answers vary. Sample: *JKL*; *MNO*
Face: Answers vary. Sample: *JKNM*; *JLOM*
Edge: Answers vary. Sample: $\overline{JM}$, $\overline{KL}$, $\overline{LO}$
Vertex: Answers vary. Sample: *J, K, L, M, N, O*

## RECALL PRIOR KNOWLEDGE

Use the ✔ **Quick Check** exercises or Chapter Pre-Test in *Assessments, Course 1*, to assess chapter readiness. For intervention suggestions see the chart below and on the following pages.

🖱 Additional online Reteach and Extra Practice worksheets from previous grades are also available. See the *Transition Guide*, Resource Planner for more information.

### 🔺 RtI Assessing Prior Knowledge

| ✔ Quick Check | *Assessments Course 1, Ch. 12* Pre-Test Items | Skill Objective | Transition Guide | 🖱 Online Resources Grades 4 and 5 |
|---|---|---|---|---|
| **1** to **3** | 1 | Identify special prisms. | Skill 48 | Reteach 5B, pp. 153–158; Extra Practice 5B, Lesson 14.1 |

Intervene with

**3** Base: Answers vary. Sample: *TUVW*; *PQRS*
Face: Answers vary. Sample: *UQRV*; *TPSW*
Edge: Answers vary. Sample: $\overline{TW}$, $\overline{SW}$, $\overline{UQ}$
Vertex: Answers vary. Sample: *P, Q, R, S, T, U, V, W*

## Finding the areas of rectangles, triangles, and trapezoids

**Rectangle**

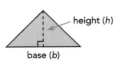

width (w)

length (ℓ)

Area of rectangle

= length · width

$A = \ell \cdot w$ or $\ell w$

**Triangle**

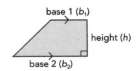

height (h)

base (b)

Area of triangle

$= \frac{1}{2} \cdot base \cdot height$

$A = \frac{1}{2} \cdot b \cdot h$ or $\frac{1}{2} bh$

**Trapezoid**

base 1 ($b_1$)

height (h)

base 2 ($b_2$)

Area of trapezoid

$= \frac{1}{2} \cdot height \cdot$ sum of parallel sides

$A = \frac{1}{2} \cdot h \cdot (b_1 + b_2)$ or $\frac{1}{2} h(b_1 + b_2)$

### ✓ Quick Check

**Find the area of each figure.**

**4**

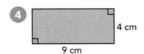

4 cm

9 cm

Area = _?_ · _?_    9; 4

      = _?_ cm²    36

**5**

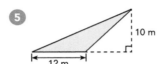

10 m

12 m

Area = $\frac{1}{2}$ · _?_ · _?_    12; 10

      = _?_ m²    60

**6**

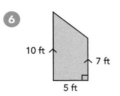

10 ft

7 ft

5 ft

Area = $\frac{1}{2}$ · _?_ · ( _?_ + _?_ )   5; 7; 10

      = $\frac{1}{2}$ · _?_ · _?_    5; 17

      = _?_ ft²    42.5

**7**

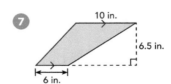

10 in.

6.5 in.

6 in.

Area = $\frac{1}{2}$ · _?_ · ( _?_ + _?_ )   6.5; 10; 6

      = $\frac{1}{2}$ · _?_ · _?_    6.5; 16

      = _?_ in.²    52

---

### ◭ RtI Assessing Prior Knowledge

| ✓ Quick Check | Assessments Course 1, Ch. 12 Pre-Test Items | Skill Objective | Intervene with | |
|---|---|---|---|---|
| | | | Transition Guide | ⊙ Online Resources Grades 4 and 5 |
| **4** to **7** | 2–4 | Find the areas of rectangles, triangles, and trapezoids | Skill 49 | Reteach 5A, pp. 159–167; Extra Practice 5A, Lessons 6.1, 6.2 |

## Finding the volumes of rectangular prisms

**Cube**

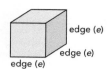

edge (e)
edge (e)
edge (e)

Volume of cube
= edge · edge · edge
$V = e \cdot e \cdot e$ or $e^3$

**Rectangular prism**

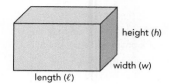

height (h)
width (w)
length (ℓ)

Volume of rectangular prism
= length · width · height
$V = \ell \cdot w \cdot h$ or $\ell w h$

## ☑ Quick Check

**Find the volume of each solid.**

**8**

8 in.
8 in.
8 in.

Volume = __?__ · __?__ · __?__   8; 8; 8

= __?__ in.³   512

**9**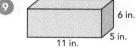

6 in.
5 in.
11 in.

Volume = __?__ · __?__ · __?__   11; 5; 6

= __?__ in.³   330

**10**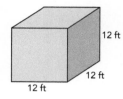

12 ft
12 ft
12 ft

Volume = __?__ · __?__ · __?__   12; 12; 12

= __?__ ft³   1,728

**11**

22 ft
13 ft
16 ft

Volume = __?__ · __?__ · __?__   16; 13; 22

= __?__ ft³   4,576

| ▲ RtI Assessing Prior Knowledge | | | | Intervene with |
|---|---|---|---|---|
| ☑ Quick Check | Assessments Course 1, Ch. 12 Pre-Test Items | Skill Objective | Transition Guide | 🖱 Online Resources Grades 4 and 5 |
| **8** to **11** | 5–6 | Find the volumes of rectangular prisms. | Skill 50 | Reteach 5B, pp. 163–164, 173–178; Extra Practice 5B, Lessons 15.1, 15.4, 15.5 |

## KEY CONCEPT

- A net of a solid is a plane figure that can be folded to form the solid.

## PACING

DAY **1** Pages 172–176

DAY **2** Pages 177–180

**Materials:** TRT28–33

**5-minute Warm Up**

Draw an example of each figure. For each figure, mark the sides that have equal lengths.

square          right triangle
rectangle       isosceles triangle
parallelogram   equilateral triangle

Check students' work.

Also available on Teacher One Stop.

---

# 12.1  Nets of Solids

**Lesson Objectives**
- Identify the nets of a prism and a pyramid.
- Identify the solid formed by a given net.

### Learn **Recognize the net of a cube.**

A cube is a type of prism. It can be cut along the red edges and flattened as shown.

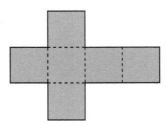

A cube has six square faces.

This figure is called a net of the cube.

More than one net may form the same solid figure. This is another net of the cube.

A net is a plane figure that can be folded to make a solid.

---

DAY **1**

### Learn **Recognize the net of a cube.**

**Model** Show students a paper cube made from a net of a cube (TRT28). Open up the cube so students can visualize how the cube can be cut along the red edges and flattened as shown in the text.

**Explain** Tell students that the figure formed is called a net of the cube. Emphasize that each face of the cube is a square.

**Ask** How many faces does the cube have? 6

**Explain** Tell students that a solid figure may have more than one net.

**Model** Distribute copies of the second net of the cube (TRT28), as shown in the text. Tell students to cut out and fold the nets along the dotted lines to form a cube like this:

**Summarize** A net of a cube is a plane figure that can be folded to form the cube.

# Hands-On Activity

**IDENTIFYING A CUBE FROM A NET**

Work in pairs.

**STEP 1** Trace and cut out each figure.

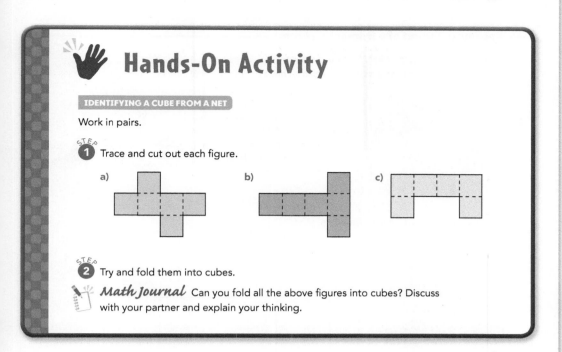

a)    b)    c)

**STEP 2** Try and fold them into cubes.

*Math Journal* Can you fold all the above figures into cubes? Discuss with your partner and explain your thinking.

## Learn Recognize the net of a rectangular prism.

This solid is a rectangular prism. It has six rectangular faces. Any two of the parallel faces can be its bases.

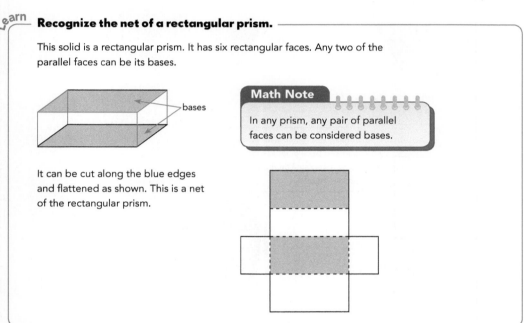

bases

**Math Note**

In any prism, any pair of parallel faces can be considered bases.

It can be cut along the blue edges and flattened as shown. This is a net of the rectangular prism.

---

## Hands-On Activity

This activity enables students to experience folding nets of a cube, and to realize that a plane figure made up of six squares is not necessarily a net of a cube. As an extension, students can be asked to try and find another net of a cube. You may want to use TRT28 for this activity, which includes nets for students to cut out.

**Caution** ///////

Some students may think that all six-square nets can form cubes. Point out that this is not always the case. Placement of the squares determines whether the net can actually be folded into a cube.

---

## Learn Recognize the net of a rectangular prism.

**Model** Show students a paper rectangular prism made from a net of a rectangular prism. Open up the rectangular prism so students can visualize how the prism can be cut along the blue edges and flattened as shown in the text.

**Explain** Tell students that the figure formed is a net of the rectangular prism.

**Ask** How many faces does the rectangular prism have? 6

**Explain** Point out to students that a rectangular prism has six faces. Lead them to deduce that for any rectangular prism, any pair of its parallel and congruent faces can be considered bases.

## Recognize the net of a triangular prism.

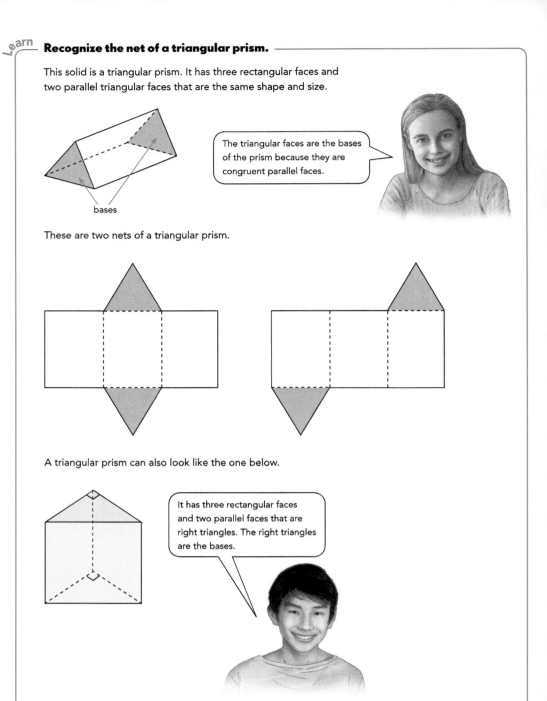

This solid is a triangular prism. It has three rectangular faces and two parallel triangular faces that are the same shape and size.

> The triangular faces are the bases of the prism because they are congruent parallel faces.

bases

These are two nets of a triangular prism.

A triangular prism can also look like the one below.

> It has three rectangular faces and two parallel faces that are right triangles. The right triangles are the bases.

## Recognize the net of a triangular prism.

**Model** Use the illustration of the triangular prism and its nets shown in the text to discuss the parts of a triangular prism. You may also want to have cut-out nets that can be folded into triangular prisms.

**Ask** Look at the prism that has purple bases. How many faces does it have? 5 What type of a triangle forms the bases of the triangular prism? equilateral triangle What shapes form the other faces? rectangles

**Model** Use the illustration of the prism whose bases are right triangles shown in the text. You may want to prepare a cut-out net for this prism.

**Ask** Look at prism that has yellow bases. What type of triangles are the bases of this prism? right triangle

**Explain** The triangular faces of a triangular prism can be right triangles, isosceles triangles, equilateral triangles, or scalene triangles.

**Summarize** The congruent parallel faces of a prism are called the bases of the prism. In a triangular prism, the triangular faces are the bases of the prism. In a cube, any pair of opposite faces can be the bases of the cube. In a rectangular prism, any pair of opposite faces can be the bases of the prism.

# Hands-On Activity

Work in pairs.

**STEP 1** Trace and cut out each net along the solid lines. Predict what figure can be formed from the net. Then fold the net to make the figure.

a)

b)

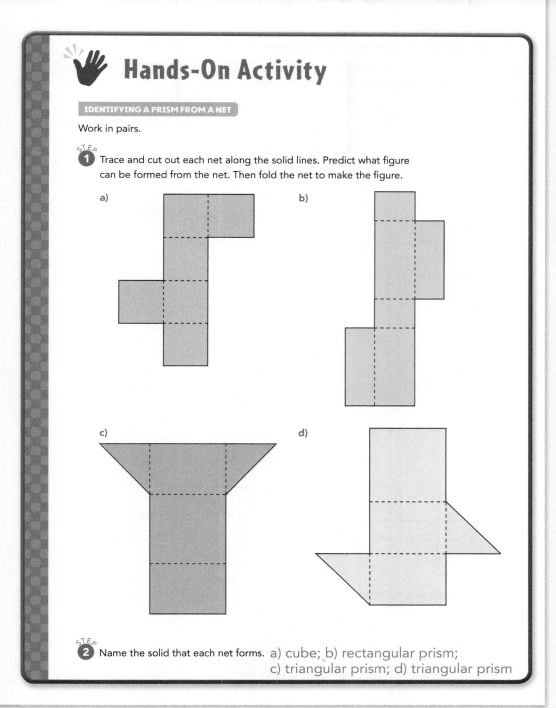

c)

d)

**STEP 2** Name the solid that each net forms. a) cube; b) rectangular prism;
c) triangular prism; d) triangular prism

## Hands-On Activity

This activity enables students to predict which solids can be formed from given nets, and then confirm their predictions by cutting out the nets and folding them to form the solids. Students can trace the nets shown in the text, or you may want to use TRT29, which has nets students can cut out.

## Guided Practice

 to 4 The questions give students practice visualizing solids formed from nets. Some students may benefit from tracing the nets shown, cutting them out, and folding them.

### 👥 DIFFERENTIATED INSTRUCTION

**Through Visual Cues**

1 If students have difficulty matching nets to a solid, suggest they start by answering two questions about the solid: 1) How many faces does it have? and 2) What shape(s) are its faces? With those two answers in mind, they can quickly assess each net and disqualify one or two solids as possible matches. Caution students that, once they have identified nets that have the correct number and type(s) of faces, they still need to mentally fold each net to determine if the faces are positioned correctly to form the solid.

## Guided Practice

**Match each solid with its net(s). There may be more than one net of each solid.**

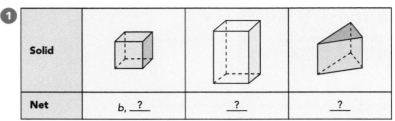

f; a and e; c and d

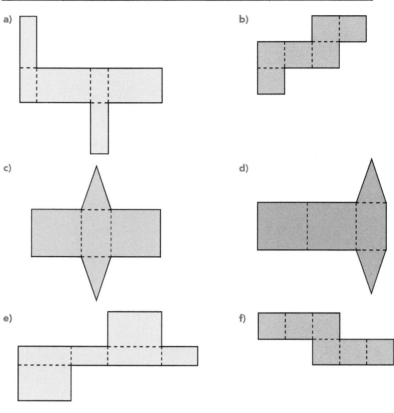

**Name the solid that each net forms.**

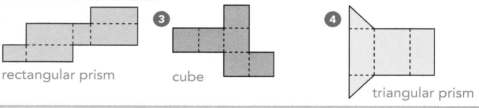

rectangular prism          cube          triangular prism

## Recognize the net of a square pyramid.

A pyramid has one base that is a polygon. The other faces are triangles that meet at a common vertex.

The solid shown below is a square pyramid. It has a square face, called the base, and four faces that are congruent isosceles triangles.

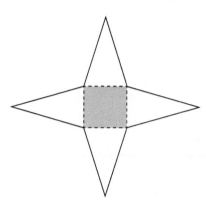

base →

> A pyramid is named by the shape of its base. So, this is a square pyramid.

These are two nets of the square pyramid.

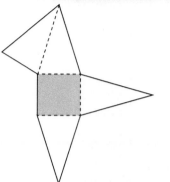

The solid shown below is a triangular pyramid.

> This triangular pyramid has an equilateral triangle for the base. The other three faces are congruent isosceles triangles.

This is a net of the triangular pyramid.

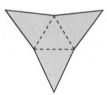

DAY 2

## Recognize the net of a square pyramid.

**Model** Use the illustration of the square pyramid shown in the text to discuss the parts of a pyramid. You may also want to have a cut-out net that can be folded into a square pyramid.

**Ask** What shape forms the base of the pyramid? Square What shapes form the other four faces? Isosceles triangles

**Model** Use the illustration of the triangular pyramid shown in the text to discuss the parts of a pyramid. You may also want to have a cut-out net that can be folded into a triangular pyramid.

**Explain** A pyramid is named by its base. This pyramid is a square pyramid. The page also shows a triangular pyramid.

**Ask** What type of triangle forms the base of the triangular pyramid? Equilateral triangle What type of triangles are the other three faces? Isosceles triangles

**Summarize** A square pyramid has a square base. A triangular pyramid has a triangular base. In both types of pyramid, the other faces are triangles.

 **Hands-On Activity**

This activity enables students to experience folding the nets of a triangular pyramid and a square pyramid. Students can trace the nets shown in the text, or you may want to use TRT30, which has nets students can cut out.

**1** Tell students that another name for a triangular pyramid is a tetrahedron.

---

👥 **DIFFERENTIATED INSTRUCTION**

**Through Visual Cues**

Once students have folded the nets into pyramids in **1**, have them shade the base of each solid one color and the other faces a different color. Point out that the triangular faces of a square pyramid are identical. Explain that, while the triangular faces of an *equilateral* triangular pyramid are identical, if the base is not equilateral, all three faces will not be identical. Then have students unfold the nets to help them visualize how nets form solids.

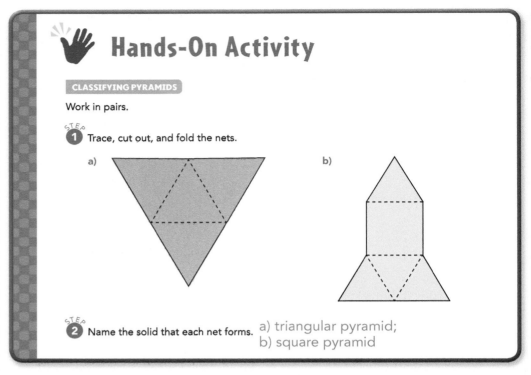

🖐️ **Hands-On Activity**

CLASSIFYING PYRAMIDS

Work in pairs.

STEP **1** Trace, cut out, and fold the nets.

a)

b)

STEP **2** Name the solid that each net forms.    a) triangular pyramid;
b) square pyramid

**Guided Practice**

**Match each solid with its net(s). There may be more than one net of each solid.**

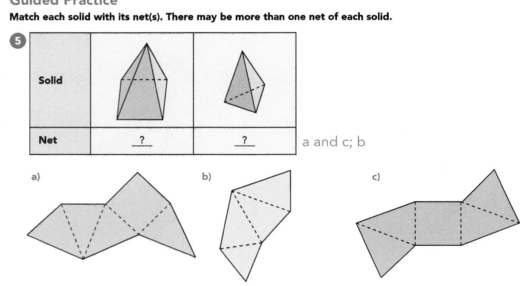

**5**

| Solid | | |
|---|---|---|
| Net | _?_ | _?_ |

a and c; b

a)    b)    c)

---

**Practice 12.1**

Basic ①–❽
Intermediate ⑨–⑭
Advanced ⑮–⑲

**Name each solid. In each solid, identify a base and a face that is not a base.** See margin.

**①**
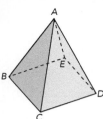

**②**
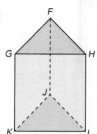

**③**
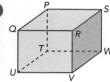

**④**
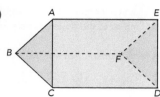

 **Name the solid that each net forms.**

**⑤**
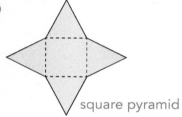
square pyramid

**⑥**
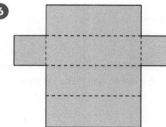
rectangular prism

**⑦**
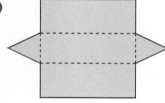
triangular prism

**⑧**
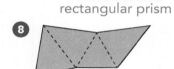
triangular pyramid

**Practice 12.1**

## Assignment Guide

DAY **1** All students should complete ❸, ❻, ⑨–⑭.

DAY **2** All students should complete ①, ②, ④, ❺, ❼ and ❽.

⑮–⑲ provide additional challenge.

Optional: *Extra Practice 12.1*
**Materials:** nets (TRT31–33)

① pyramid; Base: *BCDE*
Lateral face: Answers vary.
Sample: *ABC; ABE; ACD: AED*

② triangular prism; Base: Answers vary. Sample: *FGH; JKL*
Lateral face: Answers vary.
Sample: *FGKJ; FHLJ*

③ cube; Base: Answers vary.
Sample: *PQRS; TUVW*
Lateral face: Answers vary.
Sample: *PQUT; RSWV*

④ triangular prism; Base: Answers vary. Sample: *ABC; EDF*
Lateral face: Answers vary.
Sample: *ABFE; BCDF*

## ▲RtI Lesson Check

| Before assigning homework, use the following ... | to make sure students ... | Intervene with ... |
|---|---|---|
| Exercises ❺ and ⑨ | • can identify a solid that a net forms and fold a net to make a solid figure | Reteach 12.1 |
| ☀EXIT **Ticket Out the Door** | • describe solids and create nets of solids. | |

**Lesson 12.1** Nets of Solids   **179**

Nets are available for certain exercises:

**9** to **11** Use TRT31.
**12** to **14** Use TRT32.
**16** to **18** Use TRT33.

**Ticket Out the Door**

Work with a partner. Write down the name of one of the solids discussed in the lesson. Without showing the name, tell your partner which shape or shapes make up the faces of the solid (including the bases) and how many of each type. Then your partner should identify the solid and draw an example of a net that will form it. Possible answer: 4 triangles and 1 square; a square pyramid.

🖱 Also available on Teacher One Stop.

**Decide if each net will form a cube. Answer Yes or No.**

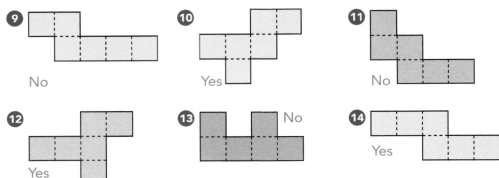

**9** No     **10** Yes     **11** No

**12** Yes     **13** No     **14** Yes

**Solve. Use graph paper.**

**15** In Exercises **9** to **14**, you identified some possible nets for a cube. There are other possible nets. Find all of the other possible nets. See margin.

**Decide if each net will form a prism. Answer Yes or No.**

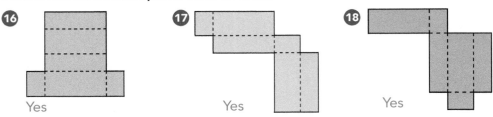

**16** Yes     **17** Yes     **18** Yes

**Copy the net of the rectangular prism shown. Then name the vertices that are not already labeled with a letter. Label the vertices.**

**19**

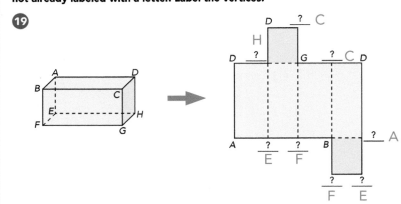

**15**

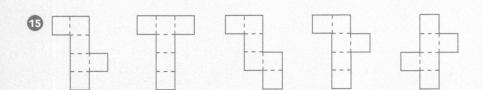

## Lesson Objective

- Find the surface area of a prism and a pyramid.

**Vocabulary**
surface area

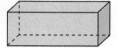 **Find the surface area of a cube.**

A wooden box is painted green all over.

The total area painted green is the surface area of the box.

A wooden cube has edges measuring 5 centimeters each. Find the surface area of the cube.

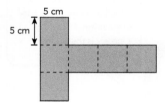
5 cm

To find the surface area, you can draw a net of the cube.

5 cm
5 cm

The net shows the six square faces of the cube.

The surface area of a cube is the area of its net.

Area of one square face = 5 · 5
= 25 cm²

$$\text{Area of one square face} = 5 \cdot 5 = 25 \text{ cm}^2$$

Surface area of cube = 6 · 25
= 150 cm²

$$\text{Surface area of cube} = 6 \cdot 25 = 150 \text{ cm}^2$$

**Math Note**

The surface area of a cube is equal to the sum of the areas of the six square faces.

If $S$ is the surface area, and $e$ is the length of an edge, then $S = 6e^2$.

## KEY CONCEPT

- The surface area of a prism or pyramid is the sum of the areas of its faces.

## PACING

DAY **1** Pages 181–183

DAY **2** Pages 184–188

**Materials:** none

 **5-minute Warm Up**

Identify the shape of each face of the following prisms or pyramids.

cube square
rectangular prism rectangle
triangular prism triangle
square pyramid triangle
triangular pyramid triangle

 Also available on Teacher One Stop.

---

 **Find the surface area of a cube.**

**Explain** Explain to students that the surface area of an object, such as the wooden box in the text, is the sum of the areas of all its faces.

**Model** Use the example in the text to demonstrate how to find the surface area of a cube.

**Ask** Look at the net of the cube. How many faces does the cube have? 6 What is the shape of each face? Square What is the length of each side of the square? 5 cm What is the area of each square? 5 × 5 = 25 cm² What is the surface area of the cube? 6 × 25 = 150 cm²

**Explain** The surface area of a cube is 6 times the area of a face. If the length of an edge is represented by $e$ and the surface area by $S$, then $S = 6(e \cdot e) = 6e^2$.

**DIFFERENTIATED INSTRUCTION**

**Through Multiple Representations**

Instead of grouping the four small faces into a single rectangle and then finding the combined area of the two bases, you may want to calculate the area of each face, then find the sum of those six areas. Emphasize that a rectangular prism has three pairs of congruent faces, as indicated by the colors of the faces here, and lead students through a calculation that focuses on the paired faces.

**Learn** **Find the surface area of a rectangular prism.**

A rectangular prism is 12 inches long, 8 inches wide, and 4 inches high. Find the surface area of the rectangular prism.

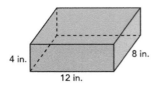

To find the surface area, draw a net of the rectangular prism.

The opposite faces of a rectangular prism are congruent rectangles. In the net, each pair of congruent faces is the same color.

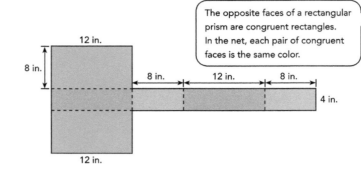

The surface area of a rectangular prism is the area of its net.

The total area of the two purple and two orange faces is equal to the area of the rectangle of length
12 + 8 + 12 + 8 = 40 inches and width 4 inches.
Total area of these four faces
= 40 · 4
= 160 in.²

Area of two green rectangular bases
= 2 · (12 · 8)
= 2 · 96
= 192 in.²

Surface area of rectangular prism
= 160 + 192
= 352 in.²

The length of the rectangle, (12 + 8 + 12 + 8) inches, is the perimeter of the base of the prism. The width, 4 inches, is the height of the prism.

**Math Note**
The surface area of a prism is equal to the perimeter of the base multiplied by the height and then added to the sum of the areas of the two bases.

**Learn** **Find the surface area of a rectangular prism.**

**Model** Use the example in the text to demonstrate how to find the surface area of a rectangular prism.

**Ask** Look at the net of the rectangular prism. How many faces does it have? 6 What is the shape of each face? A rectangle Now look at the two purple and two orange rectangles. What single shape do these four rectangles form? Another rectangle What is the length of this rectangle? 12 + 8 + 12 + 8 = 40 in. What is the width of this rectangle? 4 in. What is its area? 40 × 4 = 160 in.² What is the length and width of each green rectangular base? 12 in. and 8 in. What is the area of each rectangular base? 12 × 8 = 96 in.² What is the

total area of the two bases? 2 × 96 = 192 in.² What is the surface area of the rectangular prism? 160 + 192 = 352 in.²

**Explain** Point out to students that (12 + 8 + 12 + 8) inches is the perimeter of the base of the prism, and 4 inches is the height of the prism. So, the surface area of a prism is equal to the perimeter of the base multiplied by the height, plus the areas of the two bases.

## Guided Practice

**Complete.**

**1** A cube has edges measuring 6 centimeters each. Find the surface area of the cube.

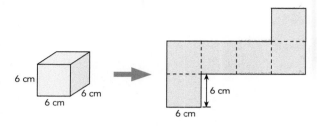

Area of one square face = __?__ · __?__  6; 6

= __?__ cm²  36

Surface area of cube = __?__ · __?__  36; 6

= __?__ cm²  216

**2** A rectangular prism measures 7 inches by 5 inches by 10 inches. Find the surface area of the prism.

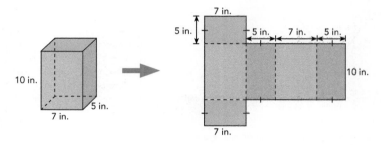

Total area of two orange and two purple faces = ( __?__ + __?__ + __?__ + __?__ ) · __?__  7; 5; 7; 5; 10

= __?__ · __?__  24; 10

= __?__ in.²  240

Area of two green rectangular bases = 2 · __?__ · __?__  7; 5

= __?__ in.²  70

Surface area of rectangular prism = __?__ + __?__  240; 70

= __?__ in.²  310

## Best Practices

**1** Write the formula for the surface area of the cube.

Surface area = 6 · 6 cm · 6 cm
= 216 cm²

Ask students to identify what each of the three terms in the formula represents. *(The first 6 stands for the 6 faces of the cube; the first "6 cm" is the length of one square face; and the second "6 cm" is the width of one square face.)*

## Guided Practice

**2** Students should be encouraged to solve using the formula Surface area of prism = perimeter of base × height + total area of the two bases. Remind students of the meaning of the tick marks shown in the net of the figure, that all sides with that mark are of equal length.

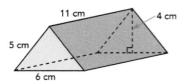

**Find the surface area of a triangular prism.**

The triangular prism shown has three rectangular faces. Its bases are congruent isosceles triangles. Find the surface area of the triangular prism.

This is a net of the triangular prism.

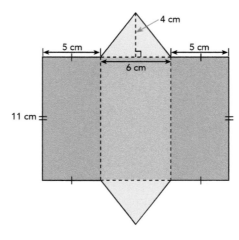

The surface area of a triangular prism is the area of its net.

Total area of two purple rectangles and orange rectangle = (5 + 6 + 5) · 11
$$= 16 \cdot 11$$
$$= 176 \text{ cm}^2$$

Area of two yellow triangular bases = $2 \cdot \left( \frac{1}{2} \cdot 6 \cdot 4 \right)$
$$= 2 \cdot 12$$
$$= 24 \text{ cm}^2$$

Surface area of triangular prism = 176 + 24
$$= 200 \text{ cm}^2$$

The surface area of the triangular prism is 200 square centimeters.

---

**DAY 2**

**Find the surface area of a triangular prism.**

**Model** Use the example in the text to demonstrate how to find the surface area of a triangular prism.

**Ask** Look at the net of the triangular prism. How many faces does it have? 5 What are the shapes of the faces? 3 rectangles and 2 isosceles triangles What single shape do the three rectangles form? Another rectangle What is the length of this rectangle? 5 + 6 + 5 = 16 cm What is the width of this rectangle? 11 cm What is its area? 16 · 11 = 176 cm² What is the base and height of each

triangular base? 6 cm and 4 cm What is the area of each triangular base? $\frac{1}{2}$ · 6 · 4 = 12 cm² What is the total area of the two bases? 2 · 12 = 24 cm² What is the surface area of the triangular prism? 176 + 24 = 200 cm²

**Explain** Point out that (5 + 6 + 5) centimeters is the perimeter of the triangular base and 11 centimeters is the height of the prism. So, the surface area of the triangular prism is also equal to perimeter of base × height + total area of two bases.

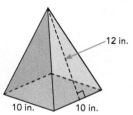

**Learn** Find the surface area of a pyramid.

This pyramid has a square base measuring 10 inches on each side. It has four faces that are congruent isosceles triangles. The height of each triangle is 12 inches. Find the surface area of the pyramid.

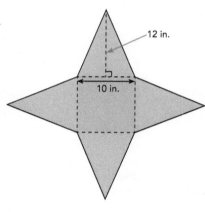

This is a net of the pyramid.

> The surface area of a pyramid is the area of its net.

Area of square base
= 10 · 10
= 100 in.²

Area of four triangles
= 4 · ($\frac{1}{2}$ · 10 · 12)
= 4 · 60
= 240 in.²

Surface area of the pyramid
= 100 + 240
= 340 in.²

The surface area of the pyramid is 340 square inches.

**Learn** **Find the surface area of a pyramid.**

**Model** Use the example in the text to demonstrate how to find the surface area of a pyramid.

**Ask** Look at the net of the pyramid. How many faces does the pyramid have? 5 What are the shapes of the faces? A square and 4 isosceles triangles What is the length of each side of the square? 10 in. What is the area of the square? 10 × 10 = 100 in.² What are the

base and the height of each triangular face? 10 in. and 12 in. What is the area of each triangular face? $\frac{1}{2}$ · 10 · 12 = 60 in.² What is the total area of the four triangular faces? 4 × 60 = 240 in.² What is the surface area of the pyramid? 100 + 240 = 340 in.²

**Summarize** Lead students to conclude that the surface area of a pyramid is the sum of the areas of its faces.

**Guided Practice**

 Encourage students to find the surface area by using the formula Surface area of prism = perimeter of base × height + total area of two bases.

In ③, watch out for students who mistakenly think that the triangular prism shown is a pyramid.

**Complete.**

③ The triangular prism shown has three rectangular faces. Its bases are congruent right triangles. Find the surface area of the triangular prism.

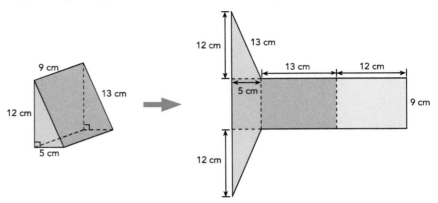

Total area of orange, purple, and yellow rectangles = ( _?_ + _?_ + _?_ ) · _?_   5; 13; 12; 9

= _?_ · _?_   30; 9

= _?_ cm²   270

Area of two green triangular bases = $2 \cdot \left( \frac{1}{2} \cdot \underline{\ ?\ } \cdot \underline{\ ?\ } \right)$ = _?_ cm²   12; 5; 60

Surface area of triangular prism = _?_ + _?_ = _?_ cm²   270; 60; 330

④ Alicia makes a pyramid that has an equilateral triangle as its base. The other three faces are congruent isosceles triangles. She measures the lengths shown on the net of her pyramid. Find the surface area of the pyramid.

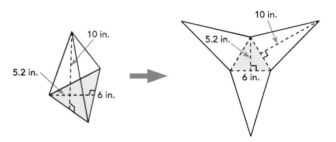

Area of yellow triangle = $\frac{1}{2} \cdot \underline{\ ?\ } \cdot \underline{\ ?\ }$ = _?_ in.²   6; 5.2; 15.6

Area of three blue triangles = $3 \cdot \frac{1}{2} \cdot \underline{\ ?\ } \cdot \underline{\ ?\ }$ = _?_ in.²   6; 10; 90

Surface area of triangular pyramid = _?_ + _?_ = _?_ in.²   15.6; 90; 105.6

# Practice 12.2

**Solve.**

① A cube has edges measuring 6 centimeters each. Find the surface area of the cube. $216 \, cm^2$

② The edge length of a cube is 3.5 inches. Find the surface area of the cube. $73.5 \, in.^2$

③ A closed rectangular tank measures 12 meters by 6 meters by 10 meters. Find the surface area of the tank. $504 \, m^2$

④ A closed rectangular tank has a length of 8.5 feet, a width of 3.2 feet, and a height of 4.8 feet. Find the surface area of the tank. $166.72 \, ft^2$

⑤ A triangular prism with its measurements is shown. Find the surface area of the prism. $660 \, cm^2$

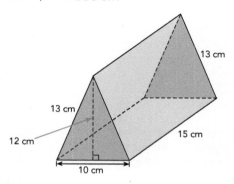

13 cm
13 cm
12 cm
15 cm
10 cm

⑥ A triangular prism with its measurements is shown. Find the surface area of the prism. $112.2 \, in.^2$

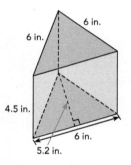

6 in.
6 in.
4.5 in.
6 in.
5.2 in.

## Practice 12.2

### Assignment Guide

**DAY 1** All students should complete ①–⑤.

**DAY 2** All students should complete ⑥–⑨.

⑩–⑪ provide additional challenge.

Optional: *Extra Practice 12.2*

---

### ▲ RtI Lesson Check

| Before assigning homework, use the following ... | to make sure students ... | Intervene with ... |
|---|---|---|
| Exercises ③, ⑤, and ⑦ | • can find the surface area of a prism or pyramid | Reteach 12.2 |
| **EXIT** Ticket Out the Door | • understand how to find the surface area of prisms and pyramids | |

**Through Modeling**

 **9** Suggest students draw a diagram of the room. **Ask:** What solid figure is formed? *(A rectangular prism)* How many faces does a rectangular prism have? *(6)* Is Ms. Jones going to paint all 6 faces of the prism? *(No)* Which faces is she going to paint? *(Just the 4 walls)* Why does the problem state the total area of the doors and windows? *(The doors and windows are on the walls but will not be painted.)*

 **Ticket Out the Door**

In your own words, explain how to find the surface area of a cube, prism, or pyramid. Possible answer: First, draw a net for the solid. Then label the dimensions of the faces in the net. Use the appropriate area formula to calculate the area of each face. Finally, find the sum of the areas of all the faces.

🖱 Also available on Teacher One Stop.

**Solve.**

 **7** A square pyramid has four faces that are congruent isosceles triangles. Find the surface area of the square pyramid if the base area is 169 square centimeters. 559 cm²

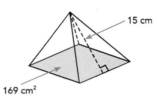

15 cm

169 cm²

**8** The faces of this solid consist of four identical trapezoids and two squares. The side lengths of the two squares are 4 centimeters and 8 centimeters. The height of each trapezoid is 12 centimeters. Find the surface area of the solid.

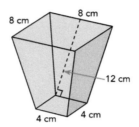

8 cm
8 cm
12 cm
4 cm    4 cm

368 cm²

**9** Ms. Jones wants to paint the walls of a rectangular room. The height of the room is 8 feet. The floor is 10.5 feet wide and 12 feet long. The doors and windows total 24 square feet and are not going to be painted. Find the total area of the walls that need to be painted. 336 ft²

**10** The base of a prism has *n* sides. Write an expression for each of the following.

a)  the number of vertices  $2n$

b)  the number of edges  $3n$

c)  the number of faces  $n + 2$

**11** The base of a pyramid has *m* sides. Write an expression for each of the following.

a)  the number of vertices  $m + 1$

b)  the number of edges  $2m$

c)  the number of faces  $m + 1$

## Lesson Objective
• Find the volume of a prism.

**Vocabulary**

cross section

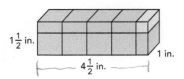

**Derive the formula for the volume of a rectangular prism.**

A rectangular prism is $4\frac{1}{2}$ inches long, 1 inch wide, and $1\frac{1}{2}$ inches high.

Find its volume.

$1\frac{1}{2}$ in.

1 in.

$4\frac{1}{2}$ in.

The volume of a cube with an edge length of 1 inch is 1 in.³. This is read as "1 cubic inch."

From the diagram, the prism is made up of four green cubes,
five blue half cubes, and one yellow quarter cube.
To find the total volume of the different sized blocks:

Volume of one green cube = 1 in.³

Volume of one blue half cube = $\frac{1}{2} \cdot 1 = \frac{1}{2}$ in.³

Volume of one yellow quarter cube = $\frac{1}{4} \cdot 1 = \frac{1}{4}$ in.³

Volume of prism = $(4 \cdot 1) + \left(5 \cdot \frac{1}{2}\right) + \left(1 \cdot \frac{1}{4}\right)$

$= 4 + \frac{5}{2} + \frac{1}{4}$

$= 6\frac{3}{4}$ in.³

Length × width × height = $4\frac{1}{2} \cdot 1 \cdot 1\frac{1}{2}$

$= \frac{9}{2} \times 1 \times \frac{3}{2}$

$= \frac{27}{4}$

$= 6\frac{3}{4}$ in.³

The volume of any rectangular prism of length $\ell$, width $w$, and height $h$ is given by

$$V = \ell wh$$

## KEY CONCEPTS
• The volume of a prism is the area of the base multiplied by the height.

• The volume of a rectangular prism is length × width × height.

## PACING

**DAY 1**   Pages 189–190

**DAY 2**   Pages 191–199

**Materials:** unit cubes

**5-minute Warm Up**

Evaluate these numerical expressions:

1. $\frac{3}{5} \times \frac{10}{7}$   $\frac{6}{7}$   2. $3\frac{3}{4} \times \frac{6}{5}$   $4\frac{1}{2}$

3. $\frac{2}{3} \times 5\frac{1}{4} \times \frac{2}{9}$   $\frac{7}{9}$

4. $1\frac{1}{2} \times \frac{5}{6} \times \frac{3}{10}$   $\frac{3}{8}$

5. $2.5 \times 4.8$   12

6. $3.2 \times 6 \times 8.3$   159.36

 Also available on Teacher One Stop.

---

**DAY 1**

**Derive the formula for the volume of a rectangular prism.**

**Model** Use the example in the text to demonstrate how to find the volume of a rectangular prism whose edges are not all whole numbers.

**Ask** What are the length, width, and height of the rectangular prism? $4\frac{1}{2}$ in., 1 in., and $1\frac{1}{2}$ in. How many green, blue, and yellow blocks make up the prism? 4, 5, 1 What fraction of the green block's volume is a blue block's volume? $\frac{1}{2}$ What fraction of a green block's volume is a yellow block's volume? $\frac{1}{4}$ What are the dimensions of each green block? 1in. by 1 in. by 1 in.

What is the volume of each green block? $1 \times 1 \times 1$ = 1 in.³ What is the volume of each blue block? $\frac{1}{2} \times 1$ = $\frac{1}{2}$ in.³ What is the volume of the yellow block? $\frac{1}{4} \times 1$ = $\frac{1}{4}$ in.³ What is the volume of the rectangular prism? $4 \times 1 + 5 \times \frac{1}{2} + 1 \times \frac{1}{4} = 6\frac{3}{4}$ in.³

**Explain** If you multiply the prism's length by its width by its height, you will get $4\frac{1}{2} \times 1 \times 1\frac{1}{2} = \frac{9}{2} \times 1 \times \frac{3}{2} = \frac{27}{4} = 6\frac{3}{4}$ in.³. So, for any rectangular prism, the volume is equal to length × width × height.

## Guided Practice

 **1** to **3** Students who have difficulty evaluating the product of length, width, and height may need to review multiplication of fractions and decimals.

---

### DIFFERENTIATED INSTRUCTION

**Through Modeling**

Be sure students recognize that, while surface area is expressed in square units, volume is expressed in cubic units. Draw a square and label its length "2 cm" and its width "2 cm." Beneath it, calculate the area: 2 cm · 2 cm = 4 cm². Point out that to find surface area, you multiply two dimensions, length and width. Each of these is measured in centimeters, so the resulting unit is cm · cm = cm². Next, draw a cube and label its length "2 cm," its width "2 cm," and its height "2 cm." Beneath it, calculate the volume: 2 cm · 2 cm · 2 cm = 8 cm³. Point out that to find volume, you multiply three dimensions: length, width, and height. Each of those dimensions is measured in centimeters, so the resulting unit is cm · cm · cm = cm³.

---

### $^{Learn}$ **Use a formula to find the volume of a rectangular prism.**

A rectangular prism measures 8.4 centimeters by 5.5 centimeters by 9 centimeters. What is the volume of the rectangular prism?

$V = \ell wh$
$= 8.4 \cdot 5.5 \cdot 9$
$= 415.8 \text{ cm}^3$

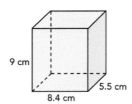

### Guided Practice

**Find the volume of each rectangular prism.**

**1** Length = $5\frac{1}{4}$ in.
Width = 6 in.
Height = 12 in.

$V = \ell wh$

$= \underline{\ \ ?\ \ } \cdot \underline{\ \ ?\ \ } \cdot \underline{\ \ ?\ \ }$  $5\frac{1}{4}; 6; 12$

$= \underline{\ \ ?\ \ } \text{ in.}^3$  378

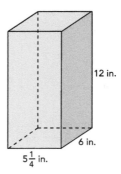

**2** Length = 8 cm
Width = 7.2 cm
Height = 3 cm

$V = \ell wh$

$= \underline{\ \ ?\ \ } \cdot \underline{\ \ ?\ \ } \cdot \underline{\ \ ?\ \ }$  8; 7.2; 3

$= \underline{\ \ ?\ \ } \text{ cm}^3$  172.8

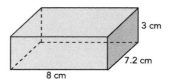

**3** Length = 4 ft
Width = 3 ft
Height = $8\frac{1}{3}$ ft

Volume = $\underline{\ \ ?\ \ }$  $\ell wh$

$= \underline{\ \ ?\ \ } \cdot \underline{\ \ ?\ \ } \cdot \underline{\ \ ?\ \ }$  $4; 3; 8\frac{1}{3}$

$= \underline{\ \ ?\ \ } \text{ ft}^3$  100

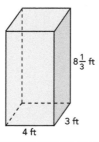

---

### $^{Learn}$ **Use a formula to find the volume of a rectangular prism.**

**Model** Use the example in the text to demonstrate how to apply the formula Volume = length × width × height to find the volume of a rectangular prism with non-whole number edges.

**Ask** What are the length, width, and height of the rectangular prism? 8.4 cm, 5.5 cm, and 9 cm. How do you find the volume of the prism? Multiply the length by the width by the height. What is the volume of the prism? 8.4 × 5.5 × 9 = 415.8 cm³

## Learn Form cross sections of prisms.

The rectangular prism below is sliced in two places: along segment $\overline{AB}$ parallel to the bases and along segment $\overline{CD}$ parallel to the bases.

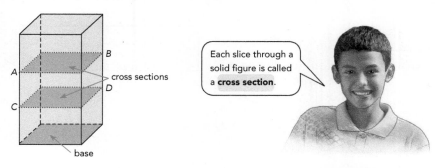

Each slice through a solid figure is called a **cross section**.

The cross section formed through $\overline{AB}$ is a rectangle that is congruent to each base.

The cross section through $\overline{CD}$ is also congruent to each base.

Any cross section of a rectangular prism that is parallel to the bases will be congruent to the bases. So, the prism has uniform cross sections.

Now, look at a triangular prism.

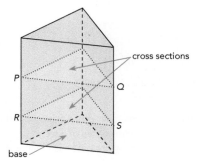

This triangular prism has right triangles for its bases. It is sliced through at both $\overline{PQ}$ and $\overline{RS}$ parallel to its bases. These cross sections are triangles that are congruent to the bases.

So, a triangular prism also has uniform cross sections when sliced parallel to the bases.

### Math Note

In general, any prism has uniform cross sections when it is sliced parallel to the bases of the prism.

---

DAY 2

## Learn Form cross sections of prisms.

**Model** Use the first illustration to show students what uniform cross sections are.

**Explain** When you slice the prism parallel to the bases, what you see is a cross section of the prism.

**Ask** What is the shape of the cross section? A rectangle What can you say about this rectangle? It is congruent to the base of the prism. Will you get the same cross section if you slice the prism anywhere parallel to the bases? Yes

**Explain** When you slice a rectangular prism parallel to the bases, the cross sections are all the same in shape

and size. You say the rectangular prism has uniform cross sections.

**Model** Use the second illustration to show what a uniform cross section of a triangular prism looks like.

**Explain** Just like the rectangular prism, a triangular prism also has uniform cross sections when sliced parallel to the bases.

**Summarize** Lead students to conclude that any prism has uniform cross sections when it is sliced parallel to its bases.

# Guided Practice

**4** Ask students what the shape of the given cross section is. Then ask whether the cross sections become smaller or larger rectangles when the cube is sliced parallel to the first cross section in each direction.

**6** Ask students what the shape of the given cross section is. Then ask whether the parallel cross sections become larger or smaller rectangles as the prism is sliced in each direction.

## Guided Practice

**Tell whether slices parallel to each given slice will form uniform cross sections. If not, explain why not.**

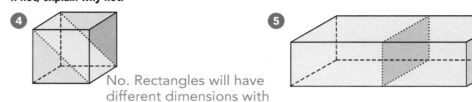

**4** No. Rectangles will have different dimensions with other cuts.

**5** Yes

**6**

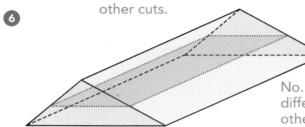

No. Rectangles will have different dimensions with other cuts.

## ᴸᵉᵃʳⁿ Use a formula to find the volume of any prism.

This is a rectangular prism.

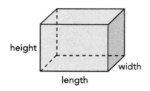

height
width
length

Volume of a rectangular prism = length · width · height
Since length · width = area of base,
volume of a prism = area of base · height.

Because all prisms have a uniform cross section when sliced parallel to the base, this formula applies to all prisms.

> Volume of a prism with uniform cross sections
> = area of base · height
> or $V = Bh$

**Caution** ▰▰▰▰▰▰▰
In the formula $V = Bh$, $B$ represents the area of the base, not a length.

## ᴸᵉᵃʳⁿ Use a formula to find the volume of any prism.

**Model** Use the example in the text to demonstrate how the volume of a rectangular prism is also equal to the area of a base multiplied by the height.

**Ask** What is the volume of a rectangular prism in terms of its length, width, and height? Length × width × height

**Ask** What is length × width equal to? Area of the base Is there another way to find the volume of a rectangular prism? Yes; Area of base × height or $V = Bh$

**Explain** Emphasize that the formula $V = Bh$ is true for all prisms with uniform cross sections. Remind students also that in the formula $V = Bh$, $B$ represents the area of the base, not a length.

a) The prism shown has bases that are parallelograms. The area of a base is 20 square inches. The height of the prism is 4 inches. Find the volume of the prism.

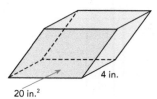

20 in.²

$V = Bh$
$= 20 \cdot 4$
$= 80$ in.³

The volume of the prism is 80 cubic inches.

b) A triangular prism with its measurements is shown. Find the volume of the prism.

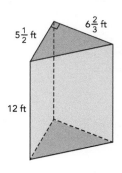

This triangular prism has a right triangle as its base.

Area of right triangle base

$= \dfrac{1}{2} \cdot 5\dfrac{1}{2} \cdot 6\dfrac{2}{3}$

$= \dfrac{1}{2} \cdot \dfrac{11}{2} \cdot \dfrac{20}{3}$

$= \dfrac{55}{3}$ ft²

$V = Bh$

$= \dfrac{55}{3} \cdot 12$

$= 220$ ft³

**Caution**

The base $b$ of the triangular base is not the same as the base $B$ of the prism.

The volume of the prism is 220 cubic feet.

**DIFFERENTIATED INSTRUCTION**

**Through Enrichment**

Draw a rectangular prism with base dimensions labeled "4 in." and "5 in.," and the height of the prism labeled "4 in." Have a volunteer calculate the volume of the prism (80 in.³). Then compare the volume and dimensions of the rectangular prism to those of the prism with parallelogram bases shown in the Learn. Tell students that the volumes of two solids are equal if the areas of their corresponding cross sections are always equal and their heights are the same. Have them research this principle known as Cavalieri's principle to see how it applies to prisms and cylinders, including oblique ones. You may want to ask students to prepare posters illustrating Cavalieri's Principle.

**Learn continued**

**Model** Use the examples in the text to demonstrate how the formula Volume of prism = area of base × height is applied.

a) **Ask** What is the shape of the base of the prism? A parallelogram What is the area of the base? 20 in.² What is the height of the prism? 4 in. How can you find the volume? By using the formula $V = Bh$ $= 20 \times 4 = 80$ in.³

b) **Ask** What is the shape of the base of the prism? A right triangle What are the base and height of this triangle? $5\dfrac{1}{2}$ ft and $6\dfrac{2}{3}$ ft What is the area of the base? $\dfrac{1}{2} \times 5\dfrac{1}{2} \times 6\dfrac{2}{3} = \dfrac{55}{3}$ ft² What is the height of the prism? 12 ft How can you find volume? $\dfrac{55}{3} \times 12 = 220$ ft³

**Explain** Emphasize that the base $b$ of the triangular base is not the same as the base $B$ of the prism.

**DIFFERENTIATED INSTRUCTION**

**Through Enrichment**

Draw an oblique version of the rectangular prism in **7** by shifting the top base to the right. Identify it as an *oblique rectangular prism*. Label all dimensions so students see that the dimensions of the prisms are identical. Use the formula $V = Bh$ to calculate the volume of the oblique prism. **Ask:** How does the volume of an oblique rectangular prism compare to the volume of a right rectangular prism with the same dimensions? *(It is the same.)*

**Caused** ///////

**8** Be sure students differentiate between the height of the trapezoid (2 ft) and the height of the prism (12 ft). First find the area of the base:

$B = \frac{1}{2} h(b_1 + b_2)$, where $h = 2$.

Then find the volume:

$V = Bh$, where $h = 12$.

---

## Guided Practice

**Find the volume of each prism.**

**7** Length = 6 cm
Width = 5.5 cm
Height = 9 cm

Area of base = \_\_?\_\_ · \_\_?\_\_  6; 5.5

= \_\_?\_\_ cm²  33

Volume of prism = \_\_?\_\_ · \_\_?\_\_  33; 9

= \_\_?\_\_ cm³  297

The volume of the prism is \_\_?\_\_ cubic centimeters.  297

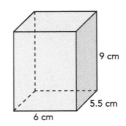

**8** Base of triangle = 10 in.
Height of triangle = $3\frac{1}{3}$ in.
Height of prism = 14 in.

Area of base = $\frac{1}{2}$ · \_\_?\_\_ · \_\_?\_\_  $3\frac{1}{3}$; 10

= \_\_?\_\_ in.²  $\frac{50}{3}$

Volume of prism = \_\_?\_\_ · \_\_?\_\_  $\frac{50}{3}$; 14

= \_\_?\_\_ in.³  $233\frac{1}{3}$

The volume of the prism is \_\_?\_\_ cubic inches.  $233\frac{1}{3}$

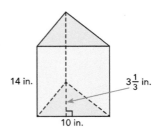

**9** Length of shorter base of trapezoid = 4 ft
Length of longer base of trapezoid = 10 ft
Height of trapezoid = 2 ft
Height of prism = 12 ft

Area of base = $\frac{1}{2}$ · \_\_?\_\_ · (\_\_?\_\_ + \_\_?\_\_)  2; 4; 10

= $\frac{1}{2}$ · \_\_?\_\_ · \_\_?\_\_  2; 14

= \_\_?\_\_ ft²  14

Volume of prism = \_\_?\_\_ · \_\_?\_\_  12; 14

= \_\_?\_\_ ft³  168

The volume of the prism is \_\_?\_\_ cubic feet.  168

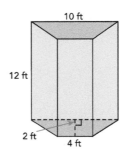

# Hands-On Activity

**Materials:**
• 27 unit cubes

**DETERMINING THE RELATIONSHIP BETWEEN VOLUME AND SURFACE AREA OF PRISMS**

Work in pairs.

 **STEP 1** Build the cube and the rectangular prism using unit cubes.

 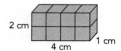

**STEP 2** Find the volume of the cube. 8 cm³
Find the volume of the rectangular prism. 8 cm³
What can you say about the volumes of the cube and the rectangular prism?
The cube and the rectangular prism have the same volume.

**STEP 3** Find the surface area of the cube. Draw its net if it helps you. 24 cm²
Find the surface area of the rectangular prism. Draw its net if it helps you. 28 cm²
What can you say about the surface areas of the cube and the rectangular prism? The surface area of the rectangular prism is greater than the surface area of the cube.

**STEP 4** Now, build these rectangular prisms using unit cubes.

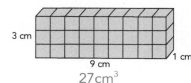
27 cm³

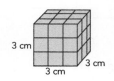
27 cm³

**STEP 5** Find the volume of the cube. Find the volume of the rectangular prism. See above.
What can you say about their volumes? Their volumes are the same.

**STEP 6** Find the surface area of the cube. Find the surface area of the rectangular prism. Draw their nets if it helps you. What can you say about their surface areas? 78 cm²; 54 cm²; See margin.

 *Math Journal* Based on the activity, what can you conclude about prisms with the same volume? Discuss with your partner and explain your thinking. While the volumes of the prisms are the same, their surface areas may not be.

---

 ## Hands-On Activity

This activity enables students to discover that solids with the same volumes need not have the same surface areas. Students can work in pairs. Each pair of students will need 27 unit cubes.

### DIFFERENTIATED INSTRUCTION

**Through Enrichment**

Tell students that four boxes are shaped like rectangular prisms. Each has a volume of 24 in.³, but all four boxes have different dimensions. **Ask:** If the length, width, and height of each box is a whole number, what are possible dimensions of the four different boxes? *(Possible answers: any combination of three whole numbers whose product is 24 such as: 24 × 1 × 1, 12 × 2 × 1, 8 × 3 × 1, 6 × 4 × 1, etc.)* What is the minimum surface area one of the boxes could have? *(A 4 in. × 3 in. × 2 in. box; surface area, 52 in.²)*

---

**6** The surface area of the rectangular prism is greater than the surface area of the cube.

## Practice 12.3

Basic ①–⑬
Intermediate ⑭–⑯
Advanced ⑰–⑳

### Assignment Guide

DAY **1** All students should complete ❶ – ❼.

DAY **2** All students should complete ❽ – ⑯.

⑰ – ⑳ provide additional challenge.

Optional: *Extra Practice 12.3*

### Caution ///////

❺ Since the group of cubes is described as a "solid," some students may not assume that there is a cube behind each of the two bottom cubes that project forward. Tell them to think of the solid as a stack of boxes (the cubes) piled against a wall.

**Solve.**

❶ A cube has edges measuring 9 inches each. Find the volume of the cube. 729 in.³

❷ A cube has edges measuring 6.5 centimeters each. Find the volume of the cube. 274.625 cm³

❸ A storage container is shaped like a rectangular prism. The container is 20 feet long, 10 feet wide, and $5\frac{1}{2}$ feet high. Find the volume of the storage container. 1,100 ft³

❹ Find the volume of the peppermint tea box on the right. 658.476 cm³

❺ The solid below is made of identical cubes. Each cube has an edge length of 2 inches. Find the volume of the solid. 72 in.³

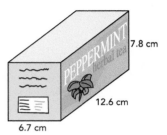

7.8 cm
12.6 cm
6.7 cm

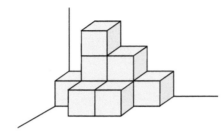

**Find the volume of the triangular prism.**

❻

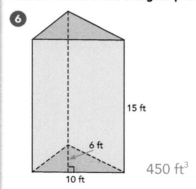

15 ft
6 ft
10 ft

450 ft³

❼

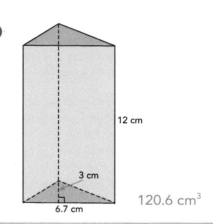

12 cm
3 cm
6.7 cm

120.6 cm³

### RtI Lesson Check

| Before assigning homework, use the following ... | to make sure students ... | Intervene with ... |
| --- | --- | --- |
| Exercises ❶ and ❸ | • can use the formula $V = \ell wh$ to find the volume of a rectangular prism | |
| Exercises ❾ and ⑪ | • can form cross sections of prisms. | Reteach 12.3 |
| Exercise ❼ | • can use the formula $V = Bh$ to find the volume of any prism | |
| Ticket Out the Door | • can use reasoning to solve a problem involving volume of a prism | |

**Tell whether slices parallel to each given slice will form uniform cross sections. If not, explain why not.**

**8**  Yes

**9** 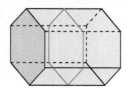 No. Circles will have different dimensions with other cuts.

**10** 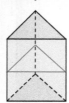 No. Squares will have different dimensions with other cuts.

**Copy the solid. Draw a slice that has the same cross section as the bases in each prism.**

**11**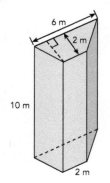

**12**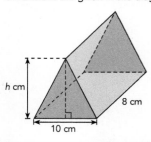

**13**

**Solve.**

**14** The bases of the prism shown are trapezoids. Find the volume of the prism.

6 m
2 m
10 m
2 m

80 m³

**15** A cube has a volume of 125 cubic inches. Find the length of its edge. 5 in.

**16** The volume of a triangular prism is 400 cubic centimeters. Two of its dimensions are given in the diagram. Find the height of a triangular base. 10 cm

h cm
8 cm
10 cm

### DIFFERENTIATED INSTRUCTION

**Through Visual Cues**

After students have completed **8** to **10**, ask them to make generalizations for prisms, cylinders, cones, and pyramids about whether multiple slices made parallel to the base will form uniform cross sections. (*Slices parallel to a base of either a prism or a cylinder will form uniform cross sections. Slices parallel to a base of either a cone or a pyramid will not form uniform cross sections.*)

### Best Practices

**11** For purposes of drawing their cross section, tell students to assume that the top and bottom of the cube are its bases.

### DIFFERENTIATED INSTRUCTION

**Through Communication**

**15** **Ask:** What do we know about the length, width, and height of a cube? (*All three dimensions must be the same.*)

**17** A cross section of the triangular prism shown below is parallel to a base. The area of the cross section is 24 square feet. The ratio of *DM* to *MA* is 3 : 5 and the length of $\overline{FO}$ is 6 feet. Find the volume of the triangular prism.

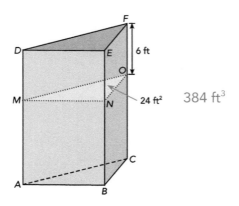

6 ft

24 ft²     384 ft³

**18** The volume of the rectangular prism shown below is 2,880 cubic inches. The cross section shown is parallel to a base. The area of the cross section is 180 square inches. The length of $\overline{AB}$ is x inches, and the length of $\overline{BC}$ is 4x inches.

a) Find the length of $\overline{AC}$.   16 in.

b) Find the value of x.   3.2

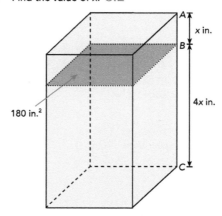

x in.

4x in.

180 in.²

**19** In the diagram of a cube shown below, points A, B, C, and D are vertices. Each of the other points on the cube is a midpoint of one of its sides. Describe a cross section of the cube that will form each of the following figures. Answers vary. Sample:

a) a rectangle  ABDC

b) an isosceles triangle  AJM

c) an equilateral triangle  EJM

d) a parallelogram  AHDF

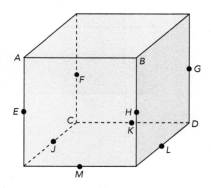

**Solve. Use graph paper.**

**20** Points A, B, C, and D form a square. The area of the square is 9 square units.

a) Find the side length of square ABCD.  3 units

b) The coordinates of point A are (2, 6). Points B and C are below $\overline{AD}$. Point B is below point A, and point D is to the right of point A. Plot the points in a coordinate plane. Connect the points in order to draw square ABCD.  See margin.

c) The points E, F, G, and H also form a square that is the same size as square ABCD. Point E is 4 units to the right of point A, and 3 units up. Points F and G are below $\overline{EH}$. Point F is below point E, and point H is to the right of point E. Plot the points in the coordinate plane. Draw $\overline{EH}$ and $\overline{GH}$ with solid lines, and $\overline{EF}$ and $\overline{FG}$ with dashed lines.  See margin.

d) Draw $\overline{AE}$, $\overline{DH}$, and $\overline{CG}$ with solid lines, and $\overline{BF}$ with a dashed line. Use the solid and dashed lines to see the figure as a solid. Name the type of prism formed.  See margin.

e) If the height of the prism is 7 units, find the volume of the prism.  63 units$^3$

**Ticket Out the Door**

A triangular prism and a rectangular prism are the same height and have the same volume. Identify a set of possible dimensions for the bases of the prisms. The area of the bases must be equal. Possible answer: The triangular prism has a triangular base with a base length of 10 cm and a height of 6 cm, and the rectangular prism has a base with a length of 6 cm and a width of 5 cm.

 Also available on Teacher One Stop.

**20** **b)**

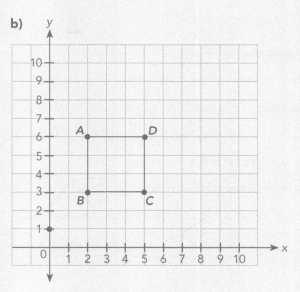

**20** **c) and d)**

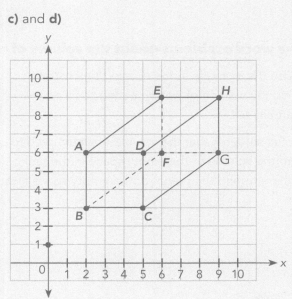

rectangular prism

**12.4** **Real-World Problems: Surface Area and Volume**

## KEY CONCEPT

- The process of problem solving involves the application of concepts, sklls, and strategies.

## PACING

**DAY 1** Pages 200–202

**DAY 2** Pages 203–208

**Materials:** none

 **5-minute Warm Up**

Identify the base and height of these prisms.

1.

2.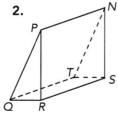

3.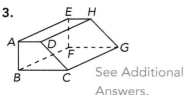

See Additional Answers.

 Also available on Teacher One Stop.

**Lesson Objective**

- Solve problems involving surface area and volume of prisms.

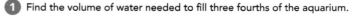
**Solve word problems about the volume of rectangular prisms.**

A rectangular fish tank 60 centimeters by 15 centimeters by 34 centimeters is $\frac{1}{3}$ full of water. Find the volume of water needed to fill the tank completely.

Volume of water needed
= Volume of empty space in the tank

Height of empty space $= \frac{2}{3} \cdot 34$

$\qquad = \frac{68}{3}$ cm

Volume of water needed to fill the tank $= 60 \cdot 15 \cdot \frac{68}{3}$    Write equation.

$\qquad = 60 \cdot 5 \cdot 68$    Divide out common factor 3.

$\qquad = 20{,}400$ cm³    Multiply.

To fill the tank, 20,400 cubic centimeters more water are needed.

**Guided Practice**
**Complete.**

1 Find the volume of water needed to fill three fourths of the aquarium.

Height of water needed $= \frac{3}{4} \cdot \underline{\ ?\ }$  14

$\qquad = \underline{\ ?\ }$ in.  $\frac{42}{4}$

Volume of water needed $= \underline{\ ?\ } \cdot \underline{\ ?\ } \cdot \underline{\ ?\ }$  25; 12; $\frac{42}{4}$

$\qquad = \underline{\ ?\ }$ in.³  3,150

The aquarium needs to have $\underline{\ ?\ }$ cubic inches of water added to it to be $\frac{3}{4}$ full.  3,150

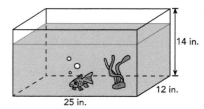

 **DAY 1**

**Solve word problems about the volume of rectangular prisms.**

**Model** Use the example in the text to demonstrate how to find the volume of water needed to fill a tank that is partially full.

**Explain** Tell students that the volume of water needed is equal to the volume of the empty space in the tank. Remind them to find the height of the empty space first.

**Ask** What fraction of the tank is filled with water? $\frac{1}{3}$

What fraction of the tank is empty space? $\frac{2}{3}$ What is the length of this empty space? 60 cm What is the width? 15 cm What is the height? $\frac{2}{3} \cdot 34 = \frac{68}{3}$ cm

What is the volume of the empty space? $60 \cdot 15 \cdot \frac{68}{3} =$ 20,400 cm³ What is the volume of water needed to fill the tank completely? 20,400 cm³

## Learn Solve word problems about surface area and volume of non-rectangular prisms.

A block of wood is a prism and has the dimensions shown in the diagram below.

a) Find the volume of the block of wood.

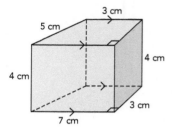

The base of the prism is a trapezoid.

Area of base
$= \frac{1}{2} h$(sum of lengths of parallel sides)

$= \frac{1}{2} \cdot 3 \cdot (3 + 7)$

$= \frac{1}{2} \cdot 3 \cdot 10$

$= 15 \text{ cm}^2$

Volume
$= Bh$

$= 15 \cdot 4$

$= 60 \text{ cm}^3$

Because all prisms have uniform cross sections when sliced parallel to the bases, you can use the formula $V = Bh$.

The volume of the block of wood is 60 cubic centimeters.

b) Find the surface area of the wooden block.

Surface area of wooden block
= perimeter of base · height + total area of two bases
$= (7 + 3 + 3 + 5) \cdot 4 + (2 \cdot 15)$
$= 18 \cdot 4 + 30$
$= 72 + 30$
$= 102 \text{ cm}^2$

The surface area of the wooden block is 102 square centimeters.

---

### Caution

a) Be sure students differentiate between the *h* in the formula for the area of the base, which represents the height of the trapezoid (3 cm), and the *h* in the formula for the volume of the prism, which represents the height of the prism (4 cm).

---

 **DIFFERENTIATED INSTRUCTION**

**Through Multiple Representations**

Some students may need clarification on how the areas of the four rectangular faces or the area of the two trapezoids were derived.

Four rectangular faces:
$A = (4 \cdot 7) + (4 \cdot 3) + (4 \cdot 3) + (4 \cdot 5)$
$\quad = 4 \cdot (7 + 3 + 3 + 5)$
$\quad = 4 \cdot 18 = 72 \text{ cm}^2$

Trapezoidal base:
$A = \frac{1}{2} h(b_1 + b_2)$
$\quad = \frac{1}{2} \cdot 3 \cdot (7 + 3)$
$\quad = \frac{1}{2} \cdot 3 \cdot 10$
$\quad = 15 \text{ cm}^2$

---

## Learn Solve word problems about surface area and volume of non-rectangular prisms.

**Model** Use the example to demonstrate how to find the volume and surface area of a prism with a non-rectangular base.

a) **Ask** How can you find the volume of the block of wood? By using the formula $V = Bh$ What is the shape of the base of this prism? A trapezoid How do you find the area of a trapezoid? By using the formula area of the base $= \frac{1}{2} h$(sum of lengths of parallel sides) What are the lengths of the parallel sides? 3 cm and 7 cm What is the height of the trapezoid? 3 cm What is the area of the trapezoid? $\frac{1}{2} \cdot 3 \cdot (3 + 7) = 15 \text{ cm}^2$ What is the height of the prism? 4 cm What is the volume of the prism? $15 \cdot 4 = 60 \text{ cm}^3$

b) **Ask** How can you find the surface area of the prism? By using the formula Surface area = perimeter of base · height + total area of two bases What is the perimeter of the trapezoidal base? $(7 + 3 + 3 + 5) = 18 \text{ cm}$

**Explain** Remind students that the height and the area of one base are already known.

**Ask** So, what is the surface area of the wooden block? $18 \cdot 4 + 2 \cdot 15 = 72 + 30 = 102 \text{ cm}^2$

## Guided Practice

 Ask students to identify the base and height of the prism. Remind them that the area of a parallelogram is the product of its base and height. Point out the two different meanings of the word "base."

 **DIFFERENTIATED INSTRUCTION**

**Through Multiple Representations**

2 Again, you may want to help some students by individually calculating the area of each face and base of the prism and then finding the sum of those areas.

---

## Guided Practice

**Complete.**

2 A metal bar has bases that are parallelograms.

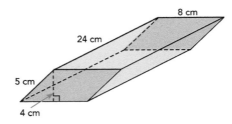

a)  Find the volume of the metal bar.

Area of parallelogram
= base of parallelogram · height of parallelogram

= __?__ · __?__   8; 4

= __?__ cm²   32

Volume of metal bar
= base of prism · height of prism

= __?__ · __?__   32; 24

= __?__ cm³   768

The volume of the metal bar is __?__ cubic centimeters.   768

b)  Find the surface area of the metal bar.

Surface area of metal bar
= perimeter of base · height + total area of 2 bases

= (__?__ + __?__ + __?__ + __?__) · __?__ + __?__ · __?__   8; 5; 8; 5; 24; 2; 32

= __?__ · __?__ + __?__   26; 24; 64

= __?__ + __?__   624; 64

= __?__ cm²   688

The surface area of the metal bar is __?__ square centimeters.   688

**Solve word problems about prisms with missing dimensions.**

A square prism of height 11 inches has a volume of 539 cubic inches.

a) Find the length of each side of the square base.

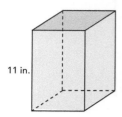

To find the length of the square base, you can first find the area of the square base.

| | |
|---|---|
| $V = Bh$ | Write formula. |
| $539 = B \cdot 11$ | Substitute. |
| $\dfrac{539}{11} = B \cdot \dfrac{11}{11}$ | Divide each side by 11. |
| $49 = B$ | Simplify. |

The area of the square base is 49 square inches.

$$\text{Length of each side of base} = \sqrt{49}$$
$$= 7 \text{ in.}$$

The length of each side of the square base is 7 inches.

b) Find the surface area of the prism.

Surface area of prism
= perimeter of base · height + area of two bases
= $(7 + 7 + 7 + 7) \cdot 11 + 2 \cdot 49$
= $28 \cdot 11 + 98$
= $308 + 98$
= $406 \text{ in.}^2$

The surface area of the prism is 406 square inches.

---

**DAY 2**

**Learn**    **Solve word problems about prisms with missing dimensions.**

**Model** Use the example in the text to demonstrate how to find the side of a square base given the volume and height of the prism.

a) **Ask** What is the formula for volume of a prism? $V = Bh$ What are you given in the problem? The volume and height of the prism Since $V = Bh$, what equation can you write? $539 = B \cdot 11$

**Explain** The equation $539 = B \cdot 11$ can be written as $11B = 539$.

**Ask** How do you solve this equation? Divide both sides by 11. So, what is $B$ equal to? $B = \dfrac{539}{11} = 49$

How is the solution $B = 49$ related to the problem? The area of the square base is 49 square inches. How can you find the length of each side of the square base? Find the square root of 49: $\sqrt{49} = 7$ in.

b) **Ask** How do you find the surface area of the prism? Use the formula Surface area = perimeter of base · height + total area of two bases What is the perimeter of the base? $4 \cdot 7 = 28$ in. So, what is the surface area of the prism? $28 \cdot 11 + 2 \cdot 49$ = $308 + 98 = 406$ in.$^2$

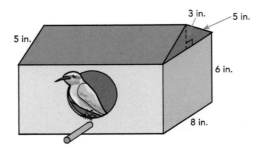

ᴸearn **Solve word problems about non-rectangular prisms with missing dimensions.**

Jacob is making a wooden birdhouse. The birdhouse is a prism with bases that are pentagons, and has the dimensions shown in the diagram. The volume of the prism is 720 cubic inches.

a)  Find the height of the prism.
    Area of pentagonal base
    = area of triangle + area of rectangle
    $= \left(\frac{1}{2} \cdot 8 \cdot 3\right) + 8 \cdot 6$
    $= 12 + 48$
    $= 60$ in.²

    | | |
    |---|---|
    | $V = Bh$ | Write formula. |
    | $720 = 60 \cdot h$ | Substitute. |
    | $\frac{720}{60} = h \cdot \frac{60}{60}$ | Divide each side by 60. |
    | $12 = h$ | Simplify. |

    The height of the prism is 12 inches.

b)  Find the surface area of the prism.

    Surface area of the prism
    = perimeter of base · height + area of two bases
    $= (5 + 6 + 8 + 6 + 5) \cdot 12 + 2 \cdot 60$
    $= 30 \cdot 12 + 120$
    $= 360 + 120$
    $= 480$ in.²

    The surface area of the prism is 480 square inches.

**Best Practices**

b) Tell students they can ignore the circular hole that is the entrance to the birdhouse. They are finding the surface area of the birdhouse before that hole is cut out.

ᴸearn **Solve word problems about non-rectangular prisms with missing dimensions.**

**Model** Use the example in the text to demonstrate how to find the height of a non-rectangular prism given the volume and the sides of the base.

a) **Ask** What is the formula for the volume of a prism $V$ in terms of its base $B$ and its height $h$? $V = Bh$ What is the volume of the prism? 720 in.³ How can you find the area of the pentagonal base? By noticing that the pentagonal base can be divided into a triangle and a rectangle. The area is the sum of those areas: Area of triangle + area of rectangle $= \frac{1}{2} \cdot 8 \cdot 3 + 8 \cdot 6 = 12 + 48 = 60$ in.² What equation can you write that relates $V$, $h$, and the base area 60 in.²? $720 = 60 \cdot h$

**Explain** You can write the equation $720 = 60 \cdot h$ as $60h = 720$.

**Ask** How do you solve the equation? Divide both sides by 60. So, what is $h$ equal to? $\frac{720}{60} = 12$ in. What is the height of the prism? 12 in.

b) **Ask** How can you find the surface area of the prism? Use the formula Surface area = perimeter of base · height + total area of two bases What is the perimeter of the base? $5 + 6 + 8 + 6 + 5 = 30$ in. What is the surface area of the prism? $30 \cdot 12 + 2 \cdot 60 = 360 + 120 = 480$ in.²

## Guided Practice

**Complete.**

**3** A candle is a square prism. The candle is 15 centimeters high, and its volume is 960 cubic centimeters.

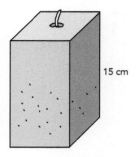

15 cm

**a)** Find the length of each side of the square base.

$$V = Bh$$

$$\underline{\ ?\ } = B \cdot \underline{\ ?\ } \quad 960;\ 15$$

$$\underline{\ ?\ } \div \underline{\ ?\ } = \underline{\ ?\ } \cdot B \div \underline{\ ?\ } \quad 960;\ 15;\ 15;\ 15$$

$$\underline{\ ?\ } = B \quad 64$$

Length of each side of base

$$= \underline{\ ?\ } \sqrt{64}$$

$$= \underline{\ ?\ } \text{ cm} \quad 8$$

The length of each side of the square base is __?__ centimeters. 8

**b)** Find the surface area of the candle.

Surface area of candle
= perimeter of base · height + area of two bases

$$= (\underline{\ ?\ } + \underline{\ ?\ } + \underline{\ ?\ } + \underline{\ ?\ }) \cdot \underline{\ ?\ } + \underline{\ ?\ } \cdot \underline{\ ?\ } \quad 8;\ 8;\ 8;\ 8;\ 15;\ 2;\ 64$$

$$= \underline{\ ?\ } \cdot \underline{\ ?\ } + \underline{\ ?\ } \quad 32;\ 15;\ 128$$

$$= \underline{\ ?\ } + \underline{\ ?\ } \quad 480;\ 128$$

$$= \underline{\ ?\ } \text{ cm}^2 \quad 608$$

The surface area of the candle is __?__ square centimeters. 608

## Guided Practice

**3** Ask students to identify the base and height of the prism. Remind them that the length of a side of a square is the square root of its area.

## Guided Practice

**4** Ask students to identify the base and height of the prism, and then ask what shapes it can be divided into. Have them name the area formulas they will need to use to find the area of the base.

**4** A storage chest is a prism with bases that are pentagons. The diagram shows some of the dimensions of the storage chest. The volume of the storage chest is 855 cubic inches.

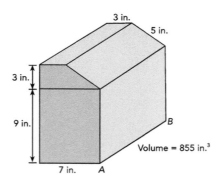

3 in.

5 in.

3 in.

9 in.

*B*

Volume = 855 in.³

7 in.  *A*

**a)** Find the height *AB* of the prism. Round your answer to the nearest hundredth.

Area of pentagonal base

= area of trapezoid + area of rectangle

$= \frac{1}{2} \cdot \underline{?} \cdot (\underline{?} + \underline{?}) + \underline{?} \cdot \underline{?}$   3; 7; 3; 9; 7

$= \underline{?} + \underline{?}$   15; 63

$= \underline{?}$ in.²   78

$V = Bh$

$\underline{?} = \underline{?} \cdot h$   855; 78

$\underline{?} \div \underline{?} = \underline{?} \cdot h \div \underline{?}$   855; 78; 78; 78

$\underline{?} \approx h$   10.96

The height of the prism is approximately __?__ inches.   10.96

**b)** Find the surface area of the prism. Round your answer to the nearest hundredth.

Surface area of prism

= perimeter of base · height + area of two bases

$\approx (\underline{?} + \underline{?} + \underline{?} + \underline{?} + \underline{?}) \cdot \underline{?} + \underline{?} \cdot \underline{?}$   7; 9; 3; 3; 5; 9; 10.96; 2; 78

$= \underline{?} \cdot \underline{?} + \underline{?}$   36; 10.96; 156

$= \underline{?} + \underline{?}$   394.56; 156

$= \underline{?}$ in.²   550.56

The surface area of the prism is approximately __?__ square inches.   550.56

**Solve.**

① Savannah has a water bottle that is a rectangular prism. The bottle measures 7 centimeters by 5 centimeters by 18 centimeters and she filled it completely with water. Then, she drank $\frac{1}{4}$ of the volume of water in her water bottle. How many cubic centimeters of water were left in the water bottle? 472.5 cm³

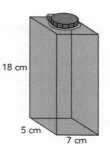
18 cm
5 cm
7 cm

② A rectangular prism has a square base with edges measuring 8 inches each. Its volume is 768 cubic inches.

a) Find the height of the prism. 12 in.

b) Find the surface area of the prism. 512 in.²

③ A triangular prism has the measurements shown.

a) Find the volume of the prism. 784 ft³

b) Find the surface area of the prism. 763.6 ft²

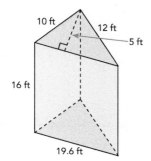
10 ft
12 ft
5 ft
16 ft
19.6 ft

④ The volume of Box A is $\frac{2}{5}$ the volume of Box B. What is the height of Box A if it has a base area of 32 square centimeters? 16 cm

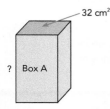
32 cm²
? Box A

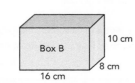
Box B
10 cm
8 cm
16 cm

### Assignment Guide

**DAY 1** All students should complete ① – ③.

**DAY 2** All students should complete ④ – ⑥.

⑦ provides additional challenge.
Optional: *Extra Practice 12.4*

### 👥 DIFFERENTIATED INSTRUCTION

**Through Communication**

④ You may want to help students through the process necessary to solve this problem. **Ask:** What are we trying to find? *(The height of Box A)* Since we know the area of the base of Box A, what other measurement will allow us to calculate its height? *(The volume of Box A)* What do we know about the volume of Box A? *(It is $\frac{2}{5}$ the volume of Box B.)* What is the volume of Box B? *(8 · 10 · 16 = 1,280 cm³)*

### 🔺 RtI Lesson Check

| Before assigning homework, use the following ... | to make sure students ... | Intervene with ... |
|---|---|---|
| Exercises ① and ③ | • can solve problems involving surface area and volume of prisms | Reteach 12.4 |
| 🚪 Ticket Out the Door | • can write and solve a real-world problem involving surface area and volume of prisms | |

## Ticket Out the Door

A triangular prism is 20 in. high. Its triangular bases have a base of 30 in. and a height of 10 in. The perimeter of its base is 66 in. Write a real-world problem involving this triangular prism. Find the surface area and volume. Real-world problems will vary. Surface area is 1,620 in.$^2$ and volume is 3,000 in.$^3$.

 Also available on Teacher One Stop.

**2** Make a list and solve the problem using guess and check.

| Length of edge of cube (ft) | Surface area (ft²) | Volume (ft³) |
|---|---|---|
| 4 | 6 · 4 · 4 = 96 | 4 · 4 · 4 = 64 |
| 5 | 6 · 5 · 5 = 150 | 5 · 5 · 5 = 125 |
| 6 | 6 · 6 · 6 = 216 | 6 · 6 · 6 = 216 |

Length of each edge of the cube: 6 ft

**5** The ratio of the length to the width to the height of an open rectangular tank is 10 : 5 : 8. The height of the tank is 18 feet longer than the width.

a) Find the volume of the tank. 86,400 ft$^3$

b) Find the surface area of the open tank. 10,440 ft$^2$

**6** Janice is making a gift box. The gift box is a prism with bases that are regular hexagons, and has the dimensions shown in the diagram.

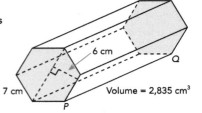

a) Find the height PQ of the prism. 22.5 cm

b) Find the surface area of the prism. 1,197 cm$^2$

**7** Container A was filled with water to the brim. Then, some of the water was poured into an empty Container B until the height of the water in both containers became the same. Find the new height of the water in both containers.

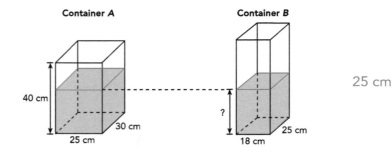

25 cm

## Brain @ Work

**1** The volume of a cube is 100 cubic inches. If each of the edges is doubled in length, what will be the volume of the cube? 800 in.$^3$

**2** The volume of a cube is x cubic feet and its surface area is x square feet, where x represents the same number. Find the length of each edge of the cube. See margin.

 ## DIFFERENTIATED INSTRUCTION

**Through Enrichment**

Because all students should be challenged, have all students try the Brain@Work exercise on this page.

For additional challenging practice and problem solving, see *Enrichment, Course 1*, Chapter 12.

# Chapter Wrap Up

## Concept Map

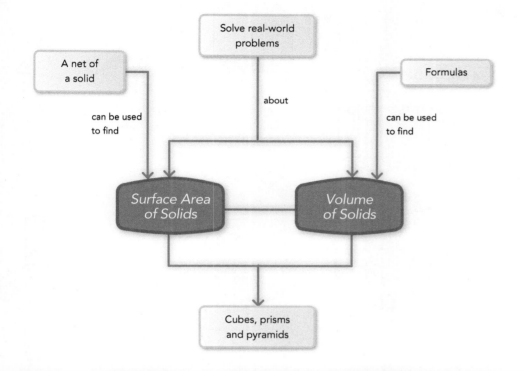

### Key Concepts

▶ The volume of a rectangular prism is the product of its length, width, and height.

▶ The volume of any prism is the product of the area of its base and its height.

▶ The surface area of a prism or pyramid is the sum of the areas of its faces.

## Vocabulary Review

Use these questions to review chapter vocabulary with students.

1. The plane figure that can be folded into a solid is a(n) __?__ of the solid. net

2. The solid with a square base and four triangular faces that meet at a point is a(n) __?__ . square pyramid

3. The sum of the areas of the faces of a prism is the __?__ of the prism. surface area

4. The shape formed when a solid is cut by a plane is a(n) __?__ of the solid.
   cross section

 Also available on Teacher One Stop.

## Chapter Assessment

Use the Chapter 12 Test A or B in *Assessments, Course 1* to assess how well students have learned the material in this chapter. These assessments appropriate for reporting results to adults at home and administrators. Test A is shown on page 213A.

## TEST PREPARATION

For additional test prep

🖱 **ExamView® Assessment Suite Course 1**

🖱 **Online Assessment System**
my.hrw.com

**1** c  **2** a  **3** b
**4** e  **5** d

# Chapter Review/Test

## Concepts and Skills

**Match each of the solid figures to its net.**

**1**   **2** 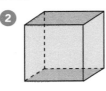  **3**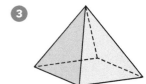

**4** 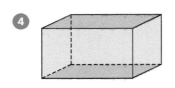  **5**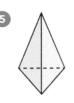

a) 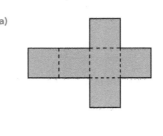  b) 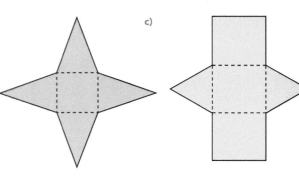  c)

d) 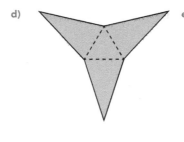  e)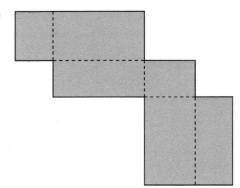

---

### ⚠ RtI  Intervention and Reteaching Recommendations

| Student Book A Review/Test Items | Assessments Chapter 12 Items | Chapter 12 Objectives | Reteach B Chapter 12 |
|---|---|---|---|
| **1** to **5** | Test A: 1 <br> Test B: 1 | **Objective 1.** Identify and recognize the nets of a prism and a pyramid. | Lesson 12.1 |

**Find the surface area of each solid.**

 **6**

8 in.
8 in.
8 in.

384 in.²

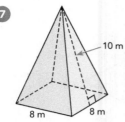 **7**

10 m

8 m     8 m

224 m²

**Find the volume of each prism.**

 **8**
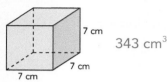

7 cm
7 cm
7 cm

343 cm³

**9**
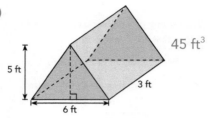

5 ft

3 ft

6 ft

45 ft³

**Solve.**

 **10** The solid below is made up of cubes, each of which has an edge length of 3 inches.

a)  What is the volume of one cube?  27 in.³

b)  What is the volume of the solid figure?  270 in.³

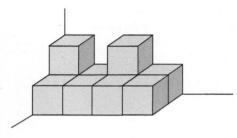

## Problem Solving

**Solve.**

 **11** A fish tank is 50 centimeters long, 30 centimeters wide, and 40 centimeters high. It contains water up to a height of 28 centimeters. How many more cubic centimeters of water are needed to fill the tank to a height of 35 centimeters?  10,500 cm³

**△RtI Intervention and Reteaching Recommendations**

| Student Book A Review/Test Items | Assessments Chapter 12 Items | Chapter 12 Objectives | Reteach B Chapter 12 |
|---|---|---|---|
| 6 to 7 | Test A: 2<br>Test B: 2 | **Objective 2.** Find the surface area of a prism and a pyramid. | Lesson 12.2 |
| 8 to 10 | Test A: 3–5<br>Test B: 3–5 | **Objective 3.** Find the volume of a prism. | Lesson 12.3 |
| 11 | Test A: 6–8<br>Test B: 6–8 | **Objective 4.** Solve problems involving the surface area and volume of prisms. | Lesson 12.4 |

**12** Find the surface area of a square pyramid given that its base area is 196 square inches and the height of each of its triangular faces is 16 inches. 644 in.²

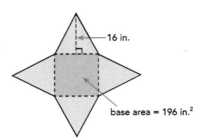

16 in.

base area = 196 in.²

**13** The volume of a rectangular prism is 441 cubic feet. It has a square base with edges that are 7 feet long.

a) Find the height of the prism. 9 ft

b) Find the surface area of the prism. 350 ft²

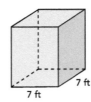

7 ft

7 ft

**14** The volume of a rectangular tank with a square base is 63,908 cubic centimeters. Its height is 64 centimeters. Find the length of an edge of one of the square bases. Round your answer to the nearest tenth of a centimeter.

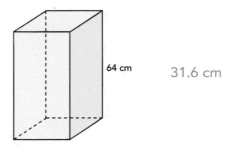

64 cm

31.6 cm

**RtI Intervention and Reteaching Recommendations**

| Student Book A Review/Test Items | Assessments Chapter 12 Items | Chapter 12 Objectives | Reteach B Chapter 12 |
|---|---|---|---|
| **12** to **14** | Test A: 6–9 <br> Test B: 6–9 | **Objective 4.** Solve problems involving the surface area and volume of prisms. | Lesson 12.4 |

**15** A rectangular container has a base that is 12 inches long and 8 inches wide. The container is filled with water to a height of 6 inches. If all the water is poured into a second container with a square base, it will rise to a height of 16 inches. What is the length of one edge of the square base of the second container? 6 in.

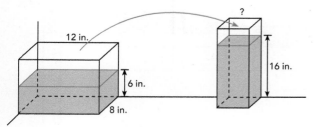

**16** Find the surface area and the volume of the prism.

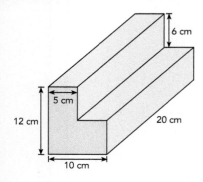

Surface area: 1,060 cm²;
Volume: 1,800 cm³

**17** Find the surface area and the volume of the prism.

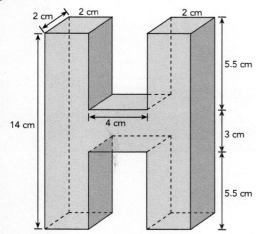

Surface area: 268 cm²;
Volume: 136 cm³

## RtI Intervention and Reteaching Recommendations

| Student Book A Review/Test Items | Assessments Chapter 12 Items | Chapter 12 Objectives | Reteach B Chapter 12 |
|---|---|---|---|
| **15** to **17** | Test A: 6–9<br>Test B: 6–9 | **Objective 4.** Solve problems involving the surface area and volume of prisms. | Lesson 12.4 |

# ASSESSMENT PAGES FOR CHAPTER 12

## Chapter 12 Tests A and B

Answer key appears in the *Assessments, Course 1*

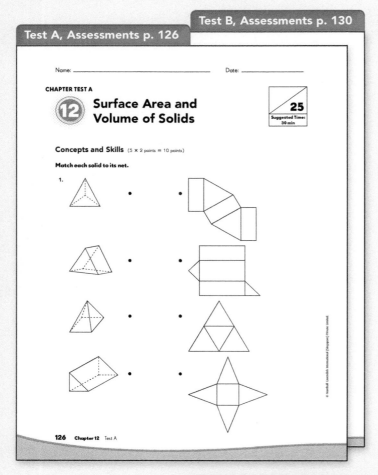

**Test B, Assessments p. 130**

**Test A, Assessments p. 126**

Name: _____   Date: _____

**CHAPTER TEST A**

**12** **Surface Area and Volume of Solids**

**25**
Suggested Time: 30 min

**Concepts and Skills** (5 × 2 points = 10 points)

**Match each solid to its net.**

1.

126   Chapter 12   Test A

---

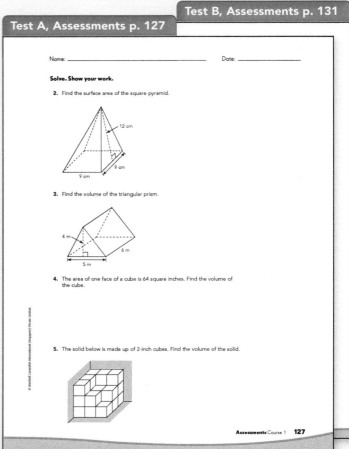

**Test B, Assessments p. 131**

**Test A, Assessments p. 127**

Name: _____   Date: _____

**Solve. Show your work.**

2. Find the surface area of the square pyramid.

12 cm
9 cm
9 cm

3. Find the volume of the triangular prism.

4 m
6 m
5 m

4. The area of one face of a cube is 64 square inches. Find the volume of the cube.

5. The solid below is made up of 2-inch cubes. Find the volume of the solid.

Assessments Course 1   **127**

---

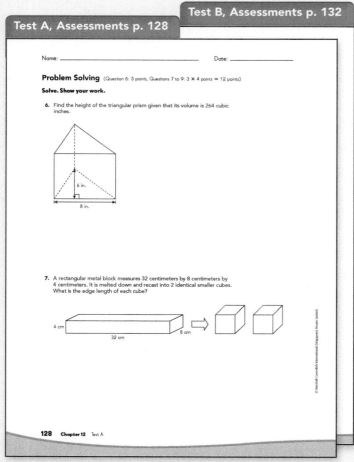

**Test B, Assessments p. 132**

**Test A, Assessments p. 128**

Name: _____   Date: _____

**Problem Solving** (Question 6: 3 points, Questions 7 to 9: 3 × 4 points = 12 points)

**Solve. Show your work.**

6. Find the height of the triangular prism given that its volume is 264 cubic inches.

6 in.
8 in.

7. A rectangular metal block measures 32 centimeters by 8 centimeters by 4 centimeters. It is melted down and recast into 2 identical smaller cubes. What is the edge length of each cube?

4 cm
32 cm
8 cm

128   Chapter 12   Test A

---

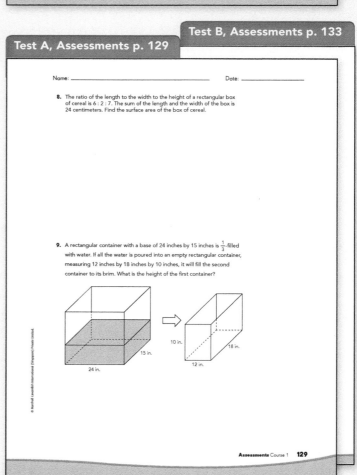

**Test B, Assessments p. 133**

**Test A, Assessments p. 129**

Name: _____   Date: _____

8. The ratio of the length to the width to the height of a rectangular box of cereal is 6 : 2 : 7. The sum of the length and the width of the box is 24 centimeters. Find the surface area of the box of cereal.

9. A rectangular container with a base of 24 inches by 15 inches is $\frac{1}{3}$-filled with water. If all the water is poured into an empty rectangular container, measuring 12 inches by 18 inches by 10 inches, it will fill the second container to its brim. What is the height of the first container?

10 in.
15 in.
18 in.
24 in.
12 in.

Assessments Course 1   **129**

## CHAPTER 13 Chapter at a Glance

Chapter at a Glance

### Additional Teaching Support

- Online Teacher's Edition
- Online Professional Development Videos

| | | CHAPTER OPENER<br>Introduction to Statistics<br>Recall Prior Knowledge | LESSON 13.1<br>Collecting and Tabulating Data<br>Pages 217–221 | LESSON 13.2<br>Dot Plots<br>Pages 222–227 |
|---|---|---|---|---|
| **LESSON AT A GLANCE** | Pacing | 2 days | 1 day | 1 day |
| | Objectives | Statistics summarize data so that information or decisions can be gathered from the data. | • Collect, organize, and tabulate data. | • Display and analyze data using a dot plot. |
| | Vocabulary | | frequency | dot plot, skewed, symmetrical, range |
| **RESOURCES** | Materials | | ruler, TRT15* | number cubes, TRT34* |
| | Lesson Resources | Student Book B, pp. 214–216<br>*Assessments Course 1*, Chapter 13 Pre-Test<br>*Transition Guide, Course 1*, Skills 51 | Student Book B, pp. 217–221<br>*Extra Practice B*, Lesson 13.1<br>*Reteach B*, Lesson 13.1<br>*Activity Book*, Lesson 13.1 | Student Book B, pp. 222–227<br>*Extra Practice B*, Lesson 13.2<br>*Reteach B*, Lesson 13.2 |
| | **Common Core** Standards for Mathematical Content | Foundational for **6.SP.4** | **6.SP.1** Recognize a statistical question.<br>**6.SP.2** Understand...data collected to answer a statistical question.<br>**6.SP.5, 6.SP.5a, 6.SP.5b** Summarize numerical data sets in relation to their context... | **6.SP.4.** Display numerical data in plots on a number line, including dot plots...<br>**6.SP.5d.** Relate...the center...to the shape of the data distribution. |
| | Mathematical Practices | **3.** Look for and use structure. **6.** Attend to precision. | **4.** Model mathematics. **5.** Use tools strategically. | **2.** Reason. **3.** Construct arguments. **4.** Model mathematics. |

*Teacher Resource Tools (TRT) are available on the Teacher One Stop.*

## Concepts and Skills Across the Courses

| GRADE 5 | COURSE 1 | COURSE 2 |
|---|---|---|
| • Represent and interpret data. (5.MD.2)<br>• Make a line plot to display measurements. (5.MD.2)<br>• Use operations on fractions to solve problems involving data in line plots. (5.MD.2) | • Develop understanding of statistical questions and variability. (6.SP.1, 6.SP.2)<br>• Display numerical data in dot plots and histograms. (6.SP.4)<br>• Summarize and describe the shape of data distributions in relation to their context. (6.SP.5, 6.SP.5a, 6.SP.5.b, 6.SP.5d) | • Use random sampling to gain information about a population and draw inferences. (7.SP. 1, 7.SP.2)<br>• Use measures of center and measures of variability to compare populations. (7.SP.3, 7.SP.4) |

| LESSON 13.3<br>Histograms<br>Pages 228–237 | CHAPTER<br>WRAP UP/REVIEW/TEST<br><br>Brain@Work<br>Pages 237–241 |
|---|---|
| 2 days | 2 days |
| • Display and analyze data using a histogram. | Reinforce, consolidate, and extend chapter skills and concepts. |
| histogram, outlier | |
| | |
| Student Book B, pp. 228–237<br>*Extra Practice B*, Lesson 13.3<br>*Reteach B*, Lesson 13.3 | Student Book A, pp. 237–241<br>*Activity Book*, Chapter 13 Project<br>*Enrichment*, Chapter 13<br>*Assessments*, Chapter 13 Test<br> ExamView® Assessment Suite Course 1 |
| **6.SP.4.** Display numerical data in plots on a number line, including… histograms…<br>**6.SP.5d.** Relate…the center…to the shape of the data distribution. | |
| **4.** Model mathematics. **5.** Use tools strategically. | **1.** Solve problems/persevere.<br>**8.** Express regularity in reasoning. |

# Additional Chapter Resources

| TECHNOLOGY |
|---|

 • Online Student eBook

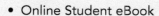

 • Interactive Whiteboard Lessons

 • Virtual Manipulatives

 • Teacher One Stop

 • ExamView® Assessment Suite Course 1

 • Online Professional Development Videos

**Every Day Counts®<br>ALGEBRA READINESS**

The May and June activities in the Pacing Chart provide:

• **Review** of solids and nets (**Ch.12: 6.G.4**)

• **Review** of variable expressions (**Ch.7: 6.EE.2**)

• **Review** of graphs of linear relationships (**Ch.12 and 9: 6.EE.9**)

# Chapter 13 Introduction to Statistics

## Frequency and Distribution

- In this chapter, students collect, organize, and tabulate data. They display data using dot plots and histograms and analyze the distribution of data.

### Tallies, frequency tables, and dot plots

- Students learn to compile tally charts and frequency tables. These display the number of times the values in a data set appear. The values in tally charts and frequency tables need not be numeric.

- Dot plots also show frequency, but they relate two sets of *numeric* data. The range of values in the set is shown on a number line. Dots above the values show each time that value appears in the set.

### Analyzing data distribution

- Students learn to analyze data distribution by observing the shape of data displayed in a dot plot.

- A normal data distribution is symmetrical about a vertical line through the center of its range. In a symmetrical distribution the mean, median, and mode are all the same number. The average value is the middle value or the value that occurs most often.

- The most famous of all statistical curves is the graph of a normal distribution: the bell curve. Shown below, it describes the outcomes of many random events such as rolling two number cubes 100 times.

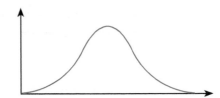

- A skewed distribution is one in which the data fall toward one side of its range. A distribution with more data points to the left of the mode is described as *left-skewed* or as having a "tail" to the left. In a skewed distribution, the mean is usually pulled toward the direction of skew. For example, in a right-skewed distribution the mean is greater than the median or mode.

## Histograms

- Students display data in histograms and analyze the distribution of data.

### From dot plots to histograms

- Students learn that, like dot plots, histograms display how often numeric values appear in a data set. Students create histograms such as the one below from data sets or from frequency tables.

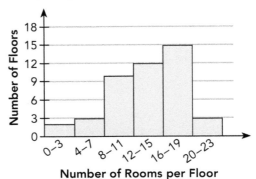

**Number of Rooms per Floor**

The range of values is shown on the horizontal axis. Their frequency is shown along the vertical axis.

- Histograms are more convenient than dot plots for displaying large sets of data. But because they group values into intervals, it is impossible to identify from a histogram either the individual values in a data set or their frequency.

- When creating a histogram, students can choose the intervals along the horizontal axis. All intervals should contain an equal portion of the range, with no data items falling between intervals.

- Students compare the shape of data displayed in a 4-interval histogram with the same data displayed in an 8-interval histogram. They discover that, although the distribution of the data set does not change, the appearance of its graph does.

### Differences from bar graphs

- Students learn that histograms differ from other bar graphs because adjacent bars in a histogram touch. This reflects the fact that bars display a continuous range of data, not discrete values or categories.

# Differentiated Instruction

## Assessment and Intervention

| | ASSESSMENT | RtI STRUGGLING LEARNERS |
|---|---|---|
| **DIAGNOSTIC** | • Quick Check in Recall Prior Knowledge in Student Book B, pp. 215–216<br>• Chapter 13 Pre-Test in *Assessments* | • Skill 51 in *Transition Guide, Course 1* |
| **ON-GOING** | • Guided Practice<br>• Lesson Check<br>• Ticket Out the Door | • Reteach worksheets<br>• Extra Practice worksheets<br>• *Activity Book*, Chapter 13 |
| **END-OF-CHAPTER** | • Chapter Review/Test<br>• Chapter 13 Test in *Assessments*<br>• ExamView® Assessment Suite Course 1 | • Reteach worksheets |

### ELL ENGLISH LANGUAGE LEARNERS

Review the terms *frequency* and *distribution*.

**Say** We use the word *frequency* to talk about how often something happens. During one half hour in the morning, hundreds of students arrive at school. In the morning, students arrive at school with *high* frequency. At night, few students arrive at school. At night, students arrive at school with *low* frequency. Line plots and histograms show frequency.

**Model** Display a sample dot plot and a histogram.

**Say** Line plots and histograms also show the *distribution* of data in a data set. To *distribute* something is to give it out or to spread it out.

**Model** Have 5 volunteers stand in a row. Distribute 30 books among them unevenly. Have students discuss how the books are distributed among the 5 students.

For definitions, see Glossary, page 301, and Online Multilingual Glossary.

### ADVANCED LEARNERS

• Students can research a subject that interests them, locate or collect a data set, and make a poster-size histogram to display the data.

• Remind students to choose a data set that can be displayed in a histogram. It must show frequency for a continuous range of values, not discrete amounts. Before students create their histograms, have them clear their ideas with you. Also have them submit a list of the data set so you can evaluate their work.

• As needed, provide direction for students, such as suggesting they choose a data set large enough to justify a histogram but that contains a manageable amount of data, and use smaller numbers to represent large values in their intervals (i.e., 30–49.9 to represent 30 to 49.9 million) Remind students to title and fully label their histograms.

To provide additional challenges use:
• *Enrichment*, Chapter 13
• Student Book B, Brain@Work problems

# CHAPTER 13

# Introduction to Statistics

## Chapter Vocabulary

Vocabulary terms are used in context in the student text. For definitions, see the Glossary at the end of the Student Book and the online Multilingual Glossary.

**dot plot** A data display similar to a line plot. It shows frequency of data on a number line using a • to represent each occurrence.

**frequency** The number of times a piece of data, such as an item or a number, occurs

**histogram** A data display that divides the range of data into equal intervals and shows how often each interval occurs in the data set. It is usually used for large sets of data.

**outlier** An extreme or rare occurrence of a value

**range** The difference between the greatest and the least number in a set of data

**skewed** A data set in which the mean, median, and mode are not all the same number

**symmetrical** A data set in which the mean, median, and mode are the same number

**BIG IDEA**

▶ Statistics summarize data so that information or decisions can be gathered from the data.

## Do you know why and how statistics are collected?

Have you ever wondered how a cafeteria manager plans for making food every day? Some statistical questions that might be asked about preparing food for the cafeteria are:
- How many students do we serve each day?
- How many students order pancakes for breakfast?

These are statistical questions because many pieces of data are needed to answer each question. Cafeteria managers need answers to questions such as these to find out how much food they will need to buy each week or how many cooks they will need to hire.

Once data have been collected, it needs to be organized so that patterns and trends can be seen. Data displays, such as graphs, can help summarize the data and make it easy to understand. Learning about statistics and data displays can help you understand and find solutions to real-world problems.

## CHAPTER OPENER

Use the chapter opener to talk about what statistical questions are, and how to apply statistics to a real-life situation.

**Ask** How do the cafeteria managers decide how many pancakes to prepare each day? Possible answer: They can look at the number of pancakes sold daily for the past few weeks. **How might this help them?** They can look for patterns in the data to predict what today's sales will be. **What kind of patterns might they look for?** Possible answer: How sales relate to days of the week or to weather.

**Explain** The collection of answers to the questions in the opener form a data set. Data sets help answer statistical questions such as: How many students eat breakfast each day? or How many pancakes do we need to cook each day? This data set can be organized and presented in data displays such as tables or graphs.

In this chapter, you will learn how to use statistics to summarize data so that information or decisions can be gathered from the data, as summarized in the **Big Idea**.

# Recall Prior Knowledge

## Interpreting data in a line plot

Michael surveyed a group of children in a music class to find out their ages.
The table below shows the results of his survey.

**Ages of Children**

| Name of Child | Age (yr) |
|---------------|----------|
| Allen | 12 |
| Brooklyn | 11 |
| Eric | 10 |
| Gianna | 12 |
| Isabelle | 12 |
| Juan | 12 |
| Lauren | 13 |
| Miguel | 12 |
| Parker | 11 |
| Vanessa | 11 |

Michael made a line plot to show the results of his survey.
Each × represents 1 student.

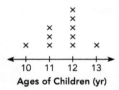

Ages of Children (yr)

Three of the students are 11 years old.
The most common age is 12 years old.
The number of students who are 10 years old and 13 years old is the same.
The total number of students in the music class is 10.
Six of the students are older than 11 years.

**Complete. Use the data in the line plot.**

The line plot shows the weight, in pounds, of cartons of apples in a store. Each × represents 1 carton of apples.

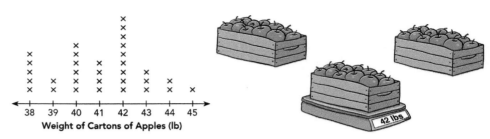

**Weight of Cartons of Apples (lb)**

① What is the weight of the lightest carton of apples? 38 lb

② What is the weight of the heaviest carton of apples? 45 lb

③ What is the difference in weight between the heaviest carton of apples and the lightest carton of apples? 7 lb

④ How many cartons weigh more than 41 pounds? 15

⑤ How many cartons weigh less than 40 pounds? 7

⑥ How many cartons weigh 44 pounds each? 2

⑦ How many cartons are there in all? 32

⑧ How many times as many cartons of apples weigh 40 pounds as the number of cartons of apples that weigh 43 pounds? Two times

⑨ The ratio of the number of cartons of apples that weigh 42 pounds to the number of cartons of apples that weigh 40 pounds is __?__. 3 : 2

⑩ The number of cartons of apples that weigh 41 pounds is __?__ % of the total number of cartons of apples. 12.5

## RECALL PRIOR KNOWLEDGE

Use the ☑ Quick Check exercises or the Chapter Pre-Test in *Assessments, Course 1*, to assess chapter readiness. For intervention suggestions, see the chart below.

🖱 Additional online Reteach and Extra Practice worksheets from previous grades are also available. See the *Transition Guide*, Resource Planner for more information.

| ▲ RtI Assessing Prior Knowledge | | | Intervene with | |
|---|---|---|---|---|
| ☑ Quick Check | *Assessments Course 1*, Ch.13 Pre-Test Items | Skill Objective | Transition Guide | 🖱 Online Resources Grades 4 and 5 |
| ① to ⑩ | 1–8 | Interpret data on a line plot. | Skill 51 | |

# 13.1 Collecting and Tabulating Data

## Lesson Objective
- Collect, organize, and tabulate data.

Vocabulary
frequency

### Learn Collect and tabulate data.

Sean wants to find how students in his class get to school.

To do this, he can collect the data by using one of the three methods.

**Method 1: Carrying out observations**

Sean can stand at the school door in the morning to observe how his classmates arrive at school.

Which method is the most efficient?

**Method 2: Conducting surveys through interviews**

Sean can interview his classmates to find out how they get to school.

**Method 3: Conducting surveys using a questionnaire**

Sean can prepare a questionnaire for his classmates to complete, such as the one below.

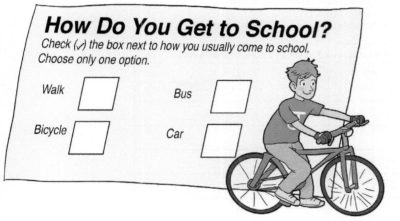

## How Do You Get to School?
Check (✓) the box next to how you usually come to school. Choose only one option.

Walk ☐     Bus ☐

Bicycle ☐     Car ☐

**Continue on next page**

---

DAY 1

### Learn Collect and tabulate data.

Use the scenario in the text to show students how to collect and tabulate data.

**Ask** What does Sean want to find out? The forms of transportation his classmates use to get to school What possible methods can he use to get the information he needs? Method 1: Carry out observations, Method 2: Conduct surveys through interviews, and Method 3: Conduct survey using a questionnaire

**Explain** Point out that carrying out observations and conducting surveys through interviews or questionnaires are ways of collecting data. The method of data collection used can affect how the data set is later interpreted.

**Ask** Which of the three methods is the most efficient? Possible answer: It is more efficient for Sean to conduct a survey through a questionnaire as this requires less time.

## 13.1 Collecting and Tabulating Data

### KEY CONCEPT
- You can collect, organize and tabulate data.

### PACING

DAY 1  Pages 217–221
**Materials:** ruler, TRT15

**5-minute Warm Up**

As a part of an event, a shopping mall is preparing door gifts for every shopper who visits it. How can they estimate the number of door gifts needed? They can find the average daily number of shoppers to estimate the number of door gifts needed.

Also available on Teacher One Stop.

## Through Language Support

Make sure students understand the meanings of *data* and *tabulate*. Explain that the plural word *data* is a collection of information, such as the number of cars in a parking lot each day or the ages of a group of people. Point out that the root of the verb *tabulate* is *table*, so tabulating data is organizing it so it is easier to analyze, such as in a table.

Help students understand the meaning of *frequency*. Explain that *frequency* describes how often each value appears in a data set. Direct students to the tables on this page. Explain that a table that shows how often each value in a data set appears is called a *frequency table*.

## Guided Practice

**1** Students practice how to fill in the frequency column by counting tally marks.

---

Sean uses a tally chart to record the results of his survey. Then he counts the tally marks to find how many students use each form of transportation.

**How My Classmates Get to School**

| How Students Get to School | Tally | Frequency |
|---|---|---|
| Walk | ﷠ ///  | 8 |
| Bus | ﷠ ﷠ /// | 13 |
| Bicycle | //// | 4 |
| Car | ﷠ | 5 |

**Frequency** refers to how often a piece of data, such as an item or a number, occurs.

Eight of Sean's classmates walk to school.
The most common form of transportation is by bus.
The least common form of transportation is by bicycle.
There is 1 more classmate who comes to school by car than by bicycle.
Sean collected data from 30 classmates altogether, excluding himself.

## Guided Practice

**Complete. Use the data in the table.**

Emma used a questionnaire to find out the number of brothers or sisters her classmates have in their families.

Then she used a tally chart to record what she had found.

**1** Copy and complete the table by counting the tally marks.

**Number of Brothers or Sisters of Emma's Classmates**

| Number of Brothers or Sisters | Tally | Frequency | |
|---|---|---|---|
| 0 | /// | ? | 3 |
| 1 | ﷠ //// | ? | 9 |
| 2 | ﷠ // | ? | 7 |
| 3 | ﷠ | ? | 5 |
| 4 | // | ? | 2 |
| 5 or more | / | ? | 1 |

---

**Learn continued**

**Ask** What does Sean use to record the results of his survey? A tally chart How does he find how many students use each form of transport? By counting the tally marks

**Explain** Emphasize that each tally mark represents a classmate of Sean's who takes a particular form of transport. "Frequency" is the number of students who select a particular form of transport. The total of the frequencies must equal the total number of classmates Sean surveyed.

**Ask** How many classmates did Sean collect the data from? 30 What is the sum of the frequencies? 30

**2** More of Emma's classmates have ___?___ brother or sister than any other number.  1

**3** ___?___ of Emma's classmates have 3 brothers or sisters in their families.  5

**4** ___?___ of Emma's classmates have 4 brothers or sisters in their families.  2

**5** How many more of Emma's classmates have 2 brothers or sisters than 5 or more brothers or sisters in their families?  6

**6** Emma has ___?___ classmates altogether.  27

---

# Hands-On Activity

**Materials:**
- blank table
- ruler
- collection of pencils

**COLLECT, TABULATE, AND INTERPRET DATA**

Work in groups of three or four.

**STEP 1** Collect a set of pencils of various lengths. Use a ruler to measure the length of each pencil to the nearest centimeter. Use tally marks to record the data.

**STEP 2** Tally your results on a table like the one below. Then count the tally marks to complete the table. Answers will vary.

| Length of Pencil (cm) | Tally | Frequency |
|---|---|---|
| ? | ? | ? |
| ? | ? | ? |
| ? | ? | ? |
| ? | ? | ? |
| ? | ? | ? |

**STEP 3** Write at least four questions about the data in the table using these phrases.

| how many pencils | shortest | longest |
|---|---|---|
| fewer than | more than | altogether |

---

## Guided Practice

Use **2** to **6** to assess students' understanding of tally marks and frequency.

## Hands-On Activity

This group activity reinforces the concept of collecting, tabulating, and interpreting data.

**1** Ask each group to assign only one member to measure the lengths of the pencils while another member records the data.

**2** Make sure students tally their results on a copy of the table.

**3** Guide students to write questions about the data they have collected and tabulated.

### Best Practices

TRT15 may be useful to students for this Hands-On Activity.

### DIFFERENTIATED INSTRUCTION

**Through Language Support**

Before students write their questions in **3**, have them use each word or phrase in a sentence unrelated to the pencil-length data in the table.

### Best Practices

❶ Point out that each row of the frequency table features a span of data values instead of a single value. Explain that large data sets are often organized into intervals such as "Below $500," "$500–$1,000," and "Over $1,000." Point out that the intervals may be chosen to divide the data set into roughly equal parts, as they are here. In other cases, the selection of intervals may reflect how the data set is going to be used. For example, suppose the Department of Transportation is recording the speed of cars on a highway. If the speed limit is 55 mph, it may choose to use only two intervals: "55 mph or less" and "Over 55 mph."

**Copy and complete the table. Solve.**

❶ A shampoo company wanted to find out more about its customers. So they asked 30 customers to indicate their income bracket:

Below $500 per week
$500–$1,000 per week
Over $1,000 per week

A tally chart was used to record the findings.

| Weekly Income | Tally | Frequency | |
|---|---|---|---|
| Below $500 | ⅟ʜ⅟ // | ? | 7 |
| $500–$1,000 | ⅟ʜ⅟ ⅟ʜ⅟ ⅟ʜ⅟ //// | ? | 19 |
| Over $1,000 | //// | ? | 4 |

How many customers have a weekly income of $1,000 or less? 26

❷ Fifty students were asked their level of satisfaction with the school's music program. The following responses were the choices provided:

(a) very satisfied (b) satisfied (c) neutral (d) dissatisfied (e) very dissatisfied.

| Level of Satisfaction | Tally | Frequency | |
|---|---|---|---|
| Very satisfied | // | ? | 2 |
| Satisfied | ⅟ʜ⅟ // | ? | 7 |
| Neutral | ⅟ʜ⅟ ⅟ʜ⅟ ⅟ʜ⅟ ⅟ʜ⅟ //// | ? | 24 |
| Dissatisfied | ⅟ʜ⅟ ⅟ʜ⅟ //// | ? | 14 |
| Very dissatisfied | //// | ? | 4 |

a) How many students are satisfied or very satisfied? 9

b) Based on the results of the survey, should the school think about changing the program? Explain your reasoning. See margin.

### ⛰️RtI Lesson Check

| Before assigning homework, use the following ... | to make sure students ... | Intervene with ... |
|---|---|---|
| Exercises ❶ to ❹ | • can collect, organize, and tabulate data | Reteach 13.1 |
| 🚪EXIT Ticket Out the Door | • can organize data into a table using reasonable intervals | |

❷ b) 18 students are dissatisfied or very dissatisfied. That is more than one-third of the students in the study. So, the school should think about changing the program.

**3** A mathematics teacher wanted to find out how many hours per week his students spent on math homework. The average number of hours reported by each student is shown.

5, 3, 6, 8, 2, 4, 2, 1, 9, 1, 9, 6, 4, 6, 5, 1, 10, 1, 5, 6, 7, 8, 6, 10, 7, 5, 2, 8

Arrange the numbers in ascending order. See margin.

| Number of Hours | Tally | Frequency |
|---|---|---|
| 0–3 | ? | ? |
| 4–7 | ? | ? |
| 8–10 | ? | ? |

*ᏝᎻᎿ ///; 8*
*ᏝᎻᎿ ᏝᎻᎿ ///; 13*
*ᏝᎻᎿ //; 7*

How many students spent more than 3 hours per week on their math homework? 20

**4** Shelly conducted a survey among her friends. She asked them to choose their favorite fruit from this list of fruits: apple, orange, strawberry, grapes, and peach. These are the data she collected:

**Favorite Fruits**

| | | | |
|---|---|---|---|
| strawberry | peach | apple | apple |
| orange | strawberry | strawberry | grapes |
| strawberry | apple | strawberry | apple |
| peach | orange | grapes | orange |
| strawberry | apple | strawberry | grapes |

Tabulate the data. See margin.

| Fruit | Tally | Frequency | |
|---|---|---|---|
| Apple | ? | ? | 5 |
| Orange | ? | ? | 3 |
| Strawberry | ? | ? | 7 |
| Grapes | ? | ? | 3 |
| Peach | ? | ? | 2 |

What is the favorite fruit of Shelly's friends? strawberry

**Best Practices**

**4** Point out that when Shelley conducted her survey, she gave her friends a list of fruits from which to choose. Explain that a survey will often restrict possible answers to a list of choices. This is especially common when large groups of people are being surveyed.

**EXIT**

**Ticket Out the Door**

Describe a context that might produce the following data set.
1, 3, 4, 4, 6, 5, 3, 2, 2, 7, 9, 11, 8
Then organize the data into three intervals and make a frequency table to display the data.
Scenarios will vary. Possible answer: The data represents the number of television programs a group of 13 students watches in one week.

Also available on Teacher One Stop.

**3** **b)** 1, 1, 1, 1, 2, 2, 2, 3, 4, 4, 5, 5, 5, 5, 6, 6, 6, 6, 6, 7, 7, 8, 8, 8, 9, 9, 10, 10

**4**

| Fruit | Tally | Frequency |
|---|---|---|
| Apple | ᏝᎻᎿ | 5 |
| Orange | /// | 3 |
| Strawberry | ᏝᎻᎿ // | 7 |
| Grapes | /// | 3 |
| Peach | // | 2 |

# KEY CONCEPTS

- You can construct a dot plot from a set of data.
- You can interpret data shown in a dot plot using the shape of the data as a guide.

## PACING

**Materials:** number cubes, TRT34

### 5-minute Warm Up

Conduct a short survey with students in your class on the type of pizzas they like. Display the data as a tally chart.

Check students' work.

 Also available on Teacher One Stop.

---

## **13.2**  Dot Plots

**Lesson Objective**

- Display and analyze data using a dot plot.

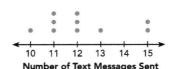

### Represent numerical data using a dot plot.

a) The number of text messages sent by some students one day is as follows. Represent the data on a dot plot.

| 12 | 11 | 10 | 15 | 13 |
|----|----|----|----|----|
| 15 | 12 | 11 | 12 | 11 |

The number of text messages spans from 10 to 15 messages.
To construct a dot plot of these numbers, draw a horizontal number line that extends from 10 to 15.

```
         •     •
   •     •     •
   •     •     •           •
+--+-----+-----+-----+-----+-----+--
  10    11    12    13    14    15
       Number of Text Messages Sent
```

The data value 10 appears once, so place one dot above the number 10 on the number line. The data value 11 appears three times, so place three dots above the number 11.
The data value 14 is absent, so there is no dot above the number 14.

> Dot plots are similar to line plots. Simply replace the ×s with dots.

---

### Represent numerical data using a dot plot.

a) **Model** Use the scenario in the text to show students how to display and analyze numerical data using a dot plot.

**Ask** What information is given in the text? The number of text messages sent by some students one day What is the range of the number of text messages sent? 10 to 15

**Model** Display the dot plot shown in the text so students can see how a dot plot for the given data set is constructed.

**Explain** The data given can be displayed more clearly on a dot plot. A dot plot is similar to a number line. The horizontal number line shows the range of the text messages sent. Each time a number appears in the data set, you draw a dot above the number on the dot plot to represent it. For example, three dots above the number 11 means that 3 students each sent eleven messages.

**Ask** How many students sent 10 messages? 1 How many students sent 11? 3 How many students sent 12? 3

**b)** Eugenia tossed a number cube, numbered 1 to 6, 20 times. She recorded the number in the table below. Represent the data on a dot plot.

| Number | 1 | 2 | 3 | 4 | 5 | 6 |
|---|---|---|---|---|---|---|
| Frequency | 2 | 3 | 6 | 1 | 5 | 3 |

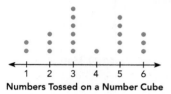

Numbers Tossed on a Number Cube

## Guided Practice

**Represent each set of data with a dot plot. Give each dot plot a title.**

**1** A group of 15 students was asked how many times they have traveled on a plane. The results are recorded in the table.

| Number of Plane Trips | 0 | 1 | 2 | 3 | 4 | 5 | 6 |
|---|---|---|---|---|---|---|---|
| Number of Students | 1 | 5 | 3 | 1 | 1 | 3 | 1 |

See margin.

**2** The results of the high jumps at a track meet are recorded in the table.

| High Jump Results (cm) | 150 | 151 | 152 | 153 | 154 | 155 |
|---|---|---|---|---|---|---|
| Number of Students | 1 | 4 | 3 | 1 | 0 | 2 |

See margin.

**Learn** — **Identifying the shape of a set of data.**

The shape of a dot plot can be either **symmetrical** or **skewed**.

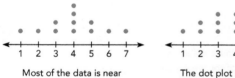 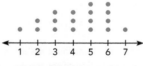 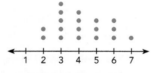

Most of the data is near the center of the range. The shape is symmetrical.

The dot plot has a "tail" on the left. The shape is left-skewed.

The dot plot has a "tail" on the right. The shape is right-skewed.

**1** – **2** See Additional Answers.

**Learn continued**

**b)** **Ask** What is given in the text? A table showing the data that Eugenia recorded What are you asked to do? Represent the data on a dot plot.

**Explain** The horizontal number line on the dot plot shows the numbers tossed on a number cube, that is, 1 to 6. The dots above each number represent the frequency or number of times the number was tossed. The vertical distance between the dots must be equal.

**Learn** **Identifying the shape of a set of data.**

**Model** Use the dot plots shown in the text to show students how to identify the shape of a dot plot.

**Explain** A dot plot can either be symmetrical or skewed. When most of the data values are near the center of the range, the shape is symmetrical. When the dot plot has a "tail" on the left, the shape is left-skewed. When the dot plot has a "tail" on the right, the shape is right-skewed.

## Guided Practice

**3** Guide students to describe the distribution using the shape and the range of the data. Suggest they use terms such as "skewed," "symmetrical," "centered," and "between."

**3** The dot plot has a "tail" on the left. The shape is left-skewed. The data values are from 1 to 5. Range: $5 - 1 = 4$ The students saved about $4 per week, and all of them saved $1 to $5 per week.

---

## Learn  Interpret data from a dot plot.

**a)** The money (in dollars) that 15 students earned by babysitting in one week is shown in the dot plot on the right. Briefly describe the distribution of the earnings of the students.

Earnings ($)

A dot plot can be described by its shape and its **range**.

This dot plot is nearly symmetrical.

These data show a nearly symmetrical dot plot centered around 20. Most of the data values are from 19 to 21.

The data values are from 17 to 24.

> The range of the data is the difference of these numbers.

Range: $24 - 17 = 7$

From these characteristics, you can describe the weekly earnings of the babysitters. They typically earn from $19 to $21 each week, but their earnings range from $17 to $24.

**b)** The number of movies that 12 students saw last month is shown in the dot plot on the right. Briefly describe the number of movies seen by the students.

Number of Movies Seen Last Month

The 12 dots represent 12 students. The dot plot has a "tail" on the right. Most of the data value are from 4 to 6, and the distribution is skewed to the right. The data values are from 3 to 8.

Range: $8 - 3 = 5$

From the description of the dot plot, you know that the students saw about 4 or 5 movies last month, and all of them saw 3 to 8 movies.

### Guided Practice

**Describe the data.**    **3** – **4** See margin.

**3** The weekly savings (in dollars) of 10 students in a class are shown in the dot plot. Briefly describe the distribution of the weekly savings of the students.

Weekly Savings ($)

---

## Learn  Interpret data from a dot plot.

**a)** **Explain** The shape and the range of the dot plot are used to describe the distribution of the earnings of the students. Emphasize that the dot plot is almost symmetrical, with most dots in the center. This means most students earn from $19 to $21 per week. Explain that the range describes the difference between the least earning and the greatest earning.

**Ask** Where are most of the dots? From $19 to $21 What is the least amount of money earned by a student? $17 What is the greatest amount of money earned by a student? $24

**b)** **Ask** What is the shape of the dot plot? Right-skewed What is the range of the distribution? 4 movies

**4** The number of points scored by 12 members of a volleyball team in a game is shown in the dot plot. Briefly describe the number of points scored by the group of players.

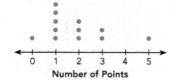

Number of Points

**4** See Additional Answers.

 # Hands-On Activity

**CONSTRUCTING A DISTRIBUTION**

Work in pairs.

**Materials:**
- 2 number cubes, numbered 1–6
- blank table

**STEP 1** – **STEP 4**, Answers will vary.

**STEP 1** Toss two number cubes. Record the difference between the two numbers in a tally chart.

**STEP 2** Repeat 20 times and add your results to another group's results. Record the results for 40 tosses in a copy of the table below.

| Difference | 0 | 1 | 2 | 3 | 4 | 5 |
|---|---|---|---|---|---|---|
| Frequency | ? | ? | ? | ? | ? | ? |

**STEP 3** Represent the data with a dot plot.

**STEP 4** Repeat **STEP 1** to **STEP 3**, but record the SUM of the two numbers each time.

a) What is the least sum you can get?

b) What is the greatest sum you can get?

 *Math Journal*    a) – c) See margin.

a) Describe the distribution of the differences.

b) Describe the distribution of the sums.

c) Discuss with your partner why one distribution is skewed, and the other is symmetric (or nearly so). Why are the shapes of the two distributions different?

## Hands-On Activity

This activity reinforces the skill of constructing a dot plot and interpreting it. Have students work in pairs.

**1** Make sure that only one student rolls the number cubes to avoid any bias in the collection of data.

**2** By combining the data collected from two groups, the students can get more data values. Explain that the more data values, the more accurate the distribution is.

### Best Practices

**2** TRT34 may be useful to students.

**3** Guide students to construct the dot plot, emphasizing the position of each dot.

**4** Students can repeat the activity to practice constructing a dot plot.

 *Math Journal*

a) Most of the data values are to the right of 1, and the distribution is right-skewed.
The data values are from 0 to 5.
Range: $5 - 0 = 5$

b) The data values are from 2 to 12.
Range: $12 - 2 = 10$
Most of the data values are near the center of the range, and the distribution is symmetrical.

c) Answers vary. Sample: The distribution for the differences is likely to be right-skewed because there is a greater chance that you will get a difference of 1 or 2 than 0, 3, 4, or 5. The probability decreases as you move from 1 to 5. The distribution for the sum is likely to be symmetrical or nearly symmetrical because there is a greater chance that you will get a sum of 6, 7, or 8 than any other number from 2 to 12.

## Practice 13.2

**DAY 1** All students should complete ①–⑧.
Optional: *Extra Practice 13.2*

### DIFFERENTIATED INSTRUCTION

**Through Visual Cues**

① Remind students that in a dot plot the entire range of values in the data set is shown on the number line, with no numbers repeated. A dot represents each value in the data set. After students construct their dot plots, point out that there are no dots above 5 on the number line. While 5 is within the range of values in the data set, the value does not actually appear in the set.

①–② See Additional Answers.

---

## Practice 13.2

Basic ①–②
Intermediate ③–⑧

**Represent each set of data with a dot plot.** ①–② See margin.

① The years of service for each of the 18 employees in a company are as follows:

| 7 | 8 | 4 | 3 | 10 | 3 |
|---|---|---|---|----|---|
| 2 | 10 | 7 | 6 | 8 | 2 |
| 1 | 4 | 11 | 12 | 6 | 9 |

② A group of 24 students was asked how many states they have visited. The results are recorded in the table.

| Number of States Visited | 0 | 1 | 2 | 3 | 4 | 5 | 6 | 7 |
|---|---|---|---|---|---|---|---|---|
| Number of Students | 2 | 4 | 5 | 2 | 2 | 6 | 2 | 1 |

**A group of teens was asked to indicate how many pairs of shoes they have in their closet. The results are shown in the dot plot. Use the dot plot to answer questions ③ to ⑤.**

Number of Pairs of Shoes

③ How many data values are there? 20

④ What conclusions can you draw with regard to the number of pairs of shoes the teens have? Most teens have 2 pairs of shoes.

⑤ What percent of the teens indicated 3 pairs of shoes in their closet? 25%

---

### ⚠ RtI Lesson Check

| Before assigning homework, use the following … | to make sure students … | Intervene with … |
|---|---|---|
| Exercise ① | • can construct a dot plot | |
| Exercise ② | • can identify the shape of a dot plot | |
| Exercises ③ and ⑧ | • can interpret a dot plot | Reteach 13.2 |
| Ticket Out the Door | • can compare the appearances and advantages of a frequency table to a dot plot | |

**The dot plot shows the number of weeks each movie that was number 1 at the box office during one year stayed in the number 1 position. Use the dot plot to answer questions 6 and 7.**

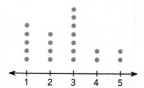

Number of Weeks as Number 1 Movie

**6** How many movies are represented by the dots altogether? 20

**7** Give a reason why more dots are above the numbers 1 to 3 than above the numbers 4 and 5 on the horizontal axis. See margin.

**Copy and complete the dot plot. Use the dot plot to answer each question.**

**8** The incomplete dot plot shows the result of a survey in which each student was asked how many dimes were in their pockets or wallets. The results for "4 dimes" are not shown. Each dot represents one student. It is known that 12.5% of the students had one dime.

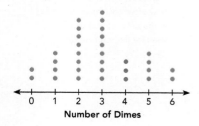

Number of Dimes

a) Find the number of students surveyed. Then complete the dot plot. 32; See above.

b) What percent of the students had either 0 or 6 dimes? 12.5%

c) What percent of the students had either 1 or 5 dimes? 25%

d) Briefly describe the distribution of the data. See margin.

**Ticket Out the Door**

In your own words compare frequency tables and dot plots as methods of displaying a data set. Describe how the data set is displayed in each and the advantages of each. Possible answer: A frequency table lists each value (or interval) in the data set, using tally marks to show the frequency of each data value. A dot plot shows the values in the data set on a number line, using dots to show the frequency of each data value. A dot plot makes it easier to see the distribution of data. A frequency table works well for both large and small sets of data.

 Also available on Teacher One Stop.

**7** Answers vary Sample: There are many good movies that come out regularly, so few movies stay at number 1 in the box office for a long time.

**8** d) Most of the data values are from 2 to 3, and the distribution is right-skewed. The data values are from 0 to 6.

Range: 6 − 0 = 6

# 13.3 Histograms

## KEY CONCEPTS

- You can construct a histogram of a data set.

- You can use a histogram to analyze and interpret data.

## PACING

DAY 1 Pages 228–231

DAY 2 Pages 232–237

**Materials:** none

### 5-minute Warm Up

Present the following data using a dot plot.

```
23 30 25 26 31 28 23 29 30
24 27 31 29 27 25 30 26 28
27 28 30 28 31 29 30 29 32
```

See Additional Answers.

 Also available on Teacher One Stop.

---

### Lesson Objective

- Display and analyze data using a histogram.

**Vocabulary**

histogram    outlier

Learn **Represent numerical data using a histogram.**

The table shows the number of minutes 25 students spent reading for pleasure one day.

| Number of Minutes | 0–29 | 30–59 | 60–89 | 90–119 | 120–149 | 150–179 | 180–209 |
|---|---|---|---|---|---|---|---|
| Frequency | 1 | 3 | 5 | 7 | 5 | 3 | 1 |

Draw a histogram to display this information.

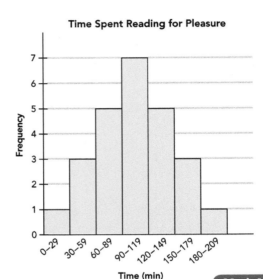

A histogram is a data display that divides the range of data into equal intervals and shows how often each interval occurs in the data set. It is usually used for large sets of data.

**Math Note**

Because the horizontal axis represents continuous intervals of time, there are no gaps between the bars.

---

DAY 1

Learn **Represent numerical data using a histogram.**

**Ask** What is given in the text? A table showing the number of minutes 25 students spent reading for pleasure one day, and a histogram

**Explain** Just like a dot plot, a histogram also represents numerical data. Because a histogram is used for large sets of data, however, the data display divides the range of data into equal intervals.

**Ask** What does the horizontal axis represent? Intervals of time Are there gaps between the bars of the histogram? No What does the height of each bar represent? The frequency for each interval of time

**Summarize** Although a histogram may look similar to a bar graph, there are many differences. A histogram always has a number line for its horizontal axis; a bar graph may show categories on its horizontal axis. A histogram has bars that meet each other, because the data set is continuous; the bars in bar graphs have gaps between them. The vertical axis of a histogram is always "Frequency"; in a bar graph it can be any numerical amounts, such as "Scores."

## Guided Practice

**Draw a histogram for each set of data.**  **–** **2** See margin.

**1** In a study of the length of several individuals of one species of fish caught, the following observations were recorded. The lengths were measured to the nearest centimeter.

| Length of Fish (cm) | 51–60 | 61–70 | 71–80 | 81–90 | 91–100 | 101–110 |
|---|---|---|---|---|---|---|
| Number of Fish | 4 | 5 | 7 | 4 | 2 | 4 |

**2** The scores obtained by 40 students in a mathematics quiz are recorded in the table below.

| Scores | 1–2 | 3–4 | 5–6 | 7–8 | 9–10 |
|---|---|---|---|---|---|
| Frequency | 8 | 8 | 10 | 9 | 5 |

### Learn Choose an appropriate interval to organize data in a histogram.

The data show the heights (in inches) of students in a class.

| | | | | | | | | | |
|---|---|---|---|---|---|---|---|---|---|
| 50 | 66 | 67 | 61 | 68 | 59 | 63 | 69 | 64 | 73 |
| 56 | 68 | 56 | 65 | 67 | 66 | 66 | 59 | 68 | 70 |
| 62 | 64 | 57 | 67 | 60 | 65 | 60 | 67 | 59 | 66 |
| 60 | 65 | 61 | 66 | 58 | 63 | 64 | 68 | 61 | 68 |

a) Group the data into 4 intervals. Display the data in a histogram.

b) Group the data into 8 intervals. Display the data in a histogram.

c) Compare the two histograms.

The greatest value in the data is 73, and the least value in the data is 50. Range: 73 − 50 = 23.

To make 4 intervals, use 23 ÷ 4, which you round up to 6 numbers in each interval. To make 8 intervals, use 23 ÷ 8, or 3 numbers in each interval.

**Continue on next page**

## Guided Practice

**1** and **2** Students practice constructing histograms. Emphasize that there is no gap between the bars.

 **DIFFERENTIATED INSTRUCTION**

**Through Enrichment**

**1** Point out the last sentence of the question stem. **Ask:** Why do you think that sentence must be included? *(If the lengths contained fractional or decimal values, they would fall between the whole number intervals.)*

### Best Practices

In **a)**, Students should keep 3 things in mind when choosing the intervals for a histogram:
1. The range of the data should be divided into equal intervals,
2. The intervals should not overlap, and
3. No values in the data set should fall between intervals (for example, fractional values if intervals are described by whole numbers only).

**1** – **2** See Additional Answers.

### Learn Choose an appropriate interval to organize data in a histogram.

**Ask** What does the data set in the box show? The heights of students in a class **What are you asked to do?** Group the data into 4 intervals, and display the data in a histogram; group the data into 8 intervals, and display the data in a histogram; compare the two histograms **Look at the data set. What is the greatest value?** 73 **What is the least value?** 50 **So, how do you get the range?** Subtract 50 from 73: 73 − 50 = 23

**Explain** So, to make 4 intervals, use 23 ÷ 4, which you round up to 6 numbers in each interval. To make 8 intervals, use 23 ÷ 8, or 3 numbers in each interval.

**Ask** Why do you need to round up when the quotient is not a whole number? Either the intervals would not contain all the data or one or more intervals would not have equal lengths.

**Through Visual Cues**

The two histograms shown here display the same data set but use different scales along their vertical axes. You may want to redraw the histogram in **b)** with vertical intervals of 3 to match the histogram in **a)**. This will help students see that the combined area of the bars (the total number of values in the data set) in both histograms is the same. It will also help students see that, when the same data set is shown divided into a greater number of (smaller) intervals, the data are more spread out.

**Best Practices**

**b)** Point out the empty interval at 53−55. **Ask:** Why is there no bar above this interval? *(There are no values between 53 and 55 in the data set.)* Because there are no gaps between intervals along the horizontal axis of a histogram, some intervals may contain no data points. If an interval contains no data points, there will be no bar above that interval.

**a)** 4 intervals

| Height (in.) | 50–55 | 56–61 | 62–67 | 68–73 |
|---|---|---|---|---|
| Frequency | 1 | 13 | 18 | 8 |

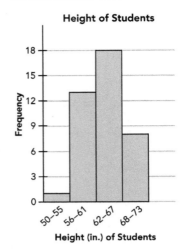

The first bar is $\frac{1}{3}$ the height between 0 and 3, so the frequency is 1.

**b)** 8 intervals

| Height (in.) | 50–52 | 53–55 | 56–58 | 59–61 | 62–64 | 65–67 | 68–70 | 71–73 |
|---|---|---|---|---|---|---|---|---|
| Frequency | 1 | 0 | 4 | 9 | 6 | 12 | 7 | 1 |

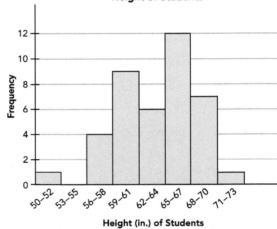

**Learn continued**

**Model** Use the histograms shown in the text to show students the data grouped into 4 and 8 intervals.

**a) Explain** With fewer intervals, there are, on average more items of data in each bar. So, the frequency of each bar will increase.

**b) Explain** With more intervals, there are, on average fewer items of data in each bar. So, the frequency of each bar will decrease.

**c)** The 4-interval histogram is easier to group and draw than the 8-interval histogram. But the spread of the data is revealed better in the 8-interval histogram. The 8-interval histogram shows that the value 50 is an **outlier** from the data. It stands apart from all the other data.

From the two histograms, we see that using more intervals reveals more about the distribution of data.

An **outlier** is an extreme or rare occurrence of a value, which is usually excluded in data analysis.

## Guided Practice

**Draw a histogram for each set of data. Solve.**  **3** – **4** See margin.

**3** The cholesterol levels (in milligram per deciliter) of 40 men are listed below.

| | | | | | | | | | |
|---|---|---|---|---|---|---|---|---|---|
| 221 | 125 | 235 | 274 | 243 | 215 | 173 | 231 | 256 | 213 |
| 270 | 210 | 223 | 161 | 220 | 238 | 180 | 201 | 218 | 198 |
| 193 | 225 | 247 | 239 | 230 | 268 | 229 | 325 | 234 | 277 |
| 218 | 282 | 207 | 265 | 227 | 189 | 239 | 253 | 212 | 159 |

**a)** Group the data into suitable intervals and tabulate them. Explain your choice of intervals.

**b)** Draw a histogram using the interval.

**4** The speeds in kilometers per hour of 40 cars on a highway were recorded as follows.

| | | | | | | | | | |
|---|---|---|---|---|---|---|---|---|---|
| 68 | 51 | 67 | 55 | 74 | 60 | 70 | 66 | 80 | 69 |
| 64 | 81 | 60 | 67 | 65 | 71 | 56 | 78 | 62 | 73 |
| 74 | 63 | 71 | 61 | 77 | 88 | 69 | 62 | 72 | 72 |
| 63 | 65 | 53 | 68 | 58 | 61 | 66 | 61 | 75 | 64 |

**a)** Group the data into suitable intervals and tabulate them. Explain your choice of intervals.

**b)** Draw a histogram using the interval.

**Learn continued**

**c) Ask** Which histogram is easier to group and draw? The 4-interval histogram Which histogram shows the spread of data better? The 8-interval histogram

**Explain** Emphasize that the 8-interval histogram reveals more about the distribution of the data. It shows that the value 50 is an outlier from the data because it stands apart from all the other data.

**Ask** Should the outlier be included in the analysis? No **Why?** Because it is a rare occurrence that is usually excluded in data analysis.

**ELL** **Vocabulary Highlight**

Help students to remember the meaning of *outlier*. Explain that 50 is an outlier in this data set. Point out that by looking at the 8-interval histogram in **b)** they can see that, 50, shown in the short bar at the left, lies out somewhere beyond the rest of the values in the set.

## Guided Practice

**3** and **4** Guide students to select the right intervals for constructing histograms.

**Caution** ///////

**3** Students who decide to break the data set into intervals of 10 may number the first interval 120–130. This interval actually includes 11 values. Every interval needs to include both the beginning and end values listed. Another common error is repeating numbers when moving from naming one interval to the next (for example, labeling one interval "160–170" and the next interval "170–180.") Remind students not to let their intervals overlap.

**3 a)**

| Cholesterol Level (mg/dL) | 120– 159 | 160– 199 | 200– 239 | 240– 279 | 280– 329 |
|---|---|---|---|---|---|
| Frequency | 2 | 6 | 21 | 9 | 2 |

For this set of data, it is suitable to use 5 intervals with a width of 40 since a cholesterol level less than 200 is desirable, a cholesterol level between 200 and 240 is borderline, while a cholesterol level greater than 240 is considered high. The outlier is 125.

**3 b)** – **4 b)** See Additional Answers.

### Learn  Interpret data from a histogram.

The histogram shows the number of digital music files each student in a class has on a computer or other electronic player. Briefly describe the data.

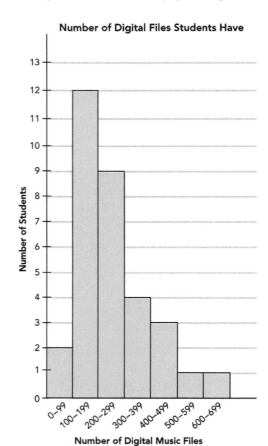

**Number of Digital Files Students Have**

There are 32 students in the class.

Most students have 100 to 299 digital music files.

The range of the data is 699.

The histogram has a "tail" to the right.

Most of the data values are to the right of the most frequent value, so the shape of the histogram is right-skewed.

## DAY 2

### Learn  Interpret data from a histogram.

**Ask** What is given in the text? A histogram showing the number of music files each student in a class has **What are you asked to do?** Describe the data.

**Explain** Interpreting the data from a histogram is the same as describing the data from a dot plot.

**Ask** How many students are there in the class? 32 What is the range of data? 699 How would you describe the shape of the data? Most of the data values are to the right of the most frequent value. So, the histogram is right-skewed.

## Guided Practice

**Describe the data.** ⑤ – ⑥ See margin.

⑤ The histogram shows the number of representatives each state sent to the U.S. Congress in 2011. Briefly describe the data.

**Congressional Representatives for Each State**

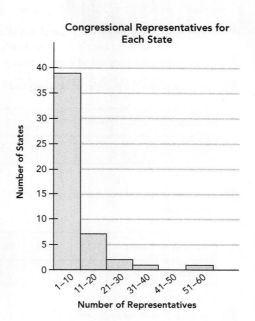

⑥ The histogram shows the highest temperature (in degrees Fahrenheit) recorded during December for one city. The temperature were recorded to the nearest degree. Briefly describe the data.

**December Temperatures**

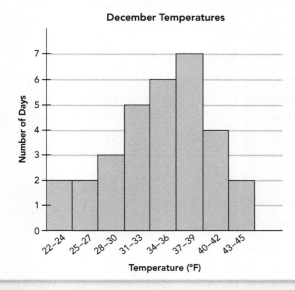

## Guided Practice

⑤ and ⑥ Students can practice describing the distribution of the data set.

⑤ Most of the states sent 1 to 10 representatives to the U.S. Congress in 2011. The histogram is skewed to the right. There is 1 state that sent 51 to 60 representatives, which is an outlier in the data.

⑥ Most of the data values are from 31°F to 39°F. The data set has a "tail" to the left, and the distribution is left-skewed. The temperatures are from 22°F to 45°F, so the range is 23°F.

## Practice 13.3

Basic **1** – **3**
Intermediate **4** – **10**
Advanced **11** – **12**

### Assignment Guide

**DAY 1** All students should complete **1** – **4**.

**DAY 2** All students should complete **5** – **10**.

**11** and **12** provide additional challenge.

Optional: *Extra Practice 13.3*

**Draw a histogram for each set of data. Include a title.** **1** – **3** See margin.

**1** The table shows the number of cans recycled by 25 households in a month.

| Number of Cans | 0–4 | 5–9 | 10–14 | 15–19 | 20–24 | 25–29 | 30–34 |
|---|---|---|---|---|---|---|---|
| Frequency | 1 | 1 | 3 | 6 | 8 | 4 | 2 |

**2** The table shows the number of points scored by a football team in 20 games of one season.

| Number of Points | 0–5 | 6–11 | 12–17 | 18–23 | 24–29 | 30–35 | 36–41 |
|---|---|---|---|---|---|---|---|
| Frequency | 1 | 4 | 6 | 5 | 3 | 0 | 1 |

**3** The table shows the keyboarding speed of 100 students in a beginning keyboarding class.

| Words per Minute | 20–29 | 30–39 | 40–49 | 50–59 | 60–69 | 70–79 | 80–89 |
|---|---|---|---|---|---|---|---|
| Frequency | 39 | 32 | 15 | 10 | 2 | 1 | 1 |

**1**

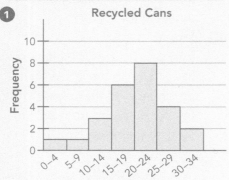

Recycled Cans

**Draw a histogram for the set of data. Include a title. Solve.**

**4** The number of sunny days in a year for 200 cities are shown in the table.

| Number of Sunny Days | 140–148 | 149–157 | 158–166 | 167–175 | 176–184 | 185–193 | 194–202 |
|---|---|---|---|---|---|---|---|
| Number of Cities | 21 | 25 | 32 | x | 31 | 24 | 19 |

**2**

Points Scored by Football Team

a) Find the value of x. 48

b) Draw a histogram to represent the data. Briefly describe the data. See margin.

c) What percent of the cities had fewer than 149 sunny days? 10.5%

d) What percent of the cities had more than 184 sunny days? 21.5%

### ▲RtI Lesson Check

| Before assigning homework, use the following ... | to make sure students ... | Intervene with ... |
|---|---|---|
| Exercise **1** | • can construct a histogram | |
| Exercises **5** and **6** | • can analyze and interpret a histogram | Reteach 13.2 |
| **EXIT** Ticket Out the Door | • can explain the similarities and differences between a dot plot and a histogram | |

**3** and **4** b) See Additional Answers.

The histogram shows the number of cars observed at one intersection at different times of the day. Use the histogram to answer questions **5** to **9**.

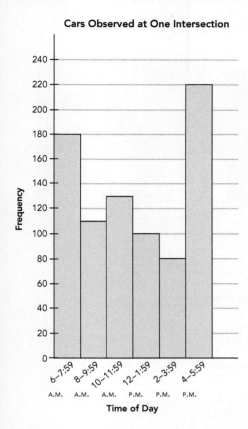

Cars Observed at One Intersection

**5** How many observations are there? 820

**6** How many fewer cars passed the intersection from 6 A.M. to 7:59 A.M. than from 4 P.M. to 5:59 P.M.? 40

**7** How many more cars passed the intersection from 10 A.M. to 11:59 A.M. than from 2 P.M. to 3:59 P.M.? 50

**8** What percent of the number of cars that passed the intersection from 4 P.M. to 5:59 P.M. was observed from 8 A.M. to 9:59 A.M.? 50%

**9** What percent of the total number of cars that passed the intersection from 6 A.M. to 5:59 P.M. was observed from 4 P.M. to 5:59 P.M.? Round your answer to the nearest percent. 27%

## Ticket Out the Door

In your own words, compare how a data set might be displayed in a dot plot and in a histogram.

Possible answer: In a dot plot, all values within the range are shown on a number line and dots are used to show the frequency of each value. In a histogram, the complete range of values, divided into equal intervals, is shown on a horizontal axis. The height of each bars represents the frequency of that interval.

🖱 Also available on Teacher One Stop.

**10** Most of the students read 1 to 15 books. The histogram is nearly symmetrical. There is 1 student who read 21 to 25 books, which is an outlier in the data.

---

The histogram shows the number of books students in a class read last month. Use the histogram to answer the question.

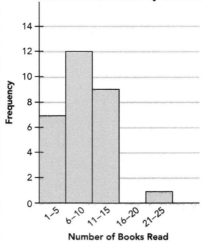

Number of Books Read by Our Class

**10** Briefly describe the data. Explain whether the histogram shows any outlier of the data set. See margin.

**Draw a histogram for the set of data. Include a title. Solve.**

**11** The sales figures for 60 pairs of one style of shoe of various sizes at a department store are given in the table.

| Size of Shoes | 6 | 6.5 | 7 | 7.5 | 8 | 8.5 | 9 | 9.5 | 10 |
|---|---|---|---|---|---|---|---|---|---|
| Number Sold | x | 8 | 22 | 16 | 4 | 3 | 3 | y | 1 |

2 pairs of shoes of at least size 9.5 were sold.

a) Find the values of x and y. $x = 2$; $y = 1$

b) What fraction of the shoes sold are smaller than size 8? $\frac{4}{5}$

c) Draw a histogram using the intervals 6–6.5, 7–7.5, 8–8.5 and so on. Briefly describe the data. See margin.

d) If shoes were to be categorized as follows:
small – sizes 6 to 7; medium – sizes 7.5 to 8.5; large – sizes 9 to 10,
draw a histogram for the above data using the new categories. See margin.

e) Compare the two histograms. When would each one be more useful? See margin.

---

**11** c)

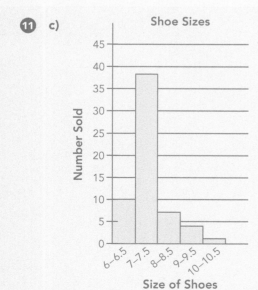

Shoe Sizes

The department store sold the greatest number of shoes with sizes 7 or 7.5. The data set has a "tail" to the right, and so the distribution is right-skewed.

**11** d)

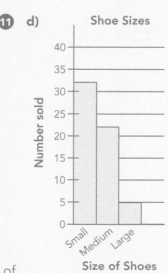

Shoe Sizes

**11** e) The first histogram, which uses more intervals, reveals more about the distribution of data. It shows the two sizes of shoes that sold the most. This histogram will be more useful when you want to find out which two shoes sizes sold best. The second histogram, which uses fewer intervals with greater width, categorizes sizes into small, medium or large. This histogram will be more useful when you want general information on which shoe sizes to stock.

**12** *Math Journal* A survey was carried out to find the number of players who scored a certain number of goals during soccer matches in a month. A histogram was drawn to display the results.

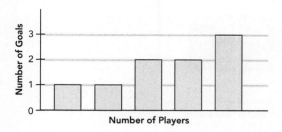

Is the histogram drawn correctly? Discuss with your partner and explain your thinking. See margin.

# Brain @ Work

The table below shows the test scores for all the students in a Spanish I course.

| Scores | 94–100 | 87–93 | 80–86 | 73–79 | 66–72 | 59–65 | 52–58 |
|---|---|---|---|---|---|---|---|
| Frequency | 40 | 50 | 25 | 15 | 10 | 5 | 5 |

The following grades are used to represent the scores.

| Scores | 94–100 | 87–93 | 80–86 | 73–79 | 66–72 | 59–65 | 52–58 |
|---|---|---|---|---|---|---|---|
| Grade | A | B | C | C | D | F | F |

**1** Draw a histogram to show the distribution of the scores. **1** – **3** See margin.

**2** Draw a bar graph to display the grades.

**3** Five students increased their scores from 79 to 89.

   a)   How would it change the histogram?

   b)   How would it change the bar graph?

 *Math Journal*
**12** Guide students to explain the errors in the histogram to their partners. The number of goals should be represented by the *x*-axis, and the *y*-axis should represent the number of players. Emphasize that there should not be spaces between the bars.

# Brain @ Work
Use the following hints and suggestions to guide students.

**1** Convert the scores into grades before they draw the histogram.

**2** Emphasize the difference between a histogram and a bar graph.

**3** Students will discover that changes in the data set will change the distribution of the histogram and the bar graph.

 *Math Journal* **12** and Brain@Work **1** – **3** See Additional Answers.

 **DIFFERENTIATED INSTRUCTION**

**Through Enrichment**

Because all students should be challenged, have all students try the Brain@Work exercise on this page.

For additional challenging practice and problem solving, see *Enrichment, Course 1,* Chapter 13.

## Chapter Wrap Up

### Concept Map

Use the notes and the flow of the concept map to review the processes of collecting, tabulating, and interpreting data to predict trends.

**CHAPTER PROJECT**

To widen students' mathematical horizons and to encourage them to think about what a statistical problem is, use the Chapter 7 project, Using Statistics to Find Solutions to Real-Life Problems, available in *Activity Book Course 1*.

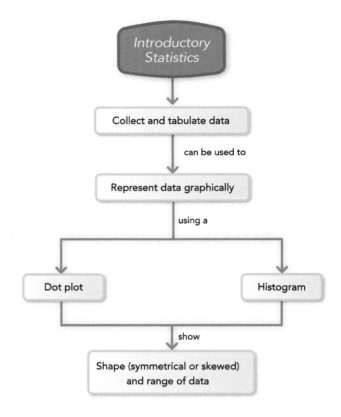

### Key Concepts

▶ Statistical questions need many pieces of data to answer. The answers to these questions require collecting data and organizing it so that it can be easily interpreted.

▶ Data, when presented in a dot plot or histogram show patterns of shape, range, and outliers. The shape of the graph may be skewed to either end of the range, or it may be symmetrical about the middle of the range.

▶ The spread of data can be represented by the range shown on a number line that is part of a dot plot or a histogram.

### Vocabulary Review

Use these questions to review chapter vocabulary with students.

1. The number of times a number appears is known as its __?__. frequency

2. A(n) __?__ is similar to a line plot. dot plot

3. A dot plot is __?__ when most of the data are distributed around the center and the two ends are evenly distributed. symmetrical

4. A distribution can be __?__ to the left or the right. skewed

5. The difference between the least and the greatest value is known as the __?__. range

6. There are no gaps between the bars in a(n) __?__. histogram

7. A(n) __?__ is usually excluded during data analysis. outlier

 Also available on Teacher One Stop.

# Chapter Review/Test

## Concepts and Skills

**Copy and complete the table. Use the set of data.**

1. The number of bedrooms in the units of a new apartment building ranged from 1 to 5. The number of bedrooms in each unit is as follows:

| | | | | |
|---|---|---|---|---|
| 2 | 1 | 3 | 4 | 5 |
| 4 | 3 | 4 | 3 | 2 |
| 3 | 4 | 2 | 1 | 4 |
| 3 | 4 | 2 | 1 | 3 |
| 5 | 1 | 3 | 4 | 3 |
| 2 | 2 | 3 | 5 | 2 |

Tabulate the data.

| Number of Bedrooms | Tally | Frequency | |
|---|---|---|---|
| 1 | ? | ? | ////; 4 |
| 2 | ? | ? | #### //; 7 |
| 3 | ? | ? | #### ////; 9 |
| 4 | ? | ? | #### //; 7 |
| 5 | ? | ? | ///; 3 |

**Draw a dot plot and a histogram for the set of data. Include a title.**

2. The table below shows the number of hours 30 teachers in a school spent correcting students' assignments.

| Number of Hours | 1 | 2 | 3 | 4 | 5 | 6 |
|---|---|---|---|---|---|---|
| Frequency | 4 | 6 | 8 | 6 | 4 | 2 |

See margin.

## Chapter Assessment

Use the Chapter 13 Test A or B in *Assessments, Course 1* to assess how well students have learned the material in this chapter. These assessments are appropriate for reporting results to adults at home and administrators. Test A is shown on page 241A.

## TEST PREPARATION

For additional test prep

- **ExamView® Assessment Suite Course 1**
- **Online Assessment System**
  my.hrw.com

2. See Additional Answers.

## RtI Intervention and Reteaching Recommendations

| Student Book B Review/Test Items | *Assessments* Chapter 13 Items | Chapter 13 Objectives | *Reteach* B Chapter 13 |
|---|---|---|---|
| 1 | Test A: 1 Test B: 1 | **Objective 1.** Collect, organize, and tabulate data. | Lesson 13.1 |
| 2 | Test A: 2–4, 10–13, Test B: 2–4, 10–13 | **Objective 2.** Display and analyze data using a dot plot. | Lesson 13.2 |

④ 44% of the runners are aged 20 to 29 years. Most of the data values are near the center of the range, and the histogram is nearly symmetrical. There is 1 runner aged 0 to 9 years, and another runner aged 50 to 59 years. These are outliers in the data.

⑤

| Length of Trout (in.) | 8–9 | 10–11 | 12–13 | 14–15 | 16–17 | 18–19 |
|---|---|---|---|---|---|---|
| Number of Trout | 3 | 8 | 24 | 9 | 5 | 1 |

The range is 18 − 8 = 10. Choosing an interval of 2 gives six intervals for the data set. A larger interval will give too few intervals, and you will not be able to see the distribution accurately.

⑥

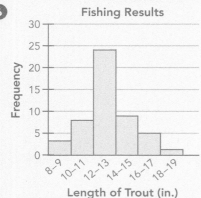

**Fishing Results**

Almost half the fish were 12 or 13 inches long. The histogram is slightly skewed to right.

The histogram shows the ages of runners in a marathon. Use the histogram to answer questions ③ and ④.

**Ages of Marathon Runners**

③ How many data values are there? 25

④ Briefly describe the distribution including any outliers in the data. See margin.

## Problem Solving

The data show the lengths (in inches) of 50 trout caught in a lake during a fishing competition. Use the data to answer questions ⑤ and ⑥.

| | | | | | | | | | |
|---|---|---|---|---|---|---|---|---|---|
| 12 | 14 | 13 | 10 | 14 | 12 | 16 | 13 | 11 | 13 |
| 16 | 12 | 8 | 13 | 12 | 11 | 13 | 15 | 12 | 13 |
| 10 | 9 | 12 | 14 | 16 | 13 | 15 | 12 | 11 | 15 |
| 13 | 12 | 12 | 10 | 13 | 8 | 12 | 16 | 13 | 12 |
| 15 | 11 | 17 | 13 | 14 | 13 | 10 | 15 | 18 | 13 |

⑤ Group the data into suitable intervals and tabulate them. Explain your choice of interval. See margin.

⑥ Draw a histogram using the interval. Briefly describe the data. See margin.

**RtI** Intervention and Reteaching Recommendations

| Student Book B Review/Test Items | Assessments Chapter 13 Items | Chapter 13 Objectives | Reteach B Chapter 13 |
|---|---|---|---|
| ③ to ⑥ | Test A: 3, 5–9<br>Test B: 3, 5–9 | **Objective 3.** Display and analyze data using a histogram. | Lesson 13.3 |

The data show the distances a golfer hits (in yards) in a long drive championship. Use the data to answer questions **7** and **8**.

| 244 | 252 | 267 | 245 | 257 | 270 | 250 | 261 | 251 | 274 |
|---|---|---|---|---|---|---|---|---|---|
| 263 | 248 | 256 | 273 | 270 | 248 | 265 | 271 | 260 | 278 |
| 254 | 250 | 255 | 252 | 249 | 263 | 273 | 268 | 256 | 269 |

**7** Group the data into suitable intervals and tabulate them. Explain your choice of interval. See margin.

**8** Draw a histogram using the interval. Briefly describe the data. See margin.

The table shows the number of cars passing a traffic light during peak hours on a Friday morning. Use the data to answer questions **9** to **11**.

| Time | 7:00–7:29 | 7:30–7:59 | 8:00–8:29 | 8:30–8:59 | 9:00–9:29 | 9:30–9:59 |
|---|---|---|---|---|---|---|
| Number of Cars | 22 | 45 | 64 | 57 | 27 | 25 |

**9** How many cars were observed altogether? 240

**10** Draw a histogram to display the data. See margin.

**11** Describe the distribution of the data. Suggest why the histogram has the shape that it does. See margin.

The quiz scores of 94 students are shown in the table. Use the data to answer questions **12** to **14**.

| Score | 14–16 | 17–19 | 20–22 | 23–25 | 26–28 | 29–31 | 32–34 | 35–37 | 38–40 |
|---|---|---|---|---|---|---|---|---|---|
| Number of Students | 17 | x | 3 | 5 | 12 | 15 | 17 | 10 | 8 |

**12** Find the value of x. 7

**13** Draw a histogram to represent the data. Describe the distribution of the data. See margin.

**14** If the 5 students who scored 23–25 all scored 26 instead, would this change where most of the data occur? Justify your answer. See margin.

**7**

| Distance of Long Drive (yd) | Frequency |
|---|---|
| 240–244 | 1 |
| 245–249 | 4 |
| 250–254 | 6 |
| 255–259 | 4 |
| 260–264 | 4 |
| 265–269 | 4 |
| 270–274 | 6 |
| 275–279 | 1 |

The range is 278 – 244 = 34. Choosing an interval of 5 gives eight intervals for the data set. A larger interval gives too few intervals, and you will not be able to see the distribution accurately.

**8**

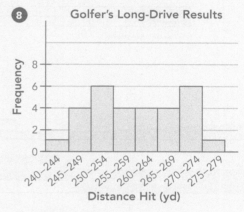

Golfer's Long-Drive Results

See below.

## RtI Intervention and Reteaching Recommendations

| Student Book B Review/Test Items | Assessments Chapter 13 Items | Chapter 13 Objectives | Reteach B Chapter 13 |
|---|---|---|---|
| **7** to **14** | Test A: 3, 5–9 Test B: 3, 5–9 | **Objective 3.** Display and analyze data using a histogram. | Lesson 13.3 |

**8** From the histogram, the two highest frequencies are at 250 to 254 yards and 270 to 274 yards. For this interval width, the distribution is quite uniform. This indicates the golfer has a wide spread of results for his long drives.

**10** – **11**, **13** – **14** See Additional Answers.

## Chapter 13 Tests A and B

Answer key appears in the *Assessments, Course 1*

---

**Test B, Assessments p. 139**

**Test A, Assessments p. 135**

Name: _____  Date: _____

CHAPTER TEST A

**13  Introduction to Statistics**

| 25 |
Suggested Time: 30 min

**Concepts and Skills** (5 × 2 points = 10 points)

**Use the given data to answer the questions.**

1. The favorite colors of 20 students are given below.

| Yellow | Red | Green | Pink | Yellow |
| Pink | Blue | Blue | Yellow | Blue |
| Yellow | Pink | Green | Blue | Green |
| Green | Blue | Yellow | Blue | Blue |

A tally chart is used to record the findings. Complete the table.

| Color | Tally | Frequency |
|-------|-------|-----------|
| Blue | | |
| Green | | |
| Pink | | |
| Red | | |
| Yellow | | |

2. The table shows the number of children in 25 families.

| Number of Children | 0 | 1 | 2 | 3 | 4 |
|--------------------|---|---|---|---|---|
| Number of Families | 3 | 7 | 8 | 5 | 2 |

Draw a dot plot to display the data.

Assessments Course 1  **135**

---

**Test B, Assessments p. 140**

**Test A, Assessments p. 136**

Name: _____  Date: _____

3. The table shows the ages of employees in a company.

| Age (years) | 20–24 | 25–29 | 30–34 | 35–39 | 40–44 |
|-------------|-------|-------|-------|-------|-------|
| Frequency | 7 | 15 | 12 | 8 | 3 |

Draw a histogram to display the data.

4. The dot plot shows the points obtained by students in a quiz. If a student needed at least 6 points to pass the quiz, how many students passed the quiz?

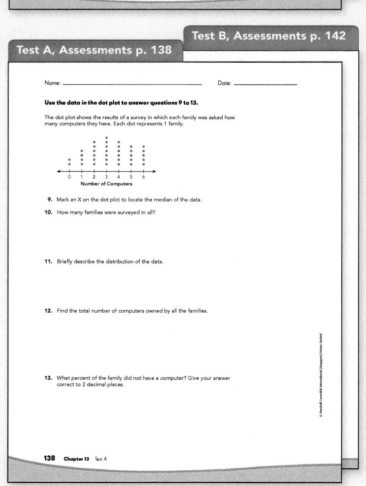

**136**  Chapter 13  Test A

---

**Test B, Assessments p. 141**

**Test A, Assessments p. 137**

Name: _____  Date: _____

5. The histogram shows the number of paper airplanes folded by students in a class. Briefly describe the distribution of the data.

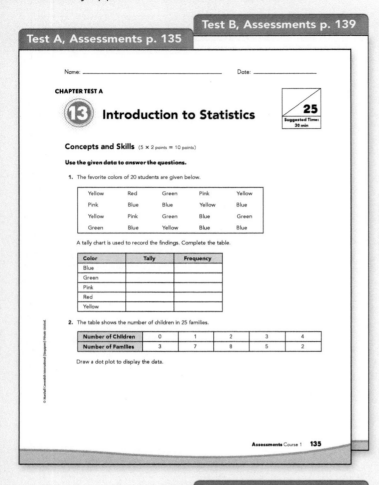

**Problem Solving** (Questions 6 to 9: 4 × 2 points = 8 points, Question 10: 1 point, Questions 11 to 13: 3 × 2 points = 6 points)

**Use the data in the table to answer questions 6 to 8.**

The table shows the masses of 50 eggs.

| Mass (grams) | 40–44 | 45–49 | 50–54 | 55–59 | 60–64 | 65–69 |
|--------------|-------|-------|-------|-------|-------|-------|
| Number of Eggs | 6 | x | 12 | 10 | 7 | 2 |

6. Find the value of x.

7. Draw a histogram to represent the data.

8. An egg with a mass of at least 60 grams is considered "large". What percent of the eggs is considered "large"?

Assessments Course 1  **137**

---

**Test B, Assessments p. 142**

**Test A, Assessments p. 138**

Name: _____  Date: _____

**Use the data in the dot plot to answer questions 9 to 13.**

The dot plot shows the results of a survey in which each family was asked how many computers they have. Each dot represents 1 family.

9. Mark an X on the dot plot to locate the median of the data.

10. How many families were surveyed in all?

11. Briefly describe the distribution of the data.

12. Find the total number of computers owned by all the families.

13. What percent of the family did not have a computer? Give your answer correct to 2 decimal places.

**138**  Chapter 13  Test A

---

# Chapter at a Glance

| | | **CHAPTER OPENER**<br>Measures of<br>Central Tendency<br><br>Recall Prior Knowledge | **LESSON 14.1**<br>Mean<br>Pages 244–250 | **LESSON 14.2**<br>Median<br>Pages 251–257 |
|---|---|---|---|---|
| **LESSON AT A GLANCE** | Pacing | 2 days | 2 days | 2 days |
| | Objectives | Measures of central tendency can be used to summarize data distributions, and help you make decisions in real-world problems. | • Find the mean of a set of data.<br>• Use the mean of a set of data to solve problems. | • Find the median of a set of data.<br>• Use the median of a set of data to solve problems. |
| | Vocabulary | | mean | median |
| **RESOURCES** | Materials | | ruler, TRT15* | TRT1*, TRT15* |
| | Lesson Resources | Student Book B,<br>    pp. 242–243<br>*Assessments Course 1*,<br>    Chapter 14 Pre-Test<br>*Transition Guide*,<br>    Course 1, Skills 52–53 | Student Book B, pp. 244–250<br>*Extra Practice B*, Lesson 14.1<br>*Reteach B*, Lesson 14.1<br>*Activity Book*, Lesson 14.1 | Student Book B, pp. 251–257<br>*Extra Practice B*, Lesson 14.2<br>*Reteach B*, Lesson 14.2 |
| | **Common Core**<br>Standards for Mathematical Content | Foundational for **6.SP.2**, **6.SP.3**, **6.SP.5** | **6.SP.2** Understand that a set of data…has a distribution which can be described by its center. **6.SP.5, 6.SP.5a, 6.SP.5c, 6.SP.5d** Summarize numerical data sets in relation to their context… | **6.SP.3** Recognize that a measure of center for a numerical data set summarizes all of its values… **6.SP.5d.** Relate…the center…to the shape of the data distribution. |
| | **Mathematical Practices** | **6.** Attend to precision.<br>**7.** Look for and use structure. | **1.** Solve problems/persevere.<br>**2.** Reason. **3.** Construct arguments.<br>**4.** Model mathematics. | **2.** Reason. **4.** Model mathematics.<br>**5.** Use tools strategically.<br>**8.** Express regularity in reasoning. |

*Teacher Resource Tools (TRT) are available on the Teacher One Stop.*

# Concepts and Skills Across the Courses

| **GRADE 5** | **COURSE 1** | **COURSE 2** |
|---|---|---|
| • Represent and interpret data. (5.MD.2)<br><br>• Make a line plot to display measurements. (5.MD.2)<br><br>• Use operations on fractions to solve problems involving data in line plots. (5.MD.2) | • Recognize measures of center (mean, median, and mode) for a numerical data set. (6.SP.3)<br><br>• Display numerical data in dot plots and histograms. (6.SP.4)<br><br>• Summarize and describe the shape of data distributions in relation to their context. (6.SP.5, 6.SP.5a, 6.SP.5.b, 6.SP.5d) | • Interpret quartiles, interquartile range, mean absolute deviation, and box plots. (6.SP.4, 6.SP.5c)<br><br>• Use random sampling to gain information about a population and draw inferences. (7.SP. 1, 7.SP.2)<br><br>• Use measures of center and measures of variability to compare and describe two populations. (7.SP.3, 7.SP.4) |

| LESSON 14.3<br>Mode<br>Pages 258–263 | LESSON 14.4<br>Real-World Problems:<br>Mean, Median, and Mode<br>Pages 264–271 | CHAPTER<br>WRAP UP/REVIEW/TEST<br>CUMULATIVE REVIEW<br>Brain@Work<br>Pages 272–279 |
|---|---|---|
| 2 days | 2 days | 3 days |
| • Find the mode of a set of data.<br>• Use the mode of a set of data to solve problems. | • Solve problems that are related to the concepts of mean, median, and mode, including selection of the measure of central tendency to be used for problems. | Reinforce, consolidate, and extend chapter skills and concepts. |
| mode | | |
| TRT1*, TRT15*, TRT35*, tape, scissors, ruler | TRT1* | |
| Student Book B, pp. 258–263<br>*Extra Practice B*, Lesson 14.3<br>*Reteach B*, Lesson 14.3 | Student Book B, pp. 264–271<br>*Extra Practice B*, Lesson 14.4<br>*Reteach B*, Lesson 14.4 | Student Book B, pp. 272–279<br>*Activity Book*, Chapter 14 Project<br>*Enrichment*, Chapter 14<br>*Assessments*, Chapter 14 Test, End-of-Course Test<br> ExamView® Assessment Suite Course 1 |
| **6.SP.4** Display numerical data in plots on a number line, including dot plots...<br>**6.SP.5d** Relate...the center...to the shape of the data distribution. | **6.SP.3** Recognize that a measure of center for a numerical data set summarizes all of its values...<br>**6.SP.5d** Relate...the center...to the context of the data. | |
| **3.** Construct arguments.<br>**4.** Model mathematics. **5.** Use tools strategically. | **1.** Solve problems/persevere.<br>**5.** Use tools strategically. **7.** Look for and use structure. **8.** Express regularity in reasoning. | **1.** Solve problems/persevere.<br>**7.** Look for and use structure. |

*Teacher Resource Tools (TRT) are available on the Teacher One Stop.*

# Additional Chapter Resources

## TECHNOLOGY

-  Online Student eBook
-  Interactive Whiteboard Lessons
-  Virtual Manipulatives
-  Teacher One Stop
-  ExamView® Assessment Suite Course 1
-  Online Professional Development Videos

## Every Day Counts®<br>ALGEBRA READINESS

**The May and June activities in the Pacing Chart provide:**

- **Review** of solids and nets **(Ch. 12: 6.G.4)**

- **Review** of variable expressions **(Ch. 7: 6.EE.2)**

- **Review** of graphs of linear relationships **(Ch. 8 and 9: 6.EE.9)**

# Math Background

# Chapter 14 Measures of Central Tendency

## Using the Mean to Solve Problems

- In this chapter, students will learn to find the mean, median, and mode of a data set, and how to solve real-world problems involving them.

### Unknown totals and missing data items

- Beyond finding means, students also learn how to find a total when given the mean of a set of data and the number of data items. They also learn how to identify a missing data item, given the mean and the rest of the values. Problems like the one below frequently appear on standardized tests.

  In five races Shani's mean time is 6.4 seconds. His four most recent times were 6.9 s, 5.8 s, 5.9 s, and 6.3 s. What was Shani's time in his first race?

  **Solution**
  First, use the mean formula to find the total time.
  Total time in 5 races = Mean · Number of races
  $$= 6.4 \cdot 5 = 32.0$$

  Next, find the total of the 4 known times.
  Total time in 4 races = 6.9 + 5.8 + 5.9 + 6.3 = 24.9

  Finally, find the difference.
  32.0 − 24.9 = 7.1
  Shani's time in his first race was 7.1 seconds.

### Weighted averages

- Students also learn how to solve another type of mean problem commonly found on standardized tests, problems involving weighted averages.

  On a math quiz, four students score 50 and six students score 70. What is the mean score?

  **Solution**
  The mean is not simply the average of 50 and 70.
  Four students scored 50: 4 · 50 = 200 points.
  Six students scored 70: 6 · 70 = 420 points.
  Mean $= \frac{(200 + 420)}{10} = \frac{620}{10} = 62$
  The mean score is 62 points.

## Choosing a Measure of Center

- In this chapter, students will relate mean, median, and mode to the distribution of a data set.

### A two-year study of data shape

- In Math in Focus, the data strand is taught over two years. Course 1 focuses on measures of center. Course 2 introduces box plots and measures of variability.

### Data shape and measures of center

- Students began their study of data shape in Chapter 13 with exploration of symmetrical and skewed distributions. In this chapter, they relate these distributions to measures of center.

- Students learn that in a symmetrical distribution, the mean, median, and mode are the same. All three measures are appropriate to describe the data set.

- Students learn that in a skewed data set, all three measures give you important information, but one may be more useful than another. The median tells which value has as many values below it as above it. The mean takes into account the effects of extreme values (outliers). For example, look at the two data sets below.

  5, 10, 15, 15, 1     5, 10, 15, 15, 55

  In both sets, the median is 15. But the mean is 9.2 in the first set and 20 in the second set.

  Which value is more useful depends on the situation. If the data sets represent savings over 5 weeks by two people, the median might help estimate how much each person could expect to save any week. The mean might be better for estimating how long it will take to save $150.

- Students find that the mode is often less useful. It is often close to the median, but it can be any value in a data set. If 20 students take a test, 15 score between 80 and 100, and 5 students score 0 (the mode), it is not particularly useful to describe the set by pointing out that the mode is 0. The median and mean better summarize the 20 students' scores.

# Differentiated Instruction

## Assessment and Intervention

| | ASSESSMENT | RtI STRUGGLING LEARNERS |
|---|---|---|
| **DIAGNOSTIC** | • Quick Check in Recall Prior Knowledge in Student Book B, pp. 243<br>• Chapter 14 Pre-Test in *Assessments* | • Skills 52–53 in *Transition Guide, Course 1* |
| **ON-GOING** | • Guided Practice<br>• Lesson Check<br>• Ticket Out the Door | • Reteach worksheets<br>• Extra Practice worksheets, Ch12–14 Cumulative Practice worksheets<br>• *Activity Book*, Chapter 14 |
| **END-OF-CHAPTER** | • Chapter Review/Test<br>• Chapter 14 Test in *Assessments*<br>• ExamView® Assessment Suite Course 1 | • Reteach worksheets |

### ELL ENGLISH LANGUAGE LEARNERS

Review the terms *mean* and *median*.

**Say** In everyday English, the word *mean* describes a person or animal that is not nice. A dog that bites people is a mean dog. In mathematics, *mean* has a very different meaning. The mean of a set of numbers is the average.

**Model** Write the formula for mean (found on page 244). List this set of values: 4, 3, 7, 2, 9. Find the mean (5).

**Say** In everyday English, a *median* is the strip of grass or concrete that separates traffic on a highway. (Show an image of a median.) The median of a highway is in the middle. In mathematics, *median* also means "middle." The median is the middle value in a data set.

**Model** Rewrite the values in the above set in ascending order. Identify and circle the middle value, 4.

For definitions, see Glossary, page 301, of Student Book and Online Multilingual Glossary.

### ADVANCED LEARNERS

• Students can create posters illustrating the effect of outliers on a data set's measures of central tendency. Have students do research in a subject that interests them to find or compile data sets that include outliers. For example, they might compile weights of various types of bears; areas or populations of a collection of nations or states; ages at which a group of famous authors published their first work; or athletic statistics.

• Have students identify the mean, median, and mode of their data sets, then exclude the outliers and find the values again. They should create posters showing how they found the mean, median, and mode as well as how outliers affected those values.

• As needed, provide direction for students, such as suggesting that they show dot plots and limit the size of their data sets to 10 to 30 items.

**To provide additional challenges use:**
• *Enrichment*, Chapter 14
• Student Book B, Brain@Work problems

CHAPTER

14

# Measures of Central Tendency

## How do blue jean companies know what customers will buy?

When blue jeans are manufactured, the quantity needed for each size depends on what retailers have ordered. It does not make economic sense to manufacture an equal number of jeans in all men's sizes from 24 inches to 44 inches. By finding a value around which most orders cluster, the production can be tailored to meet the demand. This helps to reduce waste in the manufacturing process.

In statistics, finding a value for a typical order is called finding a measure of central tendency. Learning how to find the various measures of central tendency is an important part of any production process from art prints to xylophones.

### Chapter Vocabulary

Vocabulary terms are used in context in the student text. For definitions, see the Glossary at the end of the Student Book and the online Multilingual Glossary.

**mean** One measure of the center of a set of data. It is found by dividing the sum of the data values by the number of data values.

**median** A measure of the center of a set of data. Once the data have been placed in numerical order, it is the middle value when the number of data items is odd, and the mean of the two middle values when the number of data items is even.

**mode** A measure of the center of a set of data. It is the value (or values) that occurs most often in the data set.

BIG IDEA

▶ Measures of central tendency can be used to summarize data distributions, and help you make decisions in real-world problems.

## CHAPTER OPENER

Use the chapter opener to talk about the use of measures of central tendency in a real-life situation.

**Ask** How do manufacturers know which sizes of jeans are the most popular? Possible answer: By knowing the quantities that are ordered for each size of jeans

**Explain** The quantities that are ordered determine which size of jeans is most popular among buyers, and which one will sell best in the market. A manufacturer uses data from past orders to predict what will be ordered six months or a year from now. This information helps reduce waste in the production process.

In this chapter, you will learn how measures of central tendency can be used to summarize data distributions, and help you make decisions in real-world problems, as summarized in the **Big Idea**.

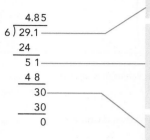

## Recall Prior Knowledge

### Dividing decimals by a whole number

Find the value of 29.1 ÷ 6.

```
      4.85
   6 ) 29.1
       24
        5 1
        4 8
          30
          30
           0
```

29 ones ÷ 6 = 4 ones R 5 ones

Regroup the remainder 5 ones.
5 ones = 50 tenths
Add the tenths.
50 tenths + 1 tenth = 51 tenths
51 tenths ÷ 6 = 8 tenths R 3 tenths

Regroup the remainder 3 tenths.
3 tenths = 30 hundredths
30 hundredths ÷ 6 = 5 hundredths

The value of 29.1 ÷ 6 is 4.85.

### ✓ Quick Check

**Divide.**

**1** 16.5 ÷ 2  8.25

**2** 48.09 ÷ 7  6.87

### Finding the average of each data set

Find the average of 12, 14, 18, 24, 36, and 40.

First, find the sum of the data values.

12 + 14 + 18 + 24 + 36 + 40 = 144

Then divide the sum by the number of data values.

The average is 144 ÷ 6 = 24.

### ✓ Quick Check

**Find the average of each data set.**

**3** 2, 4, 16, 18  10

**4** 3, 5, 7, 8, 21, 31  12.5

**5** $14, $30, $32, $50  $31.50

**6** 25 ft, 32 ft, 46 ft, 55 ft, 78 ft  47.2 ft

## RECALL PRIOR KNOWLEDGE

Use the ✓ **Quick Check** exercises or the Chapter Pre-Test in *Assessments, Course 1*, to assess chapter readiness. For intervention suggestions, see the chart below.

🖱 Additional online Reteach and Extra Practice worksheets from previous grades are also available. See the *Transition Guide*, Resource Planner for more information.

### ▲ RtI Assessing Prior Knowledge

| ✓ Quick Check | *Assessments Course 1, Ch.14* Pre-Test Items | Skill Objective | Transition Guide | Online Resources Grades 4 and 5 |
|---|---|---|---|---|
| **1** to **2** | 1–4 | Divide decimals by a whole number | Skill 52 | |
| **3** to **6** | 5–7 | Find the average of each data set | Skill 53 | Reteach 4A, pp. 95–100 Extra Practice 4A, Lesson 5.1 |

## KEY CONCEPTS

- You can calculate the mean of a set of data.

- You can calculate the mean of a set of data using a dot plot.

- You can find the missing term of a set of data, given the mean.

## PACING

DAY **1** Pages 244–246

DAY **2** Pages 247–250

**Materials:** ruler, TRT15

### 5-minute Warm Up

**Solve.**

1. David cuts a one-meter ribbon into 4 equal pieces. What is the length of each piece of ribbon in meters? $1 ÷ 4 = 0.25$

2. How do you find the average of 23, 34 and 33? Find the sum of the numbers and divide the answer by 3.

 Also available on Teacher One Stop.

---

## 14.1  Mean

**Lesson Objectives**

- Find the mean of a set of data.
- Use the mean of a set of data to solve problems.

**Vocabulary**

mean

**Learn  Understand the concept of mean.**

Finding the mean of a set of data is one way to summarize all the values in a data set with a single number.

To find the mean of a set of items, find the sum of all the items and then divide the sum by the number of items.

$$\text{Mean} = \frac{\text{sum of a set of items}}{\text{number of items}}$$

For example, Aaron has the following three mathematics test scores.

| Test | Score |
|------|-------|
| 1 | 65 |
| 2 | 74 |
| 3 | 80 |

One way to describe the set of test scores is to find the average or mean of the three test scores.

**Math Note**

Another word for average is mean.

Mean score for the three tests

$$= \frac{\text{total score for the three tests}}{\text{number of tests}}$$

$$= \frac{65 + 74 + 80}{3}$$

$$= \frac{219}{3}$$

$$= 73$$

So, Aaron's mean score for the three tests is 73.

---

DAY **1**

**Learn  Understand the concept of mean.**

**Model**  Use the example in the text to show students how to find the mean of a set of data.

**Ask**  What is "mean?" It is the sum of all the items divided by the number of items in a set of data. What is another word for "mean?" Average

**Explain**  Finding the mean of a set of data is one way of summarizing or describing the set of data.

**Ask**  What information is given in the example? Aaron's 3 mathematics test scores How can you find the mean of Aaron's scores? By using the formula

$$\text{Mean} = \frac{\text{total score of three tests}}{\text{number of tests}}$$

$$= \frac{65 + 74 + 80}{3}$$

$$= \frac{219}{3}$$

$$= 73$$

What is the mean of Aaron's three scores? 73

## Guided Practice

**Complete.**

Four boys have heights of 154 centimeters, 157 centimeters, 160 centimeters, and 165 centimeters.

**1** What is the total height of the four boys?

Total height

$= \underline{\ ?\ } + \underline{\ ?\ } + \underline{\ ?\ } + \underline{\ ?\ }$  154; 157; 160; 165

$= \underline{\ ?\ }$ cm  636

The total height of the four boys is $\underline{\ ?\ }$ centimeters.  636

**2** What is the mean height of the four boys?

Mean height

$= \dfrac{\text{total height}}{\text{number of boys}}$

$= \underline{\ ?\ } \div \underline{\ ?\ }$  636; 4

$= \underline{\ ?\ }$ cm  159

The mean height of the four boys is $\underline{\ ?\ }$ centimeters.  159

**Complete. Use the data in the table.**

The table shows the temperature at noon from Monday to Friday in one city.

**Temperature in Degrees Fahrenheit (°F)**

| Monday | Tuesday | Wednesday | Thursday | Friday |
|--------|---------|-----------|----------|--------|
| 52°F | 51°F | 49°F | 48°F | 54°F |

**3** What was the mean temperature at noon from Monday to Friday?

Mean temperature

$= \dfrac{\text{total temperature}}{\text{number of days}}$

$= \dfrac{\underline{\ ?\ } + \underline{\ ?\ } + \underline{\ ?\ } + \underline{\ ?\ } + \underline{\ ?\ }}{\underline{\ ?\ }}$  52; 51; 49; 48; 54  5

$= \dfrac{\underline{\ ?\ }}{\underline{\ ?\ }}$  $\dfrac{254}{5}$

$= \underline{\ ?\ }$ °F  50.8

The mean temperature at noon from Monday to Friday was $\underline{\ ?\ }$ °F.  50.8

## Guided Practice

**1** to **3** Reinforce students' understanding of the concept of mean.

### Best Practices

Building off of the Learn on page 244, create a data set of 6–12 test scores that you can revisit at the start of each lesson. You can find the mean, median, and mode, and discuss the distribution of data as well as which measure of center best describes the set. Skew the data to the left or right so that the mean, median, and mode are not identical.

 **DIFFERENTIATED INSTRUCTION**

**Through Modeling**

Repeat the computations in **1** and **2** with a second set of four heights: 159 cm, 159 cm, 159 cm, and 159 cm. Ask students to compare the mean to the mean they found for the first set of four values. *(It is the same.)* When the mean of a set of four values is 159 cm, they can treat that data set as if all four values are 159 cm.

## Guided Practice

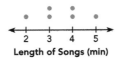

**Find the mean of a data set using a dot plot.**

There are six songs in an album. The dot plot shows the length of each song in minutes. Each dot represents 1 song.

Length of Songs (min)

To find the mean, first calculate the total length of the six songs. Then divide the total length of the songs by the number of songs.

1 song of length 2 min ⟶ 1 × 2 = 2 min
2 songs of length 3 min ⟶ 2 × 3 = 6 min
2 songs of length 4 min ⟶ 2 × 4 = 8 min
1 song of length 5 min ⟶ 1 × 5 = 5 min

$$\text{Mean} = \frac{\text{total length of songs}}{\text{number of songs}}$$
$$= \frac{2+6+8+5}{6}$$
$$= \frac{21}{6}$$
$$= 3.5 \text{ min}$$

The mean length of the six songs is 3.5 minutes.

### Guided Practice

**Complete. Use the data in the dot plot.**

A group of volunteers was selling coupons to raise money for a food pantry. The dot plot on the right shows the number of coupons sold by each volunteer. Each dot represents 1 volunteer.

Number of Coupons

④ __?__ volunteers sold 8 coupons each. ⟶ __?__ × __?__ = __?__ coupons sold  3; 3; 8; 24

⑤ __?__ volunteers sold 9 coupons each. ⟶ __?__ × __?__ = __?__ coupons sold  2; 2; 9; 18

⑥ __?__ volunteers sold 10 coupons each. ⟶ __?__ × __?__ = __?__ coupons sold  3; 3; 10; 30

⑦ __?__ coupons were sold altogether.  72

⑧ There were __?__ volunteers altogether.  8

⑨ The mean number of coupons sold by the group of volunteers was __?__.  9

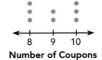

**Find the mean of a data set using a dot plot.**

**Model** Use the scenario in the text to show students how to find the mean of a data set by using a dot plot.

**Ask** What data are given in the dot plot? Number of songs in an album and length of each song in minutes How many songs have a length of 2 minutes? 3 minutes? 4 minutes? 5 minutes? 1; 2; 2; 1 What is the total length of the songs? 21 min How many songs are there altogether? 6 songs How do you find the mean length of the six songs? First, calculate the total length of the six songs. Then divide the total length of the songs by the number of songs.

**Explain** To find the mean, use the formula

$$\text{Mean} = \frac{\text{total length of songs}}{\text{number of songs}}$$
$$= \frac{2+6+8+5}{6}$$
$$= \frac{21}{6}$$
$$= 3.5 \text{ min}$$

**Ask** What is the mean length of the six songs? 3.5 min

## Learn — Find the total and a missing number from the mean.

Geraldine recorded a set of six numbers and found the mean to be 11.2.
After she accidentally erased one of the numbers, she had only five numbers left:
2.3, 6.5, 8.8, 12.4, and 16.0. Find the missing number.

Total of the six numbers = mean × number of given numbers
$$= 11.2 \times 6$$
$$= 67.2$$

Total of the five numbers left = 2.3 + 6.5 + 8.8 + 12.4 + 16.0
$$= 46$$

$$67.2 - 46 = 21.2$$

So, the missing number is 21.2.

> You can find the total of a set of items by multiplying the mean by the number of items.
>
> Total of a set of items
> = mean × number of items

## Guided Practice

**Solve.**

10. Jay's mean score for four quizzes is 8. His scores for the first three quizzes are 7.5, 8, and 9. What is Jay's score for the last quiz?

Total score for the four quizzes = mean score × number of quizzes
$$= \underline{\ ?\ } \times \underline{\ ?\ } \quad 8; 4$$
$$= \underline{\ ?\ } \quad 32$$

Total score for the first three quizzes $= \underline{\ ?\ } + \underline{\ ?\ } + \underline{\ ?\ } \quad 7.5; 8; 9$
$$= \underline{\ ?\ } \quad 24.5$$

$\underline{\ ?\ } - \underline{\ ?\ } = \underline{\ ?\ } \quad 32; 24.5; 7.5$

Jay's score for the last quiz is $\underline{\ ?\ }$.  7.5

11. Sarah's mean number of points scored for four video games is 7,500. How many points must she score in the fifth video game so that her mean score becomes 7,700?  8,500 points

## Guided Practice

**10** and **11** Students practice finding the missing number in a set of data using the mean.

### Caution

**11** Because Sarah wants to increase her mean score from 7,500 to 7,700 with a fifth score, some students may mistakenly just add 200 to the mean score and say that the fifth score must be 7,700. Explain that for Sarah to raise the mean 200 points across 5 scores, she must add 5 · 200 = 1,000 points to the total points scored. So, the fifth score must be 7,500 + 1,000 = 8,500.

---

**DAY 2**

## Learn — Find the total and a missing number from the mean.

**Ask** What information is given in the text? The mean of a set of six numbers that Geraldine recorded **What are you asked to find?** The missing number that Geraldine accidentally erased from the set

**Explain** To find the missing number, first you have to find the total of the six numbers.

**Ask** How do you find the total of the six numbers? Multiply the mean by the number of items. So, total of

six numbers = mean × number of given numbers = 11.2 × 6 = 67.2. Then, find the total of the five numbers that were left. So, 2.3 + 6.5 + 8.8 + 12.4 + 16.0 = 46. **How do you find the missing number?** Subtract the total of the five numbers that were left from the total of the six numbers.

**Explain** So, 67.2 − 46 = 21.2. The missing number is 21.2.

**Hands-On Activity**

This activity reinforces the concepts of collecting and tabulating data before finding the mean. Have students work in groups of 5.

**1** Make sure that students measure from the tip of the longest finger to the base of the palm.

**2** Have students use their data to find the mean.

**3** Guide students to find the hand length of the new student given the increase in the mean.

## Best Practices

A Teacher Resource Tool that students may find useful for this Hands-On Activity is a blank table (TRT15).

---

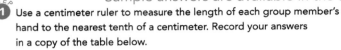 **Hands-On Activity**

**Materials:**
- centimeter ruler
- blank table

**FINDING MEAN AND USING MEAN TO SOLVE PROBLEMS**

Work in groups of five. All answers will vary, depending on the group. Sample answers are available in the solution key.

**STEP 1** Use a centimeter ruler to measure the length of each group member's hand to the nearest tenth of a centimeter. Record your answers in a copy of the table below.

**Hand Size of Group Members**

| Name | Length of Hand (cm) |
| --- | --- |
| ? | ? |
| ? | ? |
| ? | ? |
| ? | ? |
| ? | ? |

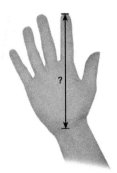

**STEP 2** Use your data to answer the following questions.

What is the longest hand length? ?

What is the shortest hand length? ?

The mean hand length of the group is ? centimeters.

**STEP 3** *Math Journal* Suppose a new student joins your group and the mean of the hand length of your group increases by 0.3 centimeter. Find the hand length of the new student to the nearest centimeter. Explain how you found your answer. Hand lengths will vary.; See margin.

---

**3** Answers vary. Possible answer:
Total hand lengths of six students
= mean length × number of hands
= 15.8 × 6
= 94.8

Total hand lengths of five students
= 15 + 16.4 + 17.5 + 14.6 + 14
= 77.5

94.8 − 77.5 = 17.3 cm

The hand length of the new student is 17.3 centimeters.

# Practice 14.1

Basic **1**–**9**
Intermediate **10**–**13**
Advanced **14**–**17**

**Find the mean of each data set.**

**1** 8, 7, 5, 9, 6, 13  8

**2** 72 L, 91 L, 65 L, 81 L, 62 L, 83 L, 75 L, 88 L  77.125 L

**3** 21.5 cm, 63.7 cm, 18.9 cm, 34.1 cm, 75.6 cm  42.76 cm

**Solve. Show your work.**

**4** The number of goals scored by seven forwards in one soccer season
were 8, 6, 4, 8, 3, 1, and 5. Find the mean number of goals scored by
the seven forwards.  5

**5** The lengths of five ropes are 3.2 meters, 5.2 meters, 2.9 meters, 6.6 meters,
and 4.5 meters. Find the mean length of these five ropes.  4.48 m

**6** The masses of six chairs are 34.5 kilograms, 42.6 kilograms, 39.8 kilograms,
40.1 kilograms, 53.4 kilograms, and 33.8 kilograms. Find their mean mass.  40.7 kg

**Use the data in the table to answer the question.**

The table shows a sprinter's times for the 100-meter dash at the first five meets
of one season.

**Time Clocked by the Sprinter**

| Meet Number | 1 | 2 | 3 | 4 | 5 |
|---|---|---|---|---|---|
| Time (s) | 10.09 | 10.14 | 10.29 | 10.07 | 9.99 |

**7** What was the sprinter's mean time for the 100-meter dash at these meets?  10.116 s

**Use the data in the dot plot to answer questions 8 and 9.**

Eight ice hockey teams competed in the quarter finals of a national championship.
The dot plot on the right shows the number of goals scored by each team.
Each dot represents 1 team.

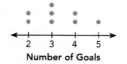
Number of Goals

**8** What was the total number of goals scored by the eight teams?  26

**9** What was the mean number of goals scored by each team?  3.25

---

Practice 14.1

## Assignment Guide

DAY **1** All students should
complete **1** – **9**.

DAY **2** All students should
complete **10** – **13**.

**14** – **17** provide additional
challenge.

Optional: *Extra Practice 14.1,
Activity Book 14.1*

---

## ⚠️ RtI Lesson Check

| Before assigning homework, use the following ... | to make sure students ... | Intervene with ... |
|---|---|---|
| Exercise **1** | • can find the mean of a set of data | |
| Exercise **8** | • can find the mean of a set of data using a dot plot | |
| Exercise **10** | • can find the missing term of a set of data, given the mean | Reteach 14.1 |
| **EXIT** Ticket Out the Door | • can explain how to find the mean of a set of data | |

**Solve. Show your work.**

**10** The mean of five numbers 3, 7, 9, 12, and *x* is 8. Find the value of *x*. 9

**11** The mean of a set of five numbers is 4.8. Given that the sixth number is *x* and the mean of these six numbers is 5.5, find the value of *x*. 9

**12** In a race, the mean time for three runners was 12.4 seconds and the mean time for another six runners was 11.5 seconds. Calculate the mean time for all the nine runners. 11.8 s

**13** The mean weight of nine apples is 7.5 ounces. Three of the apples have a mean weight of 8 ounces. Find the mean weight of the other six apples. 7.25 oz

**14** The mean of six numbers is 45. Four of the numbers are 40, 38, 46, and 51. If the remaining two numbers are in the ratio 2 : 3, find the two numbers. 38 and 57

**15** A data set consists of three numbers, *a*, *b*, and *c*. Write an algebraic expression, in terms of *a*, *b*, and *c*, to represent the mean of the new set of numbers obtained by

a) adding 5 to every number in the set. $\dfrac{a + b + c + 15}{3}$

b) doubling every number in the set. $\dfrac{2a + 2b + 2c}{3}$

c) halving every number in the set. $\dfrac{a + b + c}{6}$

**16** The table shows the mean scores of three classes in a history test.

**Mean Scores by Three Classes**

| Class | Mean Number of Points |
|-------|----------------------|
| A | 8 |
| B | 6 |
| C | 9 |

The mean score of all the students in classes A and B combined is 6.8. The mean score of all the students in classes B and C combined is 7. If the number of students in classes A, B, and C are denoted by *a*, *b*, and *c* respectively, find the ratio *a* : *b* : *c*. 4 : 6 : 3

 **17** *Math Journal* Find five different numbers whose mean is 12. Explain your strategy. Answers vary. Sample: 10, 11, 12, 13, and 14

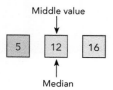

# 14.2 Median

## Lesson Objectives
- Find the median of a set of data.
- Use the median of a set of data to solve problems.

**Vocabulary**
median

### Learn — Understand the concept of median.

Barbara drew three number cards from a box and wanted to know the middle value, or median, of these values. The median is a second way to summarize the values in a data set with a single number.

First, she arranged the numbers from the least to the greatest.

Middle value

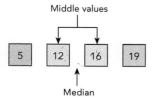

5 | 12 | 16

Median

> When a data set has an **odd** number of values, you can identify the middle value, or median, by inspection. The number of values less than the median equals the number of values greater than the median.

Then she identified the middle value, 12. So, the median of the three numbers is 12.

Barbara then picked another number, 19, from the box. She arranged these numbers in order again.

Middle values

5 | 12 | 16 | 19

Median

> When a data set has an **even** number of values, identify the two middle values. The median is the mean of these two middle values.

Mean of the two middle values $= \dfrac{12 + 16}{2}$

$= \dfrac{28}{2}$

$= 14$

So, the median of the four numbers is 14.

**Caution** ///////

Remember, the data must be in order before you look for the middle value or values. The data can be arranged from least to greatest, or greatest to least.

---

## 14.2 Median

### KEY CONCEPTS
- You can use the median of a set of data to solve problems.
- You can find the median of a set of data using a dot plot.
- You can compare the median and mean of a set of data.

### PACING
**DAY 1** Pages 251–252
**DAY 2** Pages 253–257
**Materials:** TRT1, TRT15

 **5-minute Warm Up**

1. Arrange 35, 21, 9, 67, 53 from least to greatest. What value is in the middle? 9, 21, 35, 53, 67; 35

2. Arrange 35, 21, 47, 9, 67, 53 from least to greatest. Find the mean of 35 and 47. 9, 21, 35, 47, 53, 67; 41

 Also available on Teacher One Stop.

---

**DAY 1**

### Learn — Understand the concept of median.

**Model** Use the example to show students how to find the median of a set of data.

**Ask** What is "median?" It is another measure of central tendency. It is the middle value when the number of items of a data set is odd. It is the mean of the two middle values when the number of items of a data set is even.

**Explain** To identify the middle value or values of the data set, you have to arrange the data from least to greatest, or greatest to least.

**Ask** How many number did Barbara draw from a box at first? 3 What were these numbers? 5, 12, and 16 Since the number of values is odd, what is the median of these data set? 12 Barbara picked another number from the box and arranged the numbers in order again. How are the numbers arranged now? 5, 12, 16, 19 What is the median of these set of numbers? 14

**Explain** To get the median 14, find the mean of the two middle values 12 and 16 like this: Mean of the two middle values $\dfrac{12 + 16}{2} = \dfrac{28}{2} = 14$. So, the median of the four numbers is 14.

Make sure that students understand the meaning of median. Some may be familiar with its everyday meaning.

**Ask:** What is a median on a divided highway? *(The grassy area between lanes of traffic on a highway)* Where does the median lie? *(In the middle of the highway)* Explain that the median value in a data set is the middle value.

## Guided Practice

**1** to **5** Check that students arrange the set of data in order before they find the median.

## Guided Practice

**Find the median of each data set.**

**1** The data set shows the weights of a group of students.

109 lb, 86 lb, 117 lb, 97 lb, 98 lb

Ordered from least to greatest:

__?__ lb, __?__ lb, __?__ lb, __?__ lb, __?__ lb  86; 97; 98; 109; 117

The median weight is __?__ pounds.  98

**2** The data set shows the volumes of water (in fluid ounces) in some containers.

The median volume of water is __?__ fluid ounces.  32

**3** The data set shows the ages of a group of people.

23 years, 36 years, 28 years, 43 years, 34 years, 29 years

The two middle values are __?__ years and __?__ years.  29; 34

Mean of the two middle values $= \dfrac{? + ?}{2} = $ __?__ yr  29; 34; 31.5

The median age is __?__ years.  31.5

**4** The data set shows the lengths of the tables that one company produces.

85 cm, 92 cm, 108 cm, 210 cm, 264 cm, 200 cm, 135 cm, 78 cm

The median length is __?__ centimeters.  121.5

**5** The data set shows the distances that a group of students ran during an exercise.

$\frac{1}{2}$ mi, $\frac{7}{8}$ mi, $\frac{3}{4}$ mi, $\frac{5}{8}$ mi

The median distance was __?__ mile.  $\dfrac{11}{16}$

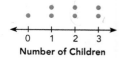

**Find the median of a data set using a dot plot.**

a) The dot plot shows the number of children in seven families living in an apartment complex. Each dot represents 1 family.

To find the median, count the dots to find the middle values.

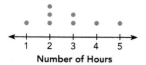

**Number of Children**

Count to the fourth dot from the left in the dot plot. Notice that the fourth and fifth dots have the same value. So, the order of the fourth and fifth dots does not matter.

There are seven families altogether.
The fourth family is in the middle because there are three families to the left and to the right of this family.
So, the median number of children is 2.

b) The dot plot shows the number of hours eight children spend on exercise every week. Each dot represents 1 child.

**Number of Hours**

First, find the middle number of hours.

There are eight children altogether. Divide this into two equal groups.
There are four children in the upper half and four children in the lower half.
So, the fourth and fifth children are in the middle.
The fourth child spends 2 hours and the fifth child spends 3 hours on exercise every week.

Then find the median number of hours.

Mean of the two values $= \dfrac{2+3}{2}$

$\qquad\qquad\qquad\quad = 2.5\ \text{h}$

So, the median is 2.5 hours.

**Best Practices**

Suggest that when identifying the median value from a dot plot, students can count from the top or bottom of each stack. To find the median value, they don't actually need to identify the middle dot; they just need to identify which value the middle dot in the set lies above.

**DAY 2**

**Find the median of a data set using a dot plot.**

a) **Ask** Have students read the scenario for the problem. What does each dot on the dot plot represent? 1 family How many families are there? 7 Will there be 1 or 2 data values in the middle of this set? 1, because the number of data values is odd. How many dots from the left will you need to count? 4, because then there will be three dots on either side of it. What number does the 4th dot from the left represent? 2

**Explain** To find the median, you can count the dots from either end of the dot plot. The 4th family is in the middle because there are 3 families to the left and 3 families to the right of this family.

b) **Explain** The dot plot shows the number of hours 8 children spend on exercise every week. Each dot represents 1 child.

**Ask** How can you find the median number of hours? First, decide which two dots represent the middle of the data: with eight pieces of data, the 4th and 5th dots represent the middle of the data set. Then, find the middle number of hours: 2 and 3. Next, find the mean of 2 and 3: $\dfrac{2+3}{2} = 2.5$ h. So, what is the median number of hours? 2.5 h

## Guided Practice

⑥ and ⑦ Students practice finding the median from a dot plot.

### Best Practices

A Teacher Resource Tool that students may find useful for ⑦ is blank number lines (TRT1).

### Best Practices

Help students to see that whenever you add a value to an existing data set, if the new value is not equal to the existing median, the median value will usually change. Direct students to the original dot plot. **Ask:** If we include a value at 98, what will the median be? *(99.5)* Why? *(The 4th and 5th values of the 8 values will be 99 and 100, so the median is 99.5.)* If instead we include a value of 100, what will the median be? *(100)* Why? *(The 4th and 5th values of the 8 values will both be 100, so the median is 100.)* After adding the values 101, 98, and 100 to the data set, when did the median change? *(When the new value was not equal to the existing median)*

## Guided Practice

**Complete. Use the data in the dot plot.**

The dot plot shows the weights of a group of immature white-tailed deer fawn. Each dot represents 1 fawn.

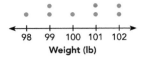

⑥ The median weight of the fawns is __?__ pounds.  100

⑦ A new fawn joins the group. It weighs 101 pounds.

   a)  Add a dot to a copy of the dot plot above to show this information.  See above.

   b)  Does this change the median of the data set?  Yes
       What is the median of the data set now?  100.5 lb

### Compare the mean and median of a data set.

Mrs. Brown took a survey to find out the number of hours the students in her class spent in the public library in two weeks. Each dot represents 1 student.

a)  Find the mean and median.

$$\text{Mean} = \frac{\text{total number of hours}}{\text{total number of students}}$$

$$= \frac{2 \times 1 + 4 \times 2 + 1 \times 3 + 1 \times 15}{8}$$

$$= \frac{28}{8}$$

$$= 3.5 \text{ h}$$

The mean is 3.5 hours.

The data set has an outlier, 15. This value makes the mean much greater than a typical value for these data.

There are eight students altogether. The fourth and fifth students are in the middle. Each of those two students spent 2 hours at the library. So, the median is 2 hours.

### Compare the mean and median of a data set.

**Model** Use the example to show students how to compare the mean and median of a data set.

a)  **Ask** What are you asked to find? Mean and median
    How can you find the mean? Calculate the total number of hours spent at the library, divided by the total number of students: $\frac{2 \times 1 + 4 \times 2 + 1 \times 3 + 1 \times 15}{8}$
    $= \frac{28}{8} = 3.5$ h. So, the mean is 3.5 h. **What is the median?** There are 8 students, so the fourth and the fifth dots are in the middle. Each of these two dots is above the value 2 on the number line. The median is 2 hours.

**Explain** For this data set, there is an outlier, 15. This value makes the mean much greater than a typical value for these data.

**b)** Which one of the two measures of central tendency, the mean or the median, better describes the data set? Justify your answer.

The mean is 3.5 hours. However, all but one student visited the library for fewer than 3.5 hours during the two weeks. So, the mean does not describe the data set well.

The median is 2 hours. It describes the data set better because most of the data values cluster around 2 hours.

## Guided Practice

**Complete. Use the data in the dot plot.**

The lowest temperatures in a town are recorded over a few days. The dot plot on the right shows these temperature readings. Each dot represents 1 temperature reading.

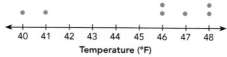

**Temperature (°F)**

**8** The mean temperature is __?__ °F.  45.5

**9** The median temperature is __?__ °F.  46.5

**10** __?__ of the temperature readings recorded are higher than the mean temperature.  6

**11** Which of the two measures of central tendency, the mean or the median, Median, better describes the data set? Justify your answer. because most of the data values cluster around 46.5°F.

---

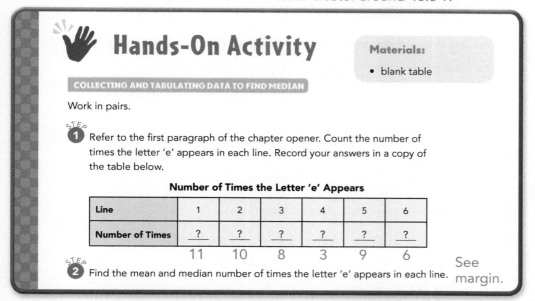

## Hands-On Activity

**Materials:**
- blank table

**COLLECTING AND TABULATING DATA TO FIND MEDIAN**

Work in pairs.

**STEP 1** Refer to the first paragraph of the chapter opener. Count the number of times the letter 'e' appears in each line. Record your answers in a copy of the table below.

**Number of Times the Letter 'e' Appears**

| Line | 1 | 2 | 3 | 4 | 5 | 6 |
|---|---|---|---|---|---|---|
| Number of Times | _?_ | _?_ | _?_ | _?_ | _?_ | _?_ |
| | 11 | 10 | 8 | 3 | 9 | 6 |

**STEP 2** Find the mean and median number of times the letter 'e' appears in each line.  See margin.

---

## Learn continued

**a) Ask** Between mean and median, which one describes the data set better? The median
Why? Because most of the data values cluster around 2 hours

## Practice 14.2

Basic **1**–**10**
Intermediate **11**–**13**
Advanced **14**–**16**

### Assignment Guide

**DAY 1** All students should
complete **1** – **8**.

**DAY 2** All students should
complete **9** – **13**.

**14** – **16** provide additional
challenge.

Optional: *Extra Practice 14.2*

**Find the median of each data set.**

**1** 9, 8, 7, 11, 7, 16, 3   8

**2** 31, 43, 12, 25, 54, 18   28

**3** 3.2, 1.5, 2.6, 3.5, 6.9, 5.8, 2.4   3.2

**4** 32.6, 72.6, 28.7, 45.4, 83.6, 69.9   57.65

**Solve. Show your work.**

**5** The number of points scored by seven students in a language test are
68, 46, 74, 58, 63, 91, and 85. Find the median score.   68

**6** The data set shows the number of goals scored by a soccer team in
eight matches.

0, 2, 3, 1, 4, 2, 5, 2

Find the median number of goals scored.   2

**7** The costs of four cell phones are $345, $400, $110, and $640. Find the
median cost.   $372.50

**8** The volumes of water, in liters, in eight containers are 3.1, 2.8, 3.2, 4.2, 3.9,
5.6, 3.7, and 4.5. Find the median volume.   3.8 L

**Use the data in the dot plots to answer questions 9 and 10.**

The dot plot shows the number of points scored by the members of a Quiz Bowl
team in a competition between School A and School B. Each dot represents one
student's points.

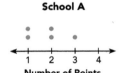

**School A**

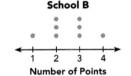

**School B**

**9** How many team members did each school have?   School A: 5;
School B: 8

**10** What was the median number of points scored by the students from

a)   School A?   2

b)   School B?   2.5

### ⛰ RtI Lesson Check

| Before assigning homework, use the following ... | to make sure students ... | Intervene with ... |
| --- | --- | --- |
| Exercise **1** | • can find the median of a set of data | |
| Exercise **9** | • can find the median of a set of data using a dot plot | Reteach 14.2 |
| Exercise **14** | • can compare the median and mean of a set of data | |
| **EXIT** *Ticket Out the Door* | • can explain how to find the median of a data set | |

**Use the data in the dot plot to answer questions ⑪ to ⑬.**

Janice bought some dinner rolls from a bakery. The dot plot shows the prices of the dinner rolls in cents. Each dot represents 1 dinner roll.

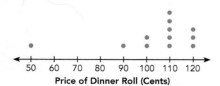

Price of Dinner Roll (Cents)

⑪ What is the mean price of the dinner rolls Janice bought? Round your answer to the nearest cent. 104 cents

⑫ What is the median price of the dinner rolls she bought? 110 cents

⑬ Which of the two measures of central tendency, the mean or the median, better describes the data set? Justify your answer.
Median, because most of the data values cluster around 110 cents.

**Solve.**

⑭ The median of a set of numbers is x. There are at least three numbers in the set. Write an algebraic expression, in terms of x, to represent the median of the new set of numbers obtained by

a) adding 3 to every number in the set. x + 3

b) doubling every number in the set. 2x

c) dividing every number in the set by 5 and then subtracting 2 from the resulting numbers. $\frac{x}{5} - 2$

d) adding 2 to the greatest number in the set. x

e) subtracting 3 from the least number in the set. x

⑮ The median of a set of three unknown numbers is 5. If the number 3 is added to the least number in the set, give an example of the original set in which

a) the median of the new set of numbers will not be equal to 5. Answers vary. Sample: 4, 5, 8

b) the median of the new set of numbers will still be equal to 5. Answers vary. Sample: 1, 5, 8

⑯ The median of a set of three unknown numbers is 5. If the number 2 is subtracted from the greatest number in the set, give an example of the original set in which

a) the median of the new set of numbers will not be equal to 5. Answers vary. Sample: 3, 5, 6

b) the median of the new set of numbers will still be equal to 5. Answers vary. Sample: 4, 5, 9

**EXIT** **Ticket Out the Door**

In your own words, describe how to find the median of a set of values. Possible answer: Put the values in ascending or descending order. If the total number of values in the set is an odd number, the median is the middle value. If the total number of values in the set is an even number, identify the two middle values, and find the mean of the two middle values.

Also available on Teacher One Stop.

## KEY CONCEPTS

- You can find the mode of a set of data.

- You can use mode to summarize a set of data.

## PACING

DAY **1** Pages 258–259

DAY **2** Pages 260–263

**Materials:** TRT1, TRT15, TRT35, tape, scissors, ruler

### 5-minute Warm Up

**Solve.**

Larry tosses a number cube with numbers 1 to 6 five times. A 2 appears once and a 4 appears three times.

**1.** What is the frequency of the number 2? 1

**2.** What is the frequency of the number 4? 3

 Also available on Teacher One Stop.

---

**14.3** Mode

**Lesson Objectives**

- Find the mode of a set of data.
- Use the mode of a set of data to solve problems.

**Vocabulary**
mode

**Learn** **Understand the concept of mode.**

Ryan tossed a number cube, numbered 1 to 6, and he recorded the data in the table.

**Number Tossed on Number Cube**

| Number Tossed | Number of Times |
|---|---|
| 1 | 1 |
| 2 | 2 |
| 3 | 2 |
| 4 | 1 |
| 5 | 3 |
| 6 | 2 |

The mode of a set of data is the value that appears most frequently. It is the third measure of central tendency.

From the table, notice that the number 5 appears most frequently.
So, the number 5 is the mode of the set of data.

You can draw a dot plot to show that the number 5 is the mode of the set of data. Each dot represents 1 toss.

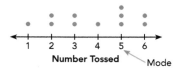

**Number Tossed**  Mode

The dot plot shows clearly that the number 5 appears most frequently.
So, the number 5 is the mode of the set of data.

**Math Note**

A set of data can have more than one mode. If all the numbers in a set of data appear the same number of times, there is no mode.

---

DAY **1**

**Learn** **Understand the concept of mode.**

**Model** Use the table and dot plot to help students understand the concept of "mode."

**Ask** What is a "mode?" A mode is the value that appears most frequently in a set of data. It is the third measure of central tendency. Look at the table, what do you think is the mode of the data set? 5 Why? Because 5 appears most frequently.

**Explain** Emphasize that it is possible for a data set to have more than one mode. For example, if one more dot appeared above the 2 in this data set, then the modes would be 2 and 5. However, if all the values appear with the same frequency, then there is no mode.

**Ask** Look at the dot plot. What does it show? It shows that the number 5 appears most frequently. So, the number 5 is the mode of the data set.

## Guided Practice

**Use the data set to complete the table. Then complete the sentence.**

Justin recorded the times for the ten runners on a track team when they ran the 100-meter dash. The data set shows the times that he recorded.

9.8 s, 9.9 s, 10.0 s, 9.9 s, 10.2 s, 10.1 s, 9.8 s, 10.3 s, 9.9 s, 10.1 s

**Times of Ten Runners**

| Time (s) | Number of Times |
|:---:|:---:|
| 9.8 | 2 |
| __?__  *9.9* | __?__  *3* |
| 10.0 | __?__  *1* |
| __?__  *10.1* | __?__  *2* |
| __?__  *10.2* | __?__  *1* |
| __?__  *10.3* | __?__  *1* |

1. The mode of this data set is __?__ seconds.  *9.9*

**Complete. Use data in the dot plot.**

Elsie likes to bowl. The dot plot shows her scores for each of the ten frames that she bowled in one game. Each dot represents her scores for one frame.

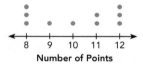

**Number of Points**

2. Elsie scored 11 points in each of __?__ frames.  *2*

3. The modes of this set of data are __?__ and __?__.  *8; 12*

When a data set has two modes, you can say that the data set is bimodal.

## Guided Practice

**1** to **3** Given a dot plot, guide students to see which values are the mode of the data set.

### Best Practices

Point out that mode can be read from a frequency table, like the one shown here. To determine mode, we often format a data set into a frequency table or dot plot because those displays make it easy to see frequency.

### DIFFERENTIATED INSTRUCTION

**Through Visual Cues**

Use **3** to discuss the range of possible modes a data set may have. **Ask:** What are the modes of this data set? *(8 and 12)* If one dot were moved from 8 to 9, what would the mode be? *(12)* And if one dot were also moved from 12 to 10, what would the mode be? *(There would be no mode. Each value would appear two times.)* Point out that a data set may have one mode, more than one, or none.

## Best Practices

To see how the data set was formatted into the bar graph, you may want to have students compile the data into a tally chart or frequency table. A Teacher Resource Tool that students may find useful is a blank table (TRT15).

## Caution

Seeing the bar graph here, some students might mistakenly think they can identify a median of a non-numeric data set by finding a middle value. For example, they may identify a median of this data set as being halfway between Chickens and Ducks because the 15th value in the graph is Chickens and the 16th is Ducks. Explain that median (and mean) can only be found for sets of numeric values. The order of the bars on a graph like this one is random. "Chickens" is listed 1st, but Ducks or Geese could just as easily be the 1st bar. There can be no middle value in a data set that is not numeric.

## Guided Practice

**4** to **6** Students practice finding the mode of a set of data.

 DAY **2**

### Learn Use mode to summarize a data set.

**Model** Use the example in the text to show students how to summarize a data set.

**Ask** What is given in the text? A non-numeric data set. Can you find the mean for this data set? No Can you find the median? Yes What is the median? Chickens Why? Because it is the data that appears most often How can you show the mode of the data set? By using a bar graph

---

 Learn **Use mode to summarize a data set.**

A farmer was placing chickens, ducks, and geese in a feeding pen. He recorded the type of birds as C, D, or G as they went into the pen. These are the data he recorded.

| | | | | | | | | | |
|---|---|---|---|---|---|---|---|---|---|
| D | C | C | C | C | G | D | C | C | C |
| D | C | D | D | C | C | C | G | D | D |
| G | C | C | D | C | C | G | D | D | G |

This data set is not numeric, so you cannot find the mean or median. However, you can find the mode of the data: chickens, because it is the data item that appears most often.

You can use a bar graph to show the mode.

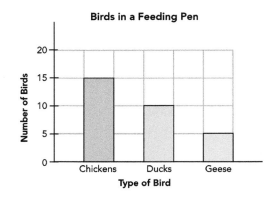

**Birds in a Feeding Pen**

Notice that the bar representing the number of chickens has the greatest height. So, the number of chickens is the greatest and the mode is chickens.

### Guided Practice

**Find the mode of each set of data.**

**4** There are 9 teachers, 88 boys, and 79 girls at a school camp. boys

**5** In a mall, there are 2 laundry shops, 14 garment shops, 3 photographic shops, 5 shoe shops, and 9 food stores. garment shops

**6** The data set shows the masses of the school bags of some students. 5.5 kg, 6.6 kg, 4.8 kg, 4.3 kg, 5.5 kg, 4.3 kg, 5.5 kg, 6.6 kg, 4.5 kg, 5.5 kg 5.5 kg

**Model** Display the bar graph shown in the text on the board so that students can see how a bar graph for the given data set is constructed.

**Explain** Look at the dot plot. Notice that the tallest bar represents the number of chickens. So, the number of chickens is the greatest and the mode is chickens.

# Hands-On Activity

## FINDING MEAN, MEDIAN, AND MODE

Work in pairs.

**Materials:**
- net of a rectangular prism, with pairs of opposite faces numbered 10, 11, or 12
- blank table
- tape
- scissors
- centimeter ruler

 **STEP 1** Cut out, fold, and tape the net of the rectangular prism provided by your teacher.

 **STEP 2** Take turns to toss the rectangular prism 40 times and record the number tossed each time.

 **STEP 3** Copy and complete your results in a table like the one below.

Answers vary. Sample:

| Number Tossed | Tally | Frequency |
|---|---|---|
| 10 | _?_ | _?_ |
| 11 | _?_ | _?_ |
| 12 | _?_ | _?_ |

HHT  HHT ; 10

HHT  HHT ; 10

HHT  HHT  HHT  HHT ; 20

 **STEP 4** From the set of data collected, find the  Answers vary. Sample:
a) mean. 11.25    b) median. 11.5    c) mode. 12

 **STEP 5**

a) Measure the area of each face to the nearest tenth of a square centimeter. Find the ratio of the total area of the faces numbered 10 to the total area of the faces numbered 11 to the total area of the faces numbered 12. 1 : 1 : 2

b) Find the ratio of the number of times the number 10 is tossed to the number of times the number 11 is tossed to the number of times the number 12 is tossed. Answers vary. Sample: About 1 : 1 : 2

c) Compare the two ratios. Why do you think you get this result?
See margin.

**STEP 6** Compare your findings with the other pairs. Answers will vary.

---

 **Hands-On Activity**

Students can practice collecting and tabulating data to find the mean, median, and mode of the set of data. Have students work in pairs.

**1** Check that students fold the rectangular prism correctly.

**2** Remind students to take turns tossing the prism.

**6** Allow some time for students to compare their results with other students.

### Best Practices

There is a Teacher Resource Tool (TRT35) for this Hands-On Activity that contains the net of the rectangular prism and a copy of the blank table. It is a square prism with edge lengths in the ratio 1 : 1 : 2.

**5** c) The two sets of ratios are nearly equal, because the larger area occurs most often.

## Practice 14.3

### Assignment Guide

**DAY 1** All students should complete ① – ⑥.

**DAY 2** All students should complete ⑦ – ⑨.

⑩ – ⑪ provide additional challenge.

Optional: *Extra Practice 14.3*

---

## Practice 14.3

Basic ① – ⑥
Intermediate ⑦ – ⑨
Advanced ⑩ – ⑪

**Find the mode or modes of each data set.**

① 5, 6, 4, 5, 8, 9, 9, 3, 4, 5    5

② 13, 31, 12, 45, 6, 19, 21, 12, 31    12 and 31

③ 8.5, 6.5, 7.8, 6.5. 6.4, 2.3, 4.5, 5.4, 7.8, 5.5, 7.8    7.8

**Find the mode.**

④ The scores of a basketball team in a series of games are 76, 85, 65, 58, 68, 72, 91, and 68. Find the mode.    68

⑤ The table shows sizes of shoes and the number of pairs of shoes sold at a shop last month.

**Number of Pairs of Shoes Sold**

| Size | 6.5 | 7 | 7.5 | 8 | 8.5 | 9 | 9.5 | 10 | 10.5 |
|------|-----|---|-----|---|-----|---|-----|----|----|
| Number of Pairs | 5 | 15 | 21 | 30 | 30 | 31 | 13 | 8 | 3 |

Find the mode.    Size 9

⑥ Tickets for a concert are priced at $20, $30, $40, $50, or $100. The table shows the number of tickets sold at each price.

**Number of Tickets Sold**

| Price ($) | Number of Tickets |
|-----------|-------------------|
| 20 | 40 |
| 30 | 55 |
| 40 | 95 |
| 50 | 84 |
| 100 | 48 |

Find the mode.    $40

---

### ▲ RtI Lesson Check

| Before assigning homework, use the following ... | to make sure students ... | Intervene with ... |
|---|---|---|
| Exercise ① | • can find the mode of a set of data | |
| Exercise ⑦ | • can use mode to summarize a set of data | Reteach 14.3 |
| **EXIT** Ticket Out the Door | • can find the mode of a set of data | |

**Make a dot plot to show the data. Use your dot plot to answer each question.**

The data set shows the number of goals scored by a soccer team in 17 matches.
3, 2, 1, 0, 2, 4, 1, 0, 2, 3, 4, 2, 3, 2, 1, 2, 5

**7** What is the mean of the data set?
Round your answer to the nearest number of goals. 2

**8** What is the median of the data set? 2

**9** What is the mode of the data set? 2

Number of Goals

**Solve. Show your work.**

**10** A class of 15 students had a spelling test consisting of 10 words.
The number of spelling mistakes made by each student in the class
is listed in the data set.

1, 2, 1, 0, 3, 1, 2, 3, 1, 2, 0, 4, 2, 3, $x$

a) If there are two modes, what are the possible values for $x$? 0, 4, 5, 6, 7, 8, 9, or 10

b) If there is exactly one mode, write a possible value for $x$, $x = 1$ and mode $= 1$, or
and the mode.  $x = 2$ and mode $= 2$

**11** The table shows the number of days of absences for 80 students in a school.

**Number of Absent Days**

| Number of Days | Number of Students |
|----------------|--------------------|
| 0 | $x$ |
| 1 | 25 |
| 2 | 17 |
| 3 | $y$ |
| 4 | 8 |

a) Find the value of $x + y$. 30

b) If the mode for this set of data is 3, write the possible values for the pair
of numbers $(x, y)$. (0, 30), (1, 29), (2, 28), (3, 27), (4, 26)

c) If the mode is equal to the median, write two possible values of $x$.
Accept any number from 16 to 24.

 **DIFFERENTIATED INSTRUCTION**

**Through Visual Cues**

**10** Suggest students create a dot plot showing the given numeric values to help them answer the questions.

 **DIFFERENTIATED INSTRUCTION**

**Through Enrichment**

**10 Ask:** If there are exactly 3 modes, what are the possible values for $x$? *(3)*

 **Ticket Out the Door**

In your own words, describe how to find the mode of a data set.
Possible answer: Use a tally chart, frequency table, or dot plot to display the data. The value or values that appear the most times is the mode.

 Also available on Teacher One Stop.

## 14.4 Real-World Problems: Mean, Median, and Mode

### KEY CONCEPTS

- You can select the mean, median, or mode as the measurement of central tendency.

- You can relate the measures of central tendency to a skewed or symmetrical distribution.

### PACING

 **DAY 1** Pages 264–265

 **DAY 2** Pages 266–271

**Materials:** TRT1

 **5-minute Warm Up**

Find the mean, median, and mode of the data below.

| 40 | 37 | 33 | 32 | 31 | 34 |
| 33 | 36 | 34 | 32 | 35 | 31 |

Mean: 34; median: 33.5; mode: 31, 32, 33 and 34.

 Also available on Teacher One Stop.

---

## 14.4 Real-World Problems: Mean, Median, and Mode

### Lesson Objective

- Solve problems that are related to the concepts of mean, median, and mode, including the selection of the measure of central tendency to be used for problems.

 **Learn** — **Decide whether to use mean, median, or mode.**

The table shows the sizes of in-line skates and the number of pairs of skates sold in a month.

**Number of Pairs of In-Line Skates Sold**

| Size | Number of Pairs |
|------|-----------------|
| 6 | 12 |
| 7 | 15 |
| 8 | 18 |
| 9 | 9 |
| 10 | 6 |

a) How many pairs of in-line skates were sold?

$12 + 15 + 18 + 9 + 6 = 60$

60 pairs of in-line skates were sold.

b) What is the mean size of the in-line skates sold?

$$\text{Mean} = \frac{\text{total of sizes of in-line skates sold}}{\text{total number of pairs sold}}$$

$$= \frac{12 \times 6 + 15 \times 7 + 18 \times 8 + 9 \times 9 + 6 \times 10}{60}$$

$$= \frac{462}{60}$$

$$= 7.7$$

The mean size of the shoes sold is 7.7.

---

**DAY 1**

**Learn** **Decide whether to use mean, median, or mode.**

**Model** Use the example in the text to show students how to decide which measure of central tendency to use.

**Ask** What does the table show? The sizes of in-line skates and the number of pairs of skates sold in a month

a) **Ask** How many pairs of in-line skates were sold?
$12 + 15 + 18 + 9 + 6 = 60$

b) **Ask** What is the mean size of the in-line skates sold?

$$\text{Mean} = \frac{12 \times 6 + 15 \times 7 + 18 \times 8 + 9 \times 9 + 6 \times 10}{60}$$

$$= \frac{462}{60} = 7.7$$

**c)** What is the modal size of the in-line skates sold?

The size of in-line skates that was sold most frequently is 8.
So, the modal size of the in-line skates sold is 8.

**d)** What is the median size of the in-line skates sold?

First, you need to find the middle sizes.

60 pairs of in-line skates were sold. Divide the skates into two equal groups.
There are 30 pairs in the upper half and 30 pairs in the lower half.
So, the thirtieth and thirty-first pairs of skates are in the middle.
The sizes of the thirtieth and thirty-first pairs of skates are both 8.

So, the median size is the mean of the two middle sizes, which is 8.

**e)** Which measure of central tendency best describes the data set?
Justify your answer.

The mean size is 7.7. However, the usual sizes for in-line skates are either
whole numbers or halves. So, the mean figure 7.7 may not be a realistic
number for describing the data set.

The mode and median are both size 8, which is a realistic number for
describing the data set. So, the mode and median may describe the data
set best.

## Guided Practice

**Solve.**

The table shows the sizes of T-shirts and the number of T-shirts displayed in a shop.

**Number of T-Shirts Being Displayed**

| Size | 8 | 10 | 12 | 14 | 16 |
|---|---|---|---|---|---|
| Number of T-Shirts | 7 | 14 | 22 | 15 | 2 |

**1** How many T-shirts are displayed in the shop? 60 T-shirts

**2** What is the mean size of the T-shirts being displayed? 11.7

**3** What is the modal size of the T-shirts being displayed? 12

**4** What is the median size of the T-shirts being displayed? 12

**5** Which measure of central tendency best describes the data set? Mode and median,
Justify your answer. because the T-shirt sizes are whole numbers and
12 is a realistic number for describing the data set.

Make sure that students
understand that *modal* is the
adjective form of *mode*.

### DIFFERENTIATED INSTRUCTION

**Through Visual Cues**

Suggest students create a dot
plot for **d)** to display the set of
values. A Teacher Resource Tool
that students may find useful is
blank number lines (TRT1).

## Guided Practice

Use **1** to **5** to assess students'
understanding of mean, median,
and mode.

---

**Learn continued**

**c) Ask** What is the modal size of the in-line skates? 8

**d) Ask** What is the median size of the in-line skates? 8

**e) Ask** Which measure of central tendency best
describes the data sheet? Mode and median

**Explain** The mean is size 7.7, while both the mode
and the median size are both 8. Since size 7.7 does
not exist, the mode and median give a more realistic
description of the data set.

Emphasize that sometimes only the mean, mode,
or median is a good descriptor of a data set. Often,
the purpose for which the data will be used will
determine which measure is best.

### DIFFERENTIATED INSTRUCTION

**Through Visual Cues**

You may want to remind students what a skewed distribution looks like. Find the tallest stack of dots. If there are more dots on one side of the tallest stack of dots than there are on the other side, the data distribution is skewed to the side that has more dots.

earn **Relate the measure of center to a skewed distribution.**

The dot plot shows the daily pocket money of a group of students. Each dot represents one student.

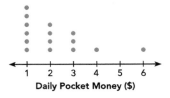

**Daily Pocket Money ($)**

In a skewed distribution, the mean and median are always different.

**a)** What is the mean daily pocket money?

$$\text{Mean} = \frac{\text{total amount of pocket money}}{\text{total number of students}}$$

$$= \frac{6 \times 1 + 4 \times 2 + 3 \times 3 + 1 \times 4 + 1 \times 6}{15}$$

$$= \frac{33}{15}$$

$$= \$2.20$$

**b)** What is the modal daily pocket money?

The greatest number of students has daily pocket money of $1.
So, the modal daily pocket money is $1.

**c)** What is the median daily pocket money?

There are 15 students altogether. The eighth student is in the middle, because there are 7 students to the left and 7 to the right of this student. So, the median daily pocket money is $2.

**d)** Which measure of central tendency best describes the data set? Justify your answer.

The mode is $1, but it represents only 6 of the 15 students. So, the mode does not describe these data well. The mean is $2.20 and the median is $2.00. Both of these numbers might be used to describe this set of data. The mean takes into account the students who have more pocket money, but the median better describes what most students have in pocket money.

**e)** Relate the measures of center to the shape of the data distribution.

The shape of the data distribution is skewed to the right. The mean gives more weight to the values on the right than the median does. So, the mean is to the right of the median.

---

**DAY 2**

earn **Relate the measure of center to a skewed distribution.**

**Model** Use the example to show students how the measures of center are related in a skewed distribution.

**Explain** Point out that in a skewed distribution, the mean and median are always different.

**a) Ask** What is the mean daily pocket money? $2.20

**b) Ask** What is the modal daily pocket money? $1

**c) Ask** What is the median daily pocket money? $2

**d) Ask** Which measure of central tendency best describes the data set? Justify your reasoning. The mode of $1 is too low to represent the whole data set. Either the mean ($2.20) or median ($2.00) would be better, because they give some representation to all the students who have more than $1 for pocket money.

**e) Ask** How can you relate the measures of center to the shape of the data distribution? The shape of the data distribution is skewed to the right. The mean gives more weight to the values on the right than the median does. So, the mean is to the right of the median.

## Guided Practice

**Solve.**

The dot plot shows the results of a survey on the number of children below 13 years old in each household. Each dot represents one household.

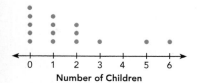

**Number of Children**

**6** Find the mean, mode, and median of the data set. Mean: 1.6; Mode: 0; Median: 1

**7** Which measure of central tendency best describes the data set? Justify your answer. See margin.

**8** Relate the measures of center to the shape of the data distribution. See margin.

---

**Learn** **Relate the measure of center to a symmetrical distribution.**

The dot plot shows the ages of students, in years, on a basketball team. Each dot represents 1 student.

**Age (yr)**

> In a symmetric or nearly symmetric distribution, the mean, median, and mode are all equal, or nearly equal.

a) Find the mean.

Mean age = $\dfrac{\text{total age of the students}}{\text{total number of students}}$

$= \dfrac{2 \times 10 + 3 \times 11 + 4 \times 12 + 3 \times 13 + 2 \times 14 + 2 \times 15}{16}$

$= \dfrac{198}{16}$

$= 12.375 \text{ yr}$

The mean is 12.375 years.

b) Find the mode.

Most students are of age 12 years. So, the mode is 12 years.

**Continue on next page**

---

## Guided Practice

**6** to **8** Students can practice describing a set of data using the mean, median, or mode.

**7** The mode is 0, but it represents only 5 of the 15 households. So, the mode does not describe the data well. The mean is 1.6 and the median is 1. Both of these numbers might be used to describe the set of data. The mean takes into account the households with 5 or 6 children, but the median better describes how many children most households have.

**8** The shape of the data distribution is skewed to the right. The mean gives more weight to the values on the right than the median does. So, the mean is to the right of the median.

---

**Learn** **Relate the measure of center to a symmetrical distribution.**

**Model** Use the example to show students how the measures of center are related in a skewed distribution.

**Explain** Point out that in a symmetrical or nearly symmetrical distribution, the mean, median, and mode are all equal, or nearly equal.

a) **Ask** What is the mean age of students? 12.375 yr

b) **Ask** What is the modal age of students? 12 yr

c) **Ask** What is the median age of the students? 12 yr

**Explain** After completing the example, help students understand how to find the median and mode just by looking at the dot plot.

**Ask** Which dot or dots slightly skew the distribution? The two dots over 15 How do you know? Without those two dots the dot plot would be perfectly symmetrical. And how would the removal of those dots change the measures of central tendency? All three measures would all be the same: 12. So what do the two dots at 15 do to the measures of central tendency? They pull the mean to the right away from the median and mode, increasing it to 12.375.

# Guided Practice

and Students practice relating the mean, median, and mode to the shape of the distribution.

 **DIFFERENTIATED INSTRUCTION**

**Through Visual Cues**

Before doing ❾ and ❿, ask students to look at the dot plot and predict approximately what the mean, median, and mode will be. *(Mode: 5; mean and median: perhaps slightly greater.)* Have them explain how they made their predictions. *(Possible answer: The mode is 5, because it has the most values. The plot would be symmetrical except for the dot at 10 and the second dot at 8.)*

 **Hands-On Activity**

Have students work in pairs. Guide them to find the mode. Explain that since the mode is 12, the most common length is 12 cm. For the median, they need to ensure that the middle term has a value of 12. The mean will always be 12 if the numbers are paired in number bonds of 24.

**c)** Find the median.

The two middles ages are both 12 years. So, the median is 12 years.

**d)** Relate the measures of center to the shape of the data distribution.

The data are well spread out and the shape of the data distribution is nearly symmetrical. Because the mode and median are the same, and the mean is slightly greater, the data set is likely to be more spread out for data greater than 12. The data set has a slight skew to the right.

## Guided Practice

**Solve.**

The dot plot shows the number of feedback forms received by a mall over a ten-week period. Each dot represents one feedback form.

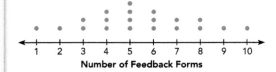

**Number of Feedback Forms**

❾ Find the mean, mode, and median of the data set. Mean: 5.4; Mode: 5; Median: 5

❿ Relate the measures of center to the shape of the data distribution. See margin.

 **Hands-On Activity**

**FINDING POSSIBLE VALUES OF MEAN, MEDIAN, AND MODE**

Work in pairs.

The lengths of 10 wallets have the same mean, median, and mode of 12 centimeters.

Explore and find a set of possible values for these lengths. Answers vary. Sample: 11 cm, 12 cm, 12 cm, 12 cm, 12 cm, 12 cm, 12 cm, 12 cm, 12 cm, 13 cm

Show your work.
(Hint: You may use a dot plot to help you.)

**Learn continued**

**c)** **Ask** What is the median age of students? 12 yr

**d)** **Ask** How can you relate the measures of center to the shape of the data distribution? The data are well spread out and the shape of the data distribution is nearly symmetrical. Because the mode and median are the same, and the mean is slightly greater, the data set is likely to be more spread out for data greater than 12. The data set has a slight skew to the right.

❿ The data are well spread out, and the shape of the data is symmetrical. Because the mode and median are the same, and the mean is slightly greater, the data set is likely to be more spread out for data greater than 5.

**Chapter 14** Measures of Central Tendency

**Find the mean, median, and mode.**

**1** Eight students took a mathematics quiz. Their scores were 85, 92, 73, 85, 68, 82, 93, and 76. Find the mean, median, and mode.
Mean: 81.75; Median: 83.5; Mode: 85

**Use the data in the table to answer questions 2 and 3.**

The table shows the results of a survey carried out on 80 families.

### Number of Children in 80 Families

| Number of Children | 0 | 1 | 2 | 3 | 4 | 5 | 6 |
|---|---|---|---|---|---|---|---|
| Number of Families | 8 | 17 | 21 | 13 | 13 | 6 | 2 |

**2** Find the mean, median, and mode. Mean: 2.4; Median: 2; Mode: 2

**3** Which measure of central tendency best describes the data set? Justify your answer. Median and mode; See margin.

**Solve. Show your work.**

The data set shows the weights of ten gerbils in ounces.

5.49, 4.48, 4.57, 4.59, 4.61, 4.57, 4.98, 4.43, 4.45, 4.58

**4** Find the mean, median, and mode. Mean: 4.675 oz; Median: 4.575 oz; Mode: 4.57 oz

**5** Which one of the weights would you delete from the list if you want the mean to be closer to the median? 5.49 oz

**Use the data in the dot plot to answer questions 6 to 9.**

The dot plot shows the number of hours nine students spent surfing the Internet one day. Each dot represents 1 student.

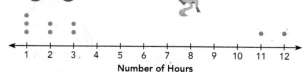

Number of Hours

**6** Find the mean, median, and mode.
Mean: 4; Median: 2; Mode: 1

**7** Give a reason why the mean is much greater than the median.
Because there are two outliers, 11 and 12.

**8** Which measure of central tendency best describes the data set? See margin.

**9** Relate the measures of center to the shape of the data distribution. See margin.

### Assignment Guide

**DAY 1** All students should complete **1** – **8**.

**DAY 2** All students should complete **9** – **16**.

**17** – **21** provide additional challenge.

Optional: *Extra Practice 14.4*
**Materials:** none

**3** The mean number of children is 2.4. It is not a realistic number for describing the data set. The median and mode are both 2, which is a realistic number for describing the data set. So, the median and the mode best describe the data set.

**8** Median; because the majority of the data values cluster around 2 hours. The mode does not describe the data set because it only represents three out of the nine students.

**9** The shape of the distribution is skewed to the right. So, the measure of center is likely to be 2, which is in the lower range.

### RtI Lesson Check

| Before assigning homework, use the following ... | to make sure students ... | Intervene with ... |
|---|---|---|
| Exercise **1** | • can select the mean, median, or mode as the measurement of central tendency | Reteach 14.4 |
| Exercises **6** and **10** | • can relate the measures of central tendency to a skewed or symmetrical distribution | |
| EXIT Ticket Out the Door | | |

**Use the data in the dot plot to answer the question.**

The dot plot shows the results of a survey on the number of brothers or sisters each student in a class has. Each dot represents 1 student.

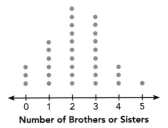

**Number of Brothers or Sisters**

**10** The data values are well spread and the shape of the data distribution is nearly symmetrical. So, the measure of center is likely to be 2, which is in the middle range.

**10** Briefly describe the data distribution and relate the measure of center to the shape of the dot plot shown. See above.

**Make a dot plot to show the data. Use your dot plot to answer questions 11 and 12.**

A box contains cards each with a number 1, 2, 3, 4, or 5 on it. In an experiment, 20 students took turns drawing a card from the box. The number written on the card was recorded before it was put back into the box.

Alice, who was the last person to draw a card, was supposed to complete the dot plot below. However, she lost the record of the experiment's results. All she could recall was the following information.

(i) There were twice as many cards with the number '3' drawn as there were cards with the number '4' drawn.

(ii) There were an equal number of cards with the numbers '1' and '5' drawn.

(iii) 5 cards with the number '2' were drawn.

(iv) 8 students drew cards that show an even number.

**11** Copy and complete the dot plot.

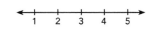

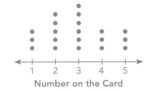

**Number on the Card**

**12** Briefly describe the data distribution and relate the measure of center to the shape of the dot plot shown. See margin.

Use the data in the table to answer questions **13** to **17**.

The table shows the number of students absent from school over a 30-day period.

**Number of Students Absent from School**

| Number of Students | 0 | 1 | 2 | 3 |
|---|---|---|---|---|
| Number of Days | 8 | 7 | 10 | 5 |

**13** What is the mode of this distribution?  2

**14** Find the mean and median number of students absent from school over the 30 days.  Mean: 1.4; Median: 1.5

**15** It is found that the mean number of students absent from school over a subsequent 20-day period is 1. Find the mean number of students absent from school over the entire 50-day period.  1.24

**16** If on one day of the 30-day period, 4 students were absent from school instead of 3, what should the mean of the distribution over the first 30-day period be? Round your answer to the nearest hundredth.  1.43

**17** If on one day of the 30-day period, 2 students were absent from school instead of 1, would the median of the distribution over the 30-day period be affected? If so, what is the new median?  Yes; 2

# Brain @ Work

In a series of six class quizzes, Tim's first four quiz scores are 3, 5, 6, and 8. The mean score of the six quizzes is 6. If the greater of the missing quiz scores is doubled, the mean score becomes $7\frac{1}{3}$. What are the two missing quiz scores?

**Tim's Test Scores**

| Test | First | Second | Third | Fourth | Fifth | Sixth |
|---|---|---|---|---|---|---|
| Score | 3 | 5 | 6 | 8 | _?_ | _?_ |

6; 8

## DIFFERENTIATED INSTRUCTION

**Through Visual Cues**

**13** to **17** Suggest students create a dot plot to display the set of values.

## Ticket Out the Door

Explain how the measures of center in a skewed distribution and in a symmetrical distribution differ. Possible answer: In a symmetrical distribution, the mean, median, and mode are all the same value. In a skewed distribution, the mean is pulled away from the median and mode, decreasing if the skew is to the left or increasing if the skew is to the right.

Also available on Teacher One Stop.

## DIFFERENTIATED INSTRUCTION

**Through Enrichment**

Because all students should be challenged, have all students try the Brain@Work exercise on this page.

For additional challenging practice and problem solving, see *Enrichment, Course 1*, Chapter 14.

Use the notes and the flow of the concept map to review the processes of finding the mean, median, and mode and using these to describe a distribution.

## CHAPTER PROJECT

To widen student's mathematical horizons and to encourage them to think beyond the concepts taught in this chapter, you may want to assign the Chapter 14 project, Number Cube Data, available in *Activity Book, Course 1*.

# Chapter Wrap Up

## Concept Map

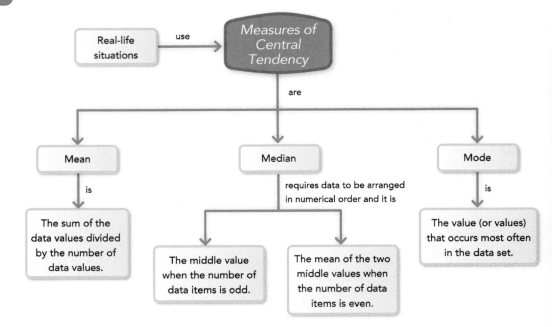

## Key Concepts

▶ The three measures of central tendency are the mean, median, and mode. Each measure is a single number summarizing all the values in a data set.

▶ Mode is the only measure that can be used to describe non-numeric data.

▶ Mean and median are both used to describe the center of a set of numeric data. The mean gives more weight to outliers and extreme values than the median does.

▶ In a symmetric or nearly symmetric data set, the mean, median, and mode will be close together.

▶ In a skewed distribution, the median and mode will be close together, but the mean will move towards the outliers.

## Vocabulary Review

Use these questions to review chapter vocabulary with students.

1. The __?__ is the value of the middle term of a set of data. median

2. "Average" is also known as __?__. mean

3. The value with the highest frequency is the __?__. mode

 Also available on Teacher One Stop.

# Chapter Review/Test

## Concepts and Skills

**Solve. Show your work.**

1. The data set shows nine students' scores in a science quiz.

   9, 6, 6, 5, 9, 10, 1, 4, 10

   Find the mean and median score. Mean: $6\frac{2}{3}$; Median: 6

2. The mean of a set of four numbers is 3.5. If a fifth number, x, is added to the data set, the mean becomes 4. Find the value of x. 6

**Make a dot plot to show the data. Use your dot plot to answer the question.** See margin.

3. The data set shows the number of vehicles at a highway intersection during morning rush hour on 15 working days.

   12, 11, 4, 6, 9, 11, 4, 6, 12, 16, 11, 10, 8, 4, 5

   Find the mean, median, and mode of the data set.
   Mean: 8.6; Median: 9; Modes: 4 and 11

## Problem Solving

**Solve. Show your work.**

The data set shows the amount of money 10 children spent in a week.

$16, $13, $11, $19, $17, $28, $15, $11, $13, $11

4. Find the mean and median amount of money spent. Mean: $15.40; Median: $14

5. Which amount of money would you delete from the list if you want the mean to be closer to the median? Explain your answer. $28; Amounts at either extreme have more effect on the mean than the median.

**Use the data in the table to answer the question.**

6. Three classes in Grade 7 took a geography test last week. The table shows the mean score of the students in each class.

   The mean score of the students in classes A and B combined is 7.25. The mean score of all the students in the three classes is 6.5.

   **Mean Score of Students in Three Classes**

   | Class | A | B | C |
   |---|---|---|---|
   | Number of Students | x | 25 | 20 |
   | Mean Score | 6 | 8 | y |

   Find the values of x and y.
   x = 15; y = 5

## CHAPTER REVIEW/TEST

### Chapter Assessment

Use the Chapter 14 Test A or B in *Assessments, Course 1* to assess how well students have learned the material in this chapter. These assessments are appropriate for reporting results to adults at home and administrators. Test A is shown on pages 274A and 274B.

## TEST PREPARATION

For additional test prep

🖱 **ExamView® Assessment Suite Course 1**

🖱 **Online Assessment System**
my.hrw.com

3.

## RtI Intervention and Reteaching Recommendations

| Student Book A Review/Test Items | Assessments Chapter 14 Items | Chapter 14 Objectives | Reteach A Chapter 14 |
|---|---|---|---|
| 1 and 2 | Test A: 1–3 <br> Test B: 1–3 | **Objective 1.** Find the mean, median, and mode of a set of data. | Lessons 14.1, 14.2, 14.3 |
| 3 to 6 | Test A: 4–15 <br> Test B: 4–15 | **Objective 2.** Use the mean, median, and mode of a set of data to solve problems. | Lesson 14.4 |

**7**

Number of Goals

**8** The shape of the distribution is skewed to the right. So, the measure of center is likely to be 2 goals, which is in the lower range.

**Make a dot plot to show the data. Use your dot plot to answer questions 7 and 8.** See margin.

The table shows the number of goals scored by a soccer team in 15 games.

**Number of Goals Scored by a Soccer Team**

| Number of Goals | 1 | 2 | 3 | 4 | 5 | 6 | 7 |
|---|---|---|---|---|---|---|---|
| Number of Games | 5 | 6 | 3 | 0 | 0 | 0 | 1 |

**7** Find the mean, median, and mode of the data set. Mean: 2.2; Median: 2; Mode: 2

**8** Briefly describe the data distribution and relate the measure of center to the distribution. See margin.

**Use the data in the dot plot to answer questions 9 to 13.**

The dot plot shows the results of a survey to find the number of computers in 30 randomly chosen families. Each dot represents 1 family.

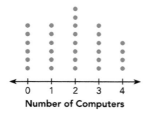

Number of Computers

**9** What is the modal number of computers? 2

**10** What is the mean number of computers? Round your answer to the hundredths place. 1.87

**11** What is the median number of computers? 2

**12** Briefly describe the data distribution and relate the measure of center to the shape of the dot plot shown. See above.

**13** A similar survey is carried out on another 15 randomly chosen families and the mean number of computers is found to be 2. If the two data sets are combined, find the mean number of computers in the combined data set. Round your answer to the nearest hundredth. 1.91

**12** The data values are well spread out and the shape of the data distribution is nearly symmetrical. So, the measure of center is likely to be 2, which is in the middle of the range.

**RtI Intervention and Reteaching Recommendations**

| Student Book A Review/Test Items | Assessments Chapter 14 Items | Chapter 14 Objectives | Reteach A Chapter 14 |
|---|---|---|---|
| 7 – 13 | Test A: 4–15 Test B: 4–15 | **Objective 2.** Use the mean, median, and mode of a set of data to solve problems. | Lesson 14.4 |

---

**Test B, Assessments p. 149**

**Test A, Assessments p. 144**

Name: _____ Date: _____

**CHAPTER TEST A**

**(14)** **Measures of Central Tendency**

☒ **25**
**Suggested Time: 30 min**

**Concepts and Skills** (5 × 2 points = 10 points)

**Solve. Show your work.**

1. The data set shows the number of passengers on eight buses.
29, 33, 41, 38, 42, 37, 36, 40
Find the mean number of passengers.

2. The number of goals scored by a football team in ten matches are
1, 3, 2, 1, 0, 3, 2, 2, 1, 1.
Find the mode and median score.

3. The mean of a set of six numbers is 4.5. If the mean of two of the numbers is 5.5, find the mean of the remaining four numbers.

**144** Chapter 14 Test A

---

**Test B, Assessments p. 150**

**Test A, Assessments p. 145**

Name: _____ Date: _____

The dot plot shows the results of a survey on the number of hours each student spends playing computer games. Use the data in the dot plot to answer questions 4 and 5.

Number of Hours Spent Playing Computer Games

4. a) Find the modal number of hours each student spends playing computer games.

   b) Find the median number of hours each student spends playing computer games.

5. Find the mean number of hours each student spends playing computer games.

Assessments Course 1 **145**

---

**Test B, Assessments p. 151**

**Test A, Assessments p. 146**

Name: _____ Date: _____

**Problem Solving** (Questions 6 and 7: 2 × 1 point = 2 points, Question 8: 2 points,
Questions 9 and 10: 2 × 1 point = 2 points,
Questions 11 and 12: 2 × 2 points = 4 points,
Question 13: 1 point, Questions 14 and 15 = 2 × 2 points = 4 points)

**Use the data set to answer questions 6 to 8.**

The data set shows the amount of Alvin's monthly savings last year.
$7, $12, $10, $12, $15, $11, $8, $9, $11, $11, $13, $10

6. Find Alvin's median monthly savings.

7. Find Alvin's mean monthly savings.

8. If Alvin had saved $1 more every month, what are his new median and new mean monthly savings?

**146** Chapter 14 Test A

---

**Test B, Assessments p. 152**

**Test A, Assessments p. 147**

Name: _____ Date: _____

**Use the data in the table to answer questions 9 to 12.**

The table shows the shoe sizes of 15 girls.

| Shoe Sizes | 4 | 5 | 6 | 7 | 8 |
|---|---|---|---|---|---|
| Number of Girls | 3 | 4 | 5 | 2 | 1 |

9. What is the modal shoe size?

10. What is the median shoe size?

11. Find the mean shoe size.

12. Which measure of central tendency best describes the distribution?

Assessments Course 1 **147**

Name: _____   Date: _____

**Use the data in the dot plot to answer questions 13 to 15.**

The dot plot shows the results of a survey to find the number of mobile phones in 30 families. Each dot represents 1 family.

Number of Mobile Phones

13. Find the median number of mobile phones.

14. Find the mean number of mobile phones. Round your answer to the nearest hundredth.

15. A similar survey is carried out on another 20 families and the mean number of mobile phones is found to be 3.6. If the two data sets are combined, find the mean number of mobile phones in the combined data set.

## TEACHER NOTES

# Cumulative Review Chapters 12–14

## Concepts and Skills

**Match each of the solid figures to its net.** (Lesson 12.1)

**1** 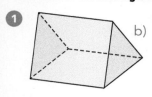 b)

**2** 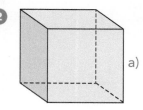 a)

**3** 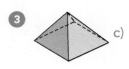 c)

a)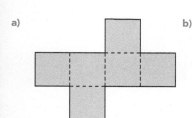

b)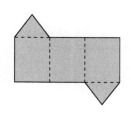

c)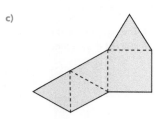

**Find the surface area and volume of each prism.** (Lessons 12.1, 12.2)

**4**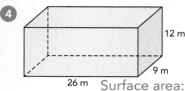
12 m
9 m
26 m

Surface area: 1,308 m²;
Volume: 2,808 m³

**5**
15 in.
12 in.
9 in.
20 in.

Surface area: 828 in.²;
Volume: 1,080 in.³

**Solve. Show your work.** (Lessons 14.1, 14.2)

**6** The data set shows the lengths (in inches) of seven pieces of wire.
7.9, 6.8, 7.6, 9.9, 10.1, 9.1, 10.9
Find the mean and median lengths of these seven pieces of wire. Mean: 8.9 in.; Median: 9.1 in.

**7** The data set shows the weights (in pounds) of 9 vases.
8.8, 8.3, 7.7, 11.6, 9.9, 8.9, 10.4, 9.6, 8.5
Find the mean and median weights of these 9 vases. Mean: 9.3 lb; Median: 8.9 lb

**8** The data set shows the heights (in feet) of 8 trees.
53, 56, 65, 61, 67, 60, 52, 48
Find the mean and median heights of these 8 trees. Mean: 57.75 ft; Median: 58 ft

## Assessment

Use Benchmark Test A or B for Chapters 12–14 in *Assessments, Course 1* to assess how well students have learned the material taught in these chapters. These assessments are appropriate for reporting results to adults at home and administrators.

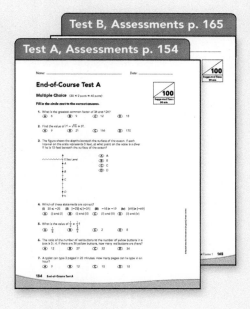

Test B, Assessments p. 165

Test A, Assessments p. 154

## TEST PREPARATION

For additional test prep

🖰 **ExamView® Assessment Suite Course 1**

🖰 **Online Assessment System**
my.hrw.com

**12 a)**

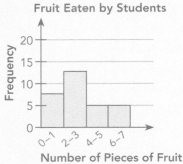

Number of Fruits

**12 b)** Answers vary. Sample:

| Number of Pieces of Fruit | 0–1 | 2–3 | 4–5 | 6–7 |
|---|---|---|---|---|
| Frequency | 7 | 13 | 5 | 5 |

**12 c)**

Fruit Eaten by Students

Frequency vs Number of Pieces of Fruit

Majority of the students ate 2 to 3 pieces of fruit during the two days. Most of the data values are to the right of the interval 2–3, so the distribution is right-skewed. Range: $7 - 0 = 7$

---

**The volume of each triangular prism is 497 cubic feet. Find the height of the triangular base. Round your answers to the nearest tenth of a foot.** (Lesson 12.3)

 **9**

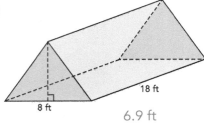

18 ft

8 ft

6.9 ft

**10**

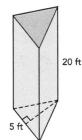

20 ft

9.9 ft

5 ft

**Solve.** (Lesson 12.3)

**11** The solid below is made of identical cubes. The volume of the solid is 405 cubic centimeters. Find the edge length of each cube.

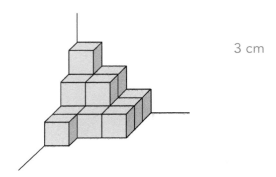

3 cm

**Draw a dot plot and a histogram for the set of data. Include a title.** (Lessons 13.2, 13.3)

**12** The number of pieces of fruits eaten in the past two days by each of 30 students was recorded below. See margin.

| | | | | | | | | | |
|---|---|---|---|---|---|---|---|---|---|
| 1 | 3 | 0 | 2 | 1 | 2 | 2 | 2 | 3 | 1 |
| 5 | 3 | 2 | 1 | 7 | 4 | 5 | 3 | 4 | 7 |
| 4 | 2 | 1 | 3 | 6 | 3 | 6 | 1 | 2 | 6 |

**a)** Represent the set of data with a dot plot.

**b)** Group the data into suitable intervals and tabulate them.

**c)** Draw a histogram using the intervals from part **b)**. Briefly describe the data.

**Describe the data.** (Lesson 13.3)

**13** The histogram shows the number of floors each building has in a particular city. Briefly describe the data.

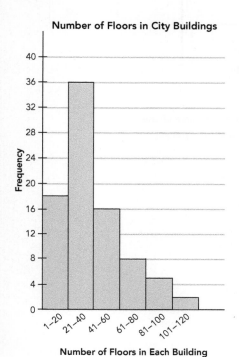

**Number of Floors in City Buildings**

Number of Floors in Each Building

There are 85 buildings in the city.

Most buildings have 21 to 40 floors.
The range of the data is 119.

The histogram has a "tail" on the right. Most of the data values are to the right of the interval 21–40, and the shape of the histogram is right-skewed.

## Problem Solving

**Draw a dot plot for each set of data. Use your dot plot to answer each question.** (Chapters 13, 14)

**14** The data set shows the number of text messages sent by Emily in 14 days.

| 1 | 5 | 7 | 3 | 7 | 0 | 3 |
|---|---|---|---|---|---|---|
| 7 | 0 | 1 | 5 | 8 | 7 | 2 |

a)  Represent the set of data with a dot plot. See margin.

b)  Find the mean, median, and mode of the data set. Mean: 4; Median: 4; Mode: 7

**14** a)

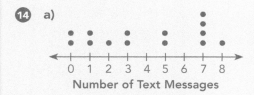

Number of Text Messages

**15** a)

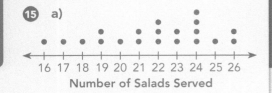

Number of Salads Served

**15** The data set shows the number of salads served in a cafe for each of 20 days.

| 23 | 22 | 24 | 26 | 19 | 21 | 24 | 26 | 21 | 16 |
|----|----|----|----|----|----|----|----|----|----|
| 22 | 20 | 18 | 24 | 25 | 17 | 22 | 23 | 19 | 24 |

a)   Represent the set of data with a dot plot.  See margin.

b)   Find the mean, median, and mode of the data set. Mean: 21.8; Median: 22; Mode: 24

**Solve. Show your work.** (Chapter 12)

**16** The square pyramid shown has congruent triangular faces. The area of one triangular face is 48 square inches. Find the surface area of the pyramid.

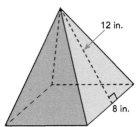

256 in.²

**17** The length of the aquarium shown is two times its width. The height of the aquarium is 18 inches. The aquarium is filled with water to a height of 16 inches. The volume of the water is 7,200 cubic inches.

a)   Find the length of the base of the aquarium.  30 in.

b)   Then find the amount of glass, in square inches, used to make the bottom and sides of the aquarium. 2,070 in.²

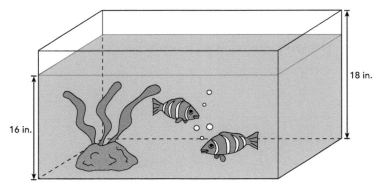

**Solve.** (Chapter 13)

**18** The table shows the number of hours each of 120 students spent helping their community in two months.

| Number of Hours | 31 – 35 | 36 – 40 | 41 – 45 | 46 – 50 | 51 – 55 | 56 – 60 | 61 – 65 | 66 – 70 | 71 – 75 |
|---|---|---|---|---|---|---|---|---|---|
| Number of Students | $x$ | 9 | 13 | 17 | 19 | 18 | 16 | 13 | $2x$ |

a) Find the value of $x$. 5

b) Draw a histogram to represent the data. See margin.
   Briefly describe the data.

c) What percent of the students spent more than 55 hours helping their community? 47.5%

d) What percent of the students spent less than 46 hours helping their community? 22.5%

**Make a dot plot to show the data. Use your dot plot to answer each question.** (Chapters 13, 14)

**19** The table shows the results of a survey to find the number of television sets in 50 randomly chosen homes.

| Number of Television Sets | 0 | 1 | 2 | 3 | 4 | 5 |
|---|---|---|---|---|---|---|
| Number of Homes | $y$ | 11 | 17 | $x$ | 6 | 2 |

The total number of homes that have 0 or 1 television set is 15.

a) Find values of $x$ and $y$. Then represent this set of data with a dot plot. $x = 10$; $y = 4$; See margin.

b) Find the mean, median, and mode of the data set. Mean: 2.18; Median: 2; Mode: 2

c) Briefly describe the data distribution and relate the measure of center to the shape of the dot plot. See margin.

d) A similar survey is carried out on another 30 randomly chosen homes and the mean number of television sets is found to be 1.9. If the two data sets are combined, find the mean number of television sets in the combined data set. 2.075

**18** b)

**Time Spent Helping the Community**

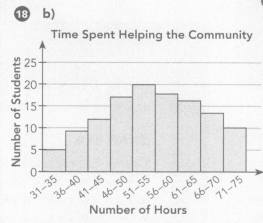

Number of Hours

Most of the data values are near the most frequent value in the interval, 51–55. The shape of the distribution is nearly symmetrical. The data values are from 31 to 75. Range: 75 − 31 = 44. The data set has a slight skew to the left.

**19** a)

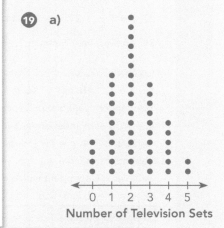

Number of Television Sets

**19** c) The data are well spread and the shape of the data distribution is nearly symmetrical. Because the mode and the median are the same, and the mean is slightly greater, the data set is likely to be more spread out for data greater than 12. The data set is slightly skewed to the right.

# Selected Answers

## Selected Answers

**CHAPTER 8**

### Lesson 8.1, Guided Practice (pp. 6–11)

**1.** 1; 4; ≠; 2; 5; ≠; 4; 7; 4    **2.** $p = 7$    **3.** $r = 8$    **4.** $k = 17$

**5.** $m = 3$    **6.** $n = 5$    **7.** $z = 15$    **8.** −; 8; −; 8; 11

**9.** $f = 9$    **10.** $g = 15$    **11.** $w = 16$    **12.** $z = 30$

**13.** ÷; 3; ÷; 3; 9    **14.** $a = 7$    **15.** $b = 5$    **16.** $m = 72$

**17.** $n = 84$    **18.** −; $\frac{3}{7}$; −; $\frac{3}{7}$; $\frac{2}{7}$    **19.** Subtract $\frac{1}{8}$;

$k = \frac{3}{4}$    **20.** Divide by 4; $p = \frac{3}{16}$

### Lesson 8.1, Practice (p. 12)

**1.** $b = 3$    **3.** $k = 15$    **5.** $t = 7$    **7.** $k = 11$    **9.** $f = 40$

**11.** $m = 9$    **13.** $c = \frac{2}{3}$    **15.** $q = 1$    **17.** $d = \frac{1}{12}$

**19.** $f = 2\frac{2}{3}$    **21.** $x = 4.5$    **23.** $j = 24.1$    **25.** $z = 5.56$

**27.** $x = 1\frac{1}{4}$    **29.** $p = 3$    **31.** $y = 27$    **33.** $k = 18\frac{2}{3}$

**35.** Answers vary. Sample: 1, $\frac{2}{5}$; 2, $\frac{4}{5}$; 3, $1\frac{1}{5}$; 4, $1\frac{3}{5}$; 5, 2

### Lesson 8.2, Guided Practice (pp. 14–19)

**1a.** $h + 7$    **1b.** $h$; 7    **1c.** $h$; $k$    **2.** $t = p + 12$;
Independent variable: $p$; Dependent variable: $t$

**3.** $n = 30 - m$; Independent variable: $m$; Dependent
variable: $n$    **4.** $c = 7b$; Independent variable: $b$;
Dependent variable: $c$    **5.** $y = \frac{x}{12}$; Independent
variable: $x$; Dependent variable: $y$

**6a.** $q = p - 2$; 2; 3; 5; 6

| Length (*p* meters) | 3 | 4 | 5 | 6 | 7 | 8 |
|---|---|---|---|---|---|---|
| Width (*q* meters) | 1 | 2 | 3 | 4 | 5 | 6 |

**6b.**

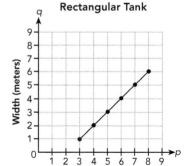

Dimensions of a
Rectangular Tank

**6c.** Yes, the rectangular tank can have a length of
5.5 meters and a width of 3.5 meters.

**7.** 8; 10; 11; $y = x + 6$    **8.** 12; 16; 20; $r = 4b$

**9.**

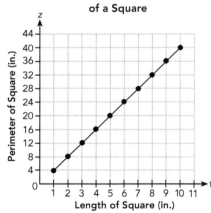

Journey

$d = 50t$

### Lesson 8.2, Practice (pp. 20–21)

**1a.** $x = w + 3$    **1b.** Independent variable: $w$; Dependent
variable: $x$    **3a.** $m = 5k$    **3b.** Independent variable: $k$;
Dependent variable: $m$    **5a.** $y = x + 8$    **5b.** 18; 19; 20;
21; 22; 23    **7a.** $P = 6b$    **7b.** 6; 12; 18; 24; 30; 36

**9a.** $z = 4t$

**9b.**

| Length of Square (*t* inches) | 1 | 2 | 3 | 4 | 5 | 6 | 7 | 8 | 9 | 10 |
|---|---|---|---|---|---|---|---|---|---|---|
| Perimeter of Square (*z* inches) | 4 | 8 | 12 | 16 | 20 | 24 | 28 | 32 | 36 | 40 |

**9c.**

Side Length and Perimeter
of a Square

**9d.** Length: 3.5 inches, Perimeter: 14 inches
Length: 7.5 inches, Perimeter: 30 inches

## Lesson 8.3, Guided Practice (pp. 24-26)

**1.**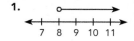

**2.**

**3.**

**4.**

**5.**

**6.**

**7.**

**8.**

Answers vary. Sample: $q = 3, 4,$ or $5$

**9.**

**10.**

Answers vary. Sample: $k = 23, 24,$ or $25$

**11.** b    **12.** c    **13.** d    **14.** a

## Lesson 8.3, Practice (pp. 27-28)

**1.** $k < 12$    **3.** $w \geq 17$    **5.** $x \geq 20$

**7.**

**9.**

**11.** $x < 9$    **13.** $x \leq 11$

**15.**

Answers vary. Sample: $p = 5, 6,$ or $7$

**17.**

Answers vary. Sample: $b = 3, 4,$ or $5$

**19.**

Answers vary. Sample: $g = 2, 3,$ or $4$

**21.**

Answers vary. Sample: $z = 7, 8,$ or $9$

**23a.** No. $x$ is more than 9.    **23b.** No. $x$ is an integer.

**25.**

**27.**

**29.**

## Lesson 8.4, Guided Practice (pp. 30-32)

**1.** 41; 23; 41; 23; 18; 18    **2.** 28    **3.** $34    **4.** 17 green beads    **5.** 125 quarters    **6a.** $x \leq 55$    **6b.** 55
**7a.** $x > 35$ or $x \geq 36$    **7b.** 36 guests    **8a.** $x < 50$
**8b.** 49 words    **9a.** $x \leq 240$    **9b.** 240 tons    **10a.** $x \geq 50$
**10b.** Alex

## Lesson 8.4, Practice (pp. 33-34)

**1.** 65    **3.** 26 words per minute    **5a.** $x > 40$;

**5b.** 41 points

**7.** $\frac{3}{7}x = 24$; 56 mountain bikes

**9.** $0.3x = 42$; 140 comic books    **11.** 54 marbles

**13a.** 60 participants    **13b.** 96 participants

## Lesson 8.4, Brain@Work (pp. 34)

5 cm

## Chapter Review/Test (pp. 36-37)

**1.** $x = 19$    **3.** $f = 5.4$    **5.** $k = 3\frac{1}{3}$    **7.** $h = 14$

**9.** $P = 12\frac{1}{2}$

**11.**

**13.**

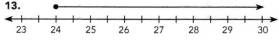

**15.**

**17.**

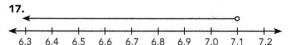

**19.** $x \geq 9$    **21.** $x < \frac{7}{10}$    **23.** $y = x + 9$    **25.** 4,030 mL

**27.** 119 pages    **29.** 24 more green counters

**31a.** $x \geq 18$    **31b.** Perimeter: 66 cm; Area: 270 cm$^2$

## CHAPTER 9

### Lesson 9.1, Guided Practice (pp. 44-46)

**1.** $P(3, 0)$, $Q(-3, 3)$, $R(-5, 1)$, $S(-6, -4)$, $T(-4, -7)$, $U(4, -5)$, and $V(3, -2)$; Quadrant II: Points $Q$ and $R$; Quadrant III: Points $S$ and $T$; Quadrant IV: Points $V$ and $U$; Point $P$ lies on the $x$-axis. It is between Quadrant I and Quadrant IV.

**2.**

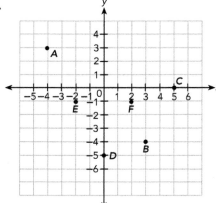

**3a.**

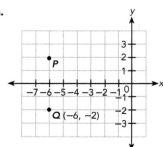

**3b.**

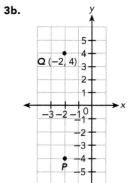

**3c.**

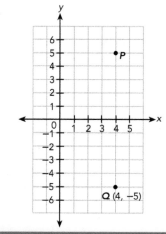

**3d.**

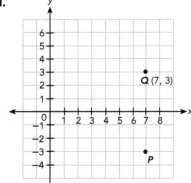

**4a.**

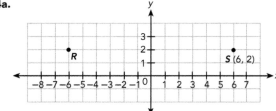

**4b.**

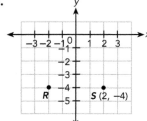

**4c.**

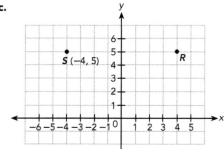

**4d.**

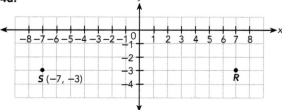

**5.**

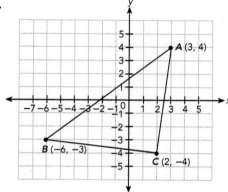

triangle

**6.**

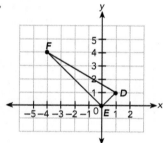

triangle

**7.**

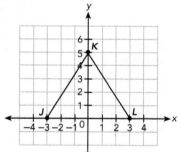

triangle

**8.**

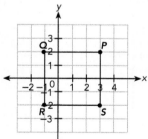

square

**9.**

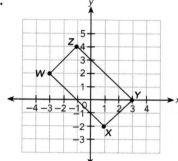

rectangle

**10.**

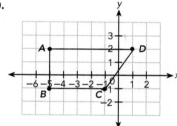

trapezoid

**11.**

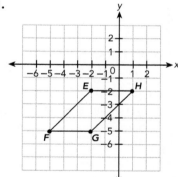

parallelogram

**12.**

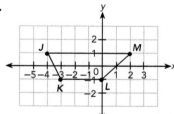

trapezoid

**13.**

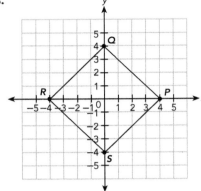

square

**14.**

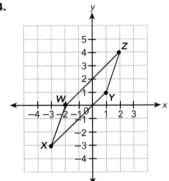

parallelogram

**Lesson 9.1, Practice** (pp. 48–49)

**1.** A (2, 6), B (6, 2), C (3, 0), D (4, −9), E (0, −2), F (−2, −4), G (−3, 0), and H (−1, 9); Quadrant I: Points A and B; Quadrant II: Point H; Quadrant III: Point F; Quadrant IV: Point D; Point C lies on the x-axis. It lies between Quadrant I and Quadrant IV. Point G lies on the x-axis. It lies between Quadrant II and Quadrant III. Point E lies on the y-axis.

It lies between Quadrant III and Quadrant IV.

**3.**

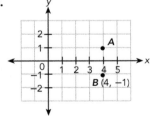

**5.**

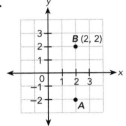

**7.**

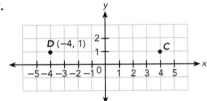

**9.**

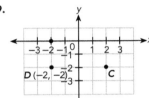

**11.**

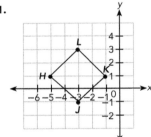

square

**13.**

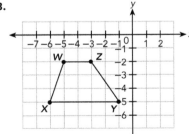

trapezoid

**15a** and **15b.**

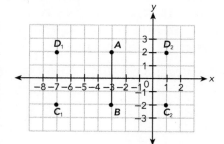

**15c.** $C_1$ (−7, −2), $D_1$ (−7, 2) and $C_2$ (1, −2), $D_2$ (1, 2)

**17.**

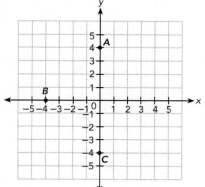

**17a.** right isosceles triangle

**17b.**

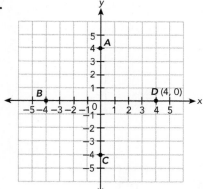

D (4, 0)

## Lesson 9.2, Guided Practice (pp. 51–57)

**1.**

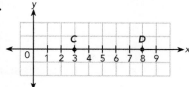

CD = 5 units

**2.**

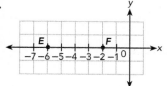

EF = 4 units

**3.**

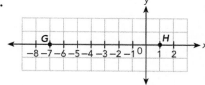

GH = 8 units

**4.**

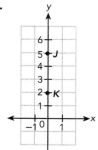

JK = 3 units

**5.**

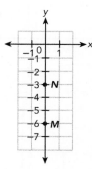

MN = 3 units

**6.**

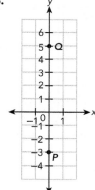

PQ = 8 units

**7.**

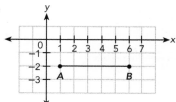

AB = 5 units

**8.**

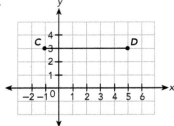

$CD$ = 6 units

**9.**

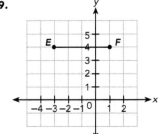

$EF$ = 4 units

**10.**

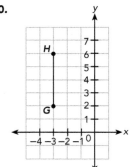

$GH$ = 4 units

**11.**

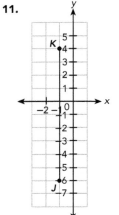

$JK$ = 10 units

**12.**

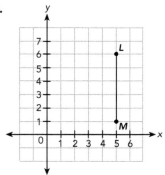

$LM$ = 5 units

**13.** $A$ (10, 20), $B$ (10, 5), and $C$ (30, 20)     **14.** 20; 5; 15; 30; 10; 20; 15; 25; 20; 60; 60     **15.** 10; 2; 2; 2; 2; 4; 4; 5; 20; 1; 4; 1; 3; 3; 5; 15; 20; 15     **16.** $P$ (16, 44), $Q$ (16, 4), $R$ (36, 4), and $S$ (36, 44)     **17.** 120 m     **18.** $T$ (16, 36)

**Lesson 9.2, Practice** (pp. 58—61)

**1.**

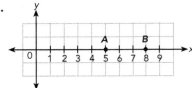

$AB$ = 3 units

**3.**

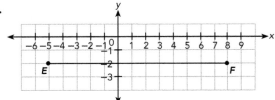

$EF$ = 13 units

**5.**

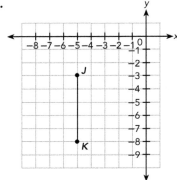

$JK$ = 5 units

**7a.**

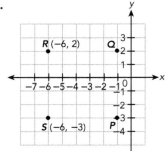

The coordinates of point $R$ are (−6, 2). The coordinates of point $S$ are (−6, −3).

**7.b**

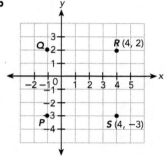

The coordinates of R are (4, 2). The coordinates of S are (4, −3).

**9a.**

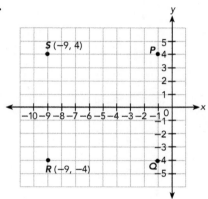

The coordinates of point R are (−9, −4). The coordinates of point S are (−9, 4).

**9b.**

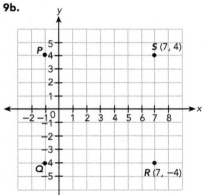

The coordinates of point R are (7, −4). The coordinates of point S are (7, 4).

**11.** A: 60 m; B: 60 m; C: 50 m; D: 50 m

**13.** Area: 15,400 m²; Perimeter: 500 m

**15.**

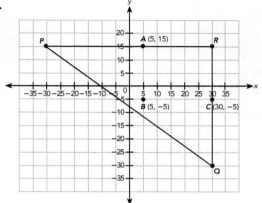

**17.** 500 m²   **19.** 180 m   **21.** 413

**Lesson 9.3, Guided Practice** (pp. 63–64)

**1.**

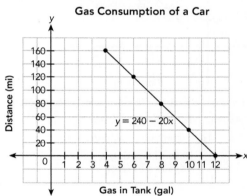

**1a.**

| Amount of Gas (x gallons) | 12 | 10 | 8 | 6 | 4 |
|---|---|---|---|---|---|
| Distance Traveled (y miles) | 0 | 40 | 80 | 120 | 160 |

**1b.** straight line or linear   **1c.** 9   **1d.** 7   **1e.** 4; 20; 4; 20; 80; 80   **1f.** x < 10   **1g.** Dependent: y; Independent: x

**2.**

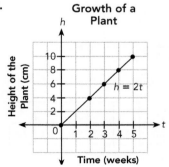

**2a.**

| Time (*t* weeks) | 0 | 1 | 2 | 3 | 4 | 5 |
|---|---|---|---|---|---|---|
| Height (*h* centimeters) | 0 | 2 | 4 | 6 | 8 | 10 |

**2b.** straight line graph or linear graph   **2c.** 6 cm

**2d.** 10 cm   **2e.** *h* < 8   **2f.** Dependent: *h*; Independent: *t*

**Lesson 9.3, Practice** (pp. 65–66)

**1.**

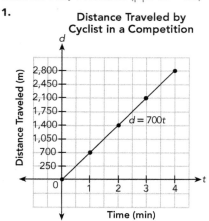

Distance Traveled by Cyclist in a Competition

$d = 700t$

**1a.** straight line graph or linear graph   **1b.** 1,750 m

**1c.** 2,450 m   **1d.** 700 m/min   **1e.** 4,900 m

**1f.** $t \geq 3$   **1g.** Dependent: *d*; independent: *t*

**3.**

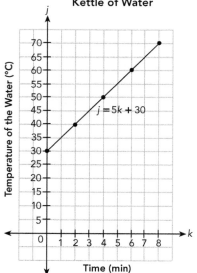

Rate of Heating a Kettle of Water

$j = 5k + 30$

**3a.**

| Time (*k* minutes) | 0 | 2 | 4 | 6 | 8 |
|---|---|---|---|---|---|
| Temperature (*j*°C) | 30 | 40 | 50 | 60 | 70 |

**3b.** 55°C   **3c.** 5°C/min   **3d.** 80°C   **3e.** $k \geq 14$

**Lesson 9.3, Brain@Work** (p. 66)

**1.**

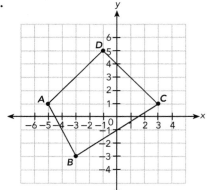

**2.**

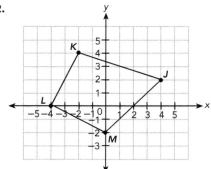

**3.**

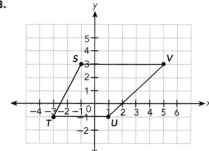

**4.** The figure formed is a quadrilateral.

**5a.**

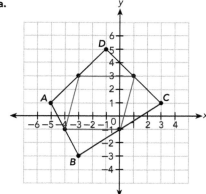

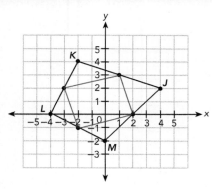

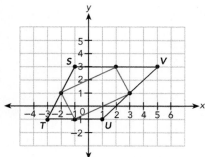

**5b.** Parallelograms. Both pairs of opposite sides are equal in length. Both pairs of opposite sides are parallel.

## Chapter Review/Test (pp. 68–71)

**1.** $A\,(-4, -3)$, $B\,(0, -6)$, $C\,(2, -4)$, $D\,(6, 3)$, and $E\,(-2, 3)$

**3.**

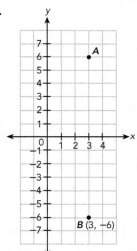

$B\,(3, -6)$

**5.**

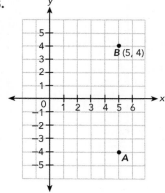

$B\,(5, 4)$

**7.**

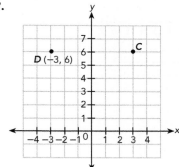

$D\,(-3, 6)$

**9.**

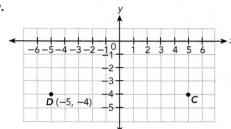

$D\,(-5, -4)$

**11.**

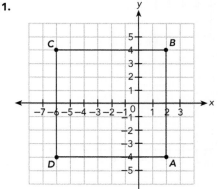

square

**13.**

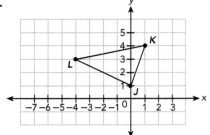

triangle

**15.**

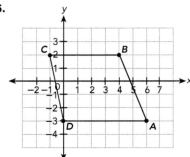

trapezoid

**17.**

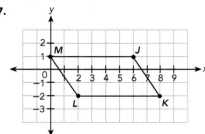

parallelogram

**19.**

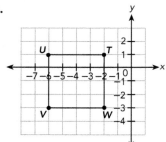

square

**21.**

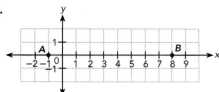

$AB$ = 9 units

**23.**

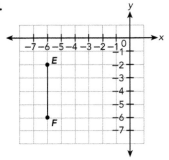

$EF$ = 4 units

**25.**

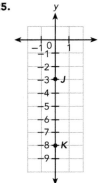

$JK$ = 5 units

**27.** $A$ (−40, 100), $B$ (−40, 20), $C$ (−60, 20), $D$ (−60, −40),
$E$ (60, −40), $F$ (60, 20), $G$ (40, 20), and $H$ (40, 100)

**29.** 160 ft

**31.**

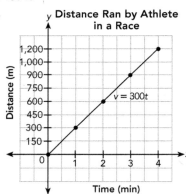

**31a.** straight line graph or linear graph   **31b.** 1,050 m

**31c.** 300 m/min   **31d.** 2,400 m   **31d.** Dependent: $v$;
Independent: $t$

## CHAPTER 10

**Lesson 10.1, Guided Practice** (pp. 79–82)

**1.** 5; 8; $\frac{1}{2}$; 5; 8; 20   **2.** 3; 4; $\frac{1}{2}$; 3; 4; 6   **3.** 2.1; 1.8; $\frac{1}{2}$;
2.1; 1.8; 1.89   **4.** 3.4; 2.7; $\frac{1}{2}$; 3.4; 2.7; 4.59   **5.** 35; $\frac{1}{2}$;

7; 35; 3.5; 35; 3.5; 3.5; 3.5; 10; 10    **6.** 36; $\frac{1}{2}$; 8; $\frac{1}{2}$; 8;

36; 4; 36; 4; 4; 4; 9; 9    **7.** 19.2; $\frac{1}{2}$; 9.6; $\frac{1}{2}$; 9.6; 19.2; 4.8;

19.2; 4.8; 4.8; 4.8; 4; 4

### Lesson 10.1, Practice (pp. 83–87)

**1.** *b*: *BC*; *h*: *AB*

**3.**

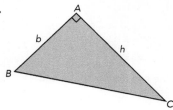

**5.**

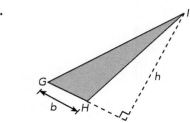

**7.** 50 cm² **9.** 9.7 in. **11.** 12.5 cm **13.** 12 cm
**15.** 330 m² **17.** 264 cm² **19.** 54 cm²

**21.**

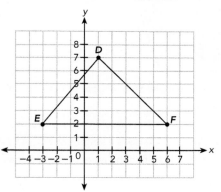

Area of triangle *DEF* = 22.5 units²

**23.**

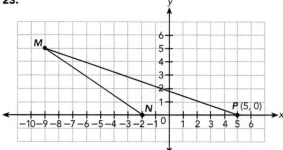

*P* (5, 0)

**25.**

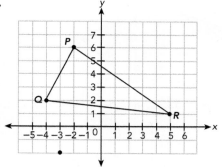

Area of triangle *PQR* = 19 units²
**27.** 487.5 cm² **29.** 32 ft²

### Lesson 10.2, Guided Practice (pp. 89–95)

**1.** 4; 7; 4; 7; 28 **2.** 3; 7; 3; 7; 21 **3.** 4; 8; 4; 8; 32 **4.** 2; 8;
2; 8; 16 **5.** 21; 12; 21; 12; 252 **6.** 24; 14.5; 24, 14.5; 348

**7.** 3; 3; 7; 10; $\frac{1}{2}$; 3; 10; 15 **8.** 4; 1; 3; 4; $\frac{1}{2}$; 4; 4; 8

**9.** 7; 7; 4; 11; $\frac{1}{2}$; 7; 11; 38.5 **10.** 7; 3; 5; 8; $\frac{1}{2}$; 7; 8; 28

**11.** 39; 25; 13; 38; $\frac{1}{2}$; 39; 38; 741 **12.** 13; 10.6; 21; 31.6;

$\frac{1}{2}$; 13; 31.6; 205.4 **13.** 22; 38; 60; 60; 30; 1,248; 30; 30;

1,248; 1,248; ÷; 30; 41.6; *DC*; 41.6; 22; 41.6; 457.6; 457.6

### Lesson 10.2, Practice (pp. 96–98)

**1.**

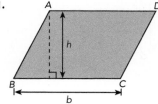

**3.**

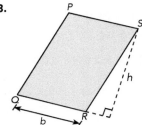

**5.** 420 in.²

**7.**

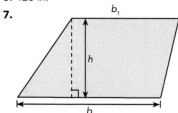

**9.**

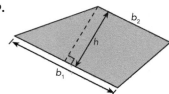

**11.** 110 cm²    **13.** 9.1 in.    **15.** 6.7 cm    **17.** 21 cm

**19.**

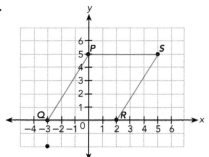

Area of parallelogram *PQRS* = 25 units²

**21.**

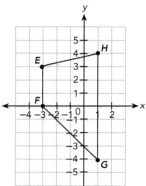

**23.** 290 cm²

Area of trapezoid *EFGH* = 22 units²

**Lesson 10.3, Guided Practice** (pp. 100–101)

**1.** 5    **2.** 6    **3.** $\frac{1}{2}$; 6; 4.1; 12.3; 5; 5; 12.3; 61.5; 61.5

**4.** $\frac{1}{2}$; 28; 24.2; 338.8; 6; 6; 338.8; 2,032.8; 2,032.8

**Lesson 10.3, Practice** (pp. 102–103)

**1.** 8    **3.** 110 cm²    **5.** 1 ft    **7.** 76.8 cm²    **9.** 199.5 cm²

**Lesson 10.4, Guided Practice** (pp. 104–108)

**1.**

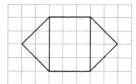

**2.** Answers vary.
Sample: two trapezoids

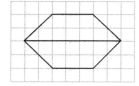

**3a.** 60; 12; 60; 6; 60; 6; 6; 6; 10; 10    **3b.** 10; 100; 100

**3c.** 100; 60; 160; 160    **4a.** 84; 5; 84; 5; 5; 5; 16.8; 12; 8;

16.8; 168; 168    **4b.** $\frac{1}{2}$; 16.8; 5; 8; 109.2; 109.2

**Lesson 10.4, Practice** (pp. 109–112)

**1.**

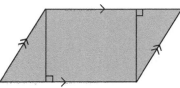

*bh*; sum of areas of the two right triangles and
the rectangle

**3.**

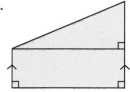

$\frac{1}{2} h(b_1 + b_2)$; sum of areas of the right triangle and
the rectangle

**5.**

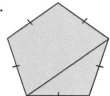

Answers vary. Sample: Sum of areas of the trapezoid
and triangle

**7.** Answers vary. Sample: I would divide it into two
triangles. I would measure the lengths of $\overline{BC}$, $\overline{AX}$, $\overline{AD}$,
and $\overline{CY}$, so that I can find the areas of the two triangles.

**9a.**

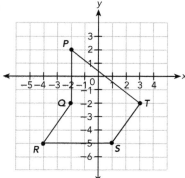

**9b.** Area of figure *PQRST* = 25 units²

**9c.**

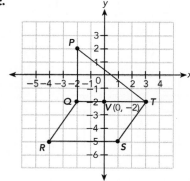

$V$ (0, −2)

**11.** 71.5 in.²     **13.** 5.5 in.

## Lesson 10.4, Brain@Work (p. 113)

**1.** 245 ft²     **2a.** (12 − $x$) centimeters

**2b.** (36 + 6$x$) square centimeters     **2c.** 12; triangle     **3.** $\frac{3}{8}$

## Chapter Review/Test (pp. 115−117)

**1.** $b$: $BC$; $h$: $AD$     **3.** 112 cm²     **5.** 1,071 cm²

**7.** 262.5 cm²     **9.** 24 cm     **11.** 667.2 cm²

# CHAPTER 11

## Lesson 11.1, Guided Practice (pp. 123−130)

**1a.** $\overline{AB}$ and $\overline{CD}$     **1b.** $\overline{ED}$. The line segment $\overline{ED}$ does not pass through the center, $O$.     **2.** 2; ÷; 6; 12; 12

**3.** 15; ÷; 2; 7

**4.**

| Circle | Radius (cm) | Diameter (cm) | Circumference (cm) |
|---|---|---|---|
| A | 7 | 14 | 44 |
| B | 21 | 42 | 132 |
| C | 10.5 | 21 | 66 |

**5.**

| Circle | Radius (cm) | Diameter (cm) | Circumference (cm) |
|---|---|---|---|
| D | 12.5 | 25 | 78.5 |
| E | 16 | 32 | 100.48 |
| F | 8.25 | 16.5 | 51.81 |

**6.** $\frac{22}{7}$; ÷; 35; 110; $\frac{1}{2}$; ÷; 110; 55; 55     **7.** 3.14; 10; 62.8; 62.8; 4; 15.7; 15.7

## Lesson 11.1, Practice (pp. 132−135)

**1.** radii     **3.** $OZ$; $OY$     **5.** diameter or $XY$     **7.** 66 in.

**9.** 17.6 ft     **11.** $15\frac{2}{5}$ ft     **13.** $17\frac{3}{5}$ cm     **15.** 25.7 cm

**17.** 38.55 ft     **19.** $37\frac{1}{2}$ cm     **21.** 100 ft     **23.** 25.12 cm

**25.** 195.32 cm     **27.** 8,792 in.     **29.** 150 cm     **31.** 213.44 ft

## Lesson 11.2, Guided Practice (pp. 138−140)

**1.** 3.14; 18; 3.14; 324; 1,017.36     **2.** 3.14; 15; 3.14; 225; 706.5; 706.5     **3.** 26; 2; 13; 3.14; 13; 3.14; 169; 530.66; 530.66     **4.** $\frac{1}{4}$; $\frac{1}{4}$; $\frac{1}{4}$; $\frac{22}{7}$; 14; $\frac{1}{4}$; $\frac{22}{7}$; 14; 14; 154; 154

**5.** 42; 21; $\frac{1}{4}$; $\frac{1}{4}$; $\frac{1}{4}$; $\frac{22}{7}$; 21; $\frac{1}{4}$; $\frac{22}{7}$; 21; 21; $346\frac{1}{2}$; $346\frac{1}{2}$

## Lesson 11.2, Practice (pp. 141−142)

**1.** 314 cm²     **3.** 308 ft²     **5.** 113.0 in.²     **7.** $38\frac{1}{2}$ cm²

**9.** 113.04 ft²     **11.** 21.5 cm²

## Lesson 11.3, Guided Practice (pp. 145−153)

**1a.** 2; 3.14; 1,736; 10,902.08; 10,900     **1b.** 11,000

**2.** $\frac{1}{2}$; 2; 3.14; 5.2; 3.14; 5.2; 16.328; 2; $\frac{1}{2}$; 3.14; 5.2; 3.14; 5.2; 16.328; 16.328; 16.328; 32.656; 33; 33     **3.** $\frac{1}{2}$; 3.14; 12; 3.14; 12; 37.68; 3.14; 12; 18.84; 37.68; 18.84; 12; 12; 80.52; 80.52     **4.** $\frac{22}{7}$; 35; $\frac{22}{7}$; 35; 35; 962.5; $\frac{22}{7}$; 35; $\frac{22}{7}$; 35; 35; 1,925; 962.5; 1,925; 2,887.5; 2,887.5     **5.** $\frac{22}{7}$; 42; $\frac{22}{7}$; 42; 42; 1,386; 42; 2; 21; 2; $\frac{1}{2}$; $\frac{22}{7}$; 21; $\frac{22}{7}$; 21; 21; 1,386; 1,386; 1,386; 2,772; 2,772     **6.** $\frac{22}{7}$; 60; $188\frac{4}{7}$; $188\frac{4}{7}$; 35; 6,600; 66; 66     **7a.** $\frac{22}{7}$; 35; 110; 110; −; 110; 110; 110; ÷; 2; 55; 55     **7b.** 220; 220; 220; ÷; 125; 1.76     **7c.** 35; 17.5; $\frac{22}{7}$; 17.5; $\frac{22}{7}$; 17.5; 17.5; $962\frac{1}{2}$; 55; 35; 1,925; 1,925; $962\frac{1}{2}$; $2,887\frac{1}{2}$; $2,887\frac{1}{2}$; 4; 721.875; 12.03125; 12; 12

## Lesson 11.3, Practice (pp. 154−158)

**1.** Area: 200.96 m²; Circumference: 50.24 m     **3a.** 77 ft²

**3b.** 36 ft     **5.** 462 cm²     **7a.** 560 m     **7b.** 11,900 m²

**9.** 886.4 ft²     **11.** 990 in.     **13.** 308 mm²     **15a.** 464 cm

**15b.** 2,016 cm²

## Lesson 11.3, Brain@Work (pp. 158−159)

**1.** 38.6 cm     **2.** 112 in.²     **3.** 21 s     **4.** 14

**Chapter Review/Test** (pp. 161—163)

**1.** Circumference: 308 cm; Area: 7,546 cm² **3.** 36 ft

**5.** 17.85 m **7.** Circumference: 31.4 in.; Area: 78.5 in.²

**9.** 130 cm **11a.** 121 cm **11b.** 24.2 cm/s

**11c.** 2,500 s **13.** 353.3 ft²

**Cumulative Review Chapters 8—11**
(pp. 164—167)

**1.**

**3.**

**5a.**
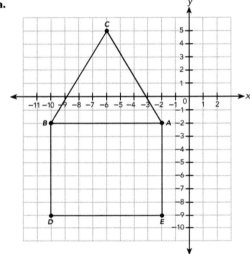

**5b.** (−6, 5) **5c.** *D* (−10, −9); *E* (−2, −9) **7.** 80 ft²

**9.** 50.24 cm² **11.** 7 mm **13.** $\frac{2}{7}b$ **15.** 40.82 cm

**17.** 44 ft² **19.** 113.64 cm² **21a.** *P* (0, 0)

**21b.** Area: 256 m²; Perimeter: 64 m **21c.** 192 m²

**23.** 40.035 m²

## CHAPTER 12

**Lesson 12.1, Guided Practice** (pp. 176—178)

**1.** f; a and e; c and d **2.** rectangular prism **3.** cube

**4.** triangular prism **5.** a and c; b

**Lesson 12.1, Practice 12.1** (pp. 179—180)

**1.** pyramid; Base: *BCDE*; Lateral face: Answers vary.
Sample: *ABC*; *ABE*; *ACD*; *AED* **3.** cube; Base: Answers
vary. Sample: *PQRS*; *TUVW*; Lateral face: Answers vary.
Sample: *PQUT*; *RSWV* **5.** square pyramid

**7.** triangular prism **9.** No **11.** No **13.** No

**15.**
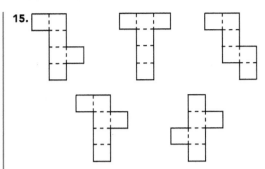

**17.** Yes

**19.**
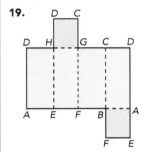

**Lesson 12.2, Guided Practice** (pp. 183—186)

**1.** 6; 6; 36; 36; 6; 216 **2.** 7; 5; 7; 5; 10; 24; 10; 240; 7;
5; 70; 240; 70; 310 **3.** 5; 13; 12; 9; 30; 9; 270; 12; 5; 60;
270; 60; 330 **4.** 6; 5.2; 15.6; 6; 10; 90; 15.6; 90; 105.6

**Lesson 12.2, Practice 12.2** (pp. 187—188)

**1.** 216 cm² **3.** 504 m² **5.** 660 cm² **7.** 559 cm² **9.** 336 ft²

**11a.** *m* + 1 **11b.** 2*m* **11c.** *m* + 1

**Lesson 12.3, Guided Practice** (pp. 190—194)

**1.** $5\frac{1}{4}$; 6; 12; 378 **2.** 8; 7.2; 3; 172.8 **3.** ℓ*wh*; 4; 3;
$8\frac{1}{3}$; 100 **4.** No. Rectangles will have different
dimensions with other cuts. **5.** Yes. **6.** No. Rectangles
will have different dimensions with other cuts. **7.** 6; 5.5;
33; 33; 9; 297; 297 **8.** $3\frac{1}{3}$; 10; $\frac{50}{3}$ ; $\frac{50}{3}$ ; 14; $233\frac{1}{3}$ ;
$233\frac{1}{3}$ **9.** 2; 4; 10; 2; 14; 14; 12; 14; 168; 168

**Lesson 12.3, Practice 12.3** (pp. 196—199)

**1.** 729 in.³ **3.** 1,100 ft³ **5.** 72 in.³ **7.** 120.6 cm³

**9.** No. Circles will have different diameters with other
slices.

**11.**

**13.**

**15.** 5 in. **17.** 384 ft³ **19a.** *ABDC* **19b.** *AJM*

**19c.** *EJM* **19d.** *AHDF*

**Lesson 12.4, Guided Practice** (pp. 200–206)

**1.** 14; $\frac{42}{4}$ ; 25; 12; $\frac{42}{4}$ ; 3,150; 3,150　**2a.** 8; 4; 32; 32; 24; 768; 768　**2b.** 8; 5; 8; 5; 24; 2; 32; 26; 24; 64; 624; 64; 688; 688　**3a.** 960; 15; 960; 15; 15; 15; 64; $\sqrt{64}$ ; 8; 8
**3b.** 8; 8; 8; 8; 15; 2; 64; 32; 15; 128; 480; 128; 608; 608
**4a.** 3; 7; 3; 9; 7; 15; 63; 78; 855; 78; 855; 78; 78; 78; 10.96; 10.96　**4b.** 7; 9; 3; 3; 5; 9; 10.96; 2; 78; 36; 10.96; 156; 394.56; 156; 550.56; 550.56

**Lesson 12.4, Practice** (pp. 207–208)

**1.** 472.5 cm³　**3a.** 784 ft³　**3b.** 763.6 ft²　**5a.** 86,400 ft³
**5b.** 10,440 ft²　**7.** 25 cm

**Lesson 12.4, Brain@Work** (p. 208)

**1.** 800 in.³

**2.** Make a list and solve the problem using guess and check.

| Length of edge of cube (ft) | Surface area (ft²) | Volume (ft³) |
|---|---|---|
| 4 | 96 | 64 |
| 5 | 150 | 125 |
| 6 | 216 | 216 |

The length of each edge of the cube is 6 feet.

**Chapter Review/Test** (pp. 210–213)

**1.** c　**3.** b　**5.** d　**7.** 224 m²　**9.** 45 ft³
**11.** 10,500 cm³　**13a.** 9 ft　**13b.** 350 ft²　**15.** 6 in.
**17.** Surface area: 268 cm²; Volume: 136 cm³

# CHAPTER 13

**Lesson 13.1, Guided Practice** (pp. 218–219)

**1.** 3; 9; 7; 5; 2; 1　**2.** 1　**3.** 5　**4.** 2　**5.** 6　**6.** 27

**Lesson 13.1, Practice** (pp. 220–221)

**1.**

| Weekly Income | Tally | Frequency |
|---|---|---|
| Below $500 | ┼┼┼ // | 7 |
| $500–$1,000 | ┼┼┼ ┼┼┼ ┼┼┼ //// | 19 |
| Over $1,000 | //// | 4 |

**3.** 1, 1, 1, 1, 2, 2, 2, 3, 4, 4, 5, 5, 5, 5, 6, 6, 6, 6, 6, 7, 7, 8, 8, 8, 9, 9, 10, 10;

| Number of Hours | Tally | Frequency |
|---|---|---|
| 0–3 | ┼┼┼ /// | 8 |
| 4–7 | ┼┼┼ ┼┼┼ /// | 13 |
| 8–10 | ┼┼┼ // | 7 |

20

**Lesson 13.2, Guided Practice** (pp. 223–225)

**1.**

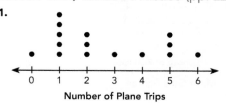

Number of Plane Trips

**2.**

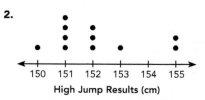

High Jump Results (cm)

**3.** The dot plot has a "tail" on the left. The shape is left-skewed. The data values are from 1 to 5. Range: 5 − 1 = 4. The students saved about $4 per week, and all of them saved $1 to $5 per week.

**4.** The dot plot has a "tail" on the right. The shape is right-skewed. The data values are from 0 to 5. Range: 5 − 0 = 5. Most of the players scored 1 point in the game, and all of them scored 0 to 5 points in the game.

**Lesson 13.2, Practice** (pp. 226–227)

**1.**

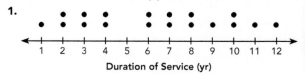

Duration of Service (yr)

**3.** 20　**5.** 25%　**7.** Answers vary. Sample: There are many good movies that come out regularly, so few movies stay at number 1 in the box office for a long time.

**Lesson 13.3, Guided Practice** (pp. 229–233)

**1.**

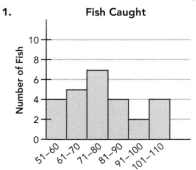

Fish Caught

**2.**

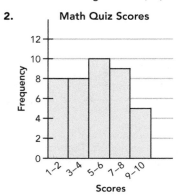

Math Quiz Scores

**3a.**

| Cholesterol Level (mg/dL) | 120–159 | 160–199 | 200–239 | 240–279 | 280–329 |
|---|---|---|---|---|---|
| Frequency | 2 | 6 | 21 | 9 | 2 |

For this set of data, it is suitable to use 5 intervals with a width of 40 since a cholesterol level less than 200 is desirable, a cholesterol level between 200 and 240 is borderline while a cholesterol level greater than 240 is considered high. The outlier is 125.

**3b.** Chlolesterol Levels in Men

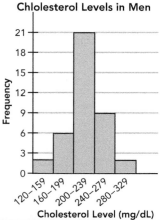

**4a.**

| Speed (km/h) | 50–54 | 55–59 | 60–64 | 65–69 | 70–74 | 75–79 | 80–84 | 85–89 |
|---|---|---|---|---|---|---|---|---|
| Frequency | 2 | 3 | 11 | 10 | 8 | 3 | 2 | 1 |

For this set of data, it is suitable to use 8 intervals with a width of 5 kilometers per hour since the tolerance for speeding is about 10% or 5 kilometers per hour above the speed limit. The outlier is 88.

**4b.**

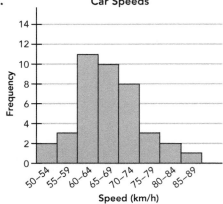

Car Speeds

**5.** Most of the states sent 1 to 10 representatives to the U.S. Congress in 2011. The histogram is right-skewed. There is 1 state that sent 51 to 60 representatives, which is an outlier in the data.     **6.** Most of the data values are from 31°F to 39°F. The data set has a "tail" to the left, and the distribution is left-skewed. The temperatures are from 22°F to 45°F, so the range is 23°F.

**Lesson 13.3, Practice** (pp. 234–237)

**1.**

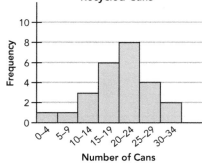

Recycled Cans

**3.**

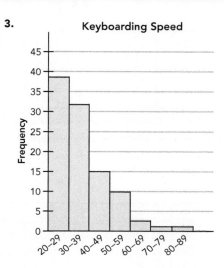

**Keyboarding Speed**

**5.** 820    **7.** 50    **9.** 27%    **11a.** $x = 2$; $y = 1$

**11b.** $\frac{4}{5}$

**11c.**

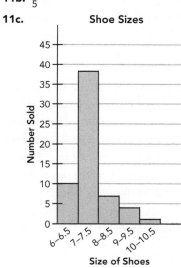

**Shoe Sizes**

The department store sold the greatest number of shoes with sizes 7 or 7.5. The data set has a "tail" to the right, and so distribution is right-skewed.

**11d.**

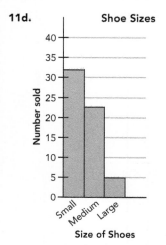

**Shoe Sizes**

**11e.** The first histogram, which uses more intervals, reveals more about the distribution of data. It shows the two sizes of shoes that sold the most. This histogram will be more useful when you want to find out which two shoe sizes sold best. The second histogram, which uses fewer intervals with greater width, categorizes sizes into small, medium or large. This histogram will be more useful when you want general information on which shoe sizes to stock.

**Lesson 13.3, Brain@Work** (p. 237)

**1.**

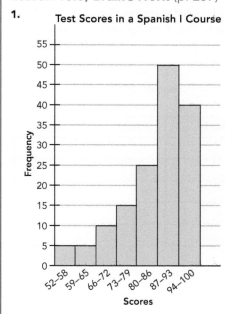

**Test Scores in a Spanish I Course**

**2.**

Grades in a Spanish I Course

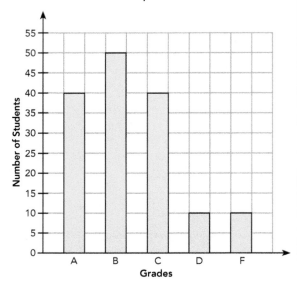

**3a.** If 5 students increased their scores from 79 to 89, then there would be 55 students with scores from 87 to 93, and 10 students with scores from 73 to 79. For the histogram, the height of the bar that represents the frequency for 87 − 93 will increase by 5, while the height of the bar that represents the frequency for 73 − 79 will decrease by 5. **3b.** For the bar graph, the height of the bar that represents the number of students who got a score of B will increase by 5, while the height of the bar that represents the number of students who got a score of C will decrease by 5.

**Chapter Review/Test** (pp. 239−241)

**1.**

| Number of Bedrooms | Tally | Frequency |
| --- | --- | --- |
| 1 | //// | 4 |
| 2 | ⧍⧍⧍ // | 7 |
| 3 | ⧍⧍⧍ //// | 9 |
| 4 | ⧍⧍⧍ // | 7 |
| 5 | /// | 3 |

**3.** 25

**5.**

| Length of Trout (in.) | 8− 9 | 10−11 | 12−13 | 14−15 | 16−17 | 18−19 |
| --- | --- | --- | --- | --- | --- | --- |
| Number of Trout | 3 | 8 | 24 | 9 | 5 | 1 |

The range is 18 − 8 = 10. Choosing an interval of 2 gives six intervals for the data set. A larger interval will give too few intervals, and you will not be able to see the distribution accurately.

**7.**

| Distance of Long Drive (yd) | 240–244 | 245–249 | 250–254 | 255–259 | 260–264 | 265–269 | 270–274 | 275–279 |
| --- | --- | --- | --- | --- | --- | --- | --- | --- |
| Frequency | 1 | 4 | 6 | 4 | 4 | 4 | 6 | 1 |

The range is 278 − 244 = 34. Choosing an interval of 5 gives eight intervals for the data set. A larger interval will give too few intervals, and you will not be able to see the distribution accurately.

**9.** 240

**11.** The most frequent value is from 8:00 A.M. to 8:29 A.M. Most of the data values are to the right of 8:00 A.M. to 8:29 A.M., and the distribution is right-skewed. The second most frequent value is from 8:30 A.M. to 8:59 A.M. The third most frequent value is from 7:39 A.M. to 7:59 A.M. These three values are significantly higher than the rest of the time, because most companies start work from 8:00 A.M. to 9:00 A.M.

**13.**

Quiz Scores of Students

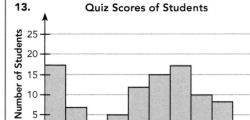

There are two peaks in the distribution of the data — one is for the interval 14–16, and the other is for the interval 32–34. Most of the data values are to the left of the interval 32–34, and the distribution is skewed to the left. The data values are from 14 to 40. Range: 40 − 14 = 26

# CHAPTER 14

### Lesson 14.1, Guided Practice (pp. 245–247)

**1.** 154; 157; 160; 165; 636; 636 **2.** 636; 4; 159; 159

**3.** 52; 51; 49; 48; 54; 5; $\frac{254}{5}$; 50.8; 50.8 **4.** 3; 3; 8; 24

**5.** 2; 2; 9; 18 **6.** 3; 3; 10; 30 **7.** 72 **8.** 8 **9.** 9

**10.** 8; 4; 32; 7.5; 8; 9; 24.5; 32; 24.5; 7.5; 7.5

**11.** 8,500 points

### Lesson 14.1, Practice (pp. 249–250)

**1.** 8 **3.** 42.76 cm **5.** 4.48 m **7.** 10.116 s

**9.** 3.25 **11.** 9 **13.** 7.25 oz **15a.** $\frac{a+b+c+15}{3}$

**15b.** $\frac{2a+2b+2c}{3}$ **15c.** $\frac{a+b+c}{6}$ **17.** Answers vary.
Sample: 10, 11, 12, 13, and 14.

### Lesson 14.2, Guided Practice (pp. 252–255)

**1.** 86; 97; 98; 109; 117; 98 **2.** 32 **3.** 29; 34; 29; 34;

31.5; 31.5 **4.** 121.5 **5.** $\frac{11}{16}$ **6.** 100

**7a.**

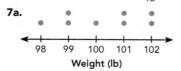

**Weight (lb)**

**7b.** Yes; 100.5 lb **8.** 45.5 **9.** 46.5 **10.** 6

**11.** Median, because most of the data values cluster
around 46.5°F.

### Lesson 14.2, Practice (pp. 256–257)

**1.** 8 **3.** 3.2 **5.** 68 **7.** $372.50 **9.** School A: 5;
School B: 8 **11.** 104 cents **13.** Median, because most
of the data values cluster around 110 cents.

**15a.** Answers vary. Sample: 4, 5, 8

**15b.** Answers vary. Sample: 1, 5, 8

### Lesson 14.3, Guided Practice (pp. 259–260)

#### Times of Ten Runners

| Time (s) | Number of Times |
|----------|-----------------|
| 9.8 | 2 |
| 9.9 | 3 |
| 10.0 | 1 |
| 10.1 | 2 |
| 10.2 | 1 |
| 10.3 | 1 |

**1.** 9.9 **2.** 2 **3.** 8; 12 **4.** boys **5.** garment shops
**6.** 5.5 kg

### Lesson 14.3, Practice (pp. 262–263)

**1.** 5 **3.** 7.8 **5.** size 9 **7.** 2 **9.** 2 **11a.** 30

**11b.** (0, 30), (1, 29), (2, 28), (3, 27), (4, 26)

**11c.** Accept any number from 16 to 24.

### Lesson 14.4, Guided Practice (pp. 265–268)

**1.** 60 T-shirts **2.** 11.7 **3.** 12 **4.** 12 **5.** Mode and
median, because the T-shirt sizes are whole numbers and
12 is a realistic number for describing the data set.

**6.** Mean: 1.6; Mode: 0; Median: 1 **7.** The mode is 0, but
it represents only 5 of the 15 households. So the mode
does not describe the data well. The mean is 1.6 and the
median is 1. Both of these numbers might be used to
describe the set of data. The mean takes into account the
households with 5 or 6 children, but the median better
describes how many children most households have.

**8.** The shape of the data distribution is right skewed.
The mean gives more weight to the values on the right
than the median does. So, the mean is to the right of the
median. **9.** Mean: 5.4; Mode: 5; Median: 5

**10.** The data are well spread out, and the shape of the
data is symmetrical. Because the mode and median are
the same, and the mean is slightly greater, the data set is
likely to be more spread out for data greater than 5.

### Lesson 14.4, Practice (pp. 269–271)

**1.** Mean: 81.75; Median: 83.5; Mode: 85 **3.** Median
and mode. The mean number of children is 2.4. It is not a
realistic number for describing the data set. The median
and mode are both 2, which is a realistic number for
describing the data set. So, the median and the mode
best describe the data set. **5.** 5.49 oz **7.** Because
there are two outliers, 11 and 12. **9.** The shape of the
distribution is right-skewed. So, the measure of center is
likely to be 2 hours, which is in the lower range.

**11.**

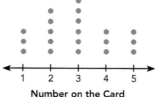

**Number on the Card**

**13.** 2 **15.** 1.24 **17.** Yes; 2

## Lesson 14.4, Brain@Work (p. 271)

**Tim's Test Scores**

| Test | First | Second | Third | Fourth | Fifth | Sixth |
|------|-------|--------|-------|--------|-------|-------|
| Score | 3 | 5 | 6 | 8 | 6 | 8 |

## Chapter Review/Test (pp. 273–274)

**1.** Mean: $6\frac{2}{3}$; Median: 6

**3.**

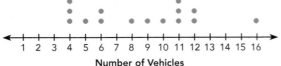

Number of Vehicles

Mean: 8.6; Median: 9; Modes: 4 and 11

**5.** $28; Amounts at either extreme have more effect on the mean than the median.

**7.**

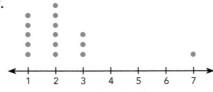

Number of Goals

Mean: 2.2; Median: 2; Mode: 2

**9.** 2   **11.** 2   **13.** 1.91

## Cumulative Review Chapters 12–14 (pp. 275–279)

**1.** b   **3.** c   **5.** Surface area: 828 in.$^2$; Volume: 1,080 in.$^3$

**7.** Mean: 9.3 lb; Median: 8.9 lb   **9.** 6.9 ft   **11.** 3 cm

**13.** There are 85 buildings in the city. Most buildings have 21 to 40 floors. The range of the data is 119. Most of the data values are to the right of the interval 21–40, and the shape of the histogram is right-skewed.

**15a.**

Number of Salads Served

**15b.** Mean: 21.8; Median: 22; Mode: 24

**17.** Length: 30 in.; Surface area: 2,070 in.$^2$

**19a.** $x = 10$; $y = 4$

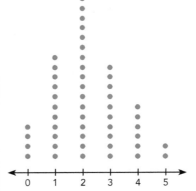

Number of Television Sets

**19b.** Mean: 2.18; Median: 2; Mode: 2   **19c.** The data are well spread and the shape of the data distribution is nearly symmetrical. Because the mode and the median are the same, and the mean is slightly greater, the data set is likely to be more spread out for data greater than 12. The data set is slightly skewed to the right.   **19d.** 2.075

# Glossary

# Glossary

## A

### absolute value

The distance from a number to 0 on the number line. It is always positive or 0.

### arc

A portion of a circle.

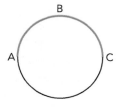

*ABC* is an arc.

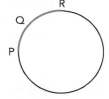

*PQR* is also an arc.

### area

The number of square units covered by a figure. It is measured in units such as square centimeter ($cm^2$), square meter ($m^2$), square inch ($in.^2$), and square foot ($ft^2$).

## B

### base (of a triangle) (*b*)

Any side of a triangle from which the height of a triangle is measured.

## C

### center (of a circle)

A point within a circle that is the same distance from all points on the circle.

### circumference

The distance around a circle.

### congruent

Having the same size and shape.

### coordinate plane

A grid formed by a horizontal number line, called the *x*-axis, and a vertical number line, called the *y*-axis, that intersect at right angles.

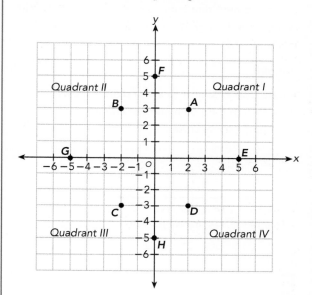

### coordinates

An ordered pair of numbers that gives the location of a point on a coordinate plane.

### cross section

The figure formed when a plane intersects a solid figure.

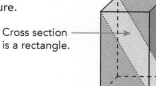

Cross section is a rectangle.

### cube

A prism that has six congruent square faces.

# D

**dependent variable**

A variable whose value depends on the value of a related independent variable.

Example: In the equation $y = x + 10$, $y$ is the dependent variable.

**diameter of a circle**

A line segment that connects two points on a circle and passes through its center; also the length of this segment.

**dot plot**

A data display similar to a line plot. It shows frequency of data on a number line using a ● to represent each occurrence.

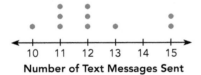

**Number of Text Messages Sent**

# E

**edge**

The line segment formed where two faces of a solid figure meet.

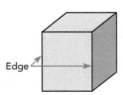

**equation**

A statement that two mathematical expressions are equal.

Example: $x + 5 = 8$, $4x = 12$ are equations.

# F

**face**

A polygon that is a flat surface of a solid figure.

**formula**

A general mathematical equation or rule.

Example: Area of triangle $= \frac{1}{2}bh$

**frequency**

The number of times a piece of data, such as an item or a number, occurs.

# H

**height (of a triangle) ($h$)**

The perpendicular distance from the base to the opposite vertex of a triangle.

**histogram**

A data display that divides the range of data into equal intervals and shows how often each interval occurs in the data set. It is usually used for large sets of data.

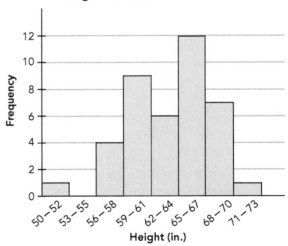

**Height of Students in a Class**

# I

### independent variable

A variable whose value determines the value of a related dependent variable.

Example: In the equation $y = x + 10$, $x$ is the independent variable.

### inequality

A mathematical sentence that compares two unequal expressions using one of the symbols $<$, $>$, $\leq$, $\geq$, or $\neq$.

# L

### linear equation

An algebraic equation that has a dependent and an independent variable. The variables have no exponents and are not multiplied together. The graph of a linear equation is a straight line.

Example: $y = x - 15$

### linear graph

A straight line graph.

### line plot

A diagram that shows frequency of data on a number line. Each × represents one occurrence.

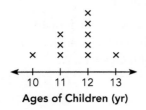

Ages of Children (yr)

# M

### mean

One measure of the center of a set of data. It is found by dividing the sum of the data values by the number of data values.

$$\text{Mean} = \frac{\text{total of a set of items}}{\text{number of items}}$$

### median

A measure of the center of a set of data. Once the data have been placed in numerical order, it is the middle value when the number of data items is odd, and the mean of the two middle values when the number of data items is even.

Examples:

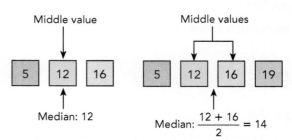

### mode

A measure of the center of a set of data. It is the value (or values) that occurs most often in the data set.

Example:

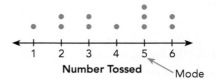

Number Tossed — Mode

## N

### negative number

A number that is less than zero.

### net

A plane figure that can be folded to make a solid.

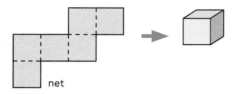

net

## O

### outlier

An extreme or rare occurrence of a value.

## P

### parallel

Always the same distance apart; planes or lines in the same plane that do not intersect.

### parallelogram

A four-sided figure in which both pairs of opposite sides are parallel and congruent.

### perimeter

The distance around a figure. It can be measured in units such as centimeter (cm), meter (m), inch (in.), or foot (ft).

### prism

A solid with two parallel congruent polygons, called bases joined by faces that are parallelograms. A prism is named by the shape of its base.

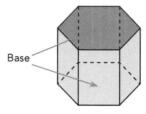

Base

Base

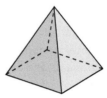

Hexagonal prism    Rectangular prism

### pyramid

A solid whose base is a polygon and whose other faces are triangles that share a common vertex.

## Q

### quadrant of a circle

A quarter of a circle.

### quadrants of a coordinate plane

The four sections of a coordinate plane formed by the axes. They are numbered Quadrant I, Quadrant II, Quadrant III, and Quadrant IV.

## R

### radius (r)

A line segment connecting the center and a point on the circle; also the length of this segment.

### radii

Plural of radius.

## range

The difference between the greatest and the least number in a set of data.

## regular polygon

A polygon whose sides are all the same length, and whose angles are all the same measure.

Examples:

## rhombus

A four-sided figure in which the opposite sides are parallel and the four sides are congruent.

# S

## semicircle

A half of a circle.

## skewed

A data set in which the mean, median, and mode are not all the same number.

Example:

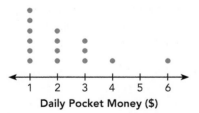

Daily Pocket Money ($)

| Mean | Median | Mode |
|------|--------|------|
| 2.2  | 2      | 1    |

So, the data set is skewed. The distribution has a "tail" on the right, so the data set is right-skewed.

## solution

A value that makes an equation true when substituted for the variable.

Example: $4x = 12$

$x = 3$

The solution of the equation $4x = 12$ is 3.

## surface area

The total area of the faces (including the bases) and curved surfaces of a solid figure.

## symmetrical

A data set in which the mean, median, and mode are the same number.

Example:

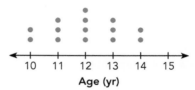

Age (yr)

| Mean | Median | Mode |
|------|--------|------|
| 12   | 12     | 12   |

So, the data set is symmetrical. The dot plot has most of the data near the center of the range.

# T

## trapezoid

A four-sided polygon with exactly one pair of parallel sides.

## triangular prism

A prism composed of two triangular bases and three faces that are parallelograms or rectangles.

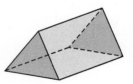

# V

**vertex**

The point at which three edges of a prism meet.

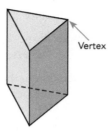

Vertex

**volume (*V*)**

The number of cubic units it takes to fill a space. It is measured in units such as cubic centimeters (cm³) or cubic inches (in.³).

# X

**x-axis**

The horizontal axis on a coordinate plane.

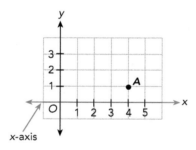

*x*-axis

# Y

**y-axis**

The vertical axis on a coordinate plane.

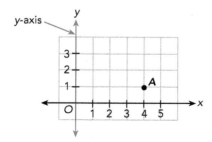

*y*-axis

# Table of Measures, Formulas, and Symbols

## Table of Measures, Formulas, and Symbols

| METRIC | CUSTOMARY |
|---|---|
| **Length** | |
| 1 kilometer (km) = 1,000 meters (m) | 1 mile (mi) = 1,760 yards (yd) |
| 1 meter = 10 decimeters (dm) | 1 mile = 5,280 feet (ft) |
| 1 meter = 100 centimeters (cm) | 1 yard = 3 feet |
| 1 meter = 1,000 millimeters (mm) | 1 yard = 36 inches (in.) |
| 1 centimeter = 10 millimeters | 1 foot = 12 inches |
| **Capacity** | |
| 1 liter (L) = 1,000 milliliters (mL) | 1 gallon (gal) = 4 quarts (qt) |
| | 1 gallon = 16 cups (c) |
| | 1 gallon = 128 fluid ounces (fl oz) |
| | 1 quart = 2 pints (pt) |
| | 1 quart = 4 cups |
| | 1 pint = 2 cups |
| | 1 cup = 8 fluid ounces |
| **Mass and Weight** | |
| 1 kilogram (kg) = 1,000 grams (g) | 1 ton (T) = 2,000 pounds (lb) |
| 1 gram = 1,000 milligrams (mg) | 1 pound = 16 ounces (oz) |

| TIME | |
|---|---|
| 1 year (yr) = 365 days | 1 week = 7 days |
| 1 year = 12 months (mo) | 1 day = 24 hours (h) |
| 1 year = 52 weeks (wk) | 1 hour = 60 minutes (min) |
| leap year = 366 days | 1 minute = 60 seconds (s) |

Centimeters
0 1 2 3 4 5 6 7 8 9 10 11 12 13 14 15 16 17 18 19 20

## CONVERTING MEASUREMENTS

| You can use the information below to convert measurements from one unit to another. | |
|---|---|
| To convert from a smaller unit to a larger unit, divide. | To convert from a larger unit to a smaller unit, multiply. |
| Example: 48 in. = __?__ ft | Example: 0.3 m = __?__ cm |

Recall: 12 in. = 1 ft
48 ÷ 12 = 4
48 in. = 4 ft

Recall: 1 m = 100 cm
0.3 × 100 = 30
0.3 m = 30 cm

## PERIMETER, CIRCUMFERENCE, AND AREA

**Square**

length ($\ell$)

length ($\ell$)

Perimeter = $4\ell$
Area = $\ell^2$

**Rectangle**

width ($w$)

length ($\ell$)

Perimeter = $2\ell + 2w$
$= 2(\ell + w)$
Area = $\ell w$

**Circle**

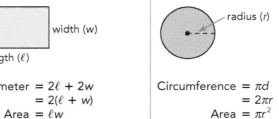

radius ($r$)

Circumference = $\pi d$
$= 2\pi r$
Area = $\pi r^2$

**Triangle**

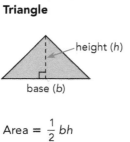

height ($h$)

base ($b$)

Area = $\frac{1}{2}bh$

**Parallelogram**

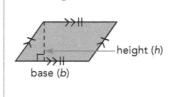

height ($h$)

base ($b$)

Area = $bh$

**Trapezoid**

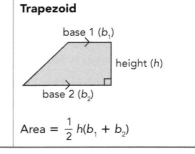

base 1 ($b_1$)

height ($h$)

base 2 ($b_2$)

Area = $\frac{1}{2}h(b_1 + b_2)$

## SURFACE AREA AND VOLUME

### Cube

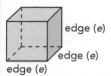

edge (*e*)
edge (*e*)
edge (*e*)

Surface Area = $6e^2$
Volume = $e^3$

### Rectangular Prism

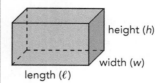

height (*h*)
width (*w*)
length (*ℓ*)

Surface Area = $2(\ell w + wh + \ell h)$
Volume = $\ell w h = Bh^*$

### Prism

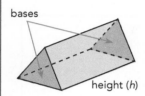

bases
height (*h*)

Surface Area
= Sum of the areas of the faces
= Perimeter of base × height + Area of two bases
Volume = $Bh^*$

### Pyramid

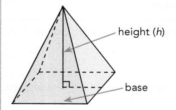

height (*h*)
base

Surface Area = Sum of the areas of the faces
Volume = $\frac{1}{3} Bh^*$

### Cylinder

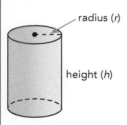

radius (*r*)
height (*h*)

Surface Area = $2\pi r^2 + 2\pi rh$
Volume = $\pi r^2 h$

### Cone

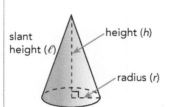

slant height (*ℓ*)
height (*h*)
radius (*r*)

Surface Area = $\pi r(\ell + r)$,
where $\ell$ is the slant height
Volume = $\frac{1}{3} \pi r^2 h$

### Sphere

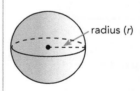

radius (*r*)

Surface Area = $4\pi r^2$
Volume = $\frac{4}{3} \pi r^3$

*$B$ represents the area of the base of a solid figure.

Centimeters

## PYTHAGOREAN THEOREM

**Right Triangle**

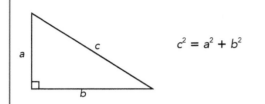

$$c^2 = a^2 + b^2$$

## PROBABILITY

Probability of an event, $A$ happening

$$P(A) = \frac{\text{Number of favorable outcomes}}{\text{Number of equally likely outcomes}}$$

Probability of an event not happening
$= 1 - P(A)$

## LINEAR GRAPHS

The slope, $m$, of a line segment joining points $P\,(x_1, y_1)$ and $Q\,(x_2, y_2)$ is given by

$m = \dfrac{y_2 - y_1}{x_2 - x_1}$ or $m = \dfrac{y_1 - y_2}{x_1 - x_2}$.

Given the slope, $m$, the equation of a line intercepting the $y$-axis at $b$ is given by $y = mx + b$.

The distance, $d$, between two points $P\,(x_1, y_1)$ and $Q\,(x_2, y_2)$ is given by

$d = \sqrt{(x_2 - x_1)^2 + (y_2 - y_1)^2}$ or $d = \sqrt{(x_1 - x_2)^2 + (y_1 - y_2)^2}$.

## RATE

Distance = Speed × Time

Average speed = $\dfrac{\text{Total distance traveled}}{\text{Total time}}$

Interest = Principal × Rate × Time

## TEMPERATURE

| | |
|---|---|
| Celsius (°C) | $C = \dfrac{5}{9} \times (F - 32)$ |
| Fahrenheit (°F) | $F = \left(\dfrac{5}{9} \times C\right) + 32$ |

## SYMBOLS

| | | | |
|---|---|---|---|
| $<$ | is less than | $|a|$ | absolute value of the number $a$ |
| $>$ | is greater than | $(x, y)$ | ordered pair |
| $\leq$ | is less than or equal to | $1:2$ | ratio of 1 to 2 |
| $\geq$ | is greater than or equal to | $/$ | per |
| $\neq$ | is not equal to | $\%$ | percent |
| $\approx$ | is approximately equal to | $\perp$ | is perpendicular to |
| $\cong$ | is congruent to | $\|\|$ | is parallel to |
| $\sim$ | is similar to | $\overleftrightarrow{AB}$ | line $AB$ |
| $10^2$ | ten squared | $\overrightarrow{AB}$ | ray $AB$ |
| $10^3$ | ten cubed | $\overline{AB}$ | line segment $AB$ |
| $2^6$ | two to the sixth power | $\angle ABC$ | angle $ABC$ |
| $2.\overline{6}$ | repeating decimal 2.66666... | $m\angle A$ | measure of angle $A$ |
| 7 | positive 7 | $\triangle ABC$ | triangle $ABC$ |
| $-7$ | negative 7 | $^\circ$ | degree |
| $\sqrt{a}$ | positive square root of the number $a$ | $\pi$ | pi; $\pi \approx 3.14$ or $\pi \approx \dfrac{22}{7}$ |
| $\sqrt[3]{a}$ | positive cube root of the number $a$ | $P(A)$ | the probability of the event $A$ happening |

Centimeters

# Credits

# Scope and Sequence Grades 4–7

## Key Differences and Distinguishing Characteristics

### Articulated Sequence

*Math in Focus*® answers the call for a coherent sequence of topics giving students time to master foundational topics, so that little repetition is required the next year. Thus, each grade level covers fewer topics but in more depth, and you will not find all topics in every grade.

- **"Missing topics"** When a topic appears to be "missing," you can be assured that it is found in either an earlier or later grade level. For example, you will find place-value concepts in grades 4 and 5, but not repeated in Course 1.

- **More advanced** As a result of not repeating topics year after year, students who use *Math in Focus*® will advance faster than students in other programs. As a result, you may find topics that seem to be "too advanced." However, you will find your students easily able to handle the challenge as long as they have had the appropriate preliminary instruction.

### Preparation for Algebra

*Math in Focus*® answers the call to prepare students for Algebra. As recommended by the Common Core State Standards, the *Math in Focus*® sequence of topics emphasizes:

- **Number sense** In Grades 4 and 5, computation algorithms for whole numbers and decimals are developed in tandem with mastery of place value concepts. In Courses 1 and 2, positive and negative numbers and the sets of integers, and rational and irrational numbers are introduced.

- **Fractions, ratios, and proportional reasoning** Significant time is allocated for in-depth work with fractions in grades 4 and 5 and with ratios, rates, and proportions in Courses 1 and 2.

- **Problem Solving** Challenging problem-solving is built into each chapter of every course. Visual models such as bar models and number lines lead students to the use of variables in algebraic expressions, equations, inequalities, and formulas.

## Developmental Continuum for Algebra

| Grades 4–5 | Course 1 | Course 2 |
|---|---|---|
| **| Concept and skill development through hands-on instruction and practice** | | |
| • place-value concepts<br>• multiplication and division algorithms for whole numbers<br>• using model drawings to solve problems involving whole numbers and fractions<br>• mental math | | |
| **| Emphasis on problem solving, skill consolidation, and a deep understanding in preparation for algebra** | | |
| | • whole numbers and their opposites in context<br>• exponents<br>• multiplying and dividing fractions and decimals<br>• ratios, rates, and percents<br>• using model drawings to solve problems involving fractions, decimals, rates, and percents | |
| **| Introductory algebra concepts in preparation for a first course in Algebra** | | |
| | • order of operations<br>• variables and algebraic expressions<br>• relating model drawings to algebraic equations<br>• graphing proportional relationships on the coordinate plane<br>• using geometric formulas | • operations with rational numbers<br>• solving one- and two-step equations using properties of equality<br>• solving one-step inequalities, and graphing the solutions on a number line<br>• applying concepts of complementary, supplementary, and vertical angles to write and solve addition equations |

View the complete Grade 4 through Course 3 Scope and Sequence at <u>www.hmheducation.com/mathinfocus</u>

| | GRADE 4 | GRADE 5 | COURSE 1 (GR 6) | COURSE 2 (GR 7) |
|---|---|---|---|---|
| **Ratios and Proportional Relationships** | | | | |
| **Ratios** | | Understand concept of ratio. Use ratios to solve problems. Find equivalent ratios. | Understand the concept of ratio and use ratio language to describe proportional relationships. Find the missing term in a pair of equivalent ratios or in a table of equivalent ratios. Plot pairs of equivalent ratios in the coordinate plane. Use tables to compare ratios. Solve multi-step real-world problems involving ratios using bar models. | Compute unit rates where the terms are given in fractional units. Explore the relationship between two quantities that vary directly or inversely. Explain what the points $(x, y)$, $(0, 0)$, and $(1, c)$ mean in a given proportional context. Solve problems involving scale drawings. Use proportional reasoning to solve multi-step ratio and percent problems. |
| **Representing Ratios** | | | Use multiplication or division to write equivalent ratios. Make tables of equivalent ratios, including whole number measurements. Use bar models to solve problems involving ratios of three quantities. | Represent quantities that vary directly or indirectly using equations. Find the constant of proportionality for quantities that vary directly or inversely from tables, graphs, verbal descriptions, or diagrams, such as scale drawings. |
| **Rates** | | | Understand the concept of a unit rate $\frac{a}{b}$ associated with a ratio $a : b$ ($b \neq 0$), and use rate language in proportional situations. Compute and compare unit rates using the division algorithm. Solve unit rate problems, including unit pricing and constant speed. | |
| **Percents** | | Solve problems with percents. Convert fractions to percents. Find a percent of a number. | Solve percent problems involving simple interest, tax, markups, discounts, and commissions. Solve multi-step percent problems involving percent increase and decrease. Solve problems involving percents, including finding the whole when the percent and its quantity are known. | Solve problems involving simple interest, sales tax, markups and markdowns, tips and commissions, and percent error. |

# SCOPE AND SEQUENCE GRADES 4–7

| | GRADE 4 | GRADE 5 | COURSE 1 (GR 6) | COURSE 2 (GR 7) |
|---|---|---|---|---|
| **The Number System** | | | | |
| **Sets and Numbers** | | Explore negative numbers in context. | Understand that positive and negative numbers can be used to describe quantities having opposite directions or values. Use positive and negative numbers to represent quantities in real-world contexts. Understand rational numbers as points on the number line. Extend number lines to represent points with negative coordinates; locate negative integers on a horizontal or vertical number line. Use negative numbers to identify and locate points in all four quadrants of the coordinate plane. Understand that the absolute value of a number is its distance from 0 on the number line. Interpret the absolute value of a rational number as magnitude for a positive or negative quantity in a given context. | Know that the set of positive and negative fractions, along with 0, make up the rational number system. Understand that some numbers, such as pi or the square root of 2, are irrational. Know that the set of real numbers is composed of the two distinct sets: rational numbers and irrational numbers. |
| **Number Representations** | Represent numbers to 100,000. | Represent numbers to 10,000,000. Represent negative numbers on a number line. | Represent fractions, decimals and integers on a number line. Relate the square of a whole number to the area of a square, and the cube of a number to the volume of a cube. Find the square or cube of a number. Find the square root or cube root of a perfect square or perfect cube, up to 150. | Write rational numbers as decimals. Understand that the decimal representation of a rational number is either terminating or repeating. Use place-value understanding to round decimals to any given place. Understand the difference between rounding a decimal and truncating it. Approximate the decimal form an irrational number using rounding. Represent irrational numbers on the number line using their decimal approximations. Approximate numbers to a given number of significant digits. |

*Math in Focus®: Singapore Math*

# SCOPE AND SEQUENCE  GRADES 4–7

| | GRADE 4 | GRADE 5 | COURSE 1 (GR 6) | COURSE 2 (GR 7) |
|---|---|---|---|---|
| **Compare and Order** | Compare and order whole numbers to 100,000.<br><br>Compare and order decimal numbers. | Compare and order whole numbers to 10,000,000. | Write, interpret, and explain statements of order for fractions and integers.<br><br>Interpret statements of inequality as statements about the relative position of two numbers on a number line.<br><br>Distinguish comparisons of absolute value from statements about order. | Compare real numbers using a number line. |
| **Place Value** | Express numbers to 100,000 in three forms. | Express numbers to 10,000,000 in various forms. | | Use place-value concepts to round decimals to a given place.<br><br>Round a number to a given number of significant digits. |
| **Fraction Concepts** | Recognize, write, and name mixed numbers and improper fractions.<br><br>Find a fraction of a set, equivalent fractions, and equivalent mixed numbers / improper fractions. | Write fractions as decimals, and vice versa.<br><br>Relate fractions to division expressions. | | |
| **Decimal Concepts** | Model decimals using tenths and hundredths.<br><br>Understand decimal notation (hundredths) as an extension of the base-ten system.<br><br>Read and write decimals that are greater than 1 or less than 1.<br><br>Compare and order decimal numbers.<br><br>Identify equivalent decimals and fractions. | Model decimal numbers using thousandths.<br><br>Understand place value concepts through thousandths.<br><br>Write decimals as fractions, and vice versa. | | Write rational numbers as decimals.<br><br>Understand that the decimal representation of a rational number is either terminating or repeating.<br><br>Understand the difference between rounding a decimal and truncating it.<br><br>Approximate the decimal form of an irrational number using rounding. |
| **Whole Number Computation: Multiplication and Division** | Apply an understanding of models for multiplication and division.<br><br>Recall multiplication facts and related division facts.<br><br>Develop fluency in multiplying multi-digit numbers.<br><br>Divide by a 1-digit number with a remainder.<br><br>Solve multi-digit multiplication and division problems. | Multiply multi-digit numbers.<br><br>Find quotients involving multi-digit dividends and divisors.<br><br>Solve whole-number multiplication and division problems.<br><br>Select the most useful form of the quotient and interpret the remainder. | Fluently divide multi-digit numbers using the standard algorithm. | Identify and compute with the number of significant digits in a whole number. |

# SCOPE AND SEQUENCE GRADES 4–7

|  | GRADE 4 | GRADE 5 | COURSE 1 (GR 6) | COURSE 2 (GR 7) |
|---|---|---|---|---|
| **Fraction Computation** | Add and subtract unlike fractions that have related denominators. | Add and subtract unlike fraction and mixed numbers. Multiply fractions, mixed numbers, and whole numbers. Divide fractions by whole numbers. Solve word problems by adding, subtracting, multiplying, and dividing fractions. | Interpret and compute quotients of fractions. Represent situations involving multiplication and division of fractions using models, such as bar models and area models. Solve real-world problems involving division of fractions by fractions. | Extend multiplication of fractions to include multiplication of rational numbers. Interpret the sum, product, or quotient of two rational numbers in a real-world context. |
| **Decimal Computation** | Add and subtract decimals. Solve problems by adding and subtracting decimals. | Add and subtract decimals to the thousandths place. Multiply and divide decimals by whole numbers. Solve problems by multiplying and dividing decimals. | Fluently multiply and divide multi-digit decimals using standard algorithms. Represent situations involving multiplication and division of decimals using models, such as bar models and area models. Solve problems by multiplying and dividing decimals, interpreting remainders to suit the context of the problem. | Solve real-world problems involving all four operations with rational numbers. |
| **Estimation and Mental Math** | Use mental math and estimation strategies to find sums, differences, products, and quotients. Decide whether an estimate or an exact answer is needed. Estimate relative sizes of amounts or distances. Round and estimate with decimals. | Use mental math and estimation strategies to estimate sums, differences, products, and quotients. Estimate sums and differences of fraction and decimal operations. Estimate products and quotients with decimals. | Estimate answers to percent problems to check for reasonableness. | Solve real-world and mathematical problems and assess reasonableness of answers using estimation and mental math strategies. |
| **Computations with Rational Numbers: Addition and Subtraction** |  |  |  | Describe situations in which opposite quantities combine to make 0. Understand the sum $p + q$ as the number located at a distance $|q|$ from $p$. Understand subtraction of a rational numbers as adding its inverse. Find the distance between two numbers on a number line using absolute value. Solve real-world problems involving addition and subtraction with rational numbers. Interpret the sum of two rational numbers in a real-world context. |

| | GRADE 4 | GRADE 5 | COURSE 1 (GR 6) | COURSE 2 (GR 7) |
|---|---|---|---|---|
| **Computations with Rational Numbers: Multiplication and Division** | | | | Apply properties of operations to multiply and divide rational numbers. Understand that the quotient of any two integers a and b is the rational number $\frac{a}{b}$ ($b \neq 0$). Understand that $-\left(\frac{p}{q}\right) = \frac{(-p)}{q} = \frac{p}{(-q)}$. Solve real-world problems involving multiplication and division of rational numbers. Interpret the product or quotient of two rational numbers in a real-world context. |

## Expressions and Equations

| | GRADE 4 | GRADE 5 | COURSE 1 (GR 6) | COURSE 2 (GR 7) |
|---|---|---|---|---|
| **Patterns** | Identify, describe, and extend numeric and nonnumeric patterns. Use a rule to describe a sequence of numbers or objects. | Identify, describe, and extend numeric patterns involving all operations. Find a rule to complete a number pattern. | | Use a number pattern to explore multiplication of negative numbers. |
| **Properties** | Represent division as the inverse of multiplication. | | Use the distributive property to factor the sum of two whole numbers, or algebraic terms with whole-number coefficients. | Use the properties of real numbers to add and subtract rational numbers. Use the properties of real numbers to extend multiplication and division of fractions to multiplication and division of rational numbers. Use the distributive property to show that $(-1)(-1) = 1$. Apply properties of real numbers to add, subtract, factor and expand algebraic expressions with rational coefficients. |
| **Number Theory** | Find all factor pairs for a whole number. Determine whether a whole number is prime or composite. Find the greatest common factor or least common multiple of two whole numbers. | Apply the least common multiple concept to finding a common denominator for two fractions. | Write a composite number as a product of its prime factors. Find the greatest common factor or least common multiple of two whole numbers. | |

Scope and Sequence

**Scope and Sequence**

|  | GRADE 4 | GRADE 5 | COURSE 1 (GR 6) | COURSE 2 (GR 7) |
|---|---|---|---|---|
| **Functional Relationships** | Understand the relationships between the numbers and symbols in formulas for area and perimeter.<br><br>Describe number relationships in context. | Understand the relationships between the numbers and symbols in formulas for surface area and volume.<br><br>Describe number relationships in context.<br><br>Graph equations from function tables. | Use variables to write equations representing two real-world quantities that change in relation to one another.<br><br>Analyze the relationship between an independent and dependent variable using graphs, tables, and equations. | |
| **Expressions / Models** | Use a variety of concrete, pictorial, and symbolic models for multiplication and division; and addition and subtraction with fractions and decimals. | Use letters as variables.<br><br>Simplify algebraic expressions.<br><br>Use the order of operations in numeric expressions with two or more operations. | Write and evaluate numerical expressions and geometric formulas involving whole-number exponents.<br><br>Write and evaluate algebraic expressions using the order of operations.<br><br>Identify parts of an expression using terms such as sum, term, product, and coefficient.<br><br>Use the properties of addition and multiplication to write equivalent expressions, including factoring a common factor from a sum.<br><br>Identify equivalent expressions and like and unlike terms of an expression.<br><br>Solve problems using variable expressions in real-world contexts. | Apply properties of real numbers to add, subtract, factor and expand algebraic expressions with rational coefficients.<br><br>Represent an expression in equivalent forms to help solve a problem.<br><br>Represent an expression using a bar model. |

|  | GRADE 4 | GRADE 5 | COURSE 1 (GR 6) | COURSE 2 (GR 7) |
|---|---|---|---|---|
| **Number Sentences, Equations, and Inequalities** | Write and solve number sentences for one-, two-, and three-step real-world problems using bar models.<br><br>Determine the missing numbers in number sentences.<br><br>Understand equality and inequality. | Write and solve number sentences and equations for one-, and two-step real-world problems.<br><br>Solve one-step equations using inverse operations.<br><br>Write and evaluate inequalities. | Use substitution to identify value(s) that make an equation or inequality true.<br><br>Write and solve addition and multiplication equations to solve real-world problems.<br><br>Write an inequality of the form $x < c$ or $x > c$ to represent a real-world situation.<br><br>Recognize that an inequality of the form $x < c$ or $x > c$ has an infinite number of solutions, and represent the solutions on a number line. | Identify equivalent equations.<br><br>Write equivalent equations using properties of equality.<br><br>Solve two-step equations of the form $ax + b = c$ and $a(x + b) = c$.<br><br>Solve equations with the variable on both sides of the equation.<br><br>Solve one-step inequalities using addition, subtraction, multiplication, or division.<br><br>Solve world problems that lead to inequalities of the form $ax + b > c$ or $ax + b < c$.<br><br>Graph the solution set of an inequality on a number line and interpret it in the context of a real-world problem. |
| **The Coordinate Plane** | Develop coordinate readiness with tables and line graphs. | Identify and plot points in the first quadrant of the coordinate plane.<br><br>Make a table of values from an equation, and plot the points these ordered pairs form in the coordinate plane. | Use negative numbers to identify and locate points in all four quadrants of the coordinate plane.<br><br>Find the length of horizontal and vertical segments in the coordinate plane.<br><br>Use tables and graphs to represent linear equations.<br><br>Solve real-world problems by graphing points in all four quadrants of the coordinate plane.<br><br>Plot pairs of equivalent rates in the coordinate plane. | Explain what the points $(x, y)$, $(0, 0)$, and $(1, c)$ mean in a given proportional context.<br><br>Find the constant of proportionality for quantities that vary directly or inversely from their graphs. |

Scope and Sequence

## SCOPE AND SEQUENCE  GRADES 4–7

| | GRADE 4 | GRADE 5 | COURSE 1 (GR 6) | COURSE 2 (GR 7) |
|---|---|---|---|---|
| **Geometry** | | | | |
| **Lines and Angles** | Draw perpendicular and parallel lines. Estimate and measure angles with a protractor. Classify angles by their angle measures. Relate $\frac{1}{4}$-, $\frac{1}{2}$-, and $\frac{3}{4}$- and full turns to the number of right angles. | Apply the sum of the angles on a straight line to solve problems. Apply the sum of the angles at a point to solve problems. Apply the vertical angles property of intersecting lines. | | Identify supplementary and complementary angles. Use supplementary, complementary, vertical and adjacent angles to write and solve simple equations for unknown angle measures. Identify parallel lines and their transversals. Identify and use corresponding angles, alternate angles, and interior angles of parallel line to solve problems. Use properties of interior angles and exterior angles of a triangle and the related sums. Construct and use angle bisectors and perpendicular bisectors. Apply the equidistant properties of angles bisectors and perpendicular bisectors to solve problems. |
| **Polygons** | Apply the properties of squares and rectangles. Find unknown angle measures and side lengths of squares and rectangles. Identify figures that form tessellations. Understand the relationships between the numbers and symbols in formulas for area and perimeter. | Apply the properties of right, isosceles, and equilateral triangles. Apply the sum of the angle measures of a triangle property. Apply the properties of a parallelogram, rhombus, and trapezoid. Show that the sum of any two side lengths of a triangle is greater than the length of the third side. | Identify regular polygons. Draw polygons in the coordinate plane given the coordinates of the vertices. Use coordinates to find the length of horizontal or vertical sides of polygons. | Solve problems involving drawings of geometric figures. Compute lengths and areas for a real figure from its scale drawing. Reproduce a scale drawing at a different scale. Construct triangles given three of its measures (angles or sides), if possible, and know when it is possible. Construct a quadrilateral from given conditions, including angle measures or lengths of sides or diagonals. |

# SCOPE AND SEQUENCE  GRADES 4–7

| | GRADE 4 | GRADE 5 | COURSE 1 (GR 6) | COURSE 2 (GR 7) |
|---|---|---|---|---|
| **Solid Figures** | | Identify and classify prisms and pyramids. Identify the solid that can be formed from a given net. Identify cylinders, spheres, and cones. Describe cylinders, spheres, and cones by the number and types of faces, edges, and vertices. Build solids using unit cubes. | Find the cross sections formed by slicing a rectangular prism. | Identify pyramids, cylinders, cones, and spheres. Find cross sections of right pyramids. Recognize that a cylinder can be thought of as a right prism with a circular base. |
| **Congruence and Symmetry** | Identify line and rotational symmetry. Relate rotational symmetry to turns and congruency. | | | |
| **Transformations** | Use transformations to form tessellations. | | | |
| **Circles** | | | Identify the center, radius, diameter, and circumference of a circle. Understand π to be the ratio of the circumference to the diameter of a circle. Solve real-world problems involving rates and circles. | |
| **Perimeter and Circumference** | Find the perimeter of composite figures. Solve problems involving the perimeter of squares, rectangles, and composite figures. | Solve problems involving the perimeter of squares, rectangles, and composite figures. | Understand how the formula for the circumference of a circle is derived. Use a formula to calculate the circumference of circles, semi-circles, and quarter circles. Solve problems involving the circumference of circles. | |

Scope and Sequence

**Scope and Sequence**

|  | GRADE 4 | GRADE 5 | COURSE 1 (GR 6) | COURSE 2 (GR 7) |
|---|---|---|---|---|
| **Area** | Identify area as an attribute of two-dimensional figures.<br><br>Connect area formula for a rectangle to the area model for multiplication.<br><br>Estimate and measure area in square units.<br><br>Compare the areas and perimeters of two plane figures.<br><br>Find the area of rectangles and composite figures. | Find the area of triangles. | Find the area of triangles, parallelograms, trapezoids, and regular polygons by decomposing into rectangles or triangles.<br><br>Find a missing dimension of a plane figure given its area and other dimension(s).<br><br>Understand how the formula for the area of a circle is derived.<br><br>Use a formula to calculate areas of circles and semi-circles.<br><br>Solve real-world problems involving the areas of triangles, parallelograms, trapezoids, regular polygons, and circles. | Use the formula for the area of a circle to find the surface area of a cylinder and cone.<br><br>Solve problems involving the areas of triangles, quadrilaterals, and other polygons. |
| **Surface Area and Volume** |  | Use the net of a rectangular prism to find its surface area.<br><br>Estimate and measure volume in cubic units. | Represent prisms and pyramids with triangular or rectangular faces using nets.<br><br>Use nets of prisms and pyramids to find the surface areas.<br><br>Find the volume of a rectangular prism with fractional edge lengths, and relate this to the formula $V = \ell wh$.<br><br>Find the volume of non-rectangular prisms using the formulas $V = Bh$.<br><br>Solve real-world problems involving surface area and volume of prisms. | Relate the volume of a pyramid to the volume of a prism and the volume of a cone to the volume of a cylinder.<br><br>Find the volume and surface area of pyramids, cylinders, cones, and spheres.<br><br>Solve problems involving the surface area and volume of figures composed of cubes and right prisms. |
| **Statistics and Probability** | | | | |
| **Classifying and Sorting** | Construct line plots, stem-and-leaf plots, tables, and line graphs. | Represent data in a double bar graph. | Represent data in frequency tables, dot plots, and histograms. | Display a data set in a box plot. |

| | GRADE 4 | GRADE 5 | COURSE 1 (GR 6) | COURSE 2 (GR 7) |
|---|---|---|---|---|
| **Interpret / Analyze Data** | Interpret tally charts, bar graphs, picture graphs, tables, and line graphs.<br><br>Find the mean (average), median, mode, and range of a data set. | Analyze data in a double bar graphs. | Recognize a statistical question.<br><br>Understand that a data set has a distribution, which can be described by its center and shape.<br><br>Recognize that a measure of center summarizes all values of a data set with a single number.<br><br>Identify measures of center of a data set and calculate each, and know when each is most useful.<br><br>Describe the overall shape of a distribution, and relate the choice of a center to the shape of the distribution.<br><br>Solve real-world problems involving the mean or median, such as finding a missing data value given the mean. | Understand that a sample can be used to gather information about a population.<br><br>Understand that a sample can be generalized to a population only if it is representative of the population.<br><br>Know that a random sample usually produces a representative sample.<br><br>Use data from a random sample to make a prediction about the population.<br><br>Use several samples of the same size to judge the variation in the predictions obtained.<br><br>Compute measures of variability for a data set: quartiles, interquartile range and mean absolution deviation.<br><br>Relate the variability of a sample to the shape of the data set, and to the context in which the data were collected.<br><br>Use measures of center and variability to compare two populations. |
| **Outcomes** | Decide whether an outcome is certain, more likely, equally likely, less likely, or impossible. | Find all possible outcomes of a compound event by listing, making a tree diagram, or multiplying. | | Represent the sample space for a compound event using a list, tree diagram, or table.<br><br>Use a Venn diagram to illustrate sample spaces and events.<br><br>Identify the outcomes of a sample space that make up an event, when the event is stated in everyday language. |

Scope and Sequence

| | GRADE 4 | GRADE 5 | COURSE 1 (GR 6) | COURSE 2 (GR 7) |
|---|---|---|---|---|
| **Expressing Probability** | Express the probability of an event as a fraction. | Determine the experimental probability of a simple event.<br><br>Compare the results of an experiment with the theoretical probability. | | Know that the probability of an event is a number between 0 and 1 inclusive.<br><br>Find the probability of complementary and mutually exclusive events.<br><br>Approximate the probability of a chance event using an appropriate sampling technique.<br><br>Compute the approximate relative frequency of a chance event from its probability.<br><br>Develop a sampling technique (probability model) for equally likely events.<br><br>Develop a sampling technique (probability model) for events that are not equally likely.<br><br>Compare the theoretical and experimental probabilities of an event.<br><br>Design and use a simulation to generate frequencies for compound events. |

Scope and Sequence

## MATHEMATICAL PROCESSES STANDARDS

| | GRADE 4 | GRADE 5 | COURSE 1 (GR 6) | COURSE 2 (GR 7) |
|---|---|---|---|---|
| **1. Make sense of problems and persevere in solving them.** | | | | |
| **Build skills through a problem-solving perspective.** | Build skills in multiplication, division, fraction concepts, data analysis, and measurement through problem solving. | Build skills in multiplication, division, concepts with fractions, decimals, ratios, and percents; data analysis, and measurement through problem solving. | Build skills in multiplication and division of fractions and decimals, ratios, and percents; algebra, data analysis, and geometry and measurement through problem solving. | Build skills in operations with integers and rational numbers; proportionality, measurement, statistics, and probability through problem solving. |
| **Plan how and use appropriate strategies, tools, and thinking skills to solve problems.** | Discuss mathematical ideas, use appropriate strategies, solve real-world problems, and explain solution methods in class. | Discuss mathematical ideas, use appropriate strategies, solve real-world problems, and explain solution methods in class. | Discuss mathematical ideas, use appropriate strategies, solve real-world problems, and explain solution methods in class. | Discuss mathematical ideas, use appropriate strategies, solve real-world problems, and explain solution methods in class. |
| **Use bar and other models consistently to persevere in problem solving.** | Use bar models to solve real-world problems involving multiplication, division, fraction concepts, data analysis, and measurement. Apply the problem-solving process in Put on Your Thinking Cap and other activities. | Use bar models to solve real-world problems involving multiplication, division, concepts with fractions, decimals, ratios, and percents; data analysis, and measurement. Apply the problem-solving process in Put on Your Thinking Cap and other activities. | Use bar models to solve real-world problems involving multiplication, division, concepts with fractions, decimals, ratios, and percents; data analysis, geometry and measurement. Apply the problem-solving process to non-routine problems in Challenging practice and Brain at Work, Chapter Projects, and other activities. | Use various models to solve multi-step real-world problems involving integers, equations, inequalities, proportions, scale drawings, formulas, probability, and statistics. Apply the problem-solving process to non-routine problems in Challenging practice and Brain at Work, Chapter Projects, and other activities. |
| **Monitor and evaluate the solution process and explain problem solving.** | Explain problem solving in Guided Practice, Math Journal, and "explain" exercises. | Explain problem solving in Guided Practice, Math Journal, and "explain" exercises. | Explain problem solving in Guided Practice, Math Journal, and "explain" exercises. | Explain problem solving in Guided Practice, Math Journal, and "explain" exercises. |
| **2. Reason abstractly and quantitatively.** | | | | |
| **Investigate mathematical ideas and models through a concrete to pictorial through abstract progression.** | Use concrete and visual models to explore concepts more deeply, formulate conjectures, and justify reasoning in Let's Explore and Hands-On activities. | Use concrete and visual models to explore concepts more deeply, formulate conjectures, and justify reasoning in Let's Explore and Hands-On activities. | Use concrete and visual models to explore concepts more deeply, formulate conjectures, and justify reasoning in Hands-On and other activities. | Use concrete and visual models to explore concepts more deeply, formulate conjectures, and justify reasoning in Hands-On, Technology, and other activities. |

Scope and Sequence

# MATHEMATICAL PROCESSES STANDARDS

| | GRADE 4 | GRADE 5 | COURSE 1 (GR 6) | COURSE 2 (GR 7) |
|---|---|---|---|---|
| **Make sense of quantities and their relationships.** | Use models to show relationships between improper fractions and mixed numbers. Apply understanding of models for multiplication and division of whole numbers. Generalize place value understanding for multiplication with multi-digit whole numbers. Analyze data shown in tables and line graphs. | Use models to show relationships between fractions and decimals. Apply understanding of models for multiplication and division of fractions and decimals by whole numbers. Generalize place value understanding for division with multi-digit whole numbers. Analyze data shown in tables, double bar graphs, line plots, stem-and-leaf plots, and line graphs. | Use models to show relationships involving fractions, decimals, percents, and ratios. Apply understanding of models for multiplication and division of fractions and decimals fractions and decimals. Generalize place value understanding for division with multi-digit decimals. Analyze the relationship between the dependent and independent variables using graphs and tables, and relate these to the equation. Use ratio and rate language in the context of a ratio relationship. Analyze data shown in frequency tables, line plots, dot plots, and histograms. | Use models to show the relationships between the types of real numbers. Apply understanding of models for operations with integers and other rational numbers. Extend place value understanding to show that all rational numbers can be written as either terminating or repeating decimals. Analyze the relationship between quantities in a proportional relationship using tables and graphs. Identify the constant of proportionality in tables, graphs, and equations. Analyze and summarize numerical data sets in frequency tables, box plots, and experiments. Use data from a random sample to draw inferences about a population. Relate symbols such as negative numbers, absolute values, and variables to real-world and mathematical situations. |
| **Investigate mathematical ideas and models.** | Explore concepts and models more deeply and justify reasoning in Let's Explore and Hands-On activities. Investigate mathematical ideas through non-routine problems in Put on Your Thinking Cap activities. | Explore concepts and models more deeply and justify reasoning in Let's Explore and Hands-On activities. Investigate mathematical ideas through non-routine problems in Put on Your Thinking Cap activities. | Explore concepts and models more deeply and justify reasoning in Hands-On and other activities. Investigate mathematical ideas through non-routine problems in Brain at Work activities. | Explore concepts and models more deeply and justify reasoning in Hands-On, Technology, and other activities. Investigate mathematical ideas through non-routine problems in Brain at Work activities. |

# MATHEMATICAL PROCESSES STANDARDS

| | GRADE 4 | GRADE 5 | COURSE 1 (GR 6) | COURSE 2 (GR 7) |
|---|---|---|---|---|
| **3. Construct viable arguments and critique the reasoning of others.** | | | | |
| **Identify, demonstrate and explain mathematical proof.** | Identify, describe, and extend numeric and nonnumeric patterns. Use properties to classify angles and lines. Show that some figures can be turned and not change shape or size (rotational symmetry). Use properties of squares and rectangles to solve problems. Analyze a data set by finding its mean, median, mode, and range. | Identify, describe, and extend numeric patterns involving all operations. Use properties to classify triangles and quadrilaterals. Apply the ideas that the sum of angles on a straight line is 180° and that the sum of angles at a point is 360°. Explain the relationships among area formulas of different polygons. Compare the results of an experiment to validate the use of theoretical probability. | Identify, describe, and extend patterns in tables of equivalent ratios. Use properties to classify prisms and pyramids. Find the area of right triangles, other triangles, special quadrilaterals, and polygons by composing into rectangles or decomposing into triangles and other shapes. Explain the relationships among the volume formulas of different prisms and pyramids. Explain the relationships among the volume formulas of different prisms and pyramids. | Identify the constant of proportionality in tables, graphs, equations, and verbal descriptions. Use properties to classify polygons, cylinders, cones, pyramids, and spheres. Use properties of complementary, supplementary, vertical, and adjacent angles to find the unknown angles in a figure. Use informal arguments to establish facts about angle sum and exterior angles of triangles. Explain the relationships among the volume formulas of prisms, cones, cylinders, and spheres. Analyze numerical data by quantitative measures of variability (such as mean absolute deviation). |
| **Use a variety of reasoning skills to communicate arguments.** | Use properties of squares and rectangles to solve problems about area and perimeter. Use the properties of operations to perform multi-digit arithmetic. | Explore the relationship among lists, tree diagrams, and multiplication to calculate combinations. Use properties of multiplication (including the distributive property) in estimation and mental math. | Use ratio and rate reasoning to solve real-world and mathematical problems, e.g., by reasoning about tables of equivalent ratios, tape diagrams, double number line diagrams, or equations. Apply the properties of operations to generate equivalent numerical and algebraic expressions. | Use activities to describe what a chance process is and explain the discrepancy between relative frequency and probability. Apply the properties of operations to add, subtract, multiply, and divide rational numbers in numerical and algebraic operations. |
| **Share and communicate mathematical thinking and ideas.** | Express ideas in Math Journal activities, using lesson vocabulary. Work together in pairs or groups in Let's Explore, Games, and other activities. | Express ideas in Math Journal activities, using lesson vocabulary. Work together in pairs or groups in Let's Explore and other activities. | Express and explain ideas in Math Journal and other activities, using lesson vocabulary. Work together in pairs or groups in Projects and other activities. | Express and explain ideas in Math Journal and other activities, using lesson vocabulary. Work together in pairs or groups in Projects and other activities. |

Scope and Sequence

# MATHEMATICAL PROCESSES STANDARDS

|  | GRADE 4 | GRADE 5 | COURSE 1 (GR 6) | COURSE 2 (GR 7) |
|---|---|---|---|---|
| **4. Model with mathematics.** | | | | |
| **Interpret phenomena through representations.** | Express numbers to 100,000 in standard, expanded, and word forms. <br> Model decimals to tenths and hundredths. | Express numbers to 10,000,000 in various forms. <br> Model decimals to thousandths. <br> Explore negative numbers in context. <br> Find equivalent ratios. | Use exponents to represent repeated multiplication. <br> Represent negative numbers on a number line and in the coordinate plane. <br> Represent solutions of inequalities on a number line. <br> Understand absolute value of a rational number as its distance from 0 on a number line. <br> Find equivalent ratios and rates. | Introduce integers and rational numbers and their definitions. <br> Introduce irrational numbers and illustrate with examples such as $\sqrt{2}$ and $\pi$. <br> Map rational and irrational numbers on the number line <br> Understand subtraction of rational numbers as adding the additive inverse. <br> Use the laws of equality to write equivalent equations. |
| **Use representations to model, organize, and record quantities.** | Translate between equivalent improper fractions and mixed numbers. <br> Use a variety of models for multi-digit multiplication and division of whole numbers. <br> Use a variety of models for addition and subtraction of fractions and decimals. <br> Use visual models and sets to represent fractions and decimals. <br> Use part/whole and comparison bar models to represent real-world problems with whole numbers, fractions, and decimals. <br> Measure perimeter and area in customary and metric units. <br> Collect data and organize it in a table. <br> Use measures of central tendency to describe typical values of data sets (social). | Translate between fractions and percents. <br> Select the most useful form of the quotient. <br> Use a variety of models for multiplication and division of fractions and decimals by whole numbers. <br> Use visual models (area models and sets) to represent problems involving fractions, decimals, ratios, and percents. <br> Use part/whole and comparison bar models to represent multi-step real-world problems with whole numbers, fractions, decimals, ratios, and percents. <br> Measure volume of a rectangular prism. <br> Use a net to find the surface area of a cube or rectangular prism. <br> Represent data in a double bar graph. <br> Represent combinations with lists, tree diagrams, and multiplication. | Translate between fractions, decimals, ratios, and percents. <br> Select the most useful form (fraction or decimal) for solving problems involving percents. <br> Use a variety of models to solve problems involving ratios, rates, and percents. <br> Use visual models (area models, sets, and number line drawings) to represent problems involving fractions, decimals, ratios, rates, and percents. <br> Use part/whole, comparison, and before and after bar models to represent multi-step real-world problems with whole numbers, fractions, decimals, ratios, rates, and percents. <br> Measure distances in the coordinate plane. <br> Use a net to find the surface area of a pyramids and prisms. <br> Represent data in a dot plots and histograms. <br> Display numerical data in plots on a number line, including line plots, dot plots, and histograms. | Translate among the various forms for rational numbers. <br> Select the most useful form of a rational number to solve real-world and mathematical problems. <br> Use activities with various models to understand sampling, chance, and probability. <br> Use various models to solve multi-step real-world problems involving integers, equations, inequalities, proportions, scale drawings, formulas, probability, and statistics. <br> Solve problems involving scale drawings of geometric figures, including measuring actual lengths and areas. <br> Identify the constant of proportionality in scale drawings and other diagrams. <br> Show how to use a random number table to simulate random samples. <br> Display data in line plots, dot plots, box plots, Venn diagrams, and histograms. <br> Use overlapping data distributions to measure the difference between two populations. |

Scope and Sequence

# MATHEMATICAL PROCESSES STANDARDS

| | GRADE 4 | GRADE 5 | COURSE 1 (GR 6) | COURSE 2 (GR 7) |
|---|---|---|---|---|
| **Use variables and coordinate grids to represent and model.** | Use boxes to represent missing addends and missing factors.<br><br>Write addition and subtraction number sentences for real-world problems with fractions and decimals.<br><br>Create a line graph from data in a table.<br><br>Use grids to model geometric transformations. | Use letters as variables to represent unknown values in equations and formulas.<br><br>Explore the use of letters as variables in expressions and inequalities.<br><br>Represent an equation as a graphed line.<br><br>Use a coordinate grid to represent equations. | Understand that a variable can represent an unknown number, or, depending on the purpose at hand, any number in a specified set.<br><br>Use letters as variables in algebraic expressions, equations, inequalities, and formulas.<br><br>Represent equivalent ratios and rates in tape diagrams, double number line diagrams, equations, or coordinate graphs.<br><br>Use a coordinate grid to represent polygons and equations. | Extend the use of variables to write and solve simple equations for an unknown angle in a figure.<br><br>Understand that rewriting a variable expression in different forms can shed light on how the quantities in a problem are related.<br><br>Identify the constant of proportionality in tables, graphs, and equations.<br><br>Use a coordinate grid to represent direct and inverse variation. |

## 5. Use appropriate tools strategically.

| | GRADE 4 | GRADE 5 | COURSE 1 (GR 6) | COURSE 2 (GR 7) |
|---|---|---|---|---|
| **Choose among tools: pencil and paper, concrete models, or technology in developing skills.** | Use paper and pencil to calculate and draw.<br><br>Use geometry tools (protractor, set squares, grid paper) to model problems.<br><br>Use technology (virtual manipulatives and computers) to model and draw.<br><br>Select appropriate formulas and units in solving problems involving perimeter and area. | Use paper and pencil to calculate and draw.<br><br>Use geometry tools (protractor, set squares, grid paper) to model problems.<br><br>Use technology (virtual manipulatives and computers) to model and draw.<br><br>Select appropriate formulas and units in solving problems involving perimeter, area, surface area, and volume.<br><br>Use a calculator to model, compute, and solve. | Use paper and pencil to calculate and draw.<br><br>Use geometry tools (protractor, set squares, grid paper) to model problems.<br><br>Use technology (virtual manipulatives and computers) to model and draw.<br><br>Select appropriate formulas and units in solving problems involving perimeter, area, surface area, and volume.<br><br>Use a calculator to model, compute and solve. | Use paper and pencil to calculate and draw.<br><br>Use geometry tools (protractor, set squares, grid paper) to model problems.<br><br>Use technology (virtual manipulatives and computers) to model and draw.<br><br>Use tools such as rulers, protractors, and technology to draw geometric figures with given conditions.<br><br>Use geometry tools to construct triangles and quadrilaterals.<br><br>Select appropriate formulas and units in solving problems involving perimeter, area, surface area, and volume.<br><br>Use a calculator to model, compute and solve problems involving rational numbers. |

# MATHEMATICAL PROCESSES STANDARDS

|  | GRADE 4 | GRADE 5 | COURSE 1 (GR 6) | COURSE 2 (GR 7) |
|---|---|---|---|---|
| **6. Attend to precision.** | | | | |
| **Communicate precisely by using mathematical language and symbols clearly in discussion with others.** | Understand and use the lesson vocabulary to explain reasoning. Interpret symbols of relation in comparing whole numbers, fractions, and decimals. Draw and label bar models, identifying parts and units. Understand decimal notation for fractions in numerical expressions. Identify and label sides and angles in polygons. Define and use symbols in geometry to identify and relate geometric figures. Express perimeter in linear units and area in square units. Use estimation to check reasonableness. (whole-number addition, subtraction, multiplication and division). | Understand and use the lesson vocabulary to explain reasoning. Interpret symbols of relation in comparing whole numbers, fractions, and decimals. Draw and label bar models, identifying parts and units. Write and interpret numerical expressions. Identify and label bases and altitudes in triangles and polygons. Use estimation to check reasonableness. (decimal addition, subtraction, multiplication and division). Express area in square units and volume in cubic units. Define and use symbols in geometry to identify and relate geometric figures. | Understand and use the lesson vocabulary to explain reasoning. Interpret symbols of relation in comparing positive and negative numbers, as well as absolute values. Recognize opposite signs of numbers as indicating locations on opposite sides of 0 on the number line or in the coordinate plane. Draw and label bar models, identifying parts and units. Identify parts of an algebraic expression using mathematical terms (sum, term, product, factor, quotient, coefficient). Understand that pi represents the relationship between the circumference and diameter of a circle. Express surface area in square units and volume in cubic units. Use estimation to check the reasonableness of multi-digit computations with decimals and percents. | Understand and use the lesson vocabulary to explain reasoning. Interpret symbols of relation in comparing real numbers. Show that all rational numbers can be written as either terminating or repeating decimals. Understand that rewriting an expression in different forms can shed light on how the quantities in a problem are related. Identify and label parts of cylinders, cones, and spheres. Understand that pi is an irrational number. Express surface area in square units and volume in cubic units. Use estimation strategies to check the reasonableness of computations with rational and irrational numbers. Write numbers to a specific number of significant digits. |
| **7. Look for and make use of structure.** | | | | |
| **Consolidate mathematical thinking.** | Present mathematical thinking through Math Journal activities. | Present mathematical thinking through Math Journal activities. | Present mathematical thinking through Math Journals, "explain" exercises, and in-class discussions. | Present mathematical thinking through Math Journals, "explain" exercises, and in-class discussions. |

Scope and Sequence

# MATHEMATICAL PROCESSES STANDARDS

| | GRADE 4 | GRADE 5 | COURSE 1 (GR 6) | COURSE 2 (GR 7) |
|---|---|---|---|---|
| **Recognize connections in mathematical ideas.** | Demonstrate that decimal notation is an extension of the base-ten system. Examine the relationship between fractions and decimals. Make connections among multiplication, division, factors, and multiples. Convert among mixed numbers and improper fractions. | Relate fractions and division. Understand the connection among fractions, decimals, ratios, and percents as ways to represent parts of a whole. Make connections among multiplication and division of fractions and decimals. Relate fractions and division. Examine the relationships between three-dimensional figures and the two-dimensional figures that form them. | Relate ratios, fractions, and rates. Understand that ratios can represent part-to part as well as part-to-whole relationships. Make connections between squares and square roots, cubes and cube roots. Convert among fractions, decimals, and percents. Examine the relationships between cross-sections of prisms and their volume. | Show that a number and its opposite have a sum of 0. Examine the relationships among integers and rational numbers. Extend understanding of operations with fractions to operations with positive and negative rational numbers. Convert among various forms of rational numbers depending on the real-world or mathematical situation. Describe the two dimensional figures that result from slicing three-dimensional figures. |

Scope and Sequence

# MATHEMATICAL PROCESSES STANDARDS

| | GRADE 4 | GRADE 5 | COURSE 1 (GR 6) | COURSE 2 (GR 7) |
|---|---|---|---|---|
| **8. Look for and express regularity in repeated reasoning.** | | | | |
| **Notice regularity in repeated calculations and monitor the process.** | Continue to use bar models to solve real-world problems involving multiplication, division, fraction concepts, data analysis, and measurement. Use the properties of operations to perform multi-digit arithmetic. Use standard algorithms for addition, subtraction, and multiplication of whole numbers. Use standard algorithms for addition and subtraction of decimals. Gain familiarity with factors and multiples. Apply formulas for perimeter and area of squares and rectangles. | Continue to use bar models to solve real-world problems involving multiplication, division, concepts with fractions, decimals, ratios, and percents; data analysis, and measurement. Use properties of multiplication (including the distributive property) in estimation and mental math. Use standard algorithms for addition, subtraction, multiplication, and division of whole numbers. Use standard algorithms for multiplication and division of decimals by whole numbers. Use factors and multiples to develop operations with fractions. Develop formulas for finding the area of triangles. Develop and apply formulas for finding the volume of a cube and a rectangular prism. | Continue to use bar models to solve real-world problems involving multiplication, division, concepts with fractions, decimals, ratios, and percents; data analysis, geometry and measurement. Apply the properties of operations to generate equivalent numerical and algebraic expressions. Apply standard algorithms for addition, subtraction, multiplication, and division of whole numbers and decimals. Apply standard algorithms for multiplication and division with fractions. Apply concept of prime factorization to finding square roots and cube roots of perfect squares and perfect cubes. Develop and apply formulas for finding the area of triangles, parallelograms, trapezoids, and regular polygons. Develop and apply formulas for finding the circumference and area of a circle. Develop and apply formulas for the surface area of prisms and pyramids and the volume of prisms. Develop and apply other formulas such as the distance formula and the interest formula. | Continue to use number lines, coordinate grids, and other visual models to solve real-world problems involving rational numbers, proportionality, geometry, measurement probability, and statistics. Apply the properties of operations to generate equivalent numerical and algebraic expressions. Extend algorithms for decimals to include rational numbers. Extend algorithms for fraction operations to operations with positive and negative rational fractions. Apply properties of operations and factorization to factor algebraic expressions with rational coefficients. Develop and apply formulas for the surface area and volume of pyramids, cones, cylinders, and spheres. Develop a probability model and use it to find probabilities of events. |

# Additional Answers

## Chapter 8

**Lesson 8.2, Practice** (p. 21)

**8c.**

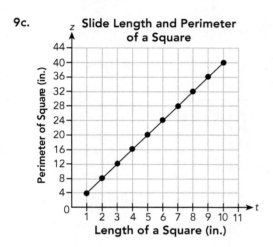

**9c.**

**Chapter Review Test** (p. 36)

**11.**

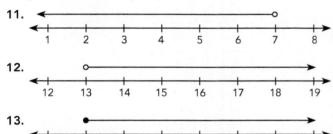

**12.**

**13.**

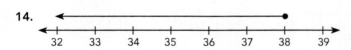

**14.**

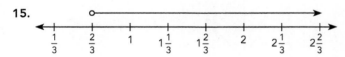

**15.**

**16.**

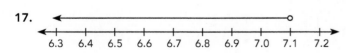

**17.**

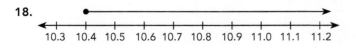

**18.**

## Chapter 9

**Lesson 9.1, 5-minute Warm Up** (p. 42)

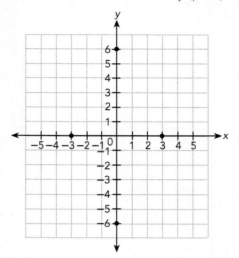

**Lesson 9.1, Guided Practice** (pp. 44–46)

**3b.**

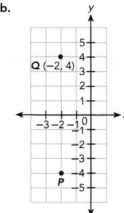

**3c.**

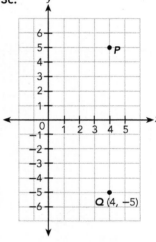

**3d.**

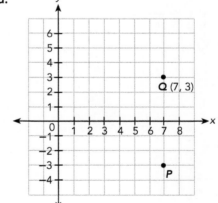

**4a.**

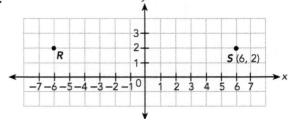

**4b.**

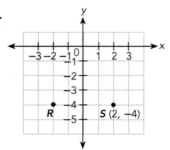

**4c.**

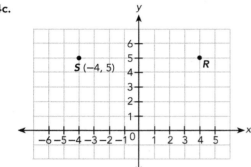

**4d.**

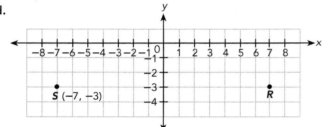

**9.**

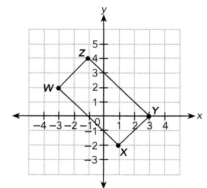

rectangle

**10.**

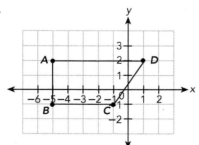

trapezoid

**11.**

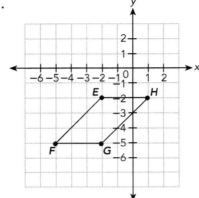

parallelogram

**12.**

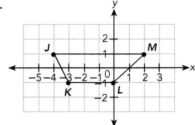

trapezoid

**13.**

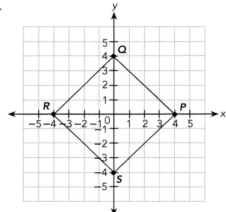

square

**14.**

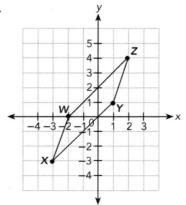

parallelogram

**2.**

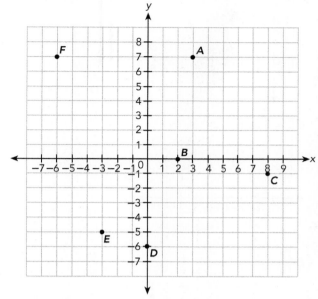

Quadrant I: Point A; Quadrant II: Point F; Quadrant III: Point E; Quadrant IV: Point C; Point B lies on the x-axis. It is between Quadrant I and Quadrant IV. Point D lies on the y-axis. It is between Quadrant III and Quadrant IV.

**5.**

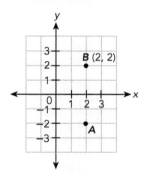

**6.**

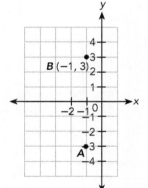

**7.**

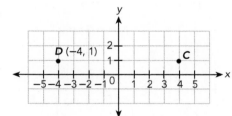

**8.**

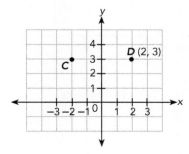

**9.**

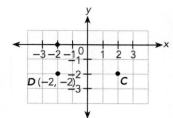

**10.**

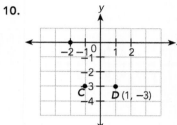

**11.**

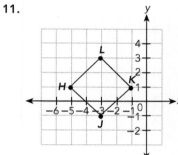

square

**12.**

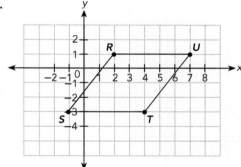

parallelogram

**13.**

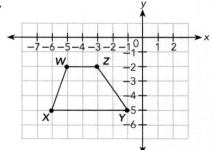

trapezoid

**14.**

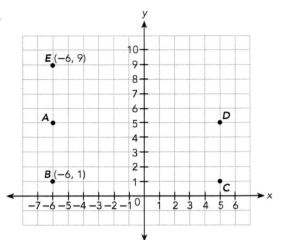

**15.**

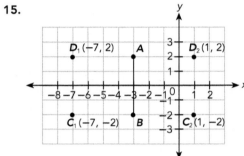

**16.**

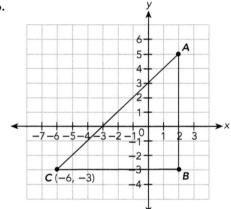

**17.**

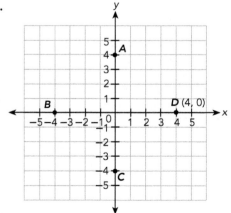

Triangle *ABC* is an isosceles triangle.

**1.**

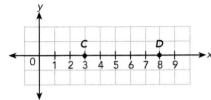

*CD* = 5 units

**2.**

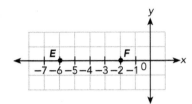

*EF* = 4 units

**3.**

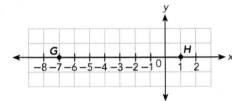

*GH* = 8 units

**4.**

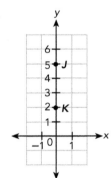

*JK* = 3 units

**5.**

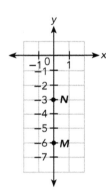

*MN* = 3 units

**6.**

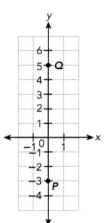

*PQ* = 8 units

**9.**

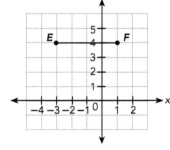

*EF* = 4 units

**10.**

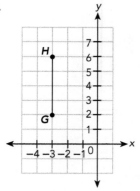

GH = 4 units

**11.**

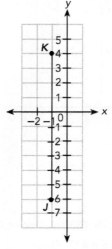

JK = 10 units

**12.**

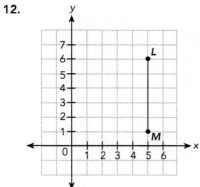

LM = 5 units

**Lesson 9.2, Practice** (p. 58)

**3.**

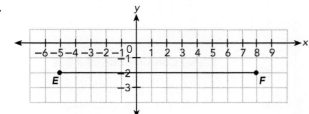

EF = 13 units

**4.**

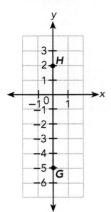

GH = 7 units

**5.**

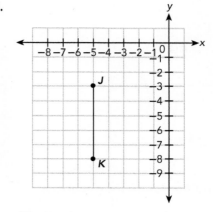

JK = 5 units

**6.**

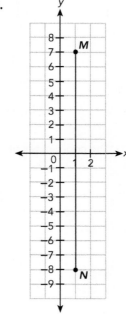

MN = 15 units

**7a.**

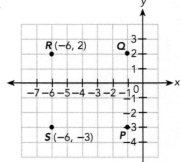

The coordinates of point R are (−6, 2). The coordinates of
point S are (−6, −3).

**7b.**

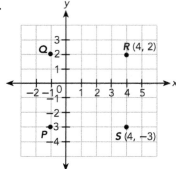

The coordinates of point R are (4, 2). The coordinates of point S are (4, −3).

**8a.**

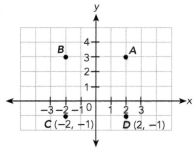

The coordinates of point C are (−2, −1). The coordinates of point D are (2, −1).

**8b.**

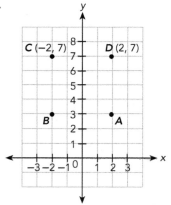

The coordinates of point C are (−2, 7). The coordinates of point D are (2, 7).

**9a.**

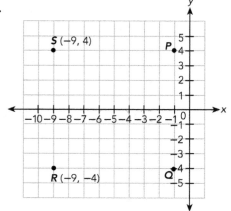

The coordinates of point R are (−9, −4). The coordinates of point S are (−9, 4).

**9b.**

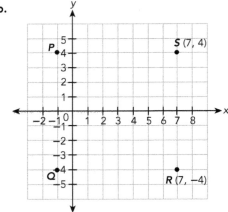

The coordinates of point R are (7, −4). The coordinates of point S are (7, 4).

**Lesson 9.3, 5-minute Warm Up** (p. 62)

| Granola bar (number) | 1 | 2 | 3 | 4 | 5 |
|---|---|---|---|---|---|
| Cost ($) | 1.50 | 3.00 | 4.50 | 6.00 | 7.50 |

**Lesson 9.3, Practice** (pp. 65−66)

**1.**

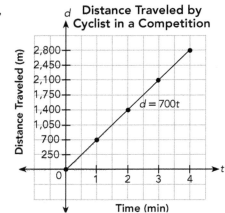

**2.**

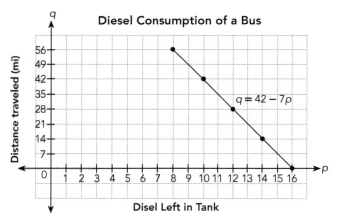

**3.**

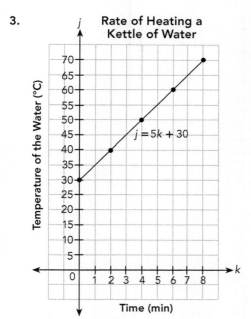

Rate of Heating a Kettle of Water

$j = 5k + 30$

Temperature of the Water (°C) / Time (min)

**Lesson 9.3, Ticket Out the Door** (p. 66)

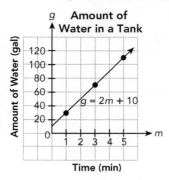

Amount of Water in a Tank

$g = 2m + 10$

Amount of Water (gal) / Time (min)

30 gal, 70 gal, 110 gal

**Lesson 9.3, Brain@Work** (p. 66)

**1. and 5a.**

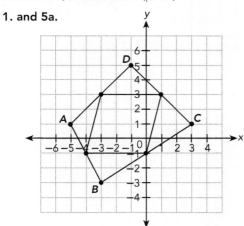

**2. and 5a.**

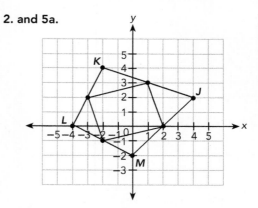

**3. and 5a.**

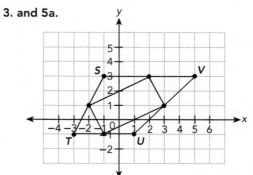

**Chapter Review Test** (pp. 68–69)

**2.**

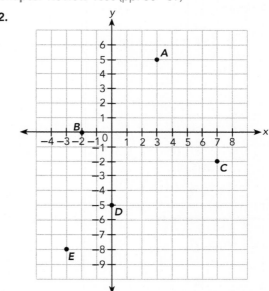

Quadrant I: Point *A*; Quadrant III: Point *E*; Quadrant IV: Point *C*; Point *B* lies on the *x*-axis. It lies between Quadrant II and Quadrant III. Point *D* lies on the *y*-axis. It lies between Quadrant III and Quadrant IV.

**3.**

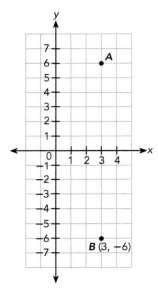

$B$ (3, −6)

**4.**

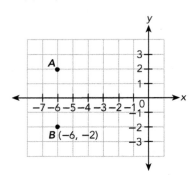

$B$ (−6, −2)

**5.**

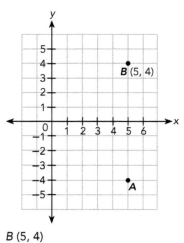

$B$ (5, 4)

**6.**

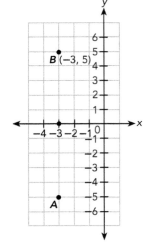

$B$ (−3, 5)

**7.**

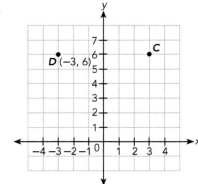

$D$ (−3, 6)

**8.**

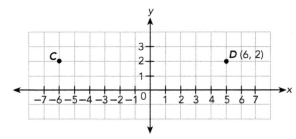

$D$ (6, 2)

**9.**

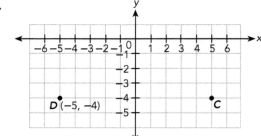

$D$ (−5, −4)

**10.**

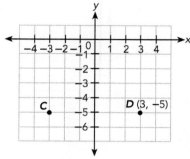

D (3, −5)

**14.**

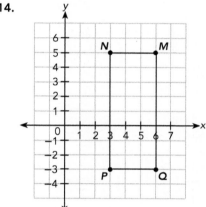

rectangle

**15.**

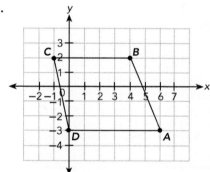

trapezoid

**16.**

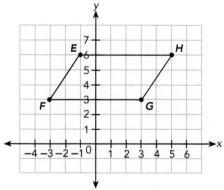

parallelogram

**17.**

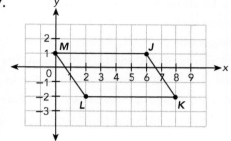

parallelogram

**18.**

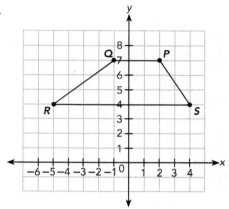

trapezoid

**19.**

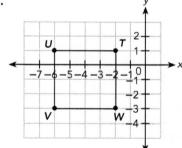

square

**20a.**

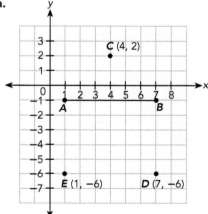

**20b.** For point C to be above $\overline{AB}$ and 2 units away from the x-axis, its y-coordinate has to be 2. For triangle ABC to be an isosceles triangle with base $\overline{AB}$, the x-coordinate of point C has to be 4 in order for AC and BC to be equal. The coordinates of C are (4, 2).     **20c.** For point D to lie 5 units below point B, the coordinates of D have to be (7, −6). For point E to lie 5 units below point A, the coordinates of E have to be (1, −6).

**21.**

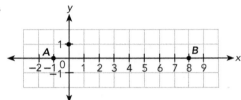

AB = 9 units

**22.**

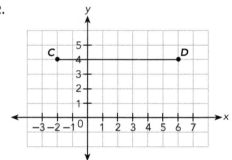

CD = 8 units

**23.**

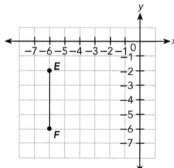

EF = 4 units

**24.**

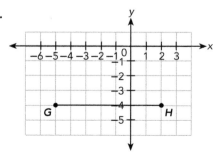

GH = 7 units

**25.**

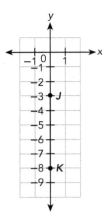

JK = 5 units

**26.**

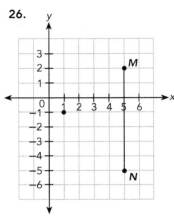

MN = 7 units

## Chapter 10

**Lesson 10.1, Practice** (p. 86)

**22.**

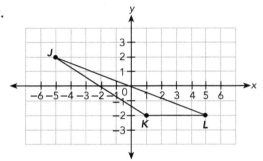

Area of triangle JKL = 8 units²

**23.**

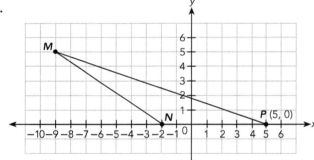

P (5, 0)

**24.**

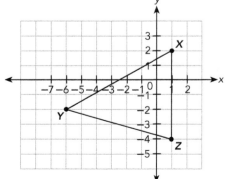

Area of triangle XYZ = 21 units²

**25.**

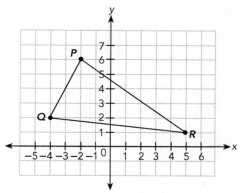

Area of triangle *PQR* = 19 units²

**Lesson 10.2, Practice** (p. 98)

**22.**

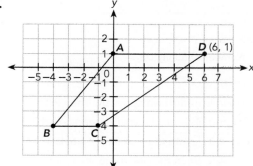

Area of trapezoid *ABCD* = 22.5 units²

**Lesson 10.4, Guided Practice** (p. 104)

**1.**

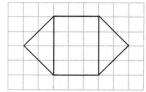

**2.** Answer vary. Sample: two trapezoids

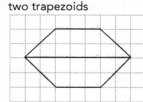

# Chapter 12

**Lesson 12.4, 5-minute Warm Up** (p. 200)

**1.** Answer vary. Sample: Base: *ABC, DEF*; Height: *AD*

**2.** Answer vary. Sample: Base: *PQR, NTS*; Height: *QT, RS, PN*

**3.** Answer vary. Sample: Base: *ABCD, EFGH*; Height: *AE, DH, CG, BF*

# Chapter 13

**Lesson 13.2, Guided Practice** (p. 223)

**1.**

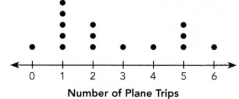

**2.**

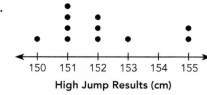

**Lesson 13.2, Guided Practice** (p. 225)

**4.** The dot plot has a "tail" on the right. The shape is right-skewed. The data values are from 0 to 5. Range: 5 − 0 = 5. Most of the players scored 1 point in the game, and all of them scored 0 to 5 points in the game.

**Lesson 13.2, Guided Practice** (p. 226)

**1.**

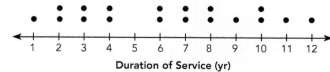

**2.**

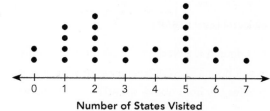

**Lesson 13.3, 5-minute Warm Up** (p. 228)

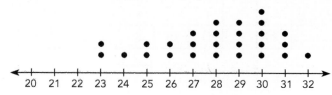

**Lesson 13.3, Guided Practice** (pp. 229–231)

**1.**

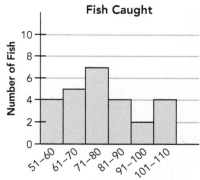

**2.**

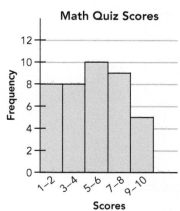

**3b.**

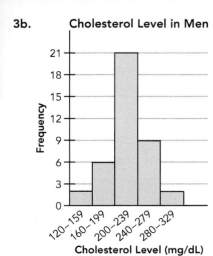

Cholesterol Level in Men

**4a.** For this set of data, it is suitable to use 8 intervals with a width of 5 miles per hour since the tolerance for speeding is about 10% or 5 miles per hour above speed limit. The outlier is 88.

| Speed (km/h) | 50–54 | 55–59 | 60–64 | 65–69 | 70–74 | 75–79 | 80–84 | 85–89 |
|---|---|---|---|---|---|---|---|---|
| Frequency | 2 | 3 | 11 | 10 | 8 | 3 | 2 | 1 |

**4b.**

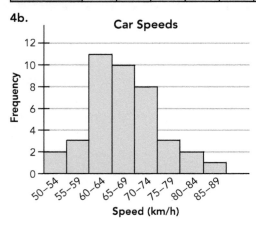

Car Speeds

Lesson 13.3, Practice (p. 234)

**3.**

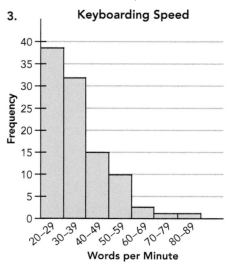

Keyboarding Speed

**4b.**

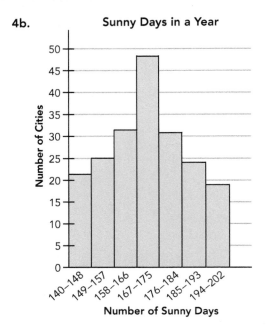

Sunny Days in a Year

Lesson 13.3, Practice (p. 237)

**12.** No, the histogram is not drawn correctly. The vertical axis should state the number or players (frequency), while the horizontal axis should state the number of goals in equal intervals on a scale. And since the horizontal axis represents a continuous scale, there should be no gaps between the bars. Also, the histogram does not have a title.

Lesson 13.3, Brain @ Work (p. 237)

**1.**

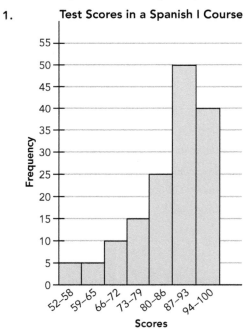

Test Scores in a Spanish I Course

**2.**

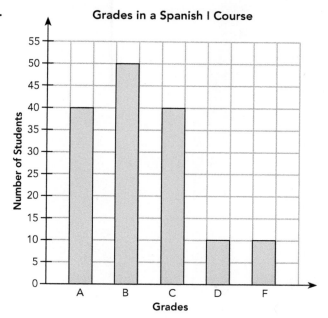

Grades in a Spanish I Course

**3a.** If 5 students increased their scores from 79 to 89, then there would be 55 students with scores from 87 to 93, and 10 students with scores from 73 to 79. For the histogram, the height of the bar that represents the frequency for 87–93 will increase by 5, while the height of the bar that represents the frequency for 73–79 will decrease by 5.   **3b.** For the bar graph, the height of the bar that represents the number of students who got a score of B will increase by 5, while the height of the bar that represents the number of students who got a score of C will decrease by 5.

**Chapter Review/Test** (pp. 239–241)

**2.   Dot plot:**

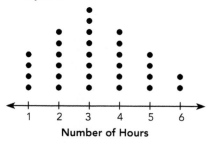

Number of Hours

**Histogram:**

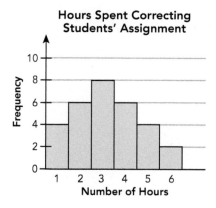

**10.**

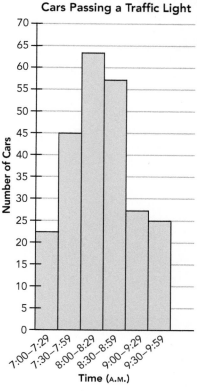

Cars Passing a Traffic Light

**11.** The most frequent value is from 8:00 A.M. to 8:29 A.M. Most of the data values are to the right of 8.00 A.M. to 8:29 A.M., and the distribution is right-skewed. The second most frequent value is 8.30 A.M. to 8:59 A.M. The third most frequent value is from 7:39 A.M. to 7:59 A.M. These three values are significantly higher than the rest of the time, because most companies start work from 8:00 A.M. to 9:00 A.M.

**13.**

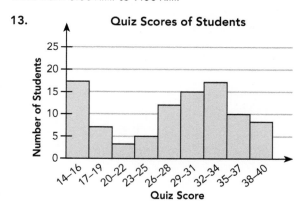

Quiz Scores of Students

There are two peaks in the distribution of the data — one is for the interval 14–16, and the other is for the interval 32–34. Most of the data values are to the left of the interval 32–34, and the distribution is left-skewed. The data values are from 14 to 40. Range: 40 − 14 = 26   **14.** No, most of the data values are still to the left of the interval 32 to 34. The distribution is still left-skewed.

# Chapter 14

Lesson 14.2, Hands-On Activity (p. 255)

**Step 2.** Mean $= \dfrac{11 + 10 + 8 + 3 + 9 + 6}{6}$

$= \dfrac{47}{6}$

$= 7\dfrac{5}{6}$

The middle number is the 24th number.

Median $= 3$

# Course 1B Index

Expressions. *See* Algebraic expression(s)

Extra Practice, *Found in* Chapter at a Glance *for each chapter in TE. For example,* 2A, 154A, 218A; 2A–2B, 168A, 214A–214B; *See also* Assessment and Intervention. *For example,* 2F, 154D, 218F; 2D, 168D, 214D; *See also* Assignment Guide *for each lesson in TE. For example,* 14, 138, 251; 12, 132, 234; *See also* Differentiated Instruction: Advanced Learners. *For example,* 2F, 154D, 218F; 2D, 168D, 214D

Factoring algebraic expressions, 2D

Factor(s), **16**, 219
    greatest common, 2E, 3, **20**, 129
    prime, **16**
    of whole number, 3

Factor trees, 20, 25, 31, 35

Factoring algebraic expressions, 242–243
    as the inverse of expanding, 242

Formula(s)
    area of circle, 118C, 136–137, 146–147
    area of parallelogram, 88
    area of rectangle, 54, 73, 75
    area of square, 73
    area of trapezoid, 88, 91, 94
    area of triangle, 75, 81, 94
    circumference of circle, 118C, 127, 143–144
    distance, 172
    graphing, 62–63
    interest, 202
    perimeter of a polygon, 41, 55
    surface area, 168C, 181–186, 200–206
    volume of non-rectangular prisms, 201
    volume of prisms, 168C, 189–195, 200–206
    volume of rectangular prism, 168C, 171, 189–190

Fraction(s), 189–191
    algebraic equations involving, 11
    common factors and, 64
    comparing, using a number line, 7–10
    comparison, 2D
    denominators of 100, 183–184
    dividing, 62C, 65–75, 101, 103, 157
    equivalent, 115–116
    expressing, 115
        as equivalent fractions
            by division, 115
            by multiplication, 115
        percent as, 187, 191
    improper, **74**
    mixed number, **74**

multiplying, 62C, 155–156, 184
on a number line, 7–10, 43–44
percent and, 182D, 185–187
to ratio, 114C
ratios as, 122–123
Real-World Problems, 94–104
in simplest form, 116
visual models, 7–10, 43–44, 65–73, 76, 103
whole number as, 96, 101

Frequency, **214**, 218

Frequency tables, 214C, 218, 219, 225, 261

Fundamental Theorem of Arithmetic, 2D

Glossary, 272–276, 301–306

Graphing in the coordinate plane, 62–64
    geometric figures in, 45, 50–57, 73, 86, 98
    points, 42–47
    relationships, 62–64

Graphs, to representing linear equations, 15–18

Greatest common factor (GCF), **2E**, 3, **20**
    with distributive property, 22–23
    to write ratios, 129

Guided Practice, 7–8, 11–13, 17, 19, 21, 23–24, 26, 30–31, 34–36, 46, 48–49, 51, 55–56, 66–67, 69, 73–74, 80, 82–84, 87–89, 91–92, 95–96, 98, 100, 102, 104, 120, 122, 123–124, 128–132, 134,136–137, 141–143, 145, 147, 160–161, 163, 165, 169–171, 173–174, 176, 186–187, 190–191, 194–195, 199–202, 205, 207, 209–211, 223–224, 227, 231, 233–236, 240, 243, 247–250; 6, 8, 10–11, 14–15, 19, 24, 26, 30, 32, 44, 46, 51, 53, 56–57, 63–64, 79–82, 89–95, 100–101, 104–108, 123, 127–128, 130, 138–140, 145–146, 148–149, 151–153, 176, 178, 183, 186, 190, 192, 194, 200–202, 205–206, 218–219, 223–225, 229, 231, 233, 245–247, 252, 254–255, 259–260, 265, 267–268
    exercises, *Throughout. See for example,* 7–8, 11–13, 17, 19, 21, 23–24, 26, 30–31, 34–36, 46–49, 51, 55–56, 66–75, 80–84, 88–92, 94–104, 119–124, 130–137, 141–147, 160–163, 165, 169–171, 173–174, 176, 186–187, 190–191, 194–195, 1 99–202, 205, 207–211; 6, 8, 10–11, 14–15, 19, 24, 26, 30, 32, 44, 46, 51, 53, 56–57, 63–64, 79–82, 89–95, 100–101, 104–108, 123, 127–128, 130, 138–140, 145–146, 148–149, 151–153, 176, 178, 183, 186, 190, 192, 194, 200–202, 205–206, 218–219, 223–225, 229, 231, 233, 245–247, 252, 254–255, 259–260, 265, 267–268

checking for reasonableness, 199, 200, 201
and decimal, 182D
expressing
    decimal as, 190
    fraction as, 189
    mixed number as, 189
finding
    amount of increase or decrease, 182E
    decrease and increase, 182E
    fraction by multiplying, 190
    part and whole, 182D
    quantity represented by, 193
    to solve problem, 204, 206, 208–210
    using a calculator, 192, 205, 206, 213
fraction and, 182D, 185–187
meaning of, 185–186
of a quantity, 193–195
Real-World Problems, 198–202
    commission, **201**
    interest, **202**
    sales tax, **199**
symbol, 185
visual models, 185, 193–198, 204–211
and unitary method, 182D

Perfect cube, **2E**, 3, **33**
cube root of, 33

Perfect square, **2E**, 4, **29**
square root of, 30–31

Pi symbol($\pi$)
on a calculator, 126
modeling, 125–126

Polygon(s)
area of, 99–101, 118C
in coordinate plane, 38C, 45, 47, 54, 98
perimeter of, 45

Positive numbers, 2D, **4–5**
on a number line, 42C

Practice

Practice exercises. *In every lesson. For example,* 14–15,
    18, 27–28, 32, 37–38; 12, 20–21, 27–28, 33–34

Prerequisite Skills
Pretest. *See* Assessment: Prior Knowledge
Prior Knowledge. *See* Assessment
Quick Check. *See* Assessment
Recall Prior Knowledge, 3, 43–44, 63–64, 115–117,
    155–158, 183–184, 219–220; 3–4, 39, 73–74,
    119–121, 169–171, 215–216, 243

Pretest. *See* Assessment: Prior Knowledge

Prime factorization, 16–17
and finding common factors, 20, 31
and finding common multiples, 25
and finding roots, 35

Prime factors, **4, 16**
product of, 2D

Prime number(s), 2D, **16**. *See also* Prime factorization
identifying, 4

Prism
cross section of, 191
identifying, 169
with missing dimensions, 202
non-rectangular, surface area and volume of, 168C,
    201
rectangular
    net of, 168C, 173
    surface area of, 168C, 182
    volume of, 168C, 171, 189–190, 200
triangular
    net of, 168C, 174
    surface area of, 168C, 184
volume of, 168C, 189–195

Problem Solving. *Throughout. See for example,* 41, 61,
    109–110, 180–181, 216–217; 116–117, 240–241
algebraic expressions, 246–250; 29–30, 37
Brain at Work, 38, 58, 107, 149, 178, 214, 246–250;
    34, 66, 113, 158–159, 237, 271
circumference and area of circle, 162–163
graphing, 70–71
inequalities, 31, 37
measures of central tendency, 273–274
parallelograms, 107

Pages listed in black type refer to Book A.
Pages listed in blue type refer to Book B.
Pages in **boldface** type show where a term is introduced.